Ex Libris:—
Dan E Gardner
7014 NE Tillamook
Portland
Ore 97213

FORKED TONGUES AND BROKEN TREATIES

FORKED TONGUES AND BROKEN TREATIES

Edited by

DONALD E. WORCESTER

ILLUSTRATED WITH PHOTOGRAPHS

THE CAXTON PRINTERS, LTD.
Caldwell, Idaho 83605
1975

Library of Congress Cataloging in Publication Data

Worcester, Donald Emmet, 1915-
Broken treaties.

Includes bibliographies.
1. Indians of North America—Treaties—Addresses, essays, lectures. I. Title.
KF8205.W67 342'.73'087 74-28285
ISBN 0-87004-246-7

Lithographed and bound in the United States of America by
The CAXTON PRINTERS, Ltd.
Caldwell, Idaho 83605
123084

The cartographers wish to acknowledge the invaluable assistance of Mr. Paul Weston of the Bureau of Indian Affairs, Portland, Oregon. Published works consulted during the preparation of the map series included: Bureau of American Ethnology — 18th Annual Report 1896-1897, Part 2 Land Cessions in the United States, Charles C. Royce; House Report — 2053 United States Government Printing Office, Washington, D.C.; Indian Tribes of North America — Bulletin 145 — Bureau of American Ethnology 1952, John R. Swanton.

Northwest Cartographic Institute
JUDITH A. FARMER, *President*

Table of Contents

List of Illustrations

MAPS

Introduction

THE DISCOVERY of continents peopled by Stone Age savages posed a number of perplexing questions for Europeans concerning the rights of the "Indians" and the legality of taking their lands. Each European nation answered these questions in its own way and in terms of its own social and cultural values. The Spaniards agonized for a century over their right to conquer the Indians and whether the Indians were rational men with souls or mere beasts without benefit of such spiritual attributes. The "dirty dog" and "noble savage" debate continued throughout the 16th century, but it did not impede the spread of the conquest. Ultimately the Spanish government decided that the Indians were indeed rational men with souls who must be converted to Christianity and not mistreated, while men in the New World made their own interpretation of what was proper treatment. The emphasis on the Black Legend of Spanish cruelty to the Indians, correct up to a point, is largely the result of Bartolomé de las Casas' lurid best-seller on the destruction of the Indians of the islands and Tierra Firme, the Spanish Main. Las Casas' work was in great demand in the lands of Spain's enemies, who took self-righteous satisfaction in seeing Spanish cruelty exposed by a Spaniard. It does not follow, however, that those enemies were more humane in their treatment of the Indians than the Spaniards. Today many more Indians remain in the lands conquered by Spain than in other parts of the Western Hemisphere, although the number of Indians in the U.S. is steadily increasing.

The English happily lacked a Las Casas to describe their treatment of the Indians to the world. In 1623, however, John Robinson, one of the Pilgrims who remained in Holland when others went to Plymouth, wrote to friends in New England suggesting that they, too, might be lacking in humanity. "Concerning the killing of those poor Indians . . .," he said, "oh, how happy a thing had it been, if you had converted some before you killed! Besides, where blood is once begun to shed, it is seldom staunched of a long time after. You will say they deserved it. I grant it; but upon what provocations and invitements by those heathenish Christians?" John Robinson ranks among the prophets of his day, for the bloodshed continued until all Indians were reduced to a hand-to-mouth existence on reservations. The Puritans saw in the "tawny sarpints" the agents of Satan, and to them warfare against the Indians was the good fight against the forces of evil. And when some catastrophe, such as a smallpox epidemic, wiped out a tribe the Puritans viewed it as the clearest evidence of divine intervention, callously assuming that the Indians had received their just desserts.

Although there were many tribal variations in cultural traits and language, there were some similarities among the Indians. The continuing struggle over tribal lands and hunting grounds created traditional enmities. Most of the tribes were willing, therefore, to help outsiders destroy their traditional foes, thereby playing an active part in their own destruction. The idea of joint action, confederation, or alliance between tribes was almost totally foreign to them, so that instead of presenting a unified front against European intruders they allowed themselves to be isolated and defeated tribe by tribe. Occasionally some Indian leader such as the Wampanoag Philip, the Ottawa Pontiac, or the Shawnee Tecumseh endeavored to unite the tribes, but with little or only temporary success.

Few Indian tribes were known by the names they called themselves. The Europeans usually learned about tribes from their neighbors, so the name frequently applied to any tribe was whatever its enemies called it. "Iroquois" was a combination of an Algonkin word for "real adder" with a French suffix. "Apache" apparently came from a Zuñi word for enemy: Apaches, like all Athapascans, called themselves "Diné," meaning "the people." The Sioux called themselves "Dakota" or "Lakota," meaning "allies." "Cheyenne" comes from the Sioux meaning "people of an alien speech." The Chopunnish received the name "Nez Perce" (pierced nose) from French traders.

In 1630 the Reverend John Cotton gave the Puritans a religious justification for their encroachment on Indian lands. "God makes room for people in three wayes," he wrote. "First, when he casts out the enemies of a people before them by lawfull warre with the inhabitants, which Godd calls them into as in Ps. 442. ... Secondly, when he gives a foreigne people favour in the eyes of any native people to come and sit downe with them either by way of purchase . . . or else when they give it in courtesie. . . . Thirdly, when he makes a Country though not altogether void of inhabitants, yet voyd in that place where they reside. Where there is a vacant place, there is liberty for the sonne of Adam or Noah to come and inhabite, though they neither buy it, nor aske their leave." According to Cotton, if God chose to provide a "vacant place" for the elect by a smallpox epidemic, there was reason for joy rather than sorrow.

Although John Eliot and Roger Williams maintained that the Indians had a right to their lands and that it was evil to enslave them, they were unable to convince many others of the correctness of their peculiar view. In 1637 the Pequot tribe tried to prevent the whites from encroaching on its lands in the Connecticut Valley. The intruders retaliated by setting fire to the Pequots' wooden village. Hundreds were burned to death; the survivors were hunted down and killed or sold into slavery. The Pequot War symbolized white-Indian competition for land thereafter. One of those who took part in the attack on the Pequots explained that it was as though "the finger of God had touched match and flint." He admitted that the screams of the burning Indians would have aroused pity "if God had not fitten the hearts of men for the service. . . ." Although the Puritans had strict laws concerning the proper methods of acquiring title to Indian lands, and generally conceded the Indians hunting rights on the lands purchased, in other regions there was less insistence on legal procedures.

Virginians at first believed that the Indians would try to become like Englishmen and that the two races could therefore live together in peace. Plans were made for educating Indian children to hasten the civilizing process, but these were abandoned after the Indian attack on the Virginia settlements in 1622. The Indians had violated natural law and thus no longer deserved friendly treatment. From that time on, the Indians were pushed farther and farther west or exterminated as the southern frontier advanced.

Although William Penn's treaty with the Indians along the Delaware was faithfully kept, the frontiersmen of western Pennsylvania disregarded Penn's policies. As one 18th-century pioneer remarked "the animals vulgarly called Indians" had no real right to the land they occupied, an attitude that prevailed along the whole frontier. An army officer declared that the "people of Kentucky will carry on private expeditions against the Indians and kill them whenever they meet them, and I do not believe there is a jury in all Kentucky who would punish a man for it."

Because of increasing friction between land-hungry frontiersmen and the Indians, the British government issued the Proclamation of 1763, which declared all land west of the crest of the Appalachians to belong to the Indians and forbade the colonists to cross that line. Only licensed agents were allowed to trade or deal with the Indians. George Washington reflected the typical American viewpoint when he said, "I can never look upon that proclamation . . . other . . . than as a temporary expedient to quiet the minds of the Indians. . . . Any person, therefore, who neglects the present opportunity of hunting out good lands, and in some measure marking and distinguishing them for his own, will never regain it." The British effort to prevent encroachment on Indian lands quickly proved a failure because it was impossible to enforce.

Governor Dunmore of Virginia replied to criticism for his failure to prevent Washington and others from sending agents into Kentucky to select land, declaring that "they do and will remove as their avidity and restlessness incite them. . . . Nor can they be easily brought to entertain any belief of the permanent obligation of treaties with those People, whom they consider, as but little removed from Brute creation."

A more extreme point of view on Indian rights to land was expressed by Hugh Brackenridge in 1782: "On what is their claim founded — Occupancy. A wild Indian with his skin painted red, and a feather through his nose, has set foot on the broad continent . . .; a second wild Indian with his ears cut in ringlets, or his nose slit like a swine . . . also sets his foot on the same extensive tract of soil. . . . I wonder if Congress or the different States would recognize the claim? I am so far from thinking the Indians have a right to the soil, that not having made better use of it . . . I conceive they have forfeited all preference to claim, and ought to be driven from it."

From the American Revolution to 1871 the United States government negotiated formal treaties with the Indian tribes as if they were virtually independent nations, yet similar formalities were not employed in initiating war on the Indians. Of the nearly four hundred treaties drawn up, more than half concerned Indian lands. Most of these treaties reduced the amount of land a tribe possessed, presumably for its own good, and solemnly guaranteed that it should retain the remainder as long as it remained a tribe.

After the Revolution, Congress assumed responsibility for Indian jurisdiction and protection formerly held by the British government. It instructed the governor of the Northwest Territory not to neglect any opportunity to extinguish Indian rights west to the Mississippi river, and he was to adhere to all treaties "unless a change of boundary, beneficial to the United States, can be obtained."

Those Americans who felt remorse over the mistreatment of the Indians were still unable to understand Indian attitudes toward property. To Americans the greatest civilizing force in the world was private property, and many men could not appreciate the Indians' refusal to embrace the American way of life and devote themselves to acquiring property. The Indians preferred, and many still do, tribal ownership of land to private ownership. As early as 1812 one American noted with bewilderment, "All they do is for the common weal, and private interest scarcely finds any place to enter."

Some whites might have been more sympathetic toward the Indians if they had shown a strong desire to accumulate private property, and submitted to becoming imitation white farmers. But what happened to the few tribes that made a sincere effort to support themselves by farming? Two of the best examples, the Cherokees and Winnebagoes, were forced to give up their lands again and again, usually with the total loss of all improvements and livestock. The Winnebagoes were forced to abandon their farms and move so many times that they finally simply gave up and took to the bottle. As one Senator remarked of the Indians:

"Their misfortune is that they hold great bodies of rich lands, which have aroused the cupidity of powerful corporations and powerful individuals."

Again and again Congress attempted to establish Indian families on individually owned small farms, but only on rare occasions was this practice ever acceptable to the Indians. When tribes such as the Cherokees and Winnebagoes did take up farming seriously, in every case envious whites soon found ways of depriving them of their lands.

Tribes were frequently referred to as "nations," and were so regarded in the treaties negotiated with them. Whites assumed that a chief had arbitrary powers to enforce his will on members of his tribe. But a chief's power was limited at best, and few chiefs had anything but the power of persuasion to induce their people to obey treaty stipulations. When unruly young warriors broke the treaties, the chiefs and their tribes were regarded as perfidious and completely untrustworthy. Yet the whites continued to make treaties and to hold the chiefs responsible for the behavior of others, over whom they had no traditional or legal control.

American frontiersmen, on the other hand, were no better controlled by their officials than the young braves insofar as abiding by treaties with the Indians was concerned. Whenever the Indians held lands coveted by the whites, the latter began pressuring them and Congress, and when the interests between whites and Indians clashed, the Indians invariably lost. As Benjamin Franklin once remarked, "it appeared to me that almost every war between the Indians and the whites has been occasioned by some injustice of the latter towards the former." In 1817 Andrew Jackson, who had the frontiersman's contempt for Indians, declared, "I have long viewed treaties with the Indians an absurdity. . . ." In the 1860s General Harney indicated that he regarded promises to Indians as sardonic jokes. He would not go among the Sioux again, he said, because they might ask him for all of the horses and cattle promised them in treaties.

The same story of land encroachment and treaty violation was repeated over and over as the frontier pushed westward. From time to time men called "prophets" arose in the desperate tribes and urged their people to abandon the ways of the whites and to return to their old ways. Among these men were the Delaware

Prophet, the Seneca Handsome Lake, whose teachings formed a religion still followed by many Iroquois, the Shawnee Prophet, who was Tecumseh's brother, and Wovoka, the Nevada Paiute who inspired the Ghost Dance.

In addition to the prophets, there were Indian leaders who clearly foresaw that their only hope of survival lay in uniting a number of tribes in the defense of their lands. King Philip was the first of these, followed by the Ottawa Pontiac, the Iroquois Joseph Brant, and the Shawnee Tecumseh. Pontiac and Tecumseh organized confederations that came fairly close to success for a time and might have succeeded, if the Indians had been familiar with confederations and alliances.

The role of Congress is not always easy to assess, for it was like a great, headless creature that moved in strange ways. Even when Congress blithely overlooked its own treaties or the frontiersmen's violations of them, it is difficult to fix blame on individuals or even groups. Some congressmen, perhaps the majority at any given time, were conscientious in fulfilling their duties. But when Congress delayed passing an appropriation bill to carry out a treaty stipulation concerning food and clothing and took no action until starving, freezing Indians rebelled, its inaction seems almost criminal.

Between 1778 and 1871 the government negotiated formal treaties with the individual tribes as it did with foreign nations. The first of these treaties, with the Delawares in 1778, provided that in the future the tribe might unite with others to form a state. Nearly four hundred separate treaties were negotiated with the various tribes, but the novel idea of statehood was abandoned for a policy of whittling down the Indian lands. In 1871, because the House of Representatives was jealous of the Senate's treaty-making prerogatives, the treaty system was abandoned in favor of "agreements." The name changed, but the theme remained the same. "The making of unfair treaties and the violation of treaty rights are the two things of which the Indian has the most right to complain . . . ," said agent McLaughlin in his book *My Friend The Indian.* As Will Rogers later remarked, "If the Indian had only known he was starving, being shotgunned off his hunting-grounds and having his squaw debauched for his own good, he'd have tried harder to be like his white brother looting the treasury. . . ."

FORKED TONGUES AND BROKEN TREATIES

Choctaws

"I acknowledge myself decisively and inconcilatly [sic] hostile to the policy of pushing Indians to the frontier—both as to its wisdom and its humanity; but . . . it has received the eulogy of scientific philanthropists, in their closets, who learn the savage character from the unerring medium of the books: and the system has been adopted by the federal government. . . ." (His underlining).

Letter from James W. Bates (congressional delegate from Arkansas Territory) to Sec. of War John C. Calhoun, November 28, 1820, Carter, *Territorial Papers*, XIX, 238.

CHAPTER 1

The Choctaw Indians: Negotiations for Survival

Arthur H. DeRosier, Jr.

UNTIL RECENTLY the history and plight of Native Americans have been one of the most neglected topics in American history. Possibly the neglect stems from the fact that this chapter of the American drama presents a side of the story most white Americans would rather forget than record. In no way does a full view of Indian history substantiate the self-portrait we accept as the essence of the American character — fair-mindedness, Judeo-Christian ethics, honesty, hard work, and individual and national integrity. Of course, Americans have never been so naive as to suggest that there are not a few unpleasant pages that mar an otherwise glorious history of orderly and dynamic growth from thirteen weak and independent entities in 1776 to fifty states that together represent one of the most powerful forces in the world today. The problem is that we have tried to accentuate the positive and forget, or at least underplay, the negative. While we have lauded the founding fathers, taken pride in such documents as the Declaration of Independence, the Gettysburg Address, and the Atlantic Charter, and marveled at our capacity for industrial development, we have dismissed with passing generalities the horrors of slavery, the rape of our environment, and the systematic destruction of the original owners of this land. Excusing past mistakes with generalizations is undoubtedly as much a trait of other people as it is Americans: it is part of human nature to prefer beauty to ugliness. But deep down in the subconsciousness of any people worthy of pride in heritage and accomplishment is the realization that someday the ledger must be

ARTHUR H. DEROSIER, JR. is Vice Chancellor for Academic Affairs and Professor of History at the University of Mississippi. He is the author of three volumes: *Through the South with a Union Soldier* (1969), *The Removal of the Choctaw Indians,* and (with others) *Four Centuries of Southern Indians* (1975). Also, he has published in various scholarly historical journals around the country more than thirty articles most of which deal with various aspects of the Indians' dilemma in America.

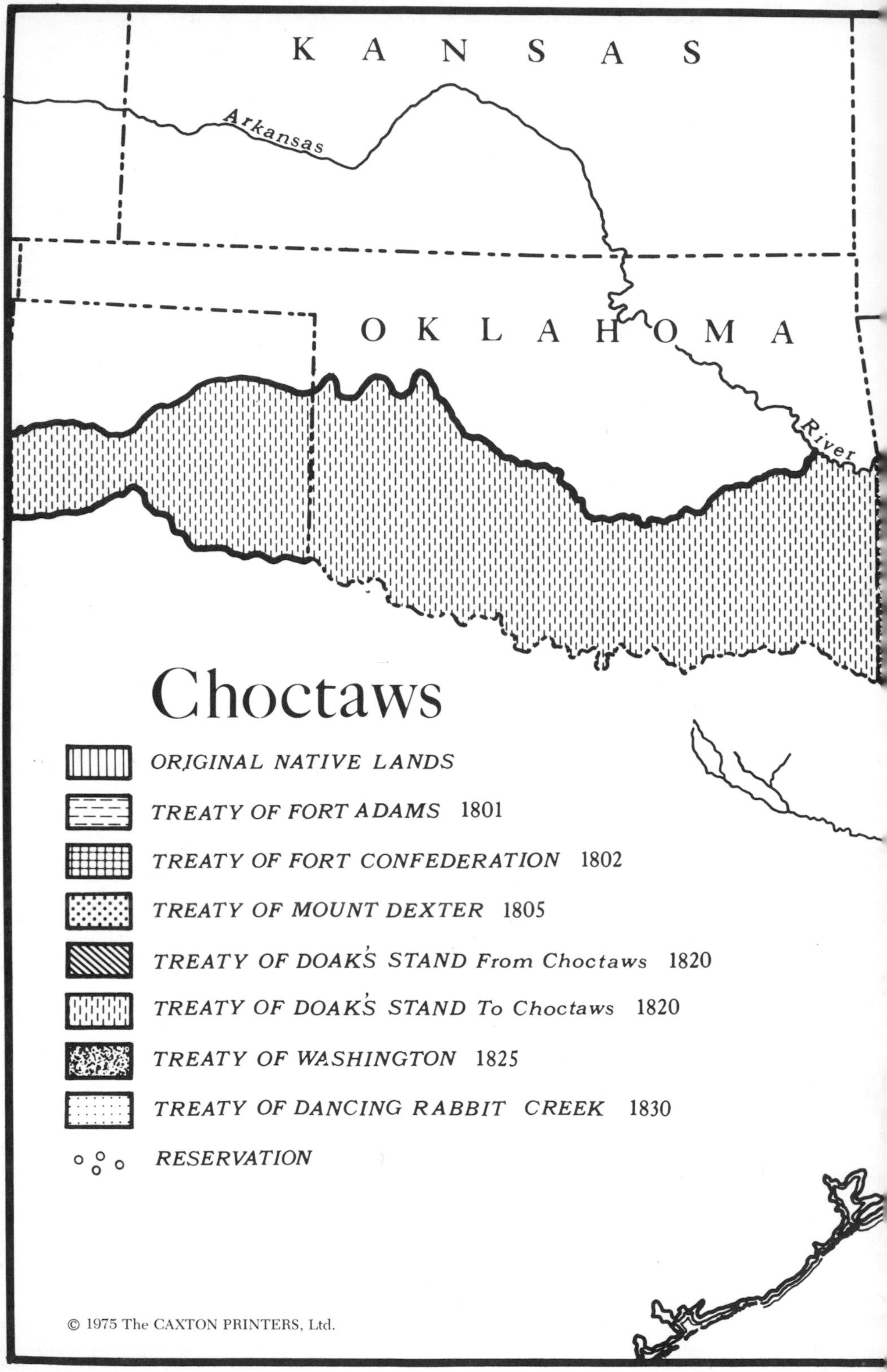
KANSAS
Arkansas
OKLAHOMA
River
Choctaws
ORIGINAL NATIVE LANDS
TREATY OF FORT ADAMS 1801
TREATY OF FORT CONFEDERATION 1802
TREATY OF MOUNT DEXTER 1805
TREATY OF DOAK'S STAND From Choctaws 1820
TREATY OF DOAK'S STAND To Choctaws 1820
TREATY OF WASHINGTON 1825
TREATY OF DANCING RABBIT CREEK 1830
RESERVATION

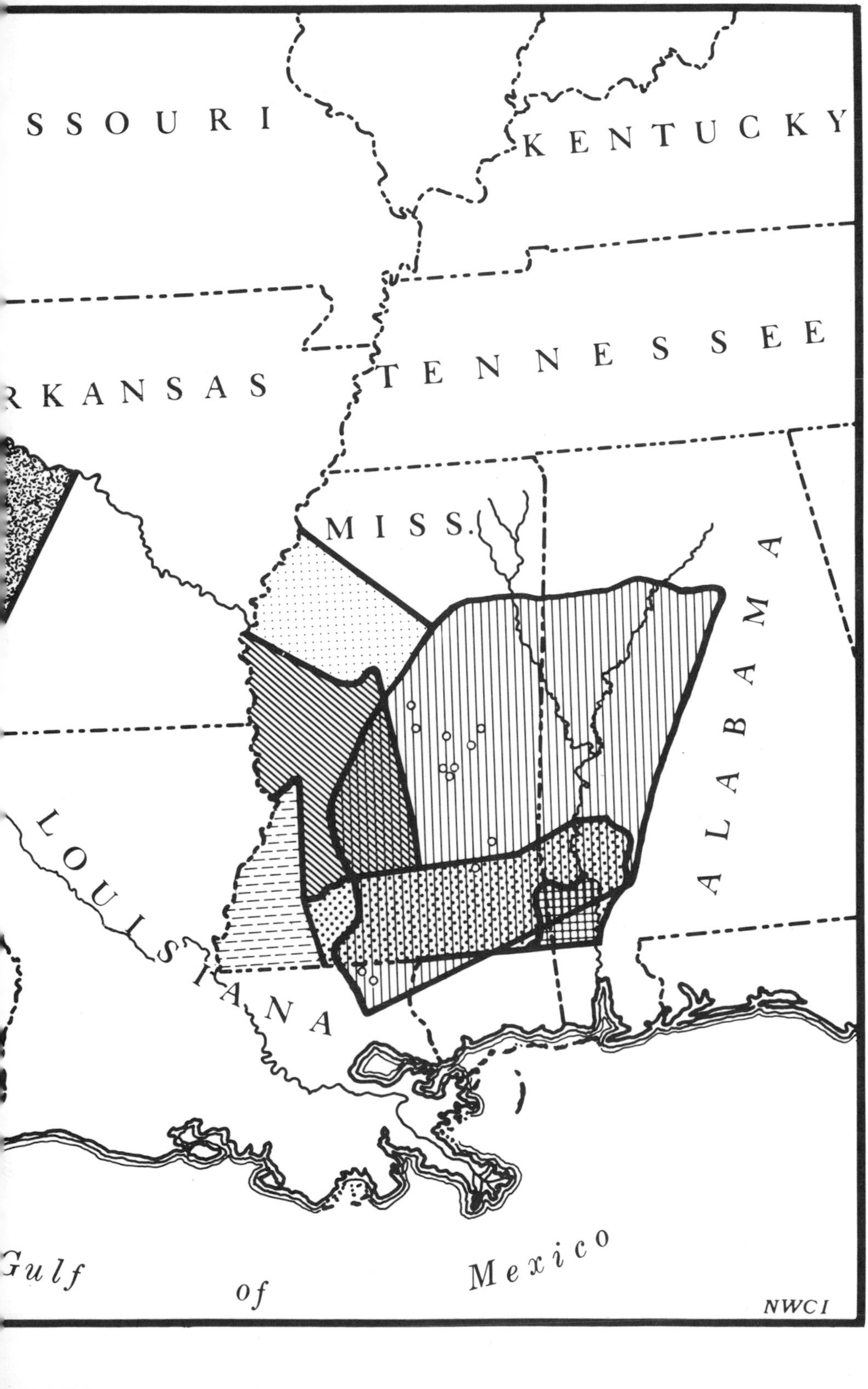
SSOURI
KENTUCKY
TENNESSEE
RKANSAS
MISS.
ALABAMA
LOUISIANA
Gulf
of
Mexico
NWCI

balanced and the whole story must be revealed. That day for the American Indians is now. For more than four hundred years, historians, anthropologists, novelists, poets, politicians, and untold others have taken refuge in the myth that the Indian was a red savage who deserved his fate and that, in reality, Spaniards, Frenchmen, Englishmen, and Americans were civilizing and Christianizing Native Americans by systematically depriving them of their heritage and their land. In this day of relevance and critical self-evaluation, Americans no longer swallow past myths and pat answers. Instead, they want to use truth and understanding to chart a new course of action to insure that the Indian's future will be better than his past. For that reason, Helen Hunt Jackson is out and Vine Deloria, Jr. is in, as evidenced by the incredible success of his 1969 *Custer Died for Your Sins*. Americans are ready to accept Deloria's statement that "it is up to us to write the final chapter of the American Indian upon this continent."

In recent years this new Indian awareness has resulted in an avalanche of volumes, scholarly essays, articles, and novels that attempt to re-evaluate past utterances on the subject. In all too many of these accounts, however, original source material has been neglected in favor of pious and subjective self-criticism. This approach simply will not do. If we are going to retrace past red-white relationships, we ought to search for the same kinds of source material that we demand while studying the Hamiltonian System or the wartime efforts of Woodrow Wilson. And, if one is willing to search and dig deep enough, Indian source material is available, though not nicely catalogued, indexed, or microfilmed. This volume is not an attempt to evaluate available source material, but it is about Indian treaties — one of the most valuable sources for research on the subject.

It amazes me to realize how little has been written on the subject of Indian treaties. Maybe it is that treaties are such obvious sources of information that we tend to overlook them; maybe it is that we feel that treaties end things, and we are looking for beginnings and middles of stories. Whatever the reason, the neglect has been monumental and the results disastrous. This is particularly true when studying the Southern Indians, who probably participated in more treaty negotiations than most Native American groups. They were subjected to so many treaties that one seems to run into the next with such rapidity that the full red-white story before 1840 appears to be one long treaty, instead of many lesser ones. One could make a good case for studying the plight of Southern Indians as one continuous treaty negotiation, but, then, the essentials of the story might be lost in the mass of names, dates, treaty sites, and treaty provisions. However, since one tribe was handled much like the next, and since the goal was always the same — the securing of Indian land — it seems more appropriate to me to concentrate in each chapter of the Southern story on one tribe and a representative treaty than to attempt a discussion of all treaties among all tribes. For that reason, in this chapter and the two that follow, we will look at the contents of three monumental treaties with the Choctaw, Cherokee, and Creek Indians and attempt not only to understand the contents of each treaty but also to learn how they were implemented and how they were thwarted.

At first glance, Indian treaties appear to be dull and lifeless documents, obviously negotiated by unsophisticated and untalented diplomats. Nothing could be further from the truth. Using the 1820 Treaty of Doak's Stand between the United States and the Choctaw Nation of Mississippi as our example, we can learn a great deal about the mentality of the day by first reading the treaty carefully without attempting to learn its specific provisions. For example, this treaty — and all other Indian treaties I have ever read — begins with the assumption that white Americans were intelligent, highly civilized, well-educated beings, and red Americans were inferior stone-age children. This is an important assumption to understand before reading a treaty's provisions because it bears directly on the contents of the document and the manner in which it was negotiated by the War Department.

The Treaty of Doak's Stand is relatively short, containing some sixteen articles. But interspersed among these articles are statements and inferences about Indian inferiority. For example, the treaty begins with the statement that it was "important for the President . . . to promote the civilization of the Choctaw Indians, by the establishment of schools amongst them. . . ." It continues by requesting that the Choctaws trade a small bit of Mississippi land for a larger amount in the West "where all who live by hunting and will not work may be collected and settled together." This short introduction in the treaty tells us much that is of prime importance in understanding the mentality of the day. It was generally assumed that all Indians were uncivilized, uneducated, and unequal. It was further assumed that Indians were not farmers and that they lived independent of each other, roaming all over the place hunting for a living.

The second assumption is easier to refute than the first because it doesn't deal in semantics. The Choctaw Nation was the largest Indian group living east of the Mississippi River, numbering around twenty-two thousand inhabitants in 1820. The people lived in communities or towns spread over most of what is today Mississippi and a bit of western Alabama. They were governed by a sophisticated political system that allowed able administrators to rise to positions of prominence while maintaining an unusual amount of individual freedom. The Nation was subdivided into three political entities — the Northwestern, the Northeastern, and the Southern districts — each with a *mingo* (principal chief), elected by the men of the district, and an elected district council. They were assisted by elected captains and subcaptains who ruled the several villages, or towns, and were responsible for implementing the district directives on the local level. Above the district level was the Nation with an elected national council that met periodically at the request of one of the mingoes. Much has been written on the political sophistication of the Choctaws and the fact that they did live together in towns, or smaller communities, and farmed the land. In fact, my studies on the tribe have shown that they were farmers second to none in America. They were the only tribal group east of the Mississippi River that harvested more crops and raised more cattle than they could consume; they were always looking for customers to whom they could sell surplus goods. But despite their agricultural achievements and political sagacity — well known by many people before 1820 — the Doak's Stand treaty begins with the assumption that Choctaws lived by hunting and were not "settled together" on the land. This general myth about all Indian tribes, handed down from 1492 onward, was so ingrained in white American thinking by 1820 that no evidence to the contrary would have been accepted by either settled Easterners or frontiersmen.

Courtesy Smithsonian Institution

Nanih Waya Mound, 1918

Also, the statement about the need "to promote . . . civilization" was, if anything, even more generally accepted by most white Americans. Since the word "civilized" is such a subjective one, the contention that Indians were uncivilized savages was simply stated and almost universally accepted by whites who made no effort to understand their red neighbors. Even today it is the "uncivilized savage" myth about Indians that Americans are least willing to abandon. If we could somehow eradicate the words "civilized," "uncivilized," and "savage" from the English language, we would have made untold progress; they are meaningless terms that render understanding impossible. The truth of the matter is that the word "civilized" is totally subjective and undefinable. It has been defined since the beginning of time in terms of what "I" feel comprises a civilized man or a civilized approach to things. There is no universality to the term because "I" is not universal. Each of us is a product of a certain nation or culture, or a combination of a few nations or heritages. Since we start with the assumption that each of us is a civilized man, it is almost impossible for us to define the word so that it applies to persons who are not a part of "our" heritage. Since Greeks, Romans, and northern Europeans were the ones who defined the components of "civilization" and "the civilized man," it is only natural that the definitions that emerged mirrored the best of those heritages. But what about the peoples of Africa, Asia, the Middle East, Eastern Europe, or, more to the point, the *skraelings* (Native Americans) that Lief Ericson met in America in 1000? Could they possibly fit the European definition of "the civilized man"? Of course not; no more so than they could meet the European definition of "beauty" or "proper dress." The definitions were not universal and could not be, but for centuries we have falsely indicted those who fall without the components as uncivilized savages who needed to be changed over in our image. Herein lies one of the great tragedies of mankind — semantics. And what is even more tragic is that we will probably never escape the trap of some definition or other.

Therefore, the Treaty of Doak's Stand, like all others, began with two indefensible assumptions: that Choctaws were uncivilized beings who needed white schooling for salvation, and that they were hunters who had not yet learned to live together. The treaty contained many other references that reinforced these basic assumptions. Article one maintained that the transformation of the Choctaws into civilized agricultural Americans was a "grand and humane object"; Article four suggested that under white tutelage the Choctaws "shall become so civilized and enlightened as to be made citizens of the United States"; and Article twelve stated that one of the government's main objects was "to promote industry and sobriety" among the Indian tribes of America. Other examples from this particular treaty could be used to reiterate the suggestion that, despite all of the War Department directives to the contrary, Americans did not believe they were negotiating with equals. But these few should suffice to show that Indian treaties were not negotiated by equal contestants sitting around a table thrashing out major points of difference. Instead, the U.S. agents approached the treaties with a feeling of superiority and the unchallengeable belief that they were dealing with children of the forest who had to be saved from their own ignorance of their low position on the scale of civilization.

The Choctaw Indians were well acquainted with the United States government before 1820. By that date they had had twenty-five years of experience negotiating with Americans to the east. In January, 1786, they negotiated and signed their first treaty with the United States — The Treaty of Hopewell — which began the American encroachment on the Choctaw tribal domain in Mississippi. The treaty contained eleven articles covering boundaries, commercial concessions, and rights and duties in future relations with the U.S. Article nine stipulated that the U.S. Congress would have exclusive right to regulate all future trade with the tribe and "to manage all their affairs in such manner as they think proper." And Article three granted the U.S. three tracts, each six miles square, for the establishment of trading posts among the tribe.

In December, 1801, the Choctaws negotiated a second treaty at the insistence of the U.S. — the Treaty of Fort Adams. It was one-sided, granting the Choctaws nothing but friendship and peace in return for 2,641,920 acres of valuable land and the privilege of constructing an east-west road through the Choctaw lands. The treaty was an obvious effort at appeasement, but it failed. The next year, the U.S. demanded continued negotiations to settle permanently the northern and eastern boundary of the Choctaw Nation. The tribe relented and surrendered a small piece of land at the October, 1802, Treaty of Fort Confederation.

In less than a year the government was back at the negotiation table with the Choctaws trying to collect debts owed to the government trading posts and Panton, Leslie and Company, a British trading firm. The result was the Treaty of Hoe Buckintoopa, which ceded to the U.S. 853,760 acres of Choctaw land in August, 1803, in lieu of payment of these debts.

Though the Treaty of Hoe Buckintoopa was a minor one generally lost among other agreements that brought the U.S. millions of acres of Choctaw land instead of thousands, it has a significance of no little importance in the treaty story. Since assuming the presidency in early 1801, Thomas Jefferson gave much time and attention to "the Indian problem." Because of his earlier thoughts and words about Indian-white equality and the need to live together at peace in the same land, many have since accepted the statement that in Thomas Jefferson the American Indians had a friend in the White House. They did not! By 1803

Jefferson, always a vote-conscious pragmatist, had developed a policy that would enable the U.S. to secure much Indian land without fighting a single battle or really even negotiating. He sincerely believed that soon Indians were going to have to abandon their tribal existence in favor of locating individual families on small farms and sending Indian children to schools offering an elementary education — with an emphasis on learning the basic elements of American law. Indians needed to learn to read and write, Jefferson preached. In addition, Indian boys needed to receive special instruction on the proper approach to agricultural and mechanical trades, and girls needed to be taught spinning and weaving. One cannot fault Jefferson's desire to educate Indians in order for them to play a significant role in a white society that was obviously going to control all the land east of the Mississippi River, and probably beyond, within a few years; it represented the best thinking of the day. The trouble lies in his preachments that Indians abandon their tribal way of life and become independent farmers. One might logically ask, why? Certainly one reason would be to adapt Indians to the white social and economic structure around them; that was the reason offered by Jefferson and leaders who followed him for the next thirty years. But there was another more sinister reason — to acquire Indian land. If tribesmen were forced to settle on a section, a half-section, or one-fourth of a section of land, the remainder of the tribal estate would be available to land-hungry white settlers. To bring this statement into sharper focus, let us deal with some actual figures. The Choctaw Nation, at the time the U.S. became a nation, numbered at least twenty-two thousand people who lived on about twenty-five million acres of land. If each person — not families as Jefferson suggested but each individual — were granted a section of land (six hundred forty acres) that would amount to a total of fourteen million eighty thousand acres, leaving an excess of eleven million acres for non-Indians to purchase from the government. If they were granted one-half of a section, the amount of land needed would be seven million forty thousand acres, leaving eighteen million excess acres; if each tribesman were granted one-fourth of a section (more likely because that was the basic unit of land purchase after the Land Law of 1800) only three million five hundred and twenty thousand acres would be necessary to house

Courtesy Mississippi Department of Archives and History

Pushmataha, Choctaw, d. 1824

twenty-two thousand tribesmen, leaving over twenty-one million acres for other people. The Jefferson suggestion foresaw, therefore, the acquisition of more than four-fifths of the Choctaw tribal estate without firing a shot or negotiating a treaty. This idea was later stated quite well by President James Monroe when he said that "the earth was given to mankind to support the greatest number of which it is capable, and no tribe of people have a right to withhold from the wants of others more than is necessary for their own support and comfort."

To acquire this land, Jefferson encouraged the growth of "factories" among the various Indian tribal groups in the East. These factories would allow tribesmen to purchase all manner of goods at fair government-regulated prices, and would also offer them a place at which they could sell or trade furs, deer skins, and other commodities. Also — and this was more important in Jefferson's thinking — the factories would encourage the Indians to purchase everything they wanted on credit. Credit was to be unlimited; Indian debt was the aim of the government. Then, when the Indians' debts were large and burdensome, the Indian agents were to call for immediate payment which, of course, the tribesmen could not meet because theirs was not a money economy. Knowing this, the government would offer an alternative — the acceptance of land in lieu of debt payment. This was the course followed by the government after 1801, and the Choctaws at Hoe Buckintoopa were the first tribal group to surrender part of their tribal estate to meet debts owed factories.

But the Choctaws did not learn from this bad experience. They had become quite dependent on the factories and continued to purchase goods on credit after 1803. By mid-1805 they were once again in financial difficulties and owed Panton, Leslie and Company forty-eight thousand dollars in back debts. When the government called upon the tribe to pay these debts, again they could not do so, and therefore reluctantly agreed to meet U.S. negotiators at Mount Dexter in the Nation to settle matters. Before the November, 1805, negotiations were completed, the Choctaws were compelled to trade 4,142,720 acres of land in southern Mississippi and southwestern Alabama for the paltry sum of $50,500 — $47,500 for Panton Leslie and Company and $3,000 for the tribe. Thus, for slightly more than eight cents per acre, the U.S. secured from the Choctaws in 1805 more land than all previous treaties combined. That was quite a bargain when we remember that the government now had an opportunity to sell the land to settlers at the minimum auction price of two dollars per acre.

Thus ended the Choctaw land cessions before 1820, except for a small amount of land ceded after the Creek War to rectify their northeastern boundary. It would be unfair to state that the U.S. broke any treaties negotiated with the Choctaws before 1820; there was no need to do so. In return for peace, harmonious relations, and balanced ledgers, the U.S. had secured approximately 7,700,000 acres — almost one-third of the Choctaw Nation. This was done without one war, without establishing one school (something the U.S. supposedly wanted to undertake), and without the expenditure of one dollar for trinkets, blankets, food, or medals.

More ominous for the Choctaws and all other eastern tribal groups was a policy expounded by Jefferson but never inaugurated during his administration — the removal of all Indians to new homes west of the Mississippi River. After the Louisiana Purchase of 1803, Jefferson believed that all eastern Indians should be transplanted onto these lands, leaving the East for white expansion. Though his preachments on this subject were never translated into action, it remains his most significant "contribution" to Indian affairs; in fact, this possibility was so attractive to white Easterners that in short order it became a national blueprint for the future, a future that was not far away. As the Choctaws entered the important treaty negotiations of 1820 at Doak's Stand, they were faced with the first effort of the U.S. government to translate this white dream into an Indian nightmare. Because of this fact, the Treaty of Doak's Stand may well be the most significant treaty ever negotiated by an American tribal group.

At the Doak's Stand treaty negotiations, the U.S. through its commissioners — Andrew Jackson and Thomas Hinds — had one goal in mind: the securing of the Choctaws' homeland for an equally large or larger estate west of the Mississippi River. The government was not naive enough to expect to achieve this goal easily or through this one treaty. But it fully expected to begin a process that would be irreversible in the future, not only for Choctaws but for all eastern Indians. After all, precedent is

Courtesy Mississippi Department of Archives and History

General Thomas Hinds

all-important in American history; if the government could establish a new precedent in 1820, it would have accomplished a task of no little significance.

The Choctaws were not totally helpless at these negotiations. President James Monroe was assisted by a secretary of war — John C. Calhoun — upon whom he depended heavily in Indian matters. For that reason, Calhoun and not Monroe was charged with charting the future course of American-Indian relations. No matter how controversial the rest of his career may have been, Calhoun was a great secretary of war who tried to combine efficiency, good judgment, and fairness in all matters of importance. For that reason he has been hailed by many as the best secretary of war the U.S. ever possessed. His contemporaries called him "the father of the War Department."

In Indian matters, Calhoun showed his mettle and his competence. He agreed with Jefferson that Indians had to be concentrated on individual holdings, educated, and removed west of the Mississippi to save them from extinction in the East. But unlike many of his contemporaries, especially Andrew Jackson, he would not force a single Indian to move to a new home, if he preferred taking his chances in the East. Many have suggested that there was really no difference between Jefferson, Calhoun, and Jackson in Indian matters, and that emphasizing his refusal to force the inevitable upon them, as Jackson would and did later, is simply dealing in semantics. I do not agree with this assessment. True, eventual removal of Indians was his goal, but his reason for pursuing this goal and the procedure he would follow in achieving it were quite different and out of step with the times. Nowhere in his correspondence, position papers, and public utterances do I detect the suggestion that Indians must be removed to make more land available for a white population desiring, above all else, more cotton land in the Old Southwest and more corn and wheat land in the Old Northwest. For most Americans, including both Jefferson and Jackson, philosophical and humanitarian reasons for removal were unnecessary and hypocritical. They wanted the land, and they would use factories, duress, and wars to acquire it. The goal was worth the risks involved. But Calhoun would not accept this position; his sense of fairness would not allow him to do so. He wanted Indian removal for another reason — to save the tribesmen from extinction. Calhoun was a pragmatist and a realist. He knew that it was utterly impossible to stop the westward expansion of America. Settlers wanted new lands and they would acquire them one way or another. They would sweep onto tribal land, squat there, and keep it no matter what the government said or did. It was just the way things were in 1820. The Indians would be subjected to constant pressure by the squatters and the worst elements of white society, and they would eventually lose. To save them from suffering and eventual death — at least tribal death, therefore, Calhoun would move them to a land as large and as rich as their present one.

Not only was Calhoun's reason for removal different from that of most of his contemporaries, but so were his procedures. No matter how important it was to remove Indians to a new and safer haven, he would not force them to leave if they chose not to take his advice. He fervently desired removal as quickly as possible, and he would help establish educational institutions to point out the need for it, but, in the final analysis, he would prefer tribal extinction to the use of force. That fact, and his removal reason, set him apart from other government leaders and rank and file Americans. It could surely jeopardize his political future, especially in his own South and its offspring, the Old Southwest, but he maintained his position from 1817 until he left office eight years later.

With Calhoun's promise of fair negotiations, encompassing the right of Indian self-determination, the Choctaws entered the Doak's Stand negotiations with a mighty weapon. This governmental position, and their own solidarity against leaving their ancient homeland, made them a formidable diplomatic foe for Jackson, Hinds, and their constituency.

But the fact of the matter is that pious utterances from Washington, D.C., do not a treaty make. Neither do they have much effect on what happens at a negotiation site in the middle of the Mississippi woods, especially when the negotiator is a strong-willed personality, such as Jackson, free from governmental restraints and a prying press. Even though Jackson promised to present the government's case fairly and to allow tribal self-determination, he was, in truth, able to employ time-honored methods of Indian negotiation — the use of whiskey, cajolery and threats followed by incredible promises that couldn't possibly be kept. All of these elements were present at Doak's Stand as Jackson employed whatever tactics he chose. He set policies and granted lands that belonged to other nations; he threatened war by angrily stating, on one occasion, "this is the last attempt, we repeat it, that will be made to treat on this side of the Mississippi. . . ." If the Choctaws did not sign the type of treaty desired, they might be forced across the river and then made to accept a *fait accompli* treaty. This was not moderation and fair-dealing, no matter how you define the terms.

With no other recourse available to them, the Choctaws signed the Treaty of Doak's Stand on October 18, 1820. They escaped losing all their land, but they did trade more than ever before — 5,169,788 acres in western and southwestern Mississippi, including the fabulously rich delta lands. This amount represented about one-third — and the best one-third — of their entire tribal holdings as of 1820. Article one of the treaty carefully stipulated the exact boundaries of the land ceded. Article two contained a much more general and less exacting description of the land ceded to the Indians in what would soon be called Indian Territory (Oklahoma). It is obvious in reading the second article that Jackson, and the government for that matter, knew practically nothing about the western country. The boundaries (mainly following rivers) granted to the Choctaws thirteen million acres of land in Arkansas Territory, Indian Territory, and Spanish Texas. The government later charged that a tragic mistake had been made in Article two, for it surely would not grant Indians land already settled by whites in Arkansas Territory and it was somewhat embarrassing to learn that through ignorance of the country they actually granted another nation's lands. But I have never been convinced that Jackson cared whether he made a mistake or not. His object was to acquire eastern land, and he cared not what he had to grant Indians to get it. At first glance, it would seem that the Choctaws were well treated, for who wouldn't trade five million acres for thirteen million in return? That argument is only viable, however, if one assumes that the Indians would be allowed to keep the thirteen million acres received. No such assumption can be made. As far back as 1803, Jefferson stated that the government would remove Indians to the west of the Mississippi and allow them to stay there until white population caught up with them. They would be moved again and again as the white population advanced. "When we shall be full on this side," Jefferson wrote, "we may lay off a range of States on the western bank [of the Mississippi River] from the head to the mouth, and so, range after range, advancing compactly as we multiply." If one accepts the inevitability of continual removal to the west as whites inexorably advance, what difference does it make how much land the government grants Indians or whose country it is located in? The only object is to get the eastern land now; the western land will take care of itself at a later date. It didn't take very long for the Choctaws to lose a goodly portion of their western cession, as we will see later in this chapter.

The rest of the treaty — articles three through sixteen — contained six general ideas that should be briefly described and discussed. Articles three, four, and fifteen were concerned with the marking of boundaries and the ownership of the eastern and western lands. Article three stipulated that both the eastern and western boundaries would be located by a commissioner appointed by the U.S. and not the Choctaws. The Indians were allowed to appoint someone to accompany the commissioner and act as a guide, for which the government would pay him two dollars per day, but the actual work was to be done and the decisions made by a representative of the United States. This was an important concession for the U.S. to receive; it opened the door to the possibility of acquiring more eastern land than listed in Article one and the surrendering of less land than was generally outlined in Article two. And if this occurred, there was no way the Choctaws could veto the action.

Articles four and fifteen contained assurances that the U.S. loved the Choctaws, honored their sovereignty, and wished them well in their future development. In Article four the government promised not to request any additional eastern lan "until the period at which said nation shall become so civilized and enlightened as to be made citizens of the United States; and Congress shall lay off a limited parcel of land for the benefit of each family or individual in the nation." No more land acquisition until Indian citizenship and Indian acceptance of American ideas on land ownership, the treaty said, but such was not to be the case. This was an important U.S. pronouncement; it contained the policies evolved by Jefferson and Calhoun to that date. But it was to be a meaningless statement that was never considered binding on the government. The Choctaws were to be called on to cede some of their western land in 1825 and all of their eastern land in 1830, but citizenship was not available until the twentieth century. Article fifteen contained a general statement that was slightly different, but desired by the tribe. It promised perpetual peace and harmony between the two peoples. It was a part of future Choctaw treaties, and those with most other nations, but was only recognized by the citizens of the U.S. as long as the Choctaws were willing to meet their demands. Articles four and fifteen were meaningless necessities that the U.S. later felt free to alter at a moment's notice.

Articles five, six, twelve and thirteen were more specific and more important articles concerning aid the U.S. would give for future tribal advancement. Article five suggested that all Choctaws living on the ceded land migrate to the West aided by generous U.S. aid. To every Indian male who left Mississippi, the government would give a blanket, kettle, rifle, bullet moulds and wipers, and ammunition enough for one year's hunting. The migrant would also be given corn enough to supply his and his family's wants for one full year from the date he left. To aid those who settle in the Indian Territory, Article six stipulated, the U.S. would appoint an Indian Agent, a factor, and a blacksmith to live amongst the western Choctaws. They would be selected by the government without consulting with the Choctaws, but the Indians could decide where in the western country they wanted these persons located. Lastly, the government would appoint a removal agent to accompany those who wanted to migrate west. Since almost no tribesmen actually did migrate west from 1821 to 1830 (some estimates indicate that as many as fifty persons migrated in this period, and others indicate as few as eight actually left), the promises made in these articles were never really needed or demanded by the Choctaws.

Articles twelve and thirteen contained interesting stipulations that were never honored by the government. The former promised that both the western and eastern Indian agents would stop the whiskey trade in the Nation. They would be granted power to confiscate all whiskey in the Nation, except that sold by the government at public places, or brought into the Nation for sale by persons with special permits issued by the Agent or the three principal Choctaw mingoes. This article was never enforced, but even if it had been, there were enough loopholes to allow a continual fountain of firewater to be available to all tribesmen who desired it. The latter article — thirteen — contained an idea totally foreign to Indians but a necessity in "civilized" society — the establishment of a police force. Article thirteen urged the Choctaw leaders to organize a "corps of light horse" consisting of thirty men — ten for each district — to maintain peace and tranquility in the eastern portion of the nation. The force was to be empowered to regulate the lawless activities of both whites and reds. The government would supply each district with two hundred dollars to establish these district corps, which would be raised and administered by the mingoes and charged with enforcing the payment of honest debts, the maintaining of order, and the removing of all "bad men" from the nation. A "bad man" was described as a lawless Indian or a white who did not have a permit from the Agent to live and work in the Choctaw Nation. The idea was novel, typically American, and totally unenforceable: also it was never put into effect. In the first place, it was inconceivable to Indians that anyone needed a police force to regulate the activities of the citizens. Secondly, the real purpose of the police force was to force Indians to pay their debts to white storeowners in the Nation. The force would never have branded any whites as "bad men" because all whites had to do to escape the jurisdiction of the corps was to get a permit from the white Agent in the nation. He, of course, would give a permit to almost anyone who asked for one, and that piece of paper automatically made a white a "good man" despite anything he might do. Such a definition is totally unacceptable, in fact absurd. And the Choctaws saw through it with ease and never established such an organization.

Articles seven and eight were concerned with funds for schools and annuities. Article seven promised that the U.S. would use funds received from the sale of fifty-four sections of one square mile each for the purpose of supporting Choctaw schools east and west of the Mississippi River. Three-fourths of the funds were to be used for schools in the east, one-fourth for schools in Indian Territory. The money would not be given to the Choctaws to establish the schools; rather the President was to be charged with the task of gathering the funds and establishing whatever schools he desired. This is a most important article; it promised the Choctaws federal aid to education, an idea not accepted by white Americans. Even if the idea may have been important, however, it didn't prove to be significant for education of either red or white in the country, for the article was never implemented. The U.S. did grant funds to a variety of religious missionary societies to establish schools, but it did not sponsor any on behalf of the United States.

Article eight was more meaningful than Article seven and contained some important educational and humanitarian stipulations. In previous treaties the U.S. had granted the Choctaws annuities of a certain sum for many years. The Choctaw mingoes had used ninety-six thousand dollars of this money — six thousand dollars a year for sixteen years — for the support of schools being established in the Nation by the American Commissioners for Foreign Missions of the Presbyterian and Congregational churches. The U.S. government was so impressed with this generosity that it promised, in Article eight, to match this sum by earmarking funds received from the sale of the ceded Choctaw land for this purpose. The government also promised to spend whatever was necessary to see to the wants of every deaf, dumb, blind, and distressed Indian in the Nation. The money would come from the matching educational grant just mentioned. If any money remained unused each year after meeting this need, it was to be parceled out in equal amounts to all members of the tribe. Both Articles seven and eight were important for a number of reasons: they show a desire by the government to make white education available to Indians (this was especially desired by Calhoun); they showed how education-conscious the Choctaws were by 1820; and they recognized the need for special attention to less fortunate members of society. Though both articles were not carried out as stipulated in the treaty, they did, especially through Article eight, bring into the tribe federal money that was used for future educational activities.

Articles ten, eleven, and fourteen included special grants and showed the willingness of the U.S. to rectify previously broken treaties. Article ten was a tricky little article seemingly binding the U.S. to pay for improvements Choctaws had made on land now ceded. The government was to pay for buildings, roads, and other improvements, but only if the tribesmen claiming compensation under this article migrated to the West. If they simply moved to a new location on the remaining Choctaw eastern land, they would not be paid. The article, of course, was meant as an incentive to migrate, but it was grossly unfair and indefensible. Improvements are improvements; those made by Indians who refused to leave Mississippi were just as valuable as those made by others who accepted the terms. It was uncalled-for duress that didn't work, but it did cause ill will among the Choctaws for years to come.

Article fourteen was a grossly unfair attempt to over-compensate the mingo who offered the least resistance to the treaty negotiations. Mingo Mushulatubbee, the son of a previous mingo with the same name, was granted a special annuity of one hundred fifty dollars a year for the remainder of his life. This was done on the pretext that the U.S. had granted a like amount to his father while he lived, but the singling out of Mushulatubbee caused much hard feeling among the other mingoes, captains, and the rank and file of the nation. It was a mistake for Mushulatubbee to accept this special consideration; it hurt his future political career in the Nation.

Article eleven included a promise by the U.S. government to pay those Choctaws who had fought with General Jackson at Pensacola during the War of 1812. They had been promised this payment in 1813, again in 1816, and now for a third time in 1820. Some had died and their descendants were not to receive payment in their name. But if they were still among the living, the U.S. would pay them in full and give as an added bonus a blanket, shirt, flap, and leggings. Many years would pass before the payment was actually made to these warriors.

Articles nine and sixteen do not fit into any categories as do the other articles, but are of prime importance. In fact, they may well have been the two most important articles in the Treaty of Doak's Stand. Article nine was an outright effort to implement the thinking of the day concerning the fate of all eastern tribesmen. It stated that all Indians who lived on ceded land could remain there on a tract one mile square to include all improvements, if they were willing to give up their tribal life and become American farmers who owned the land with a deed and paid taxes on it. Indians who did so would surrender their Indianness and become regular tax-paying Americans. If they chose to retain their Indian heritage and migrate to the West, the Article continued, they would receive all of the benefits stipulated elsewhere in the treaty for migrants. Either way the U.S. could not lose: either the Indians became ordinary Americans, subject to the laws of the land, the state in which they resided, and the local units of government, as Jefferson had suggested before 1803, or they migrated west as Jefferson and other government officials had desired after 1803. No Choctaws chose to accept the former opportunity, and only a few the latter, but the article showed that by 1820 the U.S. was, indeed, endeavoring to carry out policy decisions that foresaw the breakup of tribal entities or removal west.

The last article — Article sixteen — is of prime importance to anyone interested in understanding the inequality that existed in red-white treaty negotiations. The article simply stated that the treaty would go into effect for both parties when it was ratified by the Senate of the U.S. and signed by the President. Nowhere in the article was there a suggestion that it needed also to be ratified by the National Council of the Choctaw Nation and signed by each mingo. This is proof positive that the U.S. looked upon Indian treaties as a one-way agreement that did not need joint approval. No such stipulation can be found in U.S. treaties with England, France, or other foreign countries. But when dealing with Indians, it was assumed that the treaty was operative as soon as the U.S. accepted it. Not only was the suggestion insulting to Indians, but it opened wide the possibility of Indian wars and conflicts between Indians and settlers on the frontier. Many treaties negotiated by Indian commissioners were not, in reality, accepted by the tribe and therefore were not in effect, but the U.S. government and its frontier settlers never considered that possibility. As long as it was negotiated by Indians and white Americans and ratified by the proper U.S. authorities in Washington, it was assumed to be in immediate effect. From that point onward, the government viewed Indian efforts to guard their land as "bad faith."

In this chapter it has been suggested that the Treaty of Doak's Stand was negotiated by U.S. commissioners who developed their own policy, and that many articles in the treaty were never carried out by the U.S. The Treaty of Doak's Stand emerges, therefore, as an important document and as a broken one. None of the articles that promised the Choctaws various benefits were put into effect before permanent removal from Mississippi in 1830. True, part of the reason for this fact was that the Choctaws refused to move to their new lands in the Indian country. The government couldn't carry into effect articles five, six, part of seven, ten, and part of twelve if the Indians refused to migrate west. Since this was a treaty in which the Choctaws surrendered a carefully stipulated portion of Mississippi land for a larger amount of land in the West, it would seem that the treaty was not broken by either the Choctaws or the U.S., if articles one and two were carried out. Proceeding on that reasoning, we must conclude that the Choctaws did not break the Treaty of Doak's Stand because they did cede to the U.S. all land promised in Article one. The U.S. did not, on the other hand, cede to the Choctaw Nation all of the land promised in Article two. As mentioned earlier, the boundaries of the western lands were loosely stated, and it was soon discovered that the government had ceded the Choctaws part of Arkansas Territory and lands in Spanish Texas. Even before the treaty was ratified, infuriated Arkansas citizens pointed out to the Senate that Jackson had ceded to the Choctaws forty thousand square miles of Arkansas Territory. Arkansas Territory had been established in 1819, and many of its settlers believed that the territory's western boundary was the one-hundredth meridian, far to the west of present-day Arkansas. The Doak's Stand treaty, then, moved the Arkansas Territory western border four hundred fifty miles east of the one-hundredth meridian, much farther east than any Arkansas settler could accept. Before the Doak's Stand negotiations ever began, in fact, seventeen townships had been put up for sale to white frontiersmen on lands ceded to the Choctaws. Many excused the mistake by claiming that Jackson made the cession because of a lack of knowledge about the geography of the area, but that is hard to accept when it is realized that seventeen townships had been surveyed and advertised for sale; a simple check with the Land Office would have established that fact before he went to Mississippi to negotiate the treaty.

Be that as it may, the U.S. now was faced with a dilemma — the ire of white frontiersmen vs. a treaty promise to the Choctaws. The map enclosed with this chapter shows how much of

Courtesy Smithsonian Institution

Mushulatubbee, Choctaw chief (from a Catlin painting)

southwestern Arkansas Territory was ceded to the Choctaws. It included five counties and, according to Henry Downs, who surveyed the eastern boundary of the new Choctaw western lands for the U.S. in September 1821, the disputed land included three thousand whites who had settled on it in good faith. He recommended that a new boundary be drawn from the mouth of the Canadian River on the Arkansas, south to the Red River.

The squabble was an interesting one because it didn't really include the Choctaws. They had a treaty that was specific enough to protect them against all encroachments. If the U.S. did not honor its grant of land, the Choctaws could reverse the procedure and retake all of their Mississippi land. But the squabble did affect other elements of American society, especially in Mississippi and Arkansas. The *Arkansas Gazette* served as the spokesman for the "injured" citizens of its Territory, and a variety of Mississippi newspapers spoke up in defense of the treaty. The *Gazette* complained that "It is no doubt good policy in the states to get rid of all the Indians within their limits as soon as possible; and in doing so, they care very little where they send them, provided they get them out of the limits of their state. The practice heretofore has been to remove those poor deluded wretches into the weakest and most remote Territories. This we consider the worst policy our government can pursue with the Indians, as the Territories into which they are sent are generally thinly populated, and consequently not able to resist the aggression of a fierce and savage enemy. . . ." The *Mississippi Gazette* replied that the Choctaws were civilized and well mannered, and advised the citizens of Arkansas Territory that they had nothing to fear from the gentle Choctaws. The editor of that paper continued: "In the course of time, the territory of Arkansas will also claim a state of independence, the Indians must then be removed from her soil — and she will set but little importance upon the arguments now volunteered for her. . . ." The *Arkansas Gazette* countered by suggesting that if the Choctaws were such nice gentle souls Mississippi should keep them to uplift her own citizens and not ship them west to Arkansas. And the blistering editorials went on and on; from 1821 to 1825 paternal Mississippi and irate Arkansas Territory pleaded special interests to an embarrassed government in Washington.

Congress finally acted in March, 1823, by adopting legislation that would redraw Arkansas Territory's western boundary to correspond with the southwestern corner of Missouri due south. Of course, it was stipulated that the Choctaws would have to accept this change in the 1820 treaty. Still, the citizens of Arkansas Territory fumed because they still stood to lose nearly nine thousand square miles of land earlier claimed. Calhoun appointed William Woodward of Arkansas and Thomas Hinds of Mississippi to meet in the latter state to obtain the Choctaws' consent. On the appointed day, Hinds didn't even show up to discuss the matter with Woodward because, as he later stated, he knew the Choctaws would not entertain any suggestions to change the boundary in Arkansas Territory. A frustrated and thoroughly angered William Woodward returned to Arkansas denouncing Hinds, the State of Mississippi, politicians in Washington, and even the Choctaws.

The boundary of western Arkansas became the major issue in the 1823 election for territorial delegate to the U.S. House of Representatives. Henry W. Conway won, ousting James Woodson Bates on the charge that he had allowed the Treaty of Doak's Stand to be ratified and had not done anything subsequently to present the case of the territory to his fellow legislators in Washington. Conway proved to be more persuasive than Bates in Washington, and in May, 1824, he led Congress in the passage of a new law that repealed the act of March, 1823, and replaced it with one setting Arkansas Territory's boundary along a north-south line forty miles west of the southwest corner of Missouri. As in the previous legislation, the implementation of the law was predicated on Choctaw acceptance. Before the tribesmen were even asked to offer a reply, the U.S. surveyed and marked the new line. This activity proved to be an unnecessary expense; the heretofore quiet but observant Choctaws had no intention of accepting this unlawful act.

To secure Choctaw consent and to resolve the dilemma, Secretary Calhoun requested that the tribe send a delegation to Washington for a new treaty negotiation. Everything possible was done to make their visit pleasant and memorable. An almost unlimited expense account was granted them for liquor, jewels, clothing, and anything else that struck their fancy. The twelve Choctaw delegates accepted the government's generosity and, indeed, enjoyed Washington to the fullest, but when the negotiations began they proved to be anything but passive, rejecting one proposal after another. When the Choctaws were finally asked what they thought would be a fair settlement, they immediately suggested a complete compliance with the treaty of 1820, plus thirty thousand dollars worth of presents over a two-year period, nine thousand dollars a year for twenty years to support an institution of higher learning among the Mississippi Choctaws, a like amount to educate their children in other colleges, and three thousand dollars annually for twenty years for the education of Choctaws who might migrate beyond the Mississippi River. Indeed, the Choctaws had become sophisticated negotiators under U.S. tutelage, requesting all these items as U.S. compensation for not having yet implemented most of the Doak's Stand provisions.

These requests were unacceptable to Calhoun, but they did provide a point from which to negotiate. Finally, on January 20, 1825, the Treaty of Washington was signed. The Choctaws relented on their western boundary contentions and ceded back to the U.S. all land east of a north-south line beginning on the Arkansas River one hundred paces east of old Fort Smith and running to the Red River. This provision deprived the tribesmen of three thousand square miles of land acquired by treaty in 1820. But they didn't allow the U.S. to break the 1820 treaty cheaply. In return for this cession the Choctaws received six thousand dollars per year perpetual annuity to be sold to the government for a lump sum settlement or continued permanently any time after twenty years; an additional six thousand dollars a year for sixteen years as promised in the Treaty of Doak's Stand and not yet delivered; a government waiver of all claims to back debts owed by the Choctaws; and U.S. compensation to all Choctaws who fought in the War of 1812. It will be noted that two of the four provisions can be discounted because they simply restated broken promises of five-years' standing. Also, it should be noted that the U.S. was still indebting Indians at trading posts — a practice that had paid off handsomely for over two decades. The Choctaws were left, therefore, with a six thousand dollar perpetual annuity which had to amount to at least one hundred twenty thousand dollars — six thousand dollars a year for twenty years — and probably would amount to many times that figure, if the Choctaws used wisdom and hardheadedness in 1845.

The sad thing about the Treaty of Washington is that once again the real losers were the Indians. They had been solemnly promised a certain area of land only to lose a goodly portion of it to insistent whites. If the U.S. made a mistake in 1820 by ceding them part of Arkansas Territory — and it is seriously doubted that Jackson did not know what he was doing — then why should the Indians have to be the ones to pay for a U.S. mistake? They did — in this treaty and most others — which made the Treaty of Washington typical and not exceptional. But the question might well be asked why it had to be this way. It had to be because it was U.S. policy, since Thomas Jefferson established it that way in the first decade of the nineteenth century, that tribal groups must give way to westward expansion to the Pacific coast and beyond whenever the government requested it.

Unfortunately for the Choctaws, the Treaty of 1825 did not settle the boundary between Arkansas Territory and the Choctaw Nation. The treaty stipulated that the new boundary had to be run as quickly as possible, and to complete that task, the Department of War selected James S. Conway of Arkansas, the brother of Territorial Delegate Henry W. Conway. He proceeded to run the line to the advantage of Arkansas and purposely included about 161,000 acres of Choctaw land in the Territory. Though the Choctaws complained for decades to come, they never recovered these lost acres. Rather, after an incredibly long series of court cases and pleas to Congress for justice, the U.S. Court of Claims finally, in January 1886, found in favor of the tribe and awarded it not the land, or even a fair price for the land, but $68,102.00 (less than fifty cents per acre) in compensation after which the land was legally incorporated into the State of Arkansas.

Worse still is the fact that much of the remaining Choctaw land in Indian Territory was lost to the Chickasaws and other tribes who were crowded into Indian Territory from the east after 1830. In the end, the Choctaws retained only what is today southeastern Oklahoma, a small portion of the original grant of 1820. The government of the United States, in the Treaty of Doak's Stand, thus began not only the process of Indian removal to land west of the mighty Mississippi, but also a series of treaties that would be broken again and again until all eastern tribes

Courtesy Smithsonian Institution

Emil John, Choctaw, 1908-1909

were removed west, concentrated on reservations, or incorporated into the general population.

SUGGESTED READING

Baird, W. David. "Arkansas's Choctaw Boundary: A Study of Justice Delayed," *The Arkansas Historical Quarterly,* XXVIII (Autumn, 1969), 203-223.

Cotterill, Robert S. *The Southern Indians: The Story of the Civilized Tribes before Removal.* Norman: University of Oklahoma Press, 1954.

Debo, Angie. *The Rise and Fall of the Choctaw Republic.* 2nd Edition. Norman: University of Oklahoma Press, 1961.

DeRosier, Arthur H. Jr. *The Removal of the Choctaw Indians.* Knoxville: The University of Tennessee Press, 1970.

Horsman, Reginold. *Expansion and American Indian Policy, 1783-1812.* East Lansing: Michigan State University Press, 1967.

Peake, Ora Brooks. *A History of the United States Factory System 1795-1822.* Denver: Sage Books, 1954.

Prucha, Francis Paul. *American Indian Policy in the Formative Years: The Indian Trade, and Intercourse Acts 1790-1834.* Cambridge: Harvard University Press, 1962.

Young, Mary Elizabeth. *Redskins, Ruffleshirts and Rednecks: Indian Allotments in Alabama and Mississippi 1830-1860.* Norman: University of Oklahoma Press, 1961.

"At this time [1838] when the liberties of a noble but unfortunate race are about to be closed down by the cupidity of an avaricious people: when a stain is about to be cast upon our National Escutcheon which the tears and regrets of after ages will never be able to remove, it becomes the duty of all the friends of humanity to raise their voices against the measures and the men who would thus entail disgrace upon this country and ruin upon its aboriginal inhabitants."

Part of preamble of resolution offered to Congress by citizens of Philadelphia, Pennsylvania in 1838.

CHAPTER 2

The Cherokee Indians: Disaster through Negotiation

Arthur H. DeRosier, Jr.

IN NOVEMBER, 1785, leaders of the Cherokee Indians and representatives of the United States government met in Hopewell, South Carolina, to negotiate a treaty of perpetual friendship and peace. It was the first treaty between this powerful eastern Indian nation and its new neighbor, the United States of America. If one reads the treaty provisions without any knowledge of the subsequent history between the two peoples, he might well suspect that it was not only the first treaty they wrote but also the last. After a short description of the boundary lines between the two nations, the negotiators, in article after article, promised that future relations between white Americans and red Cherokees would be a model of fair-dealing, mutual respect, and peaceful co-existence. The treaty was one long hymn to sanity as the U.S. promised that the Hopewell agreement was "definitive"; that "the Indians may have full confidence in the justice of the United States . . . "; and that "if any citizen of the United States, or other person not being an Indian, shall attempt to settle on any [Cherokee] lands . . . such person shall forfeit the protection of the United States, and the Indians may punish him or not as they please." The treaty seemed to please everyone present, and it was negotiated in an atmosphere of lighthearted anticipation. How could anyone alive at that time have foreseen the terror that was to follow? It was utterly impossible that any living person could have predicted that during the next fifty years the Cherokees would have to withstand more pressure, endure more threats, negotiate more treaties, and suffer more indignities than any other eastern tribal group. The chapter of American history begun at Hopewell in 1785 ended at New Echota in 1835, and the "trail of tears" it sanctioned defies description. No movie or

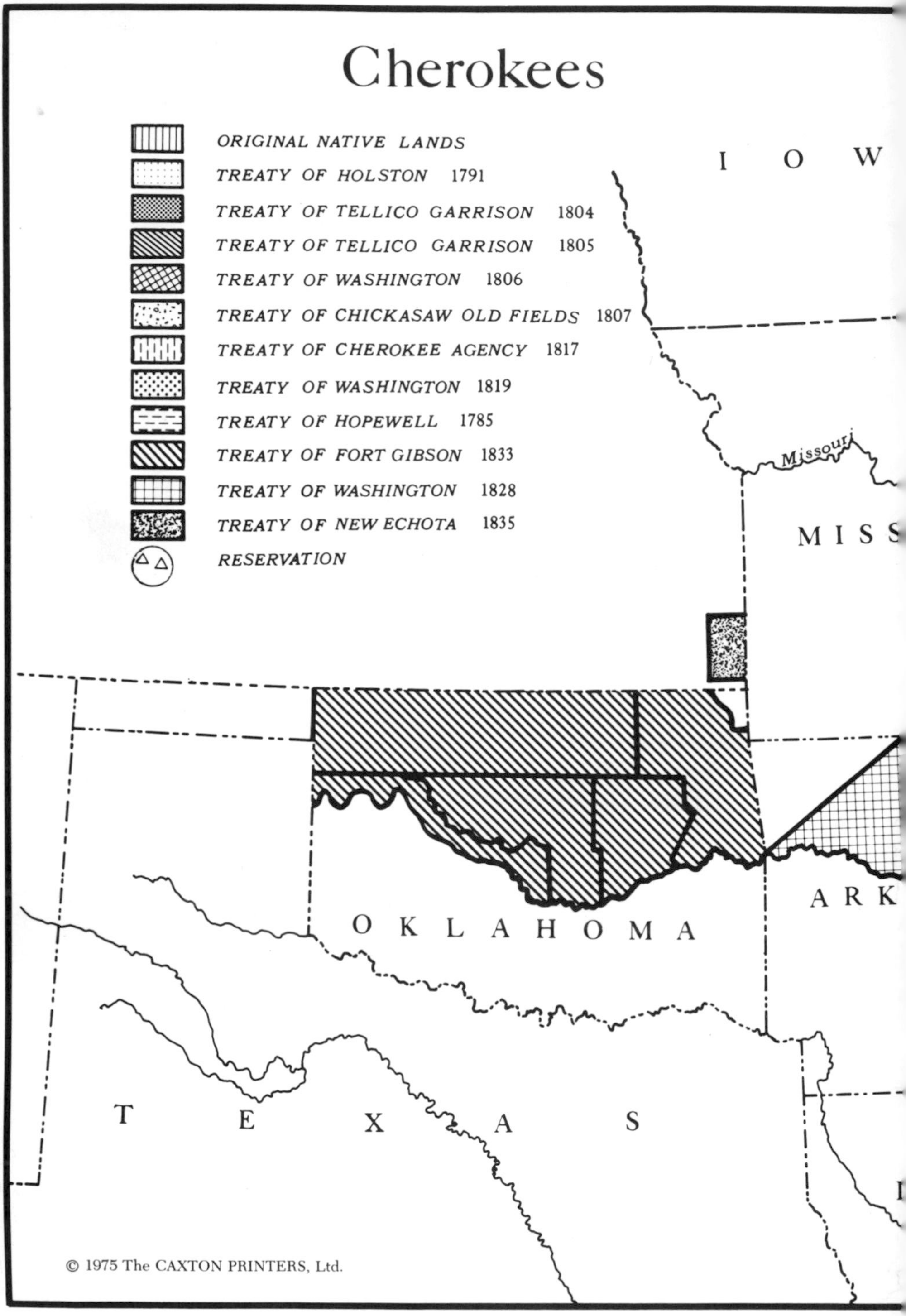
Cherokees
ORIGINAL NATIVE LANDS
TREATY OF HOLSTON 1791
TREATY OF TELLICO GARRISON 1804
TREATY OF TELLICO GARRISON 1805
TREATY OF WASHINGTON 1806
TREATY OF CHICKASAW OLD FIELDS 1807
TREATY OF CHEROKEE AGENCY 1817
TREATY OF WASHINGTON 1819
TREATY OF HOPEWELL 1785
TREATY OF FORT GIBSON 1833
TREATY OF WASHINGTON 1828
TREATY OF NEW ECHOTA 1835
RESERVATION
I O W
Missouri
M I S S
A R K
O K L A H O M A
T E X A S
© 1975 The CAXTON PRINTERS, Ltd.

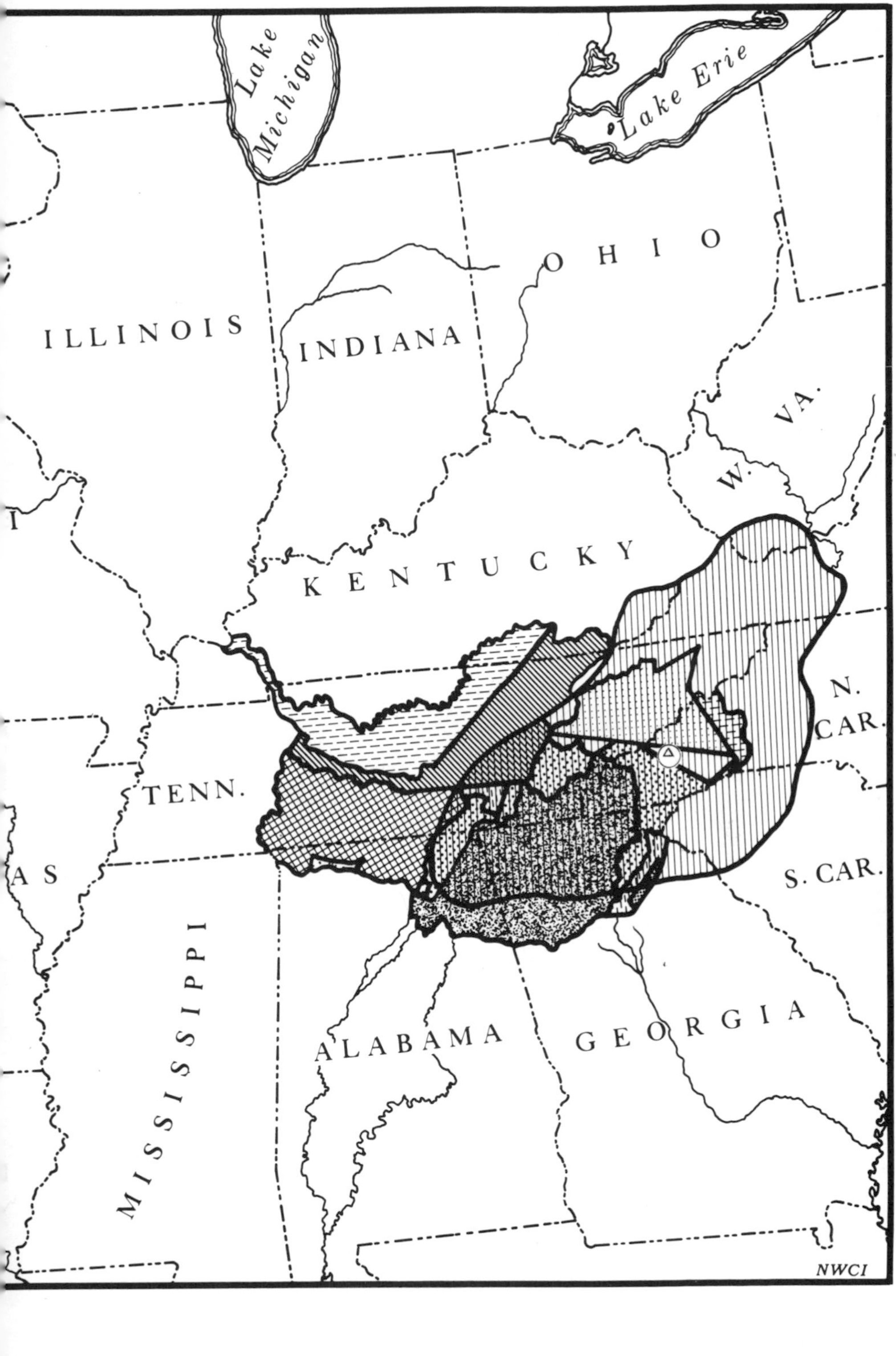
Lake Michigan
Lake Erie
ILLINOIS
INDIANA
OHIO
W. VA.
KENTUCKY
N. CAR.
TENN.
S. CAR.
MISSISSIPPI
ALABAMA
GEORGIA
NWCI

Courtesy Smithsonian Institution

Stalking Turkey, Cherokee chief, painted in London, 1762

TV screen writer could have written such a drama; it was beyond human contemplation. And yet it happened! The promise of perpetual occupancy offered the Cherokees in 1785 was replaced in 1835 by the option of annihilation or total westward removal. The pathos of the drama was summed up well in January 1833 by an editorial in the *Cherokee Phoenix* which stated, in part: "The beautiful and beloved country of the Cherokees is now passing into the occupancy of the Georgians. . . . [Our land] is wedged with settlers, and droves of land hunters, to which the Indians daily cry, and it is literally, 'Robery! Robery!' "

The Cherokee removal story has fascinated and haunted white Americans for over one hundred years. More has been written about this tribe than any other east of the mighty Mississippi. When one ponders this fact, in the light of the relative neglect accorded tribes of equal size and accomplishment, he finds it difficult to explain. It is not because the Cherokees were the first to go; actually they were one of the last eastern tribes to surrender their ancient homeland. It is not because they occupied the choicest soil in the land-hungry East; they lived in a hilly and even mountainous country that contained some of the least desired cotton land of the Old Southwest. Possibly it is because they did not live on the far-off fringes of the Old Southwest or Old Northwest as did the Sauk and Fox and the Chickasaws. Their close proximity to the southeastern states not only made the Cherokees newsworthy but also brought them into contact and conflict with the earliest trans-Appalachian migrants. Their interest to historians and novelists might also stem from the fact that the Cherokees adopted many of the "white man's ways" in the early nineteenth century, an adoption which in no way protected them from the label of "savage" and eventual removal, as missionaries predicted it would. Whatever the reason, one thing is sure — the Cherokees have not been forgotten in American history as have so many other tribal groups.

Cherokee relations with white Europeans date back to 1540 when Hernando de Soto moved through their nation on his way north from Florida and west to the Mississippi River. The settlement of Carolina in 1670 brought whites back to the general vicinity; the Cherokees negotiated their first treaty with South Carolinians in 1721, ceding land for promised protection and perpetual friendship. From that date until the last eastern treaty in December, 1835 — the Treaty of New Echota — the Cherokees negotiated thirty-eight treaties with English and United States governments and refused almost yearly to negotiate other agreements. No other eastern tribe — and possibly national tribe — signed more treaties with the U.S. than did the Cherokees. All contained the inevitable promises that no future cessions would be requested and that Cherokee ownership of the remaining lands was recognized and honored. And, of course, as soon as the ink dried and the treaty was ratified, the government was back requesting new boundaries so that whites who had illegally settled on Indian land could live within the United States once again.

Because of the availability of many fine volumes on the Cherokees it is not necessary to spend much time introducing the tribe and pointing out significant milestones in its history. This has been done admirably by others, especially Henry Thompson Malone, Grace Steele Woodward, and Thurman Wilkins. Also, we will not concern ourselves with all thirty-eight treaties negotiated by the tribe which, taken together, achieved not friendship and co-existence but removal and death. Rather, this chapter will attempt to show how the U.S. approached the Cherokees in the latter part of the eighteenth and early nineteenth centuries; how the Cherokees handled their more powerful white neighbors; and how the treaty story led inevitably and inexorably to tribal removal. Broken treaty promises will be highlighted along the way. The main object, however, will be to analyze the negotiations and contents of the final removal agreement — the Treaty of New Echota — and to show how its terms led to the infamous Cherokee "trail of tears."

As is true with most American tribal groups, little is known about the early history of the Cherokees. Most of the major Southern tribes migrated to that area from the West and are lumped together into what is called the Muskogean linguistic group. For example, the Choctaws and Chickasaws probably migrated southeasterly from the Siouan lands of Minnesota and the Dakotas. Such was not the case with the Cherokees. They were originally Iroquoian and trace their previous residence back to upstate New York or western Pennsylvania. Some time during the pre-Columbian period, probably because of pressure

Courtesy The New York Historical Society

Cherokee man, 1820, wearing coat made of trade blanket

exerted by enemy tribes in the area or dissatisfaction with the lands they occupied, they left the Iroquois country and migrated south, following the Appalachian Mountains to their southern terminus, where they developed a nation second to none in size east of the Mississippi. By the eighteenth century, when white European colonists first contacted the tribe, the so-called Cherokee Country was, indeed, something to behold. It stretched as far north as the Ohio river and as far south as the headwaters of the Savannah river. It included much of what is today Kentucky, Tennessee, western North and South Carolina, southwestern Virginia, northeastern Alabama, and the northern half of Georgia. Because tribesmen settled in various parts of this vast holding, and because Cherokees and most other tribes abhorred the idea of central administration, the nation included four general areas: the Over Hill region below the Cumberland River in Tennessee along the Tellico river; the Middle Towns on the Little Tennessee and Tuckasegee rivers; the Lower Settlements along the upper reaches of the Savannah river; and the Valley Towns located west of the Middle Towns. In all, probably eighteen thousand tribesmen lived on these lands making the Cherokee Nation second only to the Choctaw Nation in size among tribal groups residing east of the Mississippi River.

Not only was the Cherokee Nation large and populous but it was also feared. As is often the case, geography has a way of shaping a people; the Cherokees were no exception. They were tough because they had to be to survive. They did not have any natural frontiers that segregated and protected them as did the Choctaws with the Gulf Coast and the Seminoles with the Gulf and the Atlantic Ocean. More than any other tribal group, the Cherokees hacked out an empire right in the middle of eastern America. It had to be taken from others and defended on all sides from those who objected or who desired to expand. To the west and southwest stood the hated Creek Confederacy almost equal in population and just as fierce: they put constant pressure on hundreds of miles of disputed boundaries in that area. To the north were the powerful Shawnees who claimed Kentucky as their ancient hunting grounds and constantly crossed the Ohio river from the north to kill Cherokees, if the occasion presented itself. To the northeast were the kindred Iroquois who hunted and raided southward along the Appalachian ridge. To the east, in the Carolinas, were the Tuscaroras doing essentially the same thing. Add to these major enemies dozens of lesser tribes who, whenever the opportunity arose, saw nothing wrong with extending their hunting and fishing expeditions on to Cherokee lands and killing a stray tribesman or two along the way. If the Cherokees were not a tough people before they migrated south, they soon became one. They had to be tough to survive, let alone to expand and prosper.

And these northern "carpetbaggers" did prosper in the South. They did it by concentrating themselves in villages in the four main tribal regions. They did not live independent of each other, wandering at will throughout their nation. Rather, they concentrated their strength at four strategic locations, lived in dozens of villages within each region, and protected the heart of their nation from interlopers. For awhile enemies might raid at will in eastern Alabama or Kentucky, but they could not penetrate the eastern Tennessee, northern Georgia, and western North Carolina heart of the Cherokee Nation. The same was true of white frontiersmen in search of western lands. In the eighteenth century they successfully established western outposts in Kentucky, but they never could have done so in the area protected by the four regions. As the following treaties will show, the Cherokee periphery was vulnerable, and the U.S. took advantage of that fact and secured millions of acres of land before 1835, but it took traitors from within to penetrate the heart of the Cherokee holdings and destroy the tribe's eastern empire.

Much could, and possibly should, be said about the accomplishments of the Cherokees as a people. They were not "primitive forest children," as suggested by Henry Malone. They were a force to be reckoned with, not only because they would fight any and all challengers, but also because they were a highly skilled and cultivated people. Their country swept from lowlands to high mountain peaks. In the valleys along rivers and creeks and on the sides of hills, they planted with skill and knowledge. They may not have produced more food than could be consumed, as did the Choctaws, but they did not live on the rich delta lands of Mississippi either. The cool mountain air produced fine strawberries and other fruits. In the spring and summer their valleys were studded with farms producing varieties of corn, peas, beans, potatoes, tobacco, and untold other agricultural commodities. Their blankets, baskets, and art objects were known far and wide for their beauty and excellence. Even today, on both the eastern and western Cherokee lands, young Cherokee artists and artisans, many unable to write their names, are producing works of art that simply amaze anyone who appreciates beauty and talent.

Though most Cherokee historians consider the early nineteenth century as the highpoint of Cherokee achievement, that belief is open to a serious challenge. During the period after 1801 the Cherokees became more and more imitative of white society. They accepted much white law, adopted white agricultural techniques and habits, and even wrote a constitution copied almost word for word from the U.S. Constitution. If one believes that white Americans were superior beings and that Indians were inferior, it logically follows that imitating whites is progress and advancement. But at least for some persons these ground rules are unacceptable. The truth of the matter is that Cherokees were vibrant, proud, and highly successful before whites ever set foot in their country. The character of the people, the lands they ruled, the food they ate, the laws they followed, and the accommodation they made with their God and Mother Nature were long established before Englishmen, colonists, or representatives of the U.S. government came into the nation with their Bibles, bottles, bullets, and belittlement of Indian society. Then, more because of a conviction of the head rather than the heart, the Cherokees tried to reach an accord with their pushy neighbors by giving in here and there. This concession was their undoing and not their salvation! I am not suggesting that they would not have been moved west had they remained pure unto themselves. That notion is sheer nonsense. But I am suggesting that they might have thought straighter and not been sold down the river by so many fifth columnists from within had they not tried to serve two "gods." When cultures get all tangled up in the minds of men, the people become confused and disaster results. So it was with the Cherokees.

The Cherokees survived well under British control. They did make concessions to His Majesty's government in 1730 and again in 1755, but the Cherokees appreciated the British approach to things. The British government, raised and nurtured on the economic philosophy of mercantilism, had no desire to see its American colonies expand into the interior of America. They were interested in American agricultural staples and American markets for finished products and not colonial desire to balance their economy and expand westward in search of independence and "the good life." Small farms were of no value to England; they produced few if any surplus staples for hungry British factories. Also, interior agriculturalists, whether plantation owners or farmers, were faced with the nearly impossible task of moving goods to a coastal city so that British vessels could transport them to England. Worse still, expanding frontiersmen irritated Indians, who then took to the warpath and forced the British government to spend fortunes in money and men to fight wars they would rather forego. To stop this expansion and to end this red-white bickering, the British issued the famous Proclamation of October 1763, which reserved the interior of eastern America to the various tribes residing there. Though the proclamation brought down upon the government the ire of infuriated colonists, it was hailed as a significant breakthrough by the Cherokees and other tribal groups. The Cherokees, therefore, had reason to think well of the British; to no one's surprise, in 1775 the Cherokees joined the British in their civil war with the thirteen seaboard American colonies.

Without a doubt the Cherokee decision to support the British in the American Revolution was their most disastrous mistake of the century. The decision may have been a natural one, but, as the 1783 Treaty of Paris confirmed, the Cherokees backed a loser. And one must pay for backing a loser. In 1777, as the result of sound defeats at the hands of Virginians and Carolinians, the nation was forced to cede to South Carolina most of its holdings in that state and to North Carolina and Virginia large tracts within their borders. The war cost the Cherokees valuable holdings on their eastern frontier.

To suggest that the Cherokees were anxious about their future relations with the all-victorious Americans in 1783 is to put the case mildly. They had fought — and fought hard — against the U.S. in the war and, along with their English allies, had lost badly. British pride may have been hurt by defeat, but Britishers returned across the Atlantic to recoup their losses and become even more powerful than before. But the Cherokees had no such ocean behind which to hide. They had to stay and face the consequences of their actions. This situation was bad enough, of course, but the Cherokees also realized that they were not a tribe hundreds of miles west of white settlements, as were the Chickasaws; they were pressed against the eastern states of Georgia, North and South Carolina, and Virginia, all of which claimed the entire Cherokee land as their own from colonial charters. If they were going to expand westward, the Cherokees would be the first surrendered to this goal. One can imagine, therefore, the amazement of these tribesmen as they sat down with American negotiators at Hopewell in late 1785 and were told that the U.S. government did not want one inch of additional Cherokee territory. All the treaty did was to establish the formal boundary between the Cherokees and the U.S., recognizing the 1777 cession that the tribe had made to the Carolinas and Virginia. In return for Cherokee acknowledgement of land losses on the eastern frontier and the right to control Cherokee trade and to allow white traders to sell their wares in the tribal domain, the U.S. solemnly promised perpetual friendship, removal of all whites living on Indian land, and strange as it may seem, the right of the Cherokees to send a deputy to Congress.

The Indians kept their part of the treaty; the U.S. did not. The Cherokees were never allowed the privilege of sending or keeping a deputy in Congress to present their side of any question, and the U.S. did nothing whatsoever toward removing whites from Cherokee lands. Not only did those already living there stay, but others also invaded the Cherokee country. President George Washington lamented in 1790 that "upwards of five hundred families have settled on the Cherokee lands." The logical answer to the dilemma was to enforce the treaty as written and signed, but the more practical answer was to issue a call for a new treaty negotiation which, hopefully, would eliminate the problem by punishing the Indians and not the whites. So it was that the Treaty of Holston was negotiated and signed in mid-1791.

In reality, the Treaty of Holston was the one that ended the war between Cherokees and Americans: it contained not a drop of generosity as had the broken Hopewell agreement. It was negotiated by the often violent and always aggressive William Blount, Governor of the Territory South of the Ohio River. The Holston treaty included the ever-present article pledging "perpetual peace and friendship between all the citizens of the United States of America, and all the individuals composing the whole Cherokee nation of Indians." From that point on, however, Blount and his government really punished the Cherokees by taking more land on the eastern frontier, all of the remaining Cherokee lands in Kentucky, and additional lands in middle Tennessee. One historian discussing this treaty generalized that the Cherokees lost "a tract of land one hundred miles broad." If anything, that statement is a generous one; the Cherokees may well have lost considerably more than one hundred miles of land. In return for the ceded land, the U.S. "solemnly guaranteed" the remaining Cherokee country, promised again to keep white settlers out of the nation, and promised "certain valuable goods" that were never listed or described, as well as one thousand dollars annually in perpetuity. Probably the most ominous provision in the treaty was article fourteen which began the process of infiltration in order to make over the Cherokees into "white Indians." The article promised that the U.S. would, from time to time, furnish free of charge "useful implements of husbandry, and further to assist the said nation in so desirable a pursuit." The assumption was that Cherokees were hunters and not farmers and should be transformed into tillers of the soil which, of course, they already were. The article also promised roads tying together the U.S. and the nation, and four white men to serve as interpreters. The Cherokees were to give these men land for "themselves and their successors in office," so they could develop model farms for the Indians to copy. There was little in the treaty to please the Cherokees, but with no alternative, they signed it on July 2, 1791.

Even the government was embarrassed by securing so much for so little and, in a moment of generosity, Secretary of War Henry Knox amended the treaty by raising the one thousand dollar annual payment to fifteen hundred dollars. Despite this modification, the treaty was undisguised larceny. All that land for only fifteen hundred dollars a year is hard to defend no matter how you define the phrase "fair-dealing." To add embarrassment to injury, the U.S. could not do anything about getting poachers off guaranteed Cherokee land. Those people simply would not move no matter how often the government screamed and threatened to drive them out with armed might. They were not going to leave, and the government might as well have saved its breath. For these reasons above all others, the U.S. summoned the Cherokees to Philadelphia in 1794 and went back to the negotiation table. A new treaty declared that the Treaty of Holston was now in effect, promised to remove recalcitrant whites from Cherokee lands, and replaced the fifteen hundred dollars annual cash payment with five thousand dollars worth of undefined goods annually that the President would give the Cherokees in perpetuity. Obviously, these goods were to help the government "civilize" the Cherokees and therefore represent a two-edged sword that might not prove to be more generous than fifteen hundred dollars a year in cold cash. Because Cherokees were stealing horses from whites illegally residing in their nation, and these intruding whites were complaining to the U.S. government about "thieving Indians," the treaty stipulated that the government would deduct fifty dollars from the annual sum for each horse stolen by a Cherokee from poachers and not returned with ninety days. Obviously, this article is totally lacking in logic. If the U.S. intended to remove white intruders, as promised in three successive treaties, there would be no whites around from whom the Indians could steal horses. If proof were needed that the U.S. had no intention of removing poachers, or if proof were ever needed that red lawbreaking was somehow worse than white lawbreaking, this treaty stipulation would provide it.

Whites continued to pour onto Cherokee lands after 1794. The Indians continued to complain and the government continued to promise action, but nothing was done to stem the tide. Finally, in 1798 U.S. negotiators met with tribal representatives in the Cherokee Council House near Tellico (in Tennessee.) The same old guarantees of perpetual friendship, Cherokee ownership of their land, and the need to drive illegal whites out were pledged by the U.S. commissioners. In return, however, the government requested some Cherokee land in the southern part of the nation on the pretext that the boundary line there was unsettled. This was actually the land that attracted most whites and they were demanding that the government get it for them in this treaty. After much negotiation and considerable Cherokee reluctance, the tribe ceded a good amount of land along its southern border in Georgia for a lump sum payment of five thousand dollars worth of "goods, wares, and merchandise," plus an annual payment of one thousand dollars in goods "in addition to the annuity already provided for." When the eighteenth century closed, the Cherokees had ceded millions of acres of their northern, southern, eastern, and western borders in return for fifteen hundred dollars annually from 1791 through 1794; five thousand dollars worth of goods annually from the latter date through 1798; a five thousand dollar gift of goods in one lump sum; and six thousand dollars a year from 1798 onward. The government did not break these promises, but all of the others, especially those relating to the removal of whites illegally residing on Cherokee lands, were forgotten before the ink dried on the treaty.

If the Cherokees hoped that these treaties had adequately appeased the white appetite for land, they were sadly mistaken. In fact, the trend these treaties began toward contracting Cherokee holdings continued at a quickening pace as the eighteenth century gave way to the nineteenth. Many historians have continued to maintain that the nineteenth century brought Cherokee advancement and improvement, while the mounting number of treaties negotiated and ratified tells us otherwise. They continue to tell us that the Cherokees entered some type of "golden age" in 1801 which lasted until 1828, when gold was discovered in northern Georgia. The evidence offered is built around the theme of Cherokee transformation to the white man's way of life. We are told that by the 1820s the Cherokees were well-adjusted "white" farmers owning twenty-two thousand cattle, thirteen hundred slaves, two thousand spinning wheels, seven hundred looms, thirty-one grist mills, ten saw mills, eight cotton gins, and sent their children to eighteen white-operated schools. Though these statistics are common knowledge, they do not prove a thing. The Cherokees were excellent farmers long before they signed their first treaty with the United States. It would be an easy task to go back into the history of the eighteenth century and bring out statistics that are just as impressive as those mentioned above. The list might not include such white inventions as looms, cotton gins, and missionary operated schools, but it would include other things just as important. What is moot is that the Cherokees were talented people who farmed and fed themselves without the white man's gadgets; they were successful hunters without the white man's guns; and they raised animals, passed on the tribal heritage to their children, lived in harmony with one another, and incidentally, treated their women with far more respect and appreciation than did white society. The advocates of the "golden age" idea also offer as evidence of progress Sequoyah's 1821 syllabary, the establishment of the *Cherokee Phoenix,* and the drafting of the Cherokee Constitution followed by the establishment of the Cherokee Republic in 1827. These were, indeed, significant moments in Cherokee history, but what do they prove? No white man made Sequoyah the genius he was. What he did may well have been one of the greatest intellectual feats in history; surely it ranks high on the list. But it only helps prove the age-old Indian contention that they are just as bright and capable of advancement as any people who ever lived. The Cherokee were not "primitive forest children" or "stone age relics" who made advancements only when white feet entered their nation. They were as capable of great good or great evil as any other people: the fact that Sequoyah ranks with Albert Einstein, Aristotle, and Thomas Edison proves that fact. Lastly, does the drafting of a constitution, the establishment of a republic, and the acceptance of spinning wheels and cotton gins represent real advancement? I think this is the important question, and it is more than a semantical one. It seems abundantly clear that the Cherokees did these things as a part of their strategy for survival. Many of them felt that if they aped their adversaries they could appease them and save their homeland. Such was not the case and they should have known better. Their constitution and republic were not hailed as a step forward by white Georgians, who were furious when they learned what the Cherokees had done. They wanted nothing at all to prolong Indian tenure on lands they couldn't wait to steal. Was contemporary society impressed by the so-called agricultural progress the Cherokees made with their looms and grist mills? Of course not; Indian acquiescence only postponed the inevitable. Those who praised the efforts at the time, missionaries and other white friends, did so because they believed it would save the Cherokees. It did not help at all; other whites cursed the "do-gooders" as much or more than they did the Indians. So it is time we stopped repeating the missionaries' propaganda about how wonderful it was that

Cherokees imitated white society; this façade only masks the obvious truth that the Cherokees were fine people before the whites came and did not need to be nudged along the road of advancement and progress. They had always been on that road.

A perfect case in point concerning supposed Cherokee advancement in the early nineteenth century revolves around the contribution made by Agent Return Jonathan Meigs to this progress. Many historians have lauded Meigs as some sort of a prophet whose goal was to save Cherokees. Henry Malone wrote, "Fate smiled on the Cherokees in 1801 with the appointment of Return Jonathan Meigs as Indian Agent." Grace Woodward, though quite pro-Cherokee in her presentation, mentioned that Cherokee "progress was furthered by agent-appointees of Presidents Washington and Adams — Silas Dinsmoor and Return Jonathan Meigs furnishing notable examples." But when we read what Thurman Watkins has to say about "Silver Eagle," as this ex-American Revolutionary War general was known to the Indians, we find that in 1807 Meigs was bribing principal chiefs with cash and gifts in order to get their signatures on a treaty ceding thousands of acres of land. The truth of the matter is that the treaties negotiated by Meigs from 1801 through his tenure of twenty-two years — nine treaties in all — show him to be neither prophet nor friend. He was a masterful agent of his government engaged ceaselessly in depriving the Cherokee Indians of their birthright. Negotiating treaties with Indians does not, of course, automatically brand him as an Indian enemy, but it does if he went about the task with no regard for the niceties of diplomacy and if he ended up taking everything from them and giving them little in return. Such was the legacy of Agent Return Meigs.

From 1801 through 1819, Meigs negotiated nine treaties and tried to arrange many more. Taking the treaties as an aggregate, we find the same pledges of friendship as in the 1790s, the same promises that white intruders would be removed, and the same promises that each cession would be the last one requested. In return for these constantly broken promises, western land, and some money and goods, the United States secured four million acres of land on all sides of the Cherokee Nation, approximately one-third of the whole nation. Taking into consideration all payments granted the Cherokees in cash and goods from 1801 through the ninth treaty in 1819, including the in perpetuity grants then in effect, we find that the Cherokees received from the government during those dates $240,700. In return, states secured four million acres (it is hard to tell exactly how much land was ceded from boundary descriptions in treaties). By 1819, the Cherokee Nation was effectively reduced to around ten million acres, about half the size it was before the American Revolution. The money and goods paid for this land were incredibly small even for Indian treaties. For example, the Cherokees received two thousand dollars in cash for a cession in 1802; five thousand dollars in money and goods, plus a one thousand dollar yearly annuity in money or goods in 1804; sixteen hundred dollars in money or goods in 1805; and two thousand dollars a year for five years in 1806.

What was even worse than selling land for paltry sums was the fact that in the 1817 treaty the Cherokees exchanged large holdings of land in Alabama, Georgia, and Tennessee for an equally large amount between the Arkansas and White rivers in Arkansas Territory. At first glance it appears that exchanging land for an equal amount elsewhere was preferable to receiving a little money and goods and nothing else. But to the tribesmen it was not. The acceptance of western land broke down the last barrier against full tribal removal in the not-too-distant future. Though the Cherokees knew all along that westward removal was the real goal of white Americans, they held tenaciously to the treaty articles that promised sovereignty to eastern lands not freely ceded. That promise was the only thread of hope the Indians had through all those years of agonizing land cessions. The Treaty of Holston in 1791 stated clearly that "The United States solemnly guarantee[s] to the Cherokee nation, all their lands not hereby ceded." From that time to 1817, the U.S. chipped away at the lands not ceded but never got the tribesmen to admit or even to consider the possibility of exchanging all their land for a new home in the West. But in 1817 the resistance was broken; part of the nation was exchanged for land elsewhere. From that time onward until the end in 1835, the Cherokees would be bombarded with requests, threats, and subterfuge all leading to an expansion of what we might call "the 1817 idea." It is easily understandable why some Indians would get tired of fighting government agents, lawless citizens, and prophets of doom and simply give up the ghost and migrate to an area hopefully free of the tensions that surrounded life in the East. Be that as it may, the acceptance of western land in 1817 made future tribal removal inevitable.

The government hoped that most of the tribesmen living on the lands ceded in 1817, and again in 1819, would pack their possessions and migrate west. Some did, but most simply moved to the remaining Cherokee holdings. To accelerate disintegration in the 1817 and 1819 treaties, the government offered heads of families living on the ceded land American citizenship and a grant of six hundred forty acres of land with improvements. This was the famous "reservations" clause. It was hoped that most would not accept the offer and would prefer a tribal existence on land in Arkansas Territory. In other words, it was written simply to look good on paper and to allow Cherokees an alternative. To the consternation of the government, many preferred accepting a reservation in Georgia or Tennessee to migrating, and many signed up for the privilege. Some moved west, more took reservations, and even more simply moved onto the remaining tribal lands.

After the Treaty of 1819 the constant pressure exerted on the Cherokees for land cessions and western removal relented for a decade. After all, the stage was now set for wholesale removal of the Cherokees and the government had an opportunity to work out the same arrangement with the other eastern tribes. So the U.S. turned its attention to the Choctaws and Chickasaws in Mississippi and the Creeks in Alabama. Also, the new Secretary of War, John C. Calhoun, was more interested in educating Indians to the need for removal than in forcing them out. If they could but realize the advantages of removal, he reasoned, they would thank the government for its benevolent efforts and leave their present homelands where frontier pressure was bringing about inevitable conflict and Indian extermination. Another reason the U.S. attempted no further negotiations with the eastern Cherokees is that the citizens of Arkansas Territory were furious with their new Cherokee neighbors and were pressuring the government to remove them elsewhere as soon as possible. It would have been senseless for the government to muddy further already dirty waters by sending more Cherokees to the troubled Territory in the 1820s. Finally, in 1828 the government settled the problem by negotiating a new treaty with the Cherokees West. The Indians surrendered their Arkansas lands for new holdings. They were also granted the use of land directly west of their new homeland running all the way to the western limits of the United States in 1828. This was the famous Cherokee Outlet that played such a prominent role in future Oklahoma history. This same treaty, with a few modifications, was renegotiated in 1833. These treaties settled the last details that had to be ironed out before the government could negotiate a final removal treaty with the Cherokees East. The government, flushed with the victory of having uprooted Choctaws, Creeks, and Chickasaws and sent them packing to other parts of the Indian Territory in the early 1830s, was now ready to turn its attention to the pesky Cherokees.

The sequence of events that led to the Treaty of New Echota began with the drafting of the 1827 Cherokee Constitution and the establishment of the Cherokee Republic with Chief John Ross as President. The constitution was drafted not out of any feeling that the past tribal government was primitive or unresponsive, but because the Cherokees' friends, especially the missionaries, believed that such a document would prove to the government and the U.S. citizens that the Cherokees had indeed become "civilized" and saw the need to copy America's great system of government. If, the missionaries reasoned, the Indians' friends could convince their countrymen that the Cherokees had been transformed from savages into yeomen farmers with a representative government, they would be accepted as decent neighbors. But the ruse didn't work. In fact, instead of delighting neighboring whites, the Cherokee Constitution infuriated them. The U.S. Constitution specifically forbade the establishment of a state within another state, Georgians screamed, and the government should punish the Cherokees by removal for attempting to erect a republic within not one but four states. A verbal battle between the tribal newspaper, the *Cherokee Phoenix*, and Georgia newspapers and their constituents ensued.

However, the disagreement over the Cherokee's constitution was soon forgotten as gold was discovered in 1828 in the Georgia Cherokee country. Land heretofore passed over by cotton farmers and planters was invaded by a veritable herd of people

Courtesy The New York Historical Society

Cherokee Indians, about 1830

staking out mining claims with no regard for tribal boundaries. Not only did the state approve of miners trampling the rights of its Cherokee neighbors, but it joined in the debauchery. Georgia almost immediately appropriated that part of the Cherokee Nation within the limits of the state and extended its laws over all the Indians living on that land. All customs and laws of the Cherokees were declared null and void. The dispossessed Indians had nowhere to turn; they abandoned their homes and lands, therefore, and withdrew to other parts of the nation. While this disgraceful spectacle was going on in Georgia, another equally incredible drama was taking place in the halls of Con-

From Smithsonian Institution

Sequoyah (George Guess). He is holding his famous Cherokee Syllabary.

gress in Washington — the passage of the Indian Removal Act of June, 1830. The bill, as passed, provided "for an exchange of . . . lands with the Indians residing in any of the states or territories, and for their removal west of the river Mississippi."

With gold as the magnet and the Washington government as

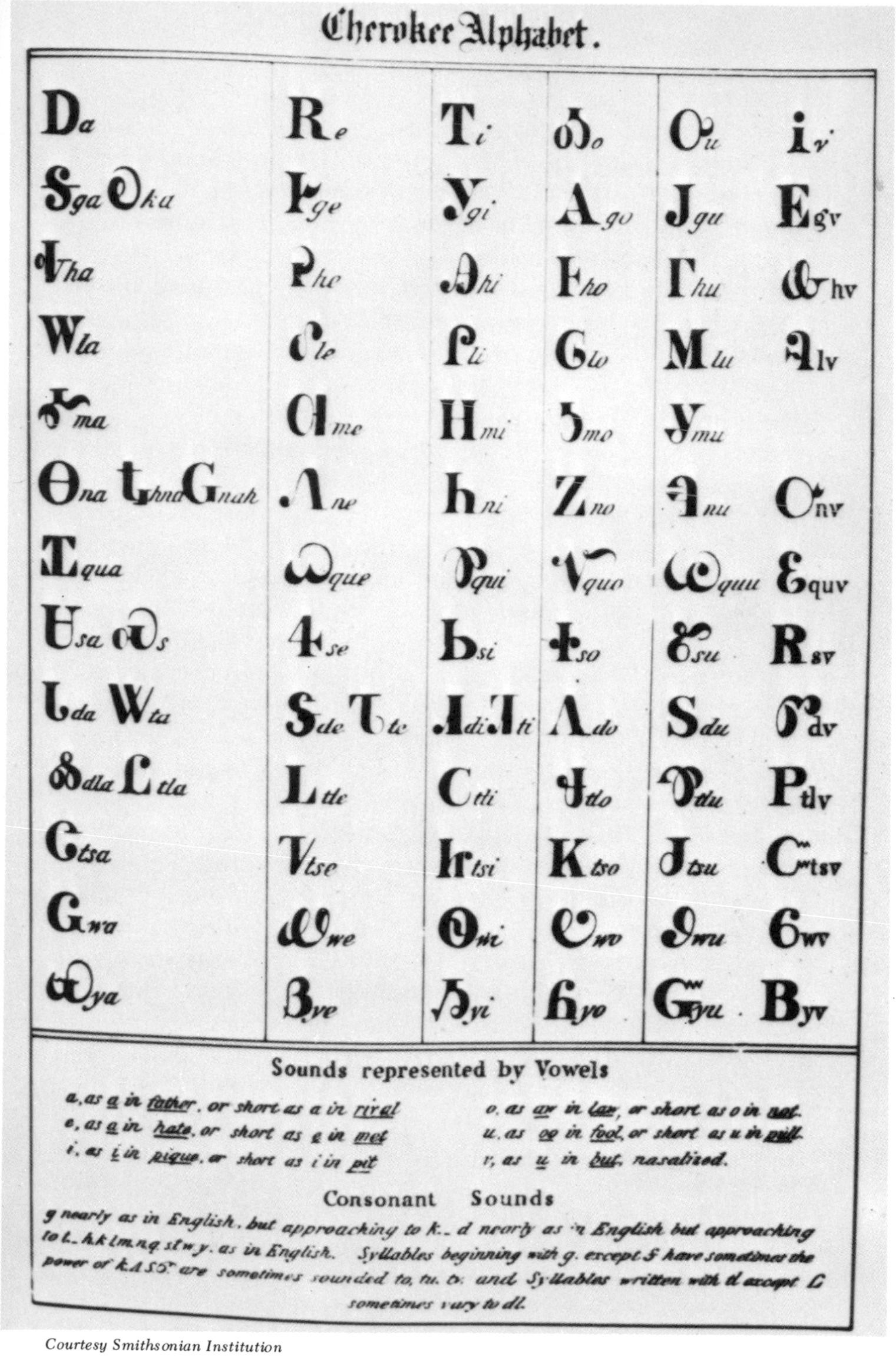

Cherokee Alphabet.

Ꭰ a	Ꭱ e	Ꭲ i	Ꭳ o	Ꭴ u	Ꭵ v
Ꭶ ga Ꭷ ka	Ꭸ ge	Ꭹ gi	Ꭺ go	Ꭻ gu	Ꭼ gv
Ꭽ ha	Ꭾ he	Ꭿ hi	Ꮀ ho	Ꮁ hu	Ꮂ hv
Ꮃ la	Ꮄ le	Ꮅ li	Ꮆ lo	Ꮇ lu	Ꮈ lv
Ꮉ ma	Ꮊ me	Ꮋ mi	Ꮌ mo	Ꮍ mu	
Ꮎ na Ꮏ hna Ꮐ nah	Ꮑ ne	Ꮒ ni	Ꮓ no	Ꮔ nu	Ꮕ nv
Ꮖ qua	Ꮗ que	Ꮘ qui	Ꮙ quo	Ꮚ quu	Ꮛ quv
Ꮜ sa Ꮝ s	Ꮞ se	Ꮟ si	Ꮠ so	Ꮡ su	Ꮢ sv
Ꮣ da Ꮤ ta	Ꮥ de Ꮦ te	Ꮧ di Ꮨ ti	Ꮩ do	Ꮪ du	Ꮫ dv
Ꮬ dla Ꮭ tla	Ꮮ tle	Ꮯ tli	Ꮰ tlo	Ꮱ tlu	Ꮲ tlv
Ꮳ tsa	Ꮴ tse	Ꮵ tsi	Ꮶ tso	Ꮷ tsu	Ꮸ tsv
Ꮹ wa	Ꮺ we	Ꮻ wi	Ꮼ wo	Ꮽ wu	Ꮾ wv
Ꮿ ya	Ᏸ ye	Ᏹ yi	Ᏺ yo	Ᏻ yu	Ᏼ yv

Sounds represented by Vowels

a, as a in father, or short as a in rival
e, as a in hate, or short as e in met
i, as i in pique, or short as i in pit
o, as aw in law, or short as o in not
u, as oo in fool, or short as u in pull
v, as u in but, nasalized.

Consonant Sounds

g nearly as in English, but approaching to k. d nearly as in English but approaching to t. h k l m n q s t w y, as in English. Syllables beginning with g, except Ꭶ have sometimes the power of k. Ꮩ Ꮪ Ꮫ are sometimes sounded to, tu, tv, and Syllables written with tl except Ꮭ sometimes vary to dl.

Courtesy Smithsonian Institution

Cherokee alphabet

the approving parent, the state of Georgia passed a series of savage laws against the Cherokees "forbidding their judicial officers to hold court or their council to meet except to ratify land cessions, forbidding them to mine their own gold, authorizing a survey of their land and its disposal by lottery to Georgians, and creating the Georgia Guard to enforce state law in their country." The Georgia legislature even passed laws against missionaries living among the Cherokees forcing them to swear allegiance to the state or be imprisoned for up to four years for noncompliance.

It is seriously doubted if any American Indian tribe was ever subjected to more concerted pressure for removal than were the Cherokees from 1829 to 1835. No holds were barred and no subterfuge was too devious to be tried. The Georgia Guards, armed thugs with the power and integrity of Gestapo agents, were everywhere terrorizing innocent tribesmen by beating them, burning their houses, abusing their women, and jailing anyone who resisted. A sympathetic Supreme Court refused to hear Cherokee pleas in Cherokee Nation vs. Georgia in 1831 because they could not qualify as a "foreign state." When the Court did decide in their favor, in the 1832 case of Worcester vs. Georgia — a case that resulted from the jailing of two missionaries who refused to take Georgia's unconstitutional oath of allegiance — Cherokee joy was dashed when President Jackson supposedly dismissed the Court's findings by saying "John Marshall has made his decision; now let him enforce it." If any people were ever forsaken, the Cherokees were in the early 1830s. Every sacred treaty promise of years long past was broken by a government that, at least momentarily, allowed brute force to reign supreme. The Washington government demanded removal west, while the rest of the nation sanctioned Georgia's self-appointed role as enforcer of the will of the people.

Was it any wonder that some previously heroic tribesmen began to crack under the strain? Most Cherokees held fast with their President, John Ross, truly believing that the tide would turn and they would somehow be miraculously saved. But others, more realistic than hopeful, began to believe that submission was necessary for salvation. They became known as the Cherokee Treaty Party and included such tribal leaders as Major Ridge, his son John Ridge, editor Elias Boudinot of the *Cherokee Phoenix,* and his brother Stand Watie. Their actions from 1832 through the New Echota treaty negotiations have been the subject of an avalanche of books, articles, doctoral dissertations, and discussions ever since. Were they traitors, as most Cherokees believed then and still do today; were they heroes saving their people from sure death as their followers believed; or were they simply normal men trying to make the best of an impossible situation? Frankly, I don't know. Most writers have eliminated the second possibility, even though Stand Watie has gone down in Cherokee history as somewhat of a folk hero because of his Civil War activities on behalf of the Confederacy. A majority of those who have written on the subject damn the Treaty Party as Indian Benedict Arnolds, but the latest volume on the subject—Thurman Wilkins's, *Cherokee Tragedy, The Story of the Ridge Family and the Decimation of a People*—makes a sound case for these people as he carefully reconstructs their side of the story. Regardless of the place members of the Treaty Party might deserve in Cherokee history, however, their break with their people in 1832 made Cherokee survival in the East even more tenuous than before.

By 1832 Elias Boudinot was writing in the *Phoenix* that emigration was inevitable; for this John Ross saw to it that he was fired from his post. In his last editorial he told his people "I have no hope"; removal was as certain as the dawning of a new day. By 1834 the Cherokee Nation had split into two openly opposing forces: the vast majority supported President John Ross and refused to consider removal; the Treaty Party was secretly negotiating with the U.S. for removal on honorable terms. As one historian has penned, "the difference of opinion between the two parties erupted into hatred."

Finally, John Ross saw that removal was inevitable and proposed selling all the eastern Cherokee lands for twenty million dollars. He hoped to use the money to move his people to Mexican soil (probably Texas) and purchase a new homeland free from the grasping hands of United States citizens. U.S. officials scoffed at the price he demanded; they knew they could get much more favorable terms from the Treaty Party. In March, 1835, therefore, they wrote a treaty in Washington with John Ridge representing his father and the other leaders favoring immediate sale and removal. This treaty was quite different from the one Ross was willing to negotiate. It promised removal for five million dollars, a figure that was much more in line with Senate opinion on the subject. John Ridge wrote his father that the treaty was liberal, at least as liberal as was possible under the circumstances, and it was being brought home for tribal action in October.

When John Ridge returned to the nation with his secret treaty and John F. Schermerhorn, a New York clergyman appointed as treaty negotiator by President Jackson, his life was in danger from a wrathful people thoroughly convinced that the Ridges and their cohorts were traitors the like of which the tribe had never before produced. The infamous arrangement was presented to the rank and file at the Cherokee Council at Red Clay on the Tennessee-Georgia border in October, 1835. The opposition was so overwhelming that even John Ridge and Elias Boudinot joined the majority and voted against it. The resourceful Schermerhorn, however, asked the Cherokees to think seriously about the generous terms offered in the treaty and to meet again at New Echota in December for further discussions on the subject. John Ross, who attended the Red Clay meeting and led the opposition to the treaty, realized that nothing new would be offered in December; and he immediately left for Washington to try again to secure twenty million dollars for the Cherokees' land.

Since John Ross would not be at the New Echota discussions in December, and since the nation had already voiced its disapproval of the treaty at Red Clay, only a small number of Cherokees journeyed to New Echota to continue discussions with John Schermerhorn. This was exactly the break that Schermerhorn needed; with the opposition leader in Washington and his supporters at home, he negotiated and signed the Treaty of New Echota with the few hundred Treaty Party members who showed up to conclude the dirty deed.

The December 29, 1835, Treaty of New Echota was, without a doubt, the most important treaty ever negotiated by the Cherokee people. It is not only an important document but also an interesting one. It contained one of the longest preambles ever attached to an Indian treaty, plus a number of supplementary articles added long after negotiations had ceased. By itself, the preamble is an incredible historical analysis of past events leading up to the treaty. It was, of course, a view of Cherokee-

American relations from the government's vantage point. If one can believe this analysis, the New Echota treaty was nothing more than the logical conclusion of a process begun in the first U.S.-Cherokee treaty fifty years earlier. In fact, the preamble maintained, "the Cherokees are anxious to make some arrangements with the Government," and the U.S. was simply honoring that request by negotiating the treaty. After discounting the opposition of Ross and a majority of the eastern Cherokees, and indicating that the Treaty Party really represented the best interests of the nation, the preamble defended the legality of the treaty by stating that "the Cherokee people, at their last October council at Red Clay, fully authorized and empowered a delegation or committee of twenty persons of their nation to enter into and conclude a treaty with the United States commissioner then present, *at that place or elsewhere* and as the people had good reason to believe that a treaty then and there be made or at a subsequent council at New Echota which the commissioners it was well known and understood, were authorized and instructed to convene for said purpose; and since said delegation have gone on to Washington City, with a view to close negotiations . . . not withstanding they were officially informed by the United States commissioner that they would not be received by the President . . . and whereas the said commissioners [William Carroll and John F. Schermerhorn] did appoint and notify a general council of the nation to convene at New Echota on the 21st day of December 1835; and informed them that the commissioners would be prepared to make a treaty with the Cherokee people who should assemble there and those who did not come they should conclude gave their assent and sanction to whatever should be transacted at this council. . . ." This statement is interesting for a number of reasons. First, it presents the government's position on the legality of the New Echota meeting. Second, it admits that the Cherokees appointed a twenty-man committee to negotiate on the tribe's behalf with John Ross as head of the committee. Third, it indicates that it was perfectly all right for the U.S. not to negotiate with the Cherokee committee since most of its members were then in Washington. Fourth, it maintained that it is perfectly all right for the government to negotiate with anyone who might show up at a meeting not sanctioned by the tribe. How each of these steps logically fitted together into an honorable whole was beyond the comprehension of the Indians in 1835; and, I might add, it is still beyond comprehension today.

Following the laborious and forced preamble were twenty articles on the subject of Cherokee removal to western lands already granted to the tribe in Indian Territory. Within two years after the ratification of the treaty by the U.S. Senate and the signing by the President, the Cherokees were to abandon all lands currently held in the east. Article 12 of the original treaty provided free of charge one hundred sixty acres to any Cherokee family head who wished to remain in the North Carolina, Tennessee, or Alabama portions of the Nation. For an unexplained reason, Georgia was noticeably missing from the states in which Cherokees could reside. Also, the heads of families would receive only one hundred sixty acres of land whereas the treaties of 1817 and 1819 specified reservations of six hundred forty acres for these persons. Lastly, the article stipulated that only heads of families "who are qualified or calculated to become useful citizens shall be entitled" to register and remain in the East. This statement would allow the commissioners charged with the job of authorizing reservations to be the sole judges of who might be qualified to be a useful citizen. Conceivably, under this statement, all Cherokees could be denied reservations in the East. We will never know if that would have happened because a supplementary article, dated March 1, 1836, removed the reservation stipulation and demanded that all Cherokees move to their western lands.

In return for all Cherokee eastern land, the U.S. promised to pay the tribe five million dollars; offered a guarantee to the seven million acres of land previously ceded in Indian Territory, plus a guarantee to the Cherokee Outlet previously provided the tribe; and, to prevent overcrowding in the Indian Territory, granted the Cherokees an additional eight hundred thousand acres in present-day southeastern Kansas adjacent to the Indian Territory holdings. The treaty made it perfectly clear, however, that the U.S. had the right to continue to maintain Fort Gibson in the Cherokee Nation West, to build any additional posts that might be necessary in the future, to construct any roads that might be needed to link these forts together with Arkansas Territory, and to secure free timber, fuels, and other materials that might be required to maintain the outposts.

The five million dollars was to be given to the leaders of the Nation in cash to be used in any way deemed appropriate by the tribe. The government also promised to invest additional money in good stocks, the interest of which could be used for specific purposes. These investments included all present annuities promised in previous treaties, plus an additional two hundred thousand dollars, with the interest to be paid yearly to the tribe and used any way its leaders saw fit; fifty thousand dollars with the interest going to help tribal orphans; and one hundred fifty thousand dollars, plus the present school funds, the interest from which could be used for schools. If the Cherokees did not like the stocks purchased for them by the government, they could, after two years' notice, cash in the stocks and reinvest the money in any other stocks which seemed better to the tribe. Lastly, the U.S. promised up to sixty thousand dollars to be used in paying off debts owed tribesmen by the U.S. government or any of its citizens, and three hundred thousand dollars to liquidate just spoliations claims necessitated by removal.

At this point, it might be worthwhile to answer the query: how much did the United States pay the Cherokee Indians for their eastern lands? It is not difficult to answer that question. The Cherokees ceded ten million acres of land in the New Echota treaty in return for eight hundred thousand acres in the West. They lost, therefore, nine million two hundred thousand acres of land in the exchange. In return they received five million four hundred thousand dollars — the cash allowance plus the investment money granted. Simple arithmetic indicates that the Cherokees received fifty-one cents an acre for their land — precious little by anyone's standard. The going rate for land in America in 1835 was a minimum of one dollar twenty-five cents per acre at auction. This means that poorer lands sold for one dollar twenty-five cents an acre or somewhere near that amount and good land sold for whatever the auction would bring above one dollar twenty-five cents an acre. Surely when one considers the excellent Cherokee land as well as the poorer mountainous or hilly land, the entire package was worth a minimum of two dollars an acre on the open market, and possibly double or triple that amount. It is not at all unreasonable to assume that John

Ross's request for twenty million dollars for the land was much nearer its minimum value than the pittance received in the December treaty.

A number of the articles concerned the removal process itself that must be concluded within two years after the ratification of the treaty. The U.S. promised to pay for all removal expenses, including a sufficient number of steamboats, baggage wagons, and agents to remove the Cherokees comfortably; physicians with ample amounts of medical supplies to take care of ailments incurred on the trip; and full subsistence for one year after arrival in the Indian Territory. If any person wished to migrate on his own — and the government encouraged this possibility —, he would be paid twenty dollars. Also, if anyone wanted to forego the one-year's full subsistence in the West, the government would pay him the lump sum of thirty-three dollars and thirty-three cents, a not overly generous sum of money. The government also promised to protect the Indian's right to remain on his present land for two full years. If the Indian was already dispossessed by rascally Georgians, or if he was dispossessed during the next two years, the government would defend the Indian's right to his land or pay him for any losses incurred. The article — Article 16 — was much too general and afforded the Cherokees no real protection for the next twenty-four months or any adequate compensation for land already lost. These were the people the treaty suggested might remove themselves as soon as possible for twenty dollars a head.

Lastly, the treaty contained a number of articles concerning the usual perpetual friendship between the two peoples and promising to pay just compensations for improvements left behind. It was stipulated that the American Board of Commissions for Foreign Missions would be adequately compensated for all of its improvements that would be abandoned. To assess the worth of these improvements, and to determine the value of all of the Cherokee improvements on the eastern land, agents were to be appointed to determine just and fair compensation. Neither the missionaries nor the Indians played any role whatsoever in determining the value of their improvements, and they later agreed that the amount received was even less than was expected — and they didn't expect much. If a Cherokee lived on land that was reserved to him forever through the reservation provisions of the treaties of 1817 or 1819, he was to be paid for the land at the fair market value. Article 13, the article that discussed this problem, stated bluntly that no matter how improved the land might be the government would pay at the going rate for unimproved land. Claimants under this article were either never paid for their land, or were paid — after much litigation — less than the one dollar twenty-five cents figure that the government received for the poorest land it put up for sale. Many tribesmen who pushed their claims actually ended up losing money. The amount they finally received was not enough to pay the lawyer's fees for pursuing the matter through the courts.

The treaty naturally included many of the timehonored stipulations that looked good on paper but that were broken continually by the government. The government again promised to pay the Cherokee warriors who fought with the U.S. in the War of 1812 and the Creek War. This was the sixth time that promise had been made and the sixth time it was to be broken. And, of course, the government also promised "perpetual peace and friendship . . . between the citizens of the United States and the Cherokee Indians," and pledged that the tribe would never be disturbed in any of its western holdings. Such was not to be the case; a glance at a tribal map today will note the conspicuous absence of the Cherokee Outlet, the Kansas lands, and some of the northeastern Oklahoma lands granted in the treaties of 1818, 1833, and 1835.

In discussing the various general categories that made up the articles of the Treaty of New Echota, mention was made in passing that this or that article was not carried out after ratification. This was not done to suggest that these articles were broken and the rest were not but to eliminate obvious examples of bad faith so that the same ground would not have to be trod in this section of the chapter. The truth of the matter is that the whole story encompassing the negotiation, ratification, and implementation of the treaty represents the ultimate in any history of broken pledges. The very fact that the government demanded removal and supported Georgia in its unlawful actions against the Cherokees is proof that the government was willing to disregard all pledges and promises made in every treaty with the Cherokees since 1785. Time and again the U.S. pledged in writing that it only desired a single piece of land and would never contemplate total removal. Each treaty contained acknowledgments of the Cherokees' ownership of its land and a promise to defend that ownership to the death. When the government decided that the Cherokees must go, however, no previous pledge caused a moment's hesitancy or a twinge of conscience. This fact presents us with a real dilemma. How can we justify spending time and effort discussing specific broken treaty articles when the whole story is one long broken pledge of honor? We might simply let it go at that, or bore any reader to death by listing every article in every treaty and showing how it was specifically broken. The latter would be an exercise in futility, and the former would explain nothing. In lieu of either alternative, I would rather suggest the totality of the broken promise and then search for meaning in the Cherokee removal. If there is no meaning in the "trail of tears" that followed the Treaty of New Echota, then there is no reason for this book. But if we can admit that the story of white-Cherokee relations — and America's relations with all Indians for that matter — is one that scars the beauty of our country and pollutes the serenity of our consciences, then we can search for answers to questions too long ignored by a proud people. To admit we were wrong is a first step, but only the first step. The ultimate aim of anyone studying Indian history, particularly America's relations with the Indians, is to find a way to improve the present and to insure that the future of America's first inhabitants will not be a duplication of the past. To study the past for its own sake is an interesting pastime, but the activity does not become meaningful unless we are willing to learn from the past. To study broken treaties for their own sake is not only rather boring, but it is a meaningless exercise of self-indulgence. But if we want to learn about the ways in which Indians were deprived of their birthright to gain knowledge and understanding, then a study of these treaties is not only important but downright necessary.

Americans seem inclined to place blame for everything wrong that happens. For some reason, we are determined to make some individual pay for mistakes that are made. This practice has had disastrous effects on the study of Indian history. Who was to blame for the Cherokee Treaty of New Echota or the ensuing "trail of tears"? We are quick to blame Andrew Jackson, or Georgia frontiersmen, or Major Ridge, or some other individual. I would like to suggest that this "need to blame" is unnecessary and unfair; it allows the real meaning of the episode to slip away undetected. The villains of the Cherokee removal were not only frontier settlers, military personnel assigned to removal, and state and federal governmental officials, as many suggest. Rather, the villain was history itself, or what we might call today "the system." All white Americans, including Spaniards, Frenchmen, Englishmen, Dutchmen, and their progeny — Americans of all backgrounds and heritages — were the culprits. We simply cannot blame one person or group for the broken treaty promises that lie around us like so many fall leaves on the ground. From the beginning of American history, people desired something that was not really theirs for the taking. Indian ownership was not considered worthy of a second thought, and nation after nation simply claimed millions of American acres and allowed their citizens to settle on the land or rob it of its minerals and animals. An international policy was thus forged and accepted by all but the wronged tribesmen. The "system," as we will call it, made land the golden fleece and allowed persons to acquire it without fair purchase from a willing seller. It is easy to point to Andrew Jackson and proclaim that his Indian policies led to the removal of the Cherokees, as well as the Choctaws, Chickasaws, and countless other Indian groups. But Jackson was only a part of the system, mirroring its aspirations and desires, and is no more to blame than the Boston merchant whose ancestors annihilated the Wampanoags, or the Spaniards who forced Florida tribesmen into missions. It is not possible or practical, of course, to hate everyone, and so we devise symbols or individuals to hate. But by doing so we lose sight of the real extent to which Indians were overwhelmed by a whole race. It is likewise hard to hate "the system" because it is an inanimate object that is hard to grasp and impossible to see.

To bring this idea into better focus, let us look for a moment at the Cherokee removal that followed the New Echota treaty. Whom do you see as the real villains? Was it the people who elected the Congressmen and Senators who passed the Indian Removal Act in 1830? Was it the President and his associates who put the act into effect? Was it the frontiersmen who forced an immediate showdown? Was it land speculators, or missionaries (who taught removal), or miners, or businessmen, or the military sent in to undertake the dirty job of actual removal?

What about the settlers who sold removal goods to the government at inflated prices? Was it the law that allowed all of this to happen? On and on we could go. But what I am really asking is whom can we blame for the Cherokee removal? The answer is all these people and thousands more; a study of the whole Cherokee removal story makes this fact painfully clear.

Since we tend to blame those who are most conspicuous, military removal agents have been singled out by many and blamed for the inhumanity of the whole trek. Even though blaming military personnel for everything under the sun is a national pastime, let us look at the record and try to determine their fault in the fiasco. The military did not participate in removal until after the Treaty of New Echota was negotiated and ratified. To enforce the treaty, the government sent General John Ellis Wool and federal troops to the nation. General Wool was so revolted by his orders to disarm and subjugate the Cherokees that he requested to be relieved of the disagreeable task. He wrote to a friend: "The whole scene since I have been in this country has been nothing but a heartrending one. . . . If I could . . . I would remove every Indian tomorrow beyond the reach of the white men, who, like vultures, are watching, ready to pounce upon their prey and strip them of everything they have. . . ." It was Wool's task to build stockades and pens into which Cherokees would be driven to be counted and then shipped like cattle to the West.

In 1838 General Winfield Scott replaced the complaining Wool and was sent into the nation with seven thousand troops to assemble the tribesmen and escort them to their new homeland. Scott arrived in the nation on May 8, 1838, after spending ten days in Washington, receiving instructions and perfecting his removal plans. Much has been made of the fact that he, too, sympathized with the Cherokees and his personal resolve was to make the removal a model of fair dealing and moderation. He even printed handbills in Athens, Tennessee, and distributed them throughout the nation pleading for Cherokees to assemble peacefully and promising every courtesy possible. He also issued a general order to his troops on May 17 which sought to impress on them the necessity of executing the treaty in a humane and merciful manner. The soldiers were instructed to show kindness to the Indians and to avoid all acts of "wanton oppression, insult, or brutality." They were even cautioned not to use indecent language during the roundup. Scott made an honest effort to insure that removal would spare the tribesmen further humiliation and suffering, or so it would seem.

But what is more important is the fact that these were fruitless gestures that could not be implemented. He was sent to the Cherokee country to execute a fraudulent treaty and remove Indians. He was told to spare no pains in executing the treaty. Regardless of Indian desires to remain, he had to capture them, incarcerate them, and transport them against their will hundreds of miles. While he was telling the troops to be merciful, he was also telling them that they must capture all tribesmen and bring them to stockades for internment until removal. In other words, they were to be kind but not to allow an Indian to escape. Despite his desires, the execution of the treaty and the capture of Indians naturally took precedence over all else. His success would be measured in Washington by Indians removed and not by the absence of curse words by soldiers. He simply could not carry out such a grim task as if he were preparing for a Sunday parade, and he knew it. The Cherokee roundup and incarceration was marred, therefore, by hardship, terror, and even death. Scott, his troops, Washington officials, observers, and Cherokees knew that it would be so. Some things, like removing Indians and gassing Jews, cannot be handled mercifully. The system does not allow such a luxury.

On May 26 the roundup began. James Mooney, an ethnologist on the scene, wrote: "Squads of troops were sent to search out with rifle and bayonet every small cabin hidden away in the coves or by the sides of mountain streams." He added that, "families at dinner were startled by the sudden gleam of bayonets in the doorway and rose up to be driven with blows and oaths along the trail that led to the stockade. Men were seized in their fields or going along the road, women were taken from their wheels and children from their play." An army private who participated in the roundup recalled years later: "I saw the helpless Cherokees arrested and dragged from their homes, and driven by bayonets into the stockades. And in the chill of a drizzling rain on an October morning I saw them loaded like cattle or sheep into wagons and started toward the west. . . . Chief Ross led in prayer and when the bugle sounded and the wagons started rolling many of the children . . . waved their little hands good-bye to their mountain homes."

From October 1838 until the spring of 1839, the Cherokees in wave after wave began their hegira from Cherokee Agency, Tennessee, north through Nashville, Hopkinsville, Kentucky and on to Golconda, Illinois, on the Ohio river. From there they crossed southern Illinois and Missouri to northeastern Indian Territory or southwestward through Arkansas heading for the same destination. It has been estimated that around four thousand Cherokees died along the way out of a total number of from sixteen thousand to eighteen thousand. One who died was Quatie Ross, the wife of Chief John Ross. A private recalled the death with these words: "I was on guard duty the night Mrs. Ross died. When relieved at midnight I did not retire, but remained around the wagons [where Quatie lay] out of sympathy for Chief Ross and at daylight was detailed . . . to assist in the burial. . . . Her uncoffined body was buried in a shallow grave . . . and the sorrowful cavalcade moved on." Where were the physicians promised in the treaty? Where was the ample supply of wagons, removal agents, food, etc. promised in the same document? Like the promises of the past, they were nowhere to be found. On and on the sordid story of the Cherokee "trail of tears" went until the inhumanity of the roundup and the removal numbs the mind. Who was to blame for all of this? Was it Scott and his troops? I think not; the fault lay with the system.

There is both a sad and happy epilogue to the Treaty of New Echota and the "trail of tears." Because individuals are blamed for the circumstances with which they struggle, Major Ridge, John Ridge, and Elias Boudinot—the leaders of the Treaty Party—were brutally murdered in Indian Territory on June 22, 1839, by John Ross's supporters who blamed them for the treason of New Echota. But out of the same treaty and removal came a ray of hope—a memorial to the tenacity of man's will to survive on his own terms. Several hundred Cherokees escaped the roundup and hid out in Smoky Mountain caves subsisting on roots and berries. Finally, a white man they could trust bought some land for them with money allowed by the government for their confiscated property, and there the Eastern Band of Cherokee Indians has remained ever since. They now number about four thousand five hundred, "living in a beautiful and picturesque region,

Courtesy Smithsonian Institution

Cherokee woman, Walini, 1888

making their living by farming and tourism — selling their crafts and recreating their history in the famous drama 'Unto These Hills.'" They survived because their will to survive was stronger than the frontiersmen's will to drive them out. They developed and prospered because that has been the Cherokees' way ever since the beginning of their tribal history. They have now been accepted by their neighbors and are allowed to pursue their beliefs unmolested. How different the history of red-white relations would have been if this practice had started a few hundred years earlier. As Angie Debo puts it, when Indians are left alone to progress under conditions of equality, they prove "that Indians [can] cook their own meal in the tipi when nobody [is] trying to burn it down."

SUGGESTED READINGS

Barry, Ada Loomis, Ed. *Yunini's Story of the Trail of Tears*. London: Fudge & Co., Ltd., 1932.

Foreman, Grant. *Indian Removal*. Norman: University of Oklahoma Press, 1932.

Foreman, Grant. *Sequoyah*. Norman: University of Oklahoma Press, 1938.

Gabriel, Ralph Henry. *Elias Boudinot Cherokee & His America*. Norman: University of Oklahoma Press, 1941.

Kilpatrick, Jack Frederick and Anna Gritts Kilpatrick, Eds. *New Echota Letters, Contributions of Samuel A. Worcester to the Cherokee Phoenix*. Dallas: Southern Methodist University Press, 1968.

Malone, Henry Thompson. *Cherokees of the Old South, A People in Transition*. Athens: The University of Georgia Press, 1956.

Van Every, Dale. *Disinherited: The Lost Birthright of the American Indians*. New York: William Morrow & Company, 1966.

Wilkins, Thurman. *Cherokee Tragedy, The Story of the Ridge Family and the Decimation of a People*. New York: The Macmillan Company, 1970.

Woodward, Grace Steele. *The Cherokees*. Norman: University of Oklahoma Press, 1963.

"These invasions of the Creek country [Red Sticks War] took place during the winter of 1813-14. The Creeks, who had known only the quick foray against the enemy and the triumphant retreat to their invincible towns, were now subjected to a pitiless extermination in the heart of their own country. In most cases they stood with desperate courage and fought to the death, neither expecting nor asking quarter."

From Angie Debo, *The Road to Disappearance*, page 80.

CHAPTER 3

The Destruction of the Creek Confederacy

Arthur H. DeRosier, Jr.

ONE OF THE major problems involved in developing the section of this volume concerned with "broken treaties" among Southern Indian tribes is that of selection. By choosing to discuss treaties with the Choctaw and Cherokee Indians in the previous two chapters, and by selecting the Creeks for the third and last chapter, a reader might assume that these three are the most important tribes in the region. That assumption is not necessarily true; in their way, broken pledges suffered by the Seminoles, Chickasaws, Catawbas, and other Southern tribal entities are just as important as those of the tribes discussed. Actually, the tribes discussed are less important than the themes they represent. In the Choctaw chapter, we examined broken promises that led to an initial exchange of that tribe's eastern homeland for a larger amount of land in Indian Territory. Next, we examined a series of broken promises that led inexorably to a final removal treaty with the Cherokees. In both cases the western land assigned to the tribes was selected by the United States. In this chapter we will concentrate on those events and promises that led to military confrontation between whites and Indians and a treaty that resulted from total defeat on the battlefield. The one common bond between the Choctaw and Cherokee discussions is the fact that both the Doak's Stand and New Echota treaties represent examples of how white America handled friendly and peaceful Southern tribesmen. We will now discuss how the United States handled defeated enemies.

The Creeks, or Muskogees, as they were sometimes called during early centuries of white expansion, lived in northern and central Alabama and most of southern Georgia when they came into contact with early white settlers. As was the case with most

Southern tribes, we are not sure when the Creeks arrived in that area or even where they came from. Most Creek historians simply indicate that they migrated from the west, probably by way of the Red River, around 800 A.D. or earlier. We do know that the original Creeks conquered or came to terms with tribes already in Alabama and Georgia and developed a powerful confederacy with some Shawnee Indians, plus the Alabama, Koasati, Hitchiti, Apalachee, Yuchi, Yamasee, Natchez, and other Indians. Through this rather unique process small tribal groups were brought into one integrated Indian nation, known as the Creek Confederacy, which was both powerful and extensive when whites arrived in North America.

Creek history is a splendid example of democracy in action. Despite the different elements that made up the Confederacy, the Creeks thought of themselves as one people united against enemy tribes located nearby, especially the Cherokees and Choctaws. In the early years, however, the Confederacy was loosely governed by leaders in the historic towns of Coweta, Cussita, Tuckabatchee, and Coosa. The people were held together by the ties of language, intermarriage between clans, frequent regional council meetings, and an annual national Council. By the eighteenth century, the Creek Confederacy consisted of approximately sixty towns, forty of which were located in what was called the Upper Towns on the Coosa and Tallapoosa rivers of Alabama and twenty in the Lower Towns located on the Ocmulgee, Flint, and Chattahoochee rivers of Georgia. Though some of the towns were naturally more important than others, none ever became the permanent capital of the Confederacy. The capital, during any given year or period of time, was the town in which lived the presiding chief of the yearly national meeting. In that way many chiefs served as the titular head of the Confederacy and many towns served as the national capital. Also, the towns were divided into two types — red or war towns and white or peace towns. As David H. Corkran in his fine book *The Creek Frontier, 1540-1783* points out, the "distinction had nothing to do with the temperament of the towns, but was traditional designation and probably related to ritualistic functions in the making of war and the making of peace." Okmulgee in the Lower Towns and Okchai in the Upper Towns were the most important white towns, and Coweta and

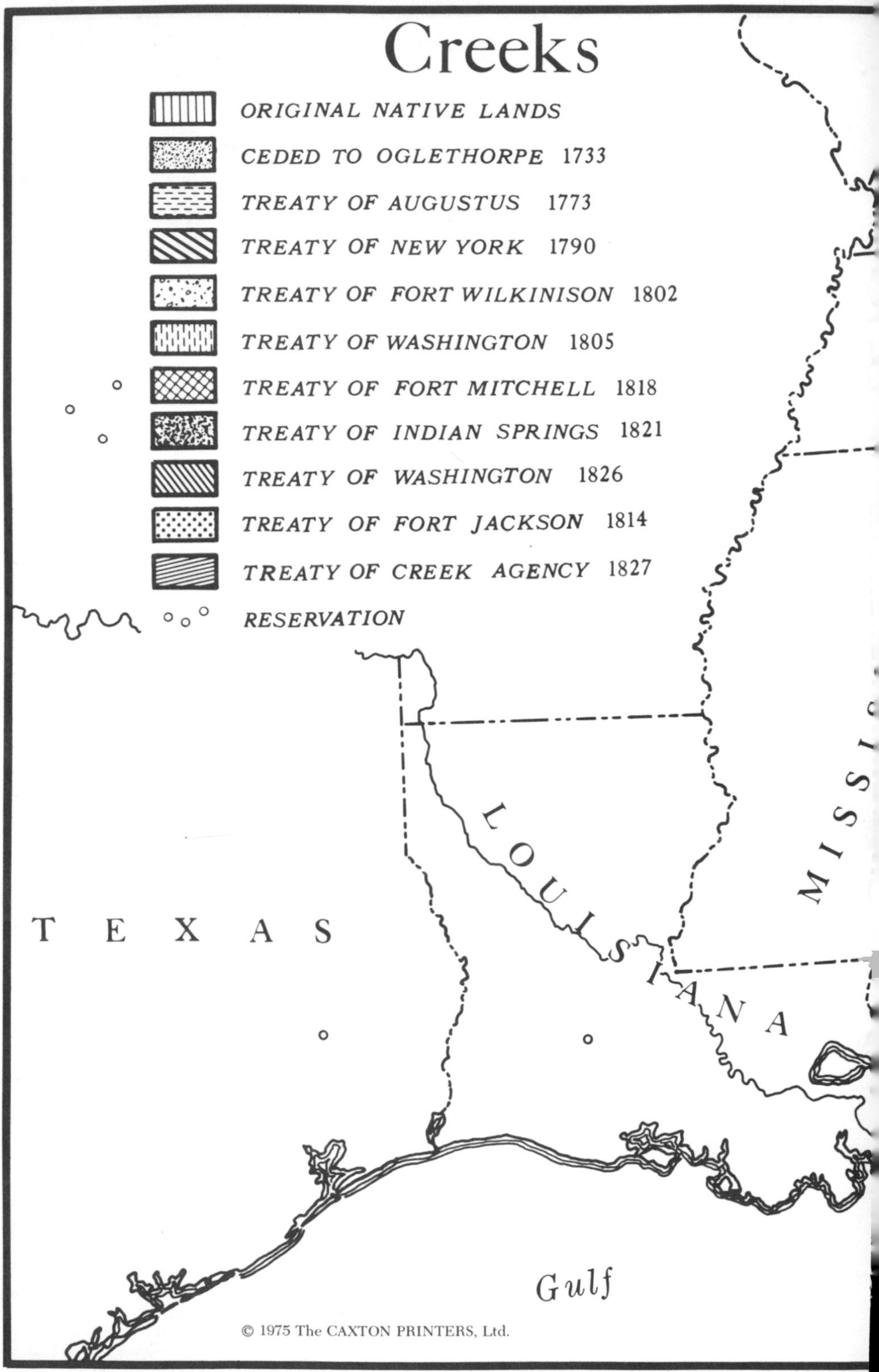
Creeks
ORIGINAL NATIVE LANDS
CEDED TO OGLETHORPE 1733
TREATY OF AUGUSTUS 1773
TREATY OF NEW YORK 1790
TREATY OF FORT WILKINISON 1802
TREATY OF WASHINGTON 1805
TREATY OF FORT MITCHELL 1818
TREATY OF INDIAN SPRINGS 1821
TREATY OF WASHINGTON 1826
TREATY OF FORT JACKSON 1814
TREATY OF CREEK AGENCY 1827
RESERVATION
TEXAS
LOUISIANA
Gulf

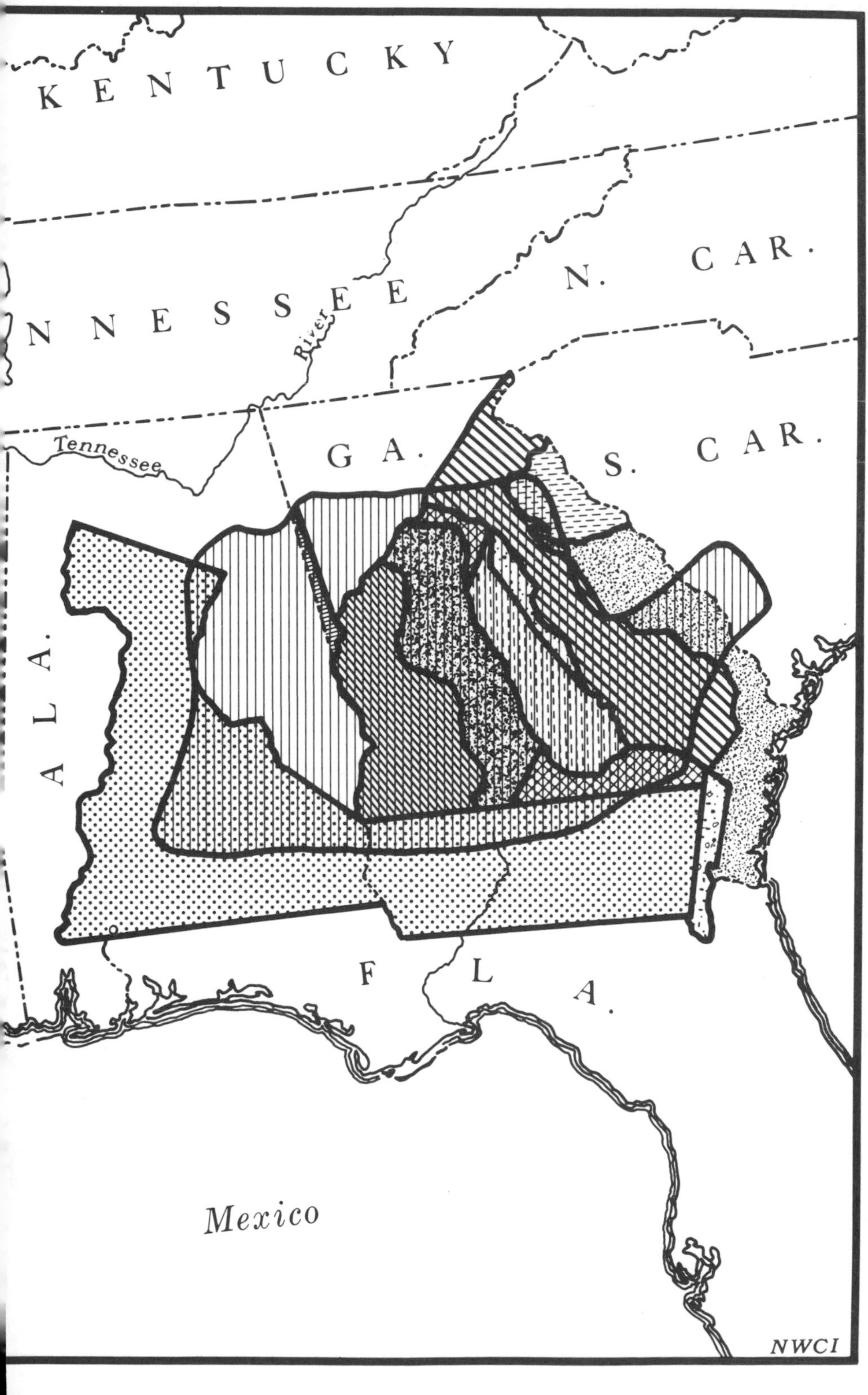
KENTUCKY
NNESSEE
N. CAR.
River
Tennessee
GA.
S. CAR.
ALA.
FLA.
Mexico
NWCI

Cussita in the Lower and Okfuskee in the Upper Towns were the most significant red towns.

Though our main task of discussing broken treaties does not allow the luxury of developing Creek social and economic life to any degree, it should be mentioned that information on this subject is available in considerable detail. The Corkran volume mentioned above is an excellent source, as is Angie Debo's *The Road to Disappearance* and John R. Swanton's *Early History of the Creek Indians and Their Neighbors.* However, it does seem appropriate to mention a few basic details about the Creeks that made them significant and somewhat unique. Their life was closely associated with the villages or towns in which they lived. Each village contained twenty-five to one hundred houses and was governed by a mico (micco) meaning "town king." A mico was identified not by his given name but by the towns he governed, hence the designations "Coweta Mico" or "Cussita Mico." This leader presided over the town council and was the most important person in the town's civil government. If the mico were old, he might be assisted by a second mico called mico-apotka — "twin chief" — who assisted him in the administration of everyday affairs. The council was composed of important townspeople who shared significantly in developing the policies that governed the town. Another group of civil officials were called henchas; they directed individual governmental activities, such as public works and tribal ceremonies. The most eloquent of the henchas was selected as the mico's speaker: it was his job to speak for the mico at official and ceremonial occasions. Separate from the civil officials were the town's war leaders who were not allowed to participate in town government. The leading warrior was called the tastanage, and though he and the other warriors were excluded from official civil functions, he was a person of no little importance in the town. Theoretically, the warriors were simply charged with fighting for the town in wars with other tribes, but because tastanages were usually strong men with iron wills they often presented proposals and gained considerable influence in the town. Most young Creek braves considered the position of tastanage more prestigious than mico and did everything possible to prove their valor and rise to the position of the town's "big warrior." Because of the different nature of the micos' and tastanages' endeavors, it

Menawa, Creek warrior

was inevitable that they should clash on matters of policy and vie for power in moments of crisis. It took a resolute, diplomatic, and strong mico to maintain civilian rule at all times. Many could not and became, in reality, nothing more than figurehead leaders under the thumb of a powerful and determined tastanage. But by and large, Creek government was controlled by civil authorities, each town was allowed an inordinate amount of self-government, and micos were responsive to the interests of the people they governed.

As serious a strain on town government as the problems between strong micos and tastanages was the division of unity caused by Creek clans. As was true with most Southern tribes, Creeks were divided into matrilineal clans. Though the tribe may have numbered as many as eighteen thousand persons in the early nineteenth century, it had fewer than ten important clans. The four major clans were the Wind, Tyger, Bear, and Eagle clans. The numerous members of these and the other clans were scattered throughout every village of the Confederacy. Warfare was carried on by clans. Punishment for crime was meted out by any member of the injured clan to any member of the clan known to be guilty of the affront. Without a doubt, clan loyalty took precedence over town or even tribal loyalty. This fact led to frequent divisions within the Confederacy, and even individual towns, and placed an additional burden on the diplomatic skills of micos who strove to maintain peace and tranquility in the face of clan vendettas and ambitious tastanages seeking individual glory or tribal victory over neighboring tribes.

As was true with most Indian tribes, the Creeks were excellent hunters. The woods they roamed were full of deer, woods buffalo, bear, wild turkey, and small game. All too often, though, contemporary Americans assume that animals and fish made up the only ingredients in an Indian's diet. Nothing could be further from the truth among Southern Indians. The Creeks, as was true with the Choctaws and Cherokees, were excellent agriculturalists. Men and women together planted corn, beans, sweet potatoes, and countless other crops in April and harvested them during the summer. During the growing season, children, old residents of the towns, and females cultivated the crops and kept the gardens free of pesky rabbits, deer, and other animals that feasted on tender leaves of food crops. Numerous white observers have testified to the agricultural skill of the Creeks and the richness of the lands they plowed. Most agreed that the Creeks were skilled farmers; in fact, the bread and hominy they made from corn soon became an important part in the diet of most white Southern frontiersmen.

Historically, the Creeks are remembered as fierce warriors equal to any other tribal group east of the Mississippi River save the Chickasaws. As was the case with the Cherokees, circumstances dictated that the Creeks be brave in war and intolerant of intruders. This was due mainly to their geographic proximity to powerful and persistent enemies. Bordering the tribe on the north were the mighty Cherokees ever mindful of their own interpretation of the correct location of the Creek-Cherokee boundary line. To the west were the small but warlike Chickasaw tribe and the more numerous Choctaws. But to the south and east were even more persistent and imaginative encroachers — Spaniards and English colonists. As if that were not bad enough, throughout much of the seventeenth and eighteenth centuries the Creeks had to contend with French intruders in Mobile and throughout southern Alabama. It is no wonder that the Creeks were ever wary of their neighbors; they knew well that no other Indian tribe was as precariously located as themselves. For that reason they trusted no outsiders, were ready to take to the warpath at a moment's notice, and developed a skill at diplomacy unequaled by any other American Indian tribe. They negotiated treaties when it served their purpose, broke them in secret arrangements with another adversary, and muddied the waters of diplomatic distrust between fellow Indians, Spaniards, Englishmen, white frontiersmen, and Frenchmen whenever the opportunity arose. The stakes were high for the Creeks, and above all else, they were determined to emerge from their "trial by encroachment" the victors, if at all possible.

By the time of the American Revolution, Georgia was still the weakest of the thirteen colonies and confined, for the most part, to a narrow strip of land along the east coast and the Savannah River. Despite that fact, the Creeks were smart enough to determine that most of their future trouble would come from that growing colony. As early as 1773, the tribe was invited to a council at Augusta by Georgia's royal governor, Sir James

Wright, who demanded a large cession of land for Creek participation in frontier warfare against English settlers. The Creeks negotiated skillfully but in the end ceded approximately two million acres of land on the upper Savannah River. Immediately settlers began pouring into the so-called "new purchase" lands and beyond, causing the Creeks to retaliate by raiding new settlements and individual homesteads. This action would have been met by British arms had not the American Revolution broken out and turned British and American attention elsewhere. What is important, though, is that the Creeks would not tolerate expansion beyond acceptable limits and stood ready to fight to the death for their homeland.

The Creeks, as was true with all neighboring tribes, did not know which side to support, if any, during the American Revolution. They hated the British for allowing frontiersmen to violate the Proclamation of 1763; they hated the Americans for stirring up trouble between tribes and encroaching on Creek land without a second thought. Unfortunately, they hated the Americans more, and they allowed that fact to convince them that the colonists would be defeated in the end. Probably they should have remained neutral and reveled in the knowledge that both sides were killing each other, but they did not. They allowed John Stuart, southern superintendent of Indian affairs, to convince them that they should take an active part on the side of Britain. Therefore, in 1778, Creek warriors, especially from the Upper Towns, began raiding outlying American settlements as far east as King's Mountain, North Carolina, and as far south as Mobile. This mistake not only cost them many warriors, but left the tribe open to American vengeance when the war ended in 1783.

Most Southern tribes came to terms with the victorious Americans shortly after the conclusion of the Revolution. But not the Creeks. In the first place, the weak American Confederation government was not strong enough to force tribes to negotiate or face stiff military confrontation. In the second place, the Creeks knew full well that Georgians would demand significantly more land than was ceded in 1773 to appease the appetites of settlers too long kept at a distance from the rich deer skins business of the interior. And in the third place, the Creeks knew that they had an ally against negotiations in the Spaniards who won back Florida in the 1783 Treaty of Paris. Spain looked with a jaundiced eye on

William Augustus Bowles, British adventurer who founded Indian state of Muscogee. From a painting by Thomas Hardy.

the expansionist tendencies of the new United States. It wanted very much to keep Americans hemmed up along the Atlantic Coast and away from Spain's possessions in Florida, Louisiana, and throughout the Southwest. If Americans were allowed to spill over the Appalachian mountains and move at will onto Indian lands in the Old Northwest and Old Southwest, Spain reasoned, they would be perilously close to Spanish lands into which frontiersmen would expand whenever the need arose. To forestall that possibility, the Spanish government determined to make an ally of the Creeks and use them to serve as a buffer zone between American and Spanish claims on the continent. And the Creeks were more than willing to comply, not because they were anxious to serve Spanish purposes but because they foresaw mutual benefits in such an arrangement. The Creeks were wise enough to see a natural bone of contention between Americans and Spaniards — expansion — and they decided to do what they could to keep the two adversaries wary of each other.

If one is going to play the dangerous game of life-and-death diplomacy, however, he had better have a good diplomat on his side. The Creeks fully realized that truism and, as fate would have it, produced at that moment the greatest diplomat in their history — Alexander McGillivray. Much has been written about McGillivray; yet the full greatness of the man is still lost among the details of his short nine-year tenure on the stage of history. From the available source material on the man, there emerges a leader whose diplomatic sagacity ranks him with the white man's Tallyrand, Metternick, and America's own John Quincy Adams. Yet, though his diplomatic ability is generally admitted, he emerges from many historians' pens as some kind of traitor, or charlatan, or sinister shadowy figure. I suspect this is mainly because many consider him a man interested only in his own welfare, a man ready to sell out his people for the first bag of gold. That assumption simply is not true. McGillivray was totally dedicated to Creek survival and was willing to do anything to achieve that goal. Only when that fact is accepted and understood, and only when one is willing to admit the lengths to which an Indian must go to combat the forces against him, can one appreciate McGillivray's contribution.

Alexander McGillivray was born in 1759 the son of a prominent Georgia trader and politician of Scottish descent, Lachlan

McGillivray, and Sehoy Marchland, a French-Indian mixed blood of the prestigious Wind clan. Young Alexander lived among the Creeks until he was fourteen, at which time his father sent him to work and to school in Savannah and Charleston. At the outbreak of the Revolutionary war, both father and son threw in their lot with the Loyalists and subsequently lost all of their property. The loss was too much for Lachlan, who promptly returned to Scotland, while Alexander stayed behind, returning to his mother's people in the Creek country. During the conflict, Alexander was fully devoted to Britain's cause, serving as a British agent among most of the Southern tribes, sending out war parties against outlying settlements, and supporting the trade aspirations of British traders among the Indians, especially Panton, Leslie & Company.

With the close of the war and his permanent return to the Upper Towns homeland of his mother, McGillivray assessed the plight of the Creeks coolly and logically. Even before the Spaniards in Florida developed their buffer-zone strategy, McGillivray realized that an alliance between the two against Georgia and America was necessary for Creek survival. He first dreamed of a confederation of all Southern Indians against the Spaniards and the Americans to compel the latter to adopt Britain's 1763 line and the former to honor it. Long before anyone ever heard of Tecumseh, McGillivray conceived of the policy "strength through union!" But by the same token, long before Tecumseh's emergence, McGillivray's hopes were dashed as historic Indian states-rights won out over union against a common foe. Then, and only then, did the emerging Creek leader turn to Spain with an offer of alliance.

The tragic post-war tale leading to eventual Creek annihilation was really begun by the Georgians and not McGillivray. In May 1783, Georgians convinced some Cherokee and Creek leaders who supported America's war effort to meet and counsel with them in Augusta. Among the few Creeks in attendance was Opothle Mico of Tallasi, an old but prominent pro-American leader. On May 31, in return for promised peace, he signed a treaty ceding a favorite Creek hunting ground between the Tugaloo and Upper Oconee rivers. Later, a council of the whole Creek Nation refused to ratify the treaty and declared it null and void. Georgians, however, steeped in the white tradition that

Indian compliance was unnecessary for ratification, began to cut up the ceded land into counties and sell tracts to willing buyers.

McGillivray countered the Georgia action by helping sponsor a general meeting of all Southern Indian nations at Pensacola in 1784. At the conference he negotiated a treaty with the Spanish authorities on behalf of the entire Creek Nation. The treaty promised a generous amount of Spanish trade and complete protection, in return for Creek obedience to any orders issued by the captain general at Havana and the promise that the tribe would forbid all whites admission to their country without a Spanish license. In addition to these terms, McGillivray was appointed the Spanish "commissary of the Creek nation" and granted a salary along with the post. It is mainly because of the salary provision, in this treaty and later ones with Spain and the U.S., that many brand McGillivray as a shyster interested only in his own well-being. That supposition is not accurate. His acceptance of the post and the salary that accompanied it was his way of convincing the Spaniards — and later the Americans — that they had "bought" his allegiance. As events clearly showed, nobody ever bought Alexander McGillivray: white assumption that they had him in their grasp was the major weapon he used to beat them at their own game.

The Creeks, led by McGillivray, vigorously disavowed the fraudulent Augusta treaty. Scouting parties were sent out to warn settlers to return east or pay the consequences for encroachment. Georgians turned to the U.S. government at New York and demanded military support for their contentions. However, all that the government could offer was a promise to send commissioners to meet with the Creeks in 1785 and negotiate a treaty. Georgians angrily retorted that they didn't need another treaty; they already had a favorable one. What they needed was enforcement and the weak Confederation could supply anything but enforcement. McGillivray was quick to see the advantage that American squabbling offered and promised to discuss matters with representatives of the U.S. government. But when the commissioners appeared, McGillivray and the other leading micos stayed at home, refusing to attend. A few micos friendly to the U.S. did attend, but they were so few that the commissioners didn't even attempt to negotiate a treaty. They chatted generally for a few days and then went home. When they left, though,

Georgia officials appeared, cajoled the micos into not only accepting the 1783 treaty but also ceding another large tract between the Altamaha and St. Mary's rivers. The state legislature ratified the treaty — the Creeks never did — and once again turned to the U.S., demanding enforcement.

All that was accomplished in 1785 was the polarization of both Creeks and Georgians; frontier depredations began again in earnest. From 1786 to 1789, Creek warriors forced Georgians back to their historic frontier; Georgia commissioners negotiated often with friendly tribesmen, securing more land and taking none; and the U.S. stood aside, unable to intercede on behalf of either side. James White, U.S. Superintendent of the Southern District, was instructed to investigate the causes of the confrontation. His report indicated that Georgians were at fault and that war with the Creeks was unthinkable at that time. He wrote Secretary of War Henry Knox that McGillivray could put six thousand warriors on the warpath at any time and that they would be fully supplied with Spanish goods, arms, and ammunition. However, he warned, if something wasn't done soon, Georgians would force the Creeks into all-out war, the results of which would be disastrous to the U.S. Lastly, he testified to the extent of McGillivray's devotion to his people by stating that Georgians had tried to bribe him by promising to return all of his family possessions confiscated during the Revolution, but the offer was spurned. If McGillivray were only interested in money, he would have accepted the offer; it was much more lucrative than the pittance he was receiving from the Spaniards. Also, on a more hopeful note, White reported that the Georgians had threatened the Spanish government in Florida with war if they did not abandon their support of the Creeks. And the threat seemed to worry the weak Spaniards; in late 1788 they notified the Creeks that they had better settle their differences with Georgia because further aid was not forthcoming. Now, White wisely hinted, was a good time to open negotiations.

The following year showed McGillivray at his best. Without Spanish aid, and with a new, more unified U.S. government with which to contend after the inauguration of George Washington in April 1789, the Creeks were for the first time on the defensive. Washington and Henry Knox, retained as Secretary of War under the new government, immediately appointed a commission to treat with the Creeks. Their instructions to the commissioners were of great importance and represent, according to Angie Debo, the "foundation of subsequent Indian policy." The Commissioners were to get the land Georgia wanted and they could spend up to forty thousand dollars to secure Creek compliance. They were also authorized to grant the Creeks a seaport, give the Creek leaders gifts, money, honorary military distinctions, offer McGillivray a rank higher than his Spanish commission, a salary to accompany the rank, and lastly the right to promise the Creeks peace and tranquility forevermore. How typical these instructions sound as they appeared again and again at almost every treaty negotiation from that time onward until every tribe was moved west, cooped up on some western reservation, or annihilated. The commissioners were also told that if they could not secure the desired lands, they were to spy on the Creeks, gather all the data they could, and then, return home to observe a war to gain the desired objective by military means. And so confident commissioners sailed from New York in 1789 armed with bribery and purchase money, and the right to threaten war. They were met at Rock Landing on the Oconee River by McGillivray and two thousand chiefs and warriors armed to the teeth and unsmiling. Two could play the game and threaten war, McGillivray reasoned. The commissioners were polite, presented their draft treaty, offered their bribes, and were left empty-handed the next day when the Creeks rejected everything, broke camp, and went home.

Without a doubt, Alexander McGillivray was playing a dangerous game in 1789. He had met the enemy, faced his verbal fire, accepted his threats of extermination, and then coolly turned away in defiance. But, in retrospect, it was the master stroke of his career. The U.S. simply did not have the armed might necessary to support its threats, and McGillivray somehow knew it. All that George Washington could do, after fuming over the turn of events, was to send a secret agent, Colonel Marinus Willett, to McGillivray with an invitation to come to New York for serious negotiations. Sensing that the U.S. finally realized that honest negotiations between equals were necessary instead of simple ratification of whatever the U.S. offered the Creeks, McGillivray accepted the invitation and journeyed to New York with twenty-five colleagues selected by the tribe. Nothing quite like that journey and treaty negotiation ever happened to Indians before or since. The wagons carrying the Creek delegation were accorded an escort that bordered on a triumphal procession. At Richmond, Fredericksburg, Philadelphia, and finally New York, they were greeted by bands, parades, mobs of cheering people, keys to cities, and honors galore. And McGillivray, knowing that such attention was thoroughly provoking the Spaniards, milked the opportunity for all it was worth.

McGillivray was well aware that the welcome he and his colleagues received along the route and in New York, the national capital, was staged by the U.S. to flatter, inflate, and soften the will of the Creek negotiators. It was no spontaneous outpouring of love for America's red neighbors. But two could play the game of ceremony to advantage. He put on his best "Indian ways," dressed extravagantly, accepted the accolades, flattered his hosts, and thereby gave them a feeling of success that worried the Spanish who sent agents to New York to observe the proceedings and report back to their Pensacola superiors. However, when the preliminaries were over and negotiations with Secretary of War Henry Knox began in late July 1790, McGillivray and his fellow micos were ready to argue and negotiate with skill. The one advantage Knox had over McGillivray was the fact that a few legitimate Creek leaders had, in fact, negotiated with Georgians on many previous occasions and ceded millions of acres of land. True, the treaties were never ratified by a national Creek council, but the documents made no mention that such ratification was necessary to become effective. McGillivray well knew that the U.S. would open the negotiations with a demand that all land previously ceded to Georgia by his overly solicitous colleagues be surrendered. This he refused to do. He was willing to make an accommodation in order to gain the desired peace with America, but he steadfastly refused to cede any more land than was absolutely necessary to gain that end. His people were tired of raiding their white neighbors. In fact, the sporadic fighting of the past six years had greatly disrupted the Confederacy and cost more lives and resources than he dared to admit. A nation of eighteen thousand could not for long hold off a neighbor boasting a population of almost four million; therefore, McGillivray negotiated with full knowledge that he would have to conclude by surrendering some land to gain peaceful co-existence with white America.

In the end, though, he surrendered more land in the Treaty of New York than he wanted to. He absolutely refused to cede land south of the Altamaha River. He did, in article four, cede all of the land west of the Ogeechee River and east of the Altamaha and Oconee rivers. The U.S. further insisted that the Creeks cede the land between the Apalachee and Oconee rivers in northeastern Georgia. McGillivray fought this demand to the end; the "Apalachee fork" land was a great hunting region and was prized by his people. But he lost this fight and ended up surrendering the prize with the warning that he was not at all sure that the Creeks back home could be persuaded to abandon that tract of land. However, by skillfully keeping the discussions on the "Apalachee fork" and by making its surrender such a hard pill to swallow, he kept American demands for other land at bay. Actually, he surrendered less land than other Creek leaders were willing to lose to guarantee peace, but that was little consolation. He did minimize the amount lost, though, by constantly inflating U.S. ego by maintaining that they had won the game of negotiation. In part, it is possible to measure McGillivray's negotiation success by studying Georgia's reaction to the final treaty. In a word, they hated the treaty and were thoroughly convinced that the U.S. had sold out their interests to gain Creek friendship and trade. Of course, this is a biased view by a land-hungry state, but Georgian discontent does indicate that the U.S. did not gain nearly all the land Georgians felt had been ceded them in earlier treaties written with their Creek neighbors.

The first Creek treaty with the U.S. was interesting in a number of other ways. Naturally, it included the perennial "perpetual peace and friendship" article, and another that solemnly guaranteed to the Confederacy "all their lands within the limits of the United States." As was the case with both the Choctaws and Cherokees, these two articles were the first ones broken by the U.S. government and its citizens. The treaty also included a strong statement in article two concerning future Creek loyalty. In an effort to win Creek allegiance away from the Spaniards, the U.S. was willing to relent on some of its territorial demands and gain instead Creek acceptance of article two which stated that the Creeks acknowledged that they were hereafter under the protection of the U.S. and "no other sovereign whatsoever." McGillivray, as well as the U.S., welcomed such a statement; now the wily diplomat had a club to hold over his reluctant Spanish allies to insure their support of his efforts to retain all guaranteed Creek land.

Taken as a whole, the Treaty of New York was a genuine effort by the U.S. to solve differences between itself and the Creek Nation. In only four articles were the Creeks asked to surrender anything. In article two they supposedly surrendered their Spanish alliance, and in article four, land. In article three the Creeks promised to return all white and black prisoners captured during the period of border warfare, and in article eleven they promised to spy on other Southern tribes and to report to the U.S. any warlike activities observed. However, because of Georgia's negative reaction to the treaty, including non-acceptance of its terms, the Creeks did not surrender the prisoners promised. Also, the promise to spy on neighbors was only windowdressing that neither side took seriously, though hurting the aspirations of hated Choctaws and Cherokees might be an attractive pastime for the Creeks.

A number of articles granted an unusual amount of protection to Creek remaining lands. In article six the U.S. stated that any citizen attempting to settle on Creek land would forfeit his right to U.S. protection and the "Creeks may punish him or not, as they please." A number of other articles tried to clarify the jurisdiction of the U.S. and Creek governments over whites or reds who broke the law within or outside the Creek Nation. None of these were ever enforced by the U.S. Whites continued to settle or hunt on Creek land at will. White crime was allowed to continue without punishment, while Indian crimes against whites brought about retaliation, punishment, and even threats of war. However, intermingled with these usual legalistic articles was one that really negated all the rest and shows, if proof is necessary, the low regard the U.S. really had for Indian territorial integrity. Article seven boldly stated that no inhabitants of the U.S. would be allowed to hunt, settle, or even enter the Creek country "without a passport first obtained from the Governor of some one of the United States, or the officer of the troops of the United States commanding at the nearest military post on the frontiers, or such other person as the President of the United

States may, from time to time, authorize to grant the same." This is an absolutely incredible statement! By allowing any governor, even the governor of New Hampshire and Rhode Island if you please, the nearest military commander, or any person designated by the President to grant such a passport without Creek permission, the U.S. was really saying that any American could grant permission to any other American to do as he pleased in the Creek Confederacy. No wonder these treaties created more problems than they solved.

The last article of note was article twelve in which the U.S., as usual, offered to lead the Creeks to "a greater degree of civilization." To accomplish that "noble" task, the U.S. promised to supply the Creeks with farm animals and implements, plus up to four agents who were to be given free land in order to live among the Indians and demonstrate by example the superiority of their way of life. McGillivray didn't mind this insult: if the U.S. wanted to make farmers out of farmers that was their business. Anyway, the tribe would get some horses, cows, and pigs for free out of the deal, he reasoned.

As usual, the treaty concluded with a statement that it would be fully effective as soon as the President and the Senate of the U.S. ratified it. This was done despite the fact that McGillivray warned that he might not be able to convince his people to ratify a treaty that surrendered the "Apalachee fork" to the U.S. Finally, it was hoped, the twelve years of Creek-U.S. warfare were at an end and peace was restored to the Southern frontier.

In every way, the Treaty of New York was the crowning achievement of Alexander McGillivray's distinguished career of service to his people. But it has not been recorded that way in the history books. In fact, it is used by many as proof positive that he was a self-seeking and devious creature. The reason for that feeling has nothing to do with the treaty itself. Rather, years after the treaty was ratified, the Alabama historian Albert James Pickett uncovered a secret arrangement negotiated by Washington, Knox, McGillivray and others at New York. According to the document, the U.S. secretly appointed McGillivray as their agent with the rank of brigadier general and a salary of twelve hundred dollars annually. Six other micos were given handsome medals and one hundred dollars annually to help McGillivray serve the cause of the U.S. in the South. In return for this money, the Creek leaders were to divert all tribal commerce away from the Spaniards and direct it to U.S. ports in the area. Without thinking further on the subject, some historians have steadfastly maintained that this secret arrangement is proof positive that McGillivray was an unprincipled and self-oriented crook who would sell out his people for a reasonable bribe. But that argument is as naive as it is incorrect. We must remember that salvation is not always a clean business offering clear-cut alternatives. McGillivray, above all else, was trying to save his people from two grasping neighbors — Spain and the United States. His only weapon was their competition for the same goal — Creek land. Therefore, he accepted a Spanish rank and money to convince that enemy of his friendship. In 1790 he did the same thing with the U.S., allowing both to believe that he was tied to their interests by the bond of bribery. But he wasn't! His acceptance of the title and money was as much a bribe in reverse as their offering of it. Proof of this statement can be seen in his activities after he left New York. He let the Spaniards know that his services had been bought by the U.S. at a higher price than they had offered. To counteract this diplomatic disaster, the Spaniards gave him a new title — Superintendent General of the Creek Nation — and an annual salary of thirty-five hundred dollars. He accepted the honor and money without surrendering his secret arrangement with the United States. Now he was in the employ of both adversaries and served neither. It is quite obvious what he was doing — saving his people by allying himself with both their enemies. He certainly didn't need the titles; he already had as many Creek titles as anyone could use. By the same token, the money was of no value to him living in a non-monetary society. But the diplomatic leverage both positions gave him was important and he knew it. No, Alexander McGillivray was not a traitor to his people; he achieved a diplomatic coup unequaled by any other Indian leader in the history of the Republic.

But the Treaty of New York settled nothing. Georgians would not even discuss the document, let alone accept it. The Creek national council would not surrender the "Apalachee fork," as McGillivray predicted. So frontier warfare commenced all over again: Georgians "swarmed into the Creek country with packs of dogs and slaughtered the game thirty or forty miles back from the border," despite treaty stipulations to the contrary. The Creeks retaliated by making frontier settlement a risky business for adventurous hunters and settlers. In the midst of this confrontation, McGillivray died on February 17, 1793 at the young age of thirty-four and thereby robbed the Creeks of their most respected leader. Border difficulties increased after McGillivray's death, intrigues with Spanish officials continued, and the mounting death toll and property loss alarmed both sides. Georgia not only claimed land acquired before 1790 but additional acreage deemed necessary for its expanding population. The major setback for the Creeks did not take place on the battlefield, but at the white man's negotiation table. In 1795, after years of conflict, Spain and the U.S. settled long-standing differences in the Treaty of San Lorenzo, thereby depriving the Creeks of their leverage on the frontier. But Georgia could not capitalize on this advantage; one of its frontiersmen, Benjamin Harrison, led a number of fellow-cutthroats on a raid in which they murdered and mutilated the bodies of twenty peaceful Creeks. They carried out the dirty deed with such ferocity that even Georgians were shocked and horrified. At this juncture, the U.S. offered to negotiate a new treaty, and the Creeks, shaken by the massacre and hurt by the San Lorenzo treaty, consented to meet the U.S. at Colerain.

The 1796 Treaty of Colerain was a most important one for both the Creeks and the U.S., despite the fact that it really was nothing more than an acceptance by both sides of the Treaty of New York. The U.S. was represented by commissioners headed by Benjamin Hawkins, a rich and influential North Carolinian destined to play a significant role in Creek history for the next two decades. The Creeks were represented by four hundred leaders headed by their spokesman, Fushatchee Mico. What is significant and even unique about this treaty is the fairness exhibited by the U.S. commissioners. Despite the fact that they represented a country much more powerful than the one faced by McGillivray in 1790, Hawkins and his colleagues, George Clymer of Pennsylvania and Andrew Pickens of South Carolina, allowed a full and uninhibited discussion of all points of friction. They did insist that the Creeks accept the Treaty of New York, including the cession of the "Apalachee fork," but nothing more. After reluctant Creek acceptance of that point, they requested permission for the U.S. to establish military and trading posts in the Creek country along the Georgia border. At first the micos protested, but then it dawned on them that there were definite advantages to having such posts nearby. Their quarrel was not with the U.S. government but its Georgia citizens. Such posts could protect the Creeks and prove to the U.S. that it was not they who raided illegally in another nation's territory. Article three granted the U.S. the right to five miles of Creek land along the southern border and five miles in the north to establish military and trading posts to protect the frontier and allow the Creeks to trade their wares for quality goods at low prices. In return, the Creeks were granted in article eight six thousand dollars worth of goods free of charge and two blacksmiths with strikers, one to be located in the Upper Towns and the other in the Lower Towns. The treaty was signed on June 29, 1796 after both sides promised that "all animosities for past grievances shall henceforth cease." It was the first treaty to which all Creeks freely consented since long before the American Revolution.

After the Treaty of Colerain, an uneasy peace settled on the Creek frontier. The Lower Creeks were well satisfied, but the Upper Creeks, more isolated and more attached to the "old ways," simply grumbled and watched to see what would happen in the future. The first result was a happy one for the Confederacy — the U.S. appointed Benjamin Hawkins as Creek agent. There is no doubt that Hawkins approached his job with an honesty and zest for fair-dealing seldom found in others entrusted with the same position. Angie Debo states that "he was the ablest man that ever represented the United States among the Creeks," and that statement is generally accepted by all other Creek historians. Though the statement is undoubtedly true, Hawkins did suffer from the same disease that infected other Indian agents; he considered the Creeks children of nature who, above all else, had to be "civilized." His reports to the U.S. were models of modesty and frank and accurate statements of conditions as they existed in the Nation. But he was always trying to make white people out of Indians. He persuaded the council to pass punishment laws, adopt a new plan of government which centralized power under his influence, and he even tried to divide up the land into individually-owned farms. He eventually made much headway among the Lower Towns because they were poorer, more devastated by past wars, and geographically closer to whites in Spanish Florida and Georgia who, through the years, had succeeded in making the people of the Lower Towns less Indian and more white in orientation. But he always had trouble with the more isolated and more prosperous Upper Towns. They had not suffered from frontier wars as had the Lower Towns or their Cherokee neighbors, and they had long maintained an independence from whites unequaled throughout the rest of the South. But the security of geography would help no longer as Georgians, Tennesseans, Carolinians, and Virginians crowded the frontier, anxious to swarm over all the best lands between Augusta and the Mississippi River. While the Lower Towns realized that survival meant accommodation, the Upper Towns faced the new day with hope of preserving most of the past. Hawkins tried to prepare them for the inevitable, but they were convinced that total submission to his ideas was unnecessary. They would rather die than become white Indians. Time would afford them that opportunity.

As was true with all other tribal groups, acquiescence to one white American demand simply prompted another. So in 1802, Hawkins, Pickens, and James Wilkinson met with the Creeks near Fort Wilkinson on the Oconee River to discuss a further cession of land. Wilkinson took the lead in the negotiations and upbraided the Creeks for murders and general thievery along the Georgia frontier. As an indemnity for these activities, he demanded a north-south sliver of land on the west bank of the Oconee and Apalachee rivers. The chiefs retorted by presenting a list of white depredations within the Creek Confederacy which Wilkinson dismissed as unworthy of comment. After a minimum of discussion, the micos present surprised the commissioners by agreeing to sell the land requested for fair compensation. They received three thousand dollars annually in perpetuity and an additional one thousand dollars for ten years. They also received ten thousand dollars worth of merchandise, while the U.S. promised to pay ten thousand dollars worth of debts owed by the Creeks to the government factory and five thousand dollars in claims by white citizens for property destroyed by the Creeks since the Treaty of Colerain. Again, the U.S. promised to supply two blacksmiths and tools free of charge for three years. The promise, without a time limit, had been made in 1796 and never carried out by the U.S. Lastly, the Creeks agreed again to allow the U.S. to establish as many forts as necessary along the eastern boundary for protection of persons on both sides of the line.

The Treaty of Fort Wilkinson was obviously a generous gesture by the Creeks to clear up frontier problems and to earn U.S. friendship. They ceded the land requested for a pittance and hoped that the gesture would relieve the constant pressure exerted by Georgians on their perennially troublesome eastern boundary. One can see the hand of Benjamin Hawkins in the treaty counseling kindness and solicitation as the best means to a bright future.

But all was not well in the Creek country. In 1798 the government of the U.S. established the Mississippi Territory in what is today much of Mississippi and Alabama. Also in 1802 Georgia formally ceded its western lands to the U.S. in return for the promise that the U.S. would work toward extinguishing all Indian title to lands within the boundaries of the state of Georgia as soon as possible. A guarantee of historic lands to the Creeks in 1802 cannot be reconciled with a promise to Georgia to extinguish Indian title soon. Diametrically opposite promises make for immediate problems, and which promise do you suppose the U.S. was most inclined to keep? As could be predicted, settlers flocked to the Mississippi Territory lands, creating trouble for the Choctaws and Chickasaws as well as the Creeks. Once again, because of pressure exerted by whites moving west, the U.S. sat down with the Creeks in 1805 to discuss the possibilities of yet another cession of land.

Despite past promises of Creek security on their present lands, the U.S. in 1805 demanded a large tract of north-south land running westward from the past cession to the Ocmulgee River in central Georgia. This was not a request for a "sliver of land" as was true in 1802, but a request for millions of acres. Once again, through the pressure exerted by Hawkins, the Creeks showed remarkable self-control and relented with little overt pressure. Not only did they cede the land demanded, but granted the right to build forts and factories on the new border, and agreed to allow the U.S. to build roads through the remaining Creek country "in such direction as shall, by the President of the United States, be considered most convenient. . . ." The U.S. could cut down trees for the road, build bridges, and interestingly enough, build an untold number of "houses of entertainment . . . for the accommodation of travelers" along the way. For these acres and privileges, the U.S. paid the Creeks two hundred six thousand — twelve thousand dollars a year for eight years and eleven thousand dollars for ten years "in money or goods." Lastly, since the U.S. had yet to send the first blacksmith into the Nation, it was once again promised that two blacksmiths and two strikers would be supplied free of charge for the next eight years.

Though the U.S. did not know it at the time, the Creeks had gone as far as they would go with the policy of appeasement. Enough is enough, they reasoned. But whites did not know that the Creeks had reached the end of their appeasement rope; possibly the Indians did not realize it themselves, for all appeared to be peaceful in the Creek Confederacy from 1800 to 1812: Benjamin Hawkins reigned supreme. Hawkins, highly successful in North Carolina and quite wealthy, considered himself the Moses of the "untutored savages" among whom he dwelled. How much grace he must be earning in heaven, Hawkins probably contemplated, as he observed the good works he was fostering in the Creek Nation. They loved and appreciated him; at least it seemed that way as some micos bestowed upon him the title "Beloved Man of the Four Nations." He could observe white man's plows, animals, clothes, and haircuts all around him during those days, at least in the Lower Towns and amongst Upper Creek sympathizers. And peace had descended upon the land — sixteen years of peace which the Creeks had not known before for centuries.

But the smug Hawkins was wrong, dead wrong. Most Creeks did what they had to do to insure peace, smouldered inwardly as they observed whiteism among their ranks and endless caravans of white people traveling through the country on U.S. roads stealing, raping, and even settling along the way. What many Creeks wanted, above all else, was a taste of the "good old days." They wanted to roam their own land sure that the only enemy they would meet was a Cherokee or Chickasaw tribesman poaching where he didn't belong. These yearnings gave way to imagining the past as perfection and the present as living hell. And these yearnings gave way to dreaming. They wanted another leader like Alexander McGillivray, who could turn back the clock and bring pride again to all members of the Confederacy. They dreamed so hard and they prayed so fervently for their messiah that they eventually found him in the person of Tecumseh. Possibly in more normal times, they would have seen faults in that impressive leader, but dreams have a way of clouding faults and emphasizing assets; and Tecumseh had many assets.

By 1810, unknown to Hawkins and even most of the Creeks, changes were in the air that would tragically affect eastern Indians and the United States which claimed at least nominal jurisdiction over them. Events with seemingly little connection have a way of meshing together into tragic moments in history. So it was that isolated episodes in the "Jefferson years" led red and white Americans inexorably to two tragic wars — the Red Sticks or Creek War of 1813-14 and the War of 1812. If Hawkins and many of his charges could not see that the Creek treaties of 1802 and 1805, in addition to subsequent thwarted requests for more land, would lead to war, how, then, could they have predicted that war between France and Britain in Europe, the invention of the cotton gin, and the grasping policies of William Henry Harrison and his followers in Indiana, would enhance the possibility of such a war? But these events did! As seen in Chapter 1, by 1805 the U.S. had adopted a policy which foresaw grabbing bits and pieces of tribal domains whenever the opportunity presented itself and the eventual removal of all eastern Indians to a new homeland west of the mighty Mississippi. The goal, once set, was never altered, even though trouble with England and France over the impressment of sailors, the rights of neutrals on the high seas, the British activities among Old Northwest Indians, among other things, forced the U.S. to pay less and less attention to their red neighbors than to problems created by foreign powers. However, during the years 1805-1810, the U.S. could afford to neglect Indians; northern tribes had been defeated badly by General Anthony Wayne and they were tolerating white encroachments, while Southern tribes were being "civilized" by a number of enthusiastic and dedicated "saviors," such as Benjamin Hawkins in the Creek country. But the respite gave Creeks, Shawnees, Choctaws, and other tribes time to contemplate what had happened to them since the U.S. became their major white adversary in 1783 — and many tribes did not like what they saw. Some tribes, such as the Choctaws and Cherokees, felt that it was the better part of valor to pursue "olive branch" foreign policy. They knew that the U.S.

ultimately wanted to uproot them completely and send tribes west, but thus far the policy was not enforced, and tribes were allowed the option of agreeing or refusing to surrender more land. Possibly the future would be different, the Choctaw mingo Pushmataha and others of like mind reasoned, but if the tribes did nothing to disturb or provoke their growing white colossus to the east the possibility of ultimate removal was less likely to come about.

Pushmataha's approach had merit and received favorable acceptance by many tribes, but not by the Creeks of Alabama and Georgia. From earliest times, they had met French, Spanish, English, and even American thrusts on the battlefield if necessary and at the negotiation table if possible. And, what is more important, their willingness to take to the warpath had paid handsome dividends on more than one occasion. Had they not been able to keep the Spaniards at bay by meeting them on the battlefield? Had they not been the last Southern tribe to sign a treaty with the U.S. and gained acceptable terms in 1796 by killing encroachers and attacking settlements? And what had happened when the Creeks accepted peaceful co-existence as their policy around 1800? The answer was the treaties of 1802 and 1805 which cost the tribe almost as much additional land as was originally ceded at New York and Colerain, to say nothing about the demands for more lands which were enunciated yearly after 1805. It is no wonder that many Creeks, mentally in search of the good old days, were willing to burn the olive branch and return to the hitherto successful policy of military confrontation.

The man who brought matters to a head and offered the alternative policy many Upper Creeks desired was not a Creek, or a Southern Indian for that matter. It was Tecumseh, a major leader of the Shawnee Indians of the Old Northwest. The tribes of that region were small, totally disorganized, and thoroughly cowed by their defeat in 1793 at Fallen Timbers. Therefore, they did not offer a formidable barrier to a territorial governor, such as William Henry Harrison, who dispossessed tribesmen from millions of acres by 1808. But in true Hegelian fashion his activities gave way to a counterweight in the person of Tecumseh. Surely, this great leader ranks among the most significant Indians ever produced in North America. In fact, Angie Debo writes, "As a statesman, orator, patriot, warrior, and as a chivalrous, generous, honorable human being, Tecumseh stands as one of the greatest Indians known to history." Heretofore, most Indians including McGillivray maintained that tribes did not have to honor treaties negotiated by other tribesmen not authorized to do so. Tecumseh rejected this thesis and instead held that all land belonged to all Indians, and therefore, no tribe could sell any part of the Indians' common heritage. At first, he did not encourage warfare; rather he felt that if all Indians would unite they could hold back the white tide pressing around them. In 1808, Tecumseh and his brother Tenskwatawa (the prophet) built Prophet's Town on Tippecanoe Creek in Indiana and traveled throughout the Old Northwest preaching their beliefs to all tribesmen who would listen. And the brothers attracted followers wherever they went. While they preached and converted, Harrison continued to meet with weak Indian leaders and acquire from them, after much socializing, additional tribal land. In 1810 Tecumseh journeyed to the capital city of Indiana Territory, Vincennes, to explain why the treaties were not binding and to warn Harrison against continuing to steal land from drunken Indians. When Harrison contended that the Indians had sold the land in fair negotiations, Tecumseh exploded and screamed: "Sell a country! Why not sell the air, the clouds and the great sea, as well as the earth? Did not the Great Spirit make them all for the use of his children?" While they sat on a bench arguing over the right of Indians to sell land to whites, Harrison maintained that Americans had always treated their red neighbors fairly. In response, Tecumseh moved closer to Harrison on the bench and the latter moved away. Tecumseh moved closer again and again and each time Harrison moved away until he reached the end of the bench and could move no further. Then, Tecumseh laughed and told Harrison that his plight was analogous to that of the Indians — they could move no further.

The fame of Tecumseh spread throughout the country, and as he continued to visit with tribes, their positive response to his preachings increased daily. Many tribes, including the Choctaws, were not convinced by his dazzling presentation, especially when he started talking about a possible war in 1811, but when he visited with the Creeks that year he was welcomed by many as the leader they were seeking. Many Creeks, especially those from the Lower Towns thoroughly controlled by Hawkins, feared him, but Tecumseh knew from his Creek reception that he was mainly among friends. After his visit, the council agreed to punish by death any mico who negotiated illegally with whites and ceded more land. Tecumseh left behind among the Creeks a relative, Seekaba, who was to instruct the new converts in the new religious Dance of the Lakes and in the use of magic red war clubs that would protect Indians when they fought whites. Part of Tecumseh's message included the need for Indians to eliminate all white symbols, such as weapons, tools, animals, and clothes. Pro-American leaders tried hard to combat Tecumseh's influence, but everywhere he went in the nation he made converts. The gods were even on his side; while he visited, a comet appeared and an earthquake rumbled across the Creek country. Here indeed was the man sent to restore the good old days to the Creek Confederacy.

Opothle Mico of the Upper Creeks became an immediate convert and the leader of the "hostiles," as Tecumseh's Creek followers were called. Trouble was in the air, and it was not long in coming. In the summer of 1812 — the same summer the U.S. went to war with Great Britain for the second time — a number of Creeks traveled to Shawnee country to attend a conference with Tecumseh. When they returned in the fall full of enthusiasm for the cause, they killed seven white families near the mouth of the Ohio River. Possibly they also killed a few more as they made their way through Kentucky and Tennessee en route to Alabama and Georgia. Tennessee officials immediately issued a call for ten thousand militiamen to attack and exterminate the Creek Nation. Hawkins warned the leaders that they must punish these murderers to avert all-out war. William McIntosh, speaker of the Lower Towns, agreed with Hawkins, but Menawa, speaker of the Upper Creeks, and later a hostile leader, hesitated to take any action against fellow-tribesmen who only did to whites what had been done to Indians for years. But Menawa realized that the murders jeopardized the safety of the entire Upper Towns region, and to forestall war, he joined McIntosh in hunting down the murderers and executed eleven of them in late April 1813.

Normally, such a wholesale execution would have ended the incident, but these were not normal times. The action simply infuriated the Upper Creek hostiles and, worse still, brought to their fold a number of equally upset neutrals who had been wavering between the preachments of Tecumseh and Hawkins. The hostiles attacked the "enforcement party," killed many of their number, and talked of war as they circulated the "magical" red war clubs from town to town accompanied by bundles of sticks indicating the number of days until a general attack. From town to town, as if by a pre-arranged signal, the war drums began their ominous cadence, and the Dance of the Lakes added wild rhythms to the scene of impending war. Hostiles began to kill livestock, fowls, and other "white" animals, while they also destroyed guns, ammunition, and farm implements gained in past treaties or given them by Hawkins. Without a doubt, war was in the air by the summer of 1813.

It is important to realize that from the beginning the Red Sticks, as the hostiles became generally known, were a minority party. Most of the Lower Creeks remained loyal to the U.S. and requested more arms and ammunition from Hawkins to attack their mischievous brethren. The Upper Towns were about evenly divided between Red Sticks and "progressives," as Hawkins called his friends. But since the Red Sticks were interspersed throughout most of the Upper Towns — and since they were the ones calling for action, they, in effect, controlled the fate of the Upper Towns. Micos and warriors who wavered or were openly progressive in the Upper region were harassed and driven out or forced to go into hiding. Progressive towns were burned to the ground. Menawa joined the hostiles and became one of their most able leaders. The McGillivray family was evenly divided, but William Weatherford (known as Red Eagle) joined the Red Sticks and became their major leader. Weatherford was the son of a white trader and Alexander McGillivray's sister Sehoy; his exploits in the impending war were such that they have passed into Creek legend and have gained for him a tribal memory second to none.

The Creek or Red Sticks War began on August 30, 1813 when Weatherford and his followers fell upon Fort Mims, a frontier fort a few miles north of Mobile. The fort contained five hundred fifty-three Americans, two hundred sixty-five of whom were soldiers and the remainder frightened civilians who understood the need for refuge from the totally possessed Red Sticks. The fort was commanded by Major Samuel Beasley, who was so inept that he didn't even shut and lock the gates despite positive knowledge that Red Sticks were lurking about. At noon, on a pre-arranged signal, the Red Sticks attacked, overwhelmed the fort, killed all but thirty-six people who escaped, and began a war destined to be the most tragic moment in Creek history. Infuriated Creeks from the Lower Towns, Choctaws, and Cherokees, firmly believing that the war was a mistake, joined three white armies sent forth to crush the recalcitrant Red Sticks.

Space does not allow a blow-by-blow account of this well-recorded war. From the beginning the Red Sticks did not have a chance to achieve victory. It is true that many Red Sticks braves and even women did not care whether they won or lost. They were frustrated and yearned to punish whites for all their sins since DeSoto arrived in 1540. Death was not feared if, before the fateful hour, each Red Stick could take a number of whites along to the happy hunting ground with him. To me, this is the major tragedy of the war. Victory as a goal is one thing, but to fight for no object other than sure death of self and adversaries is something else. Maybe the suicidal furor of the Creek Red Sticks proves that Indians are sub-human beasts, as many have maintained. However, I choose not to accept that simplistic answer. Rather, the war proves to me that some people cannot and will not accept total humiliation at the hands of a relentless adversary. For centuries eastern Indians were subjected to almost indescribable inhumanity by various white colonizers. Some accepted their fate meekly; others fought to win or survive through negotiation; still others chose to die on the battlefield. From the safety of hindsight, I have often wondered which course I would have followed. I honestly do not know, but I am convinced that the Red Sticks War is a blot on American and not Creek history.

Three armies were set in motion against the Red Sticks — one from Mississippi Territory under the command of Gen. Ferdinand Clairborne and the Choctaw mingo Pushmataha; another containing many Cherokees attacked from Georgia under the command of the always inept and often lost John Floyd; and the third from Tennessee commanded by Andrew Jackson, whose exploits in the war launched one of the most famed rags-to-riches stories in American history. Clairborne's army met with success in western Alabama, winning the significant Battle of the Holy Ground. Floyd offered a severe test to the Red Sticks, but his army was eventually driven from the field. Even Andrew Jackson, plagued by bad health and an army of militiamen more intent on mustering out and returning home than killing Indians, suffered two initial defeats. However, the resourceful Jackson overcame all obstacles and finally met the major Red Sticks army well entrenched at the Horseshoe Bend of the Tallapoosa River. The day of the battle, March 27, 1814, was a day that will long be remembered in the history of American-Indian warfare.

At the battle Jackson commanded an army of two thousand men and was opposed by Red Eagle with eight hundred warriors well entrenched and willing to fight to the bitter end. The Horseshoe was a deep bend in the river covering about one hundred acres filled with gullies, brush, timber, and log breastworks. Jackson surrounded the Horseshoe and attacked. There was a hard fight at the breastworks but the Americans, with superior firepower, overran them. "Arrows, and spears, and balls were flying," recorded an ensign with Jackson, "swords and tomahawks gleaming in the sun." That part of the battle ended when the last Indian lay dead. Still Jackson's army pressed on. Though he hated Indians with a fervor peculiar to frontiersmen, Jackson offered more than once to end the carnage if the Red Sticks would surrender. They did not; so the Americans took the one hundred acres inch by inch. When the day was over, at least seven hundred fifty-nine of the eight hundred Red Sticks lay dead, while Jackson suffered fewer than two hundred casualties. But Red Eagle escaped, and word reached Jackson that he was rallying the remaining Red Sticks for yet another battle. The rumor was not true; by May Red Sticks refugees were heading toward Florida and future life among their relatives — the Seminoles.

The eventual surrender of Weatherford has since become an important legend in Creek history. Supposedly, Jackson fumed and fussed over the fact that he did not have an opportunity personally to kill Red Eagle at Horseshoe Bend. He swore, though, that he would kill the man if ever the opportunity presented itself. As legend records it, one day in July Jackson was leaving his quarters and an Indian approached him asking, "General Jackson?" "Yes," replied Jackson. "I am Bill Weatherford," the man stated simply, whereupon Jackson replied (according to the version you read), "I am glad to see you, Mr. Weatherford," or "How dare you show yourself at my tent after having murdered the women and children at Fort Mims!" They went inside Jackson's tent and talked. "I am come," Red Eagle said, "to give myself up. I can oppose you no longer. I have done you much injury. I should have done you more . . . [but] my warriors are killed. . . . I am in your power. Dispose of me as you please. . . . But I beg you to send for the women and children of the war party, who have been driven to the woods without an ear of corn. . . . They never did any harm. But kill me, if the white people want it." Marquis James in his classic, *The Life of Andrew Jackson,* states that Jackson was greatly impressed with Red Eagle, offered him a cup of brandy, promised to help the women and children, and offered the Indian his hand while promising that he would not be executed. "Red Eagle took it," James comments, "and strode from the ruined fort in which his mother had been born — vanishing from the view of the astonished soldiery, and from history, a not entirely graceless figure."

Whether or not Jackson was as gracious to Weatherford as legend records is subject to debate, but he certainly did not inflict a very gracious treaty on his adversaries. The Treaty of Fort Jackson was a victor's peace if ever there were one. The treaty was important for a number of reasons: first, it was the product of Jackson's own thinking with a minimum of help from the government he represented; second, it punished the friendly Lower Creeks more than it did the Red Sticks of the Upper Towns; third, it made Jackson a national hero; and fourth, it destroyed forever Creek power in the South. The treaty contained an interesting preamble which, in clause after clause, blamed the Creeks for all the problems evident on the Southern frontier since 1783. It stated, in part, "that prior to the conquest of that part of the Creek nation hostile to the United States, numberless aggressions had been committed against the peace, the property, and the lives of citizens of the United States, and those of the Creek nation in amity with her, at the mouth of Duck river, Fort Mimms, and elsewhere, contrary to national faith. . . ." Of course, nothing was said about Georgians' wronging Indians, but then, a victor's preamble is permitted to take liberties with history.

With one or two exceptions, the thirty-five Creek leaders gathered at Fort Jackson to accept Jackson's peace were all members of the pro-American wing of the Creek Nation. First, they had to accept a strongly worded confession of war guilt and then cede twenty-two million acres of their Georgia and Alabama land — the largest single cession of land extracted from any Southern Indian tribe in history. Nothing in the treaty was negotiable. A person can always tell a victor's peace from one in which American commissioners are simply requesting land. Previous treaty articles all began with such neutral phrases as "it is hereby agreed," or "it is hereby stipulated," but almost every article in the Fort Jackson treaty begins with the words "the United States demand." And so they did! For our purposes in studying different broken treaties, the Fort Jackson treaty is the best example possible to show what the U.S. would take if it were left free to include in the treaty anything it wanted to.

In taking the twenty-two million acres shown on the map included with this chapter, Jackson realized that he was extracting more land from his friends than his enemies. But it was the land most desired by whites at the time. He did provide, however, that any friendly Creek losing land in the treaty would receive a one-mile square reservation where he now lived, as long as the Indian were willing to be subjected to the laws of the state and federal government. However, nowhere in the treaty did he establish a procedure to differentiate the friendly Indians from the Red Sticks. He didn't even state who would make the determination and, therefore, left the door wide open to all types of future problems for progressives. Georgia and Alabama surely would want to keep down the number of one-mile square tracts lost to anxious white purchasers. And how could an Indian prove that he was friendly? All Creeks were later assumed to be guilty unless proved beyond a shadow of a doubt to be innocent. How could that be done? Leaving the problem up to Hawkins was surely what Jackson had in mind, but Hawkins died shortly after the war, thereby dashing any hope of retribution for the overwhelming number of loyal Lower Creeks.

Of the nine articles in the treaty, seven were demands by the U.S. on the Creeks. Article one included all particulars about the twenty-two million acre land cession; articles two and three guaranteed the Creeks their remaining territory, provided they abandon all intercourse with the British; article four granted the U.S. the right to build roads, military posts, and trading houses on the remaining land; article five forced the Creeks to surrender all persons and property taken in the war; article six required that the Creeks surrender all Red Sticks still in the nation to the U.S.; and article nine forced the nation to "ratify and confirm the preceding articles."

On only one occasion in the treaty — article seven — did Jackson show any humanity at all. "The Creek nation being reduced to extreme want," the article stated, "the United States, from motives of humanity, will continue to furnish gratuitously the necessaries of life, until the crops of corn can be considered competent to yield the nation a supply, and will establish trading houses in the nation, . . . to enable the nation, by industry and economy, to procure clothing." A careful reading of the article forces one to define generosity in the broadest possible way. It is ridiculous to state that there is much generosity in the stipulation that one is willing to build stores at which tribesmen could buy clothing. They had no money to buy clothing! Also, it was kind of Jackson to offer to feed the tribe until the next crop became available — almost a year later — but Jackson had no extra food to give. Throughout the war, he had continually complained about the fact that his army was being starved to death by a government almost totally without supply facilities. Even if he wanted to, he couldn't feed the Creeks. Therefore, article seven was just another promise that was broken before the ink dried on the document.

Because the treaty did not cede to the U.S. Creek land in eastern Alabama and western Georgia, the Upper Creeks, in reality, were allowed to return home and farm as in the past. But the poor progressives, loyal to the U.S. through thick and thin, were severely punished by the loss of much of their land. And the tribe received no payment for the ceded land which more than disheartened them. But constant complaints about the unfairness of the treaty did force the U.S. to review that portion of the treaty; and Congress, in 1817, appropriated eighty-five thousand dollars for the Lower Creeks and in 1853 awarded them another one hundred ten thousand dollars. But in passing, it is interesting to note that for slightly more than one hundred ninety-five thousand dollars the U.S. got land which it sold to settlers for eleven million, two hundred fifty thousand dollars during the next forty years. As one historian has written, "from the white man's point of view it had been a very satisfactory war."

The most satisfactory aspect of the war from the Creek vantage point was that at least they had the satisfaction of knowing that the U.S. would not break this treaty. One need never break a document in which he gives up nothing in return for vast holdings of land. The most satisfying aspect of the war from America's viewpoint, however, was not securing the land but breaking Creek power in the East forever. The tribe now lay helpless and susceptible to the whims of a government that could afford to be generous for the next decade. But when more land was needed, the Creeks were removed from their remaining Georgia lands in 1827 and their Alabama lands in 1835 with little or no difficulty. As was true with their Choctaw and Cherokee neighbors who chose the "olive branch" approach with no more success than Creek "warpath" diplomacy, they ended up in Oklahoma, there to remain to this day.

It seems appropriate to conclude with a 1972 insult to the Creeks which is not only unforgivable but shows that many white Americans still don't respect Creeks as equal human beings caught up in the drama of history. The February 10, 1972, issue of *The Daily Oklahoman* (Oklahoma City) includes a story that is as nauseating as it is insulting. It seems that the Macon, Georgia, Chamber of Commerce has invited many Creek Indians to return to the Macon area. Why? To accept jobs that might attract tourists to the area, the newspaper reported. "The jobs would include work at Georgia tourist attractions where Indians would work as craftsmen for a trading post, museum curators and tour guides . . .," the paper continued. For enriching white Georgians with the tourist dollar and "playing Indian savage," the Chamber of Commerce promises that the jobs will pay around five thousand dollars a year — enough to keep the tribesmen off welfare but not enough to help them live in dignity. I wonder what Alexander McGillivray or Red Eagle would have replied to such an offer.

SUGGESTED READINGS

Caughey, John Walton. *McGillivray of the Creeks.* 2nd Edit. Norman: University of Oklahoma Press, 1959.

Corkran, David H. *The Creek Frontier, 1540-1783.* Norman: University of Oklahoma Press, 1967.

Cotterill, R.S. *The Southern Indians, The Story of the Civilized Tribes before Removal.* 3rd Edit. Norman: University of Oklahoma Press, 1966.

Debo, Angie. *A History of the Indians of the United States.* Norman: University of Oklahoma Press, 1970.

Debo, Angie, *The Road to Disappearance.* Norman: University of Oklahoma Press, 1941.

Halbert, H.S. and T.H. Ball. *The Creek War of 1813 and 1814.* University, Alabama: University of Alabama Press, 1969.

James, Marquis. *The Life of Andrew Jackson.* New York: Garden City Publishing Co., Inc., 1940.

Swanton, John R. *Early History of the Creek Indians and Their Neighbors. Bulletin No. 73* of The Bureau of American Ethnology. Washington: Bureau of American Ethnology, 1922.

Wright, J. Leitch, Jr. *William Augustus Bowles, Director General of the Creek Nation.* Athens: University of Georgia Press, 1967.

Many Americans agreed with Phillip H. Sheridan when he exclaimed: "This outbreak does not look to me, as being originated by the actions of bad white men, or the sale of whiskey to Indians by traders. It is the result of the restless nature of the Indian who has no profession but arms and naturally seeks for war and plunder when the grazing gets high enough to feed his ponies."

CHAPTER 4

The Southern Cheyennes

Emmett M. Essin, III

THEY CALLED themselves T sis tsis′ tas, "those bred similarly." The Sioux called them Shā hī′ ē la or Shā hī′ e na, "people speaking language not understood." White men, who more often than not learned a tribe's name from its enemies, referred to the tribe as Cheyenne, and the name stuck.

French explorers and traders were the first white men to encounter the Cheyennes. A map drawn by Joliet placed them north of the Sioux near the mouth of the Wisconsin River. In 1684 the cartographer Jean Baptiste Louis Fraquelin placed the tribe in the Minnesota River Valley. Later traders told of trading with Cheyennes near the Sheyenne River in eastern North Dakota. It was here that the Cheyennes acquired horses and began to trade for glass beads. In 1802 Francis Marie Perrie de Lac visited a large group of Cheyennes on the banks of the Missouri near the boundary of North and South Dakota. Pierre-Antoine Tabeau spent the winter of 1804-1805 wandering with a Cheyenne band in the eastern part of the Black Hills.

The Cheyennes maintained amiable but somewhat distant relations with the early Europeans. Whenever they met, both groups were content merely to barter — the whites for pelts and the Indians for beads and then iron ware, rifles, gunpowder, and horses. Later the French Canadians and English fur company agents refined the trading practices. Living for months at a time with different bands of the tribe and inevitably taking squaws as companions or wives in each band, they established more enduring ties, and some became members of the tribe. These men did

---

Emmett M. Essin, III received a Ph.D. from Texas Christian University. He is presently an Associate Professor of History at East Tennessee State University where he teaches courses in the American West and Spanish Borderlands. He has published several articles in American western and cultural history.

not change the Cheyennes' way of life but mildly corrupted them, teaching them to appreciate the conveniences of a supposedly more advanced civilization.

The first-known Americans to contact the Cheyennes were members of the Lewis and Clark expedition. On Monday, October 1, 1804, as the explorers were ascending the Missouri River, they met Jean Vallé who told them that the previous year he had "wintered 300 Leagues up the Chien River under the Black mountains," and had visited with the Cheyennes. From Vallé's remarks Clark concluded that the "Cheyenne Indians are about 300 Lodges" and that they "Steel horses from the Spanish Settlements to the S.W." Ten days later Clark wrote that he saw "some of the Chien or Dog Indians. . . . This nation is at war with the Crow Indians & have 3 children prisoners." He added that the Cheyennes had established a brisk trade with the "Rickarees" (Arikaras). On December 1, six Cheyenne warriors visited the expedition's headquarters at Fort Mandan. Lewis and Clark told the Cheyennes to keep the peace and gave them tobacco and trinkets. According to Clark, the Indians "departed well satisfied with our Councils and advice."

On the return trip down the Missouri in 1806 Lewis and Clark held "councils" with most of the tribes along the way. Reaching the Arikara villages on August 21, they discovered a large number of Cheyennes and some Mandans trading with the "Ricarees." Clark met with the chiefs of each tribe on the bank of the river and delivered the same speech he had delivered to other tribes around the mouth of the Yellowstone River. The Cheyennes and other representatives therefore probably heard something similar to the following:

Children. The Great Spirit has given a fair and bright day for us to meet together in his View that he may inspect us in this all we say and do.

Children. I take you all by the hand as the children of your Great father the President of the U. States of America who is the great chief of all the white people towards the rising sun.

Children. This Great Chief who is Benevolent, just, wise, & bountifull has sent me . . . to all his read children on the Missouri and its waters quite to the great lake of the West where the land ends and the (sun) sets on the face of the great water, to know their wants and inform him of them on our return.

Children. The object of my comeing to see you is not to do you injurey but to do you good the Great Chief of all the white people who has more goods at his command than could be piled up in the circle of your camp, wishing that all his

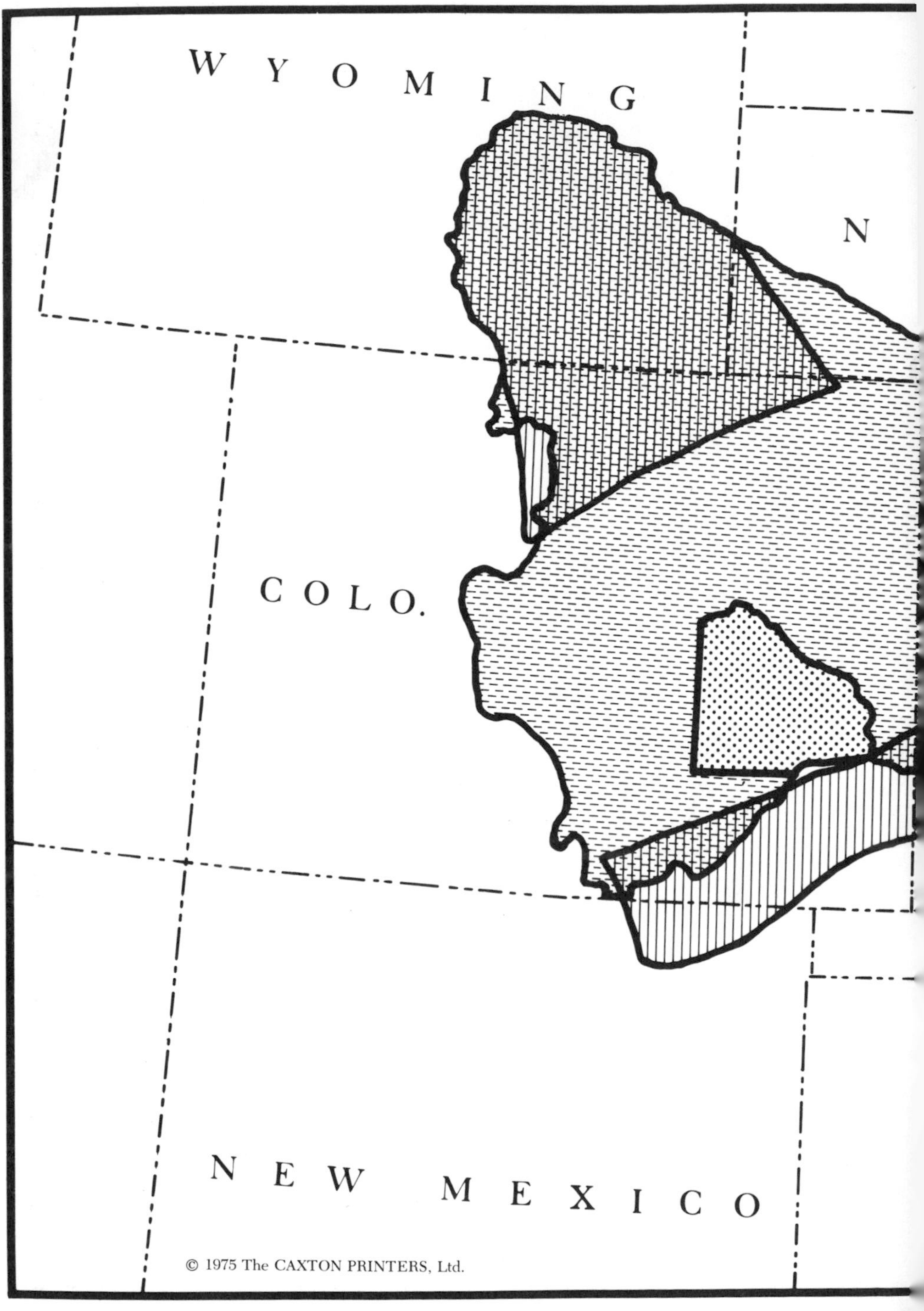
WYOMING
N
COLO.
NEW MEXICO

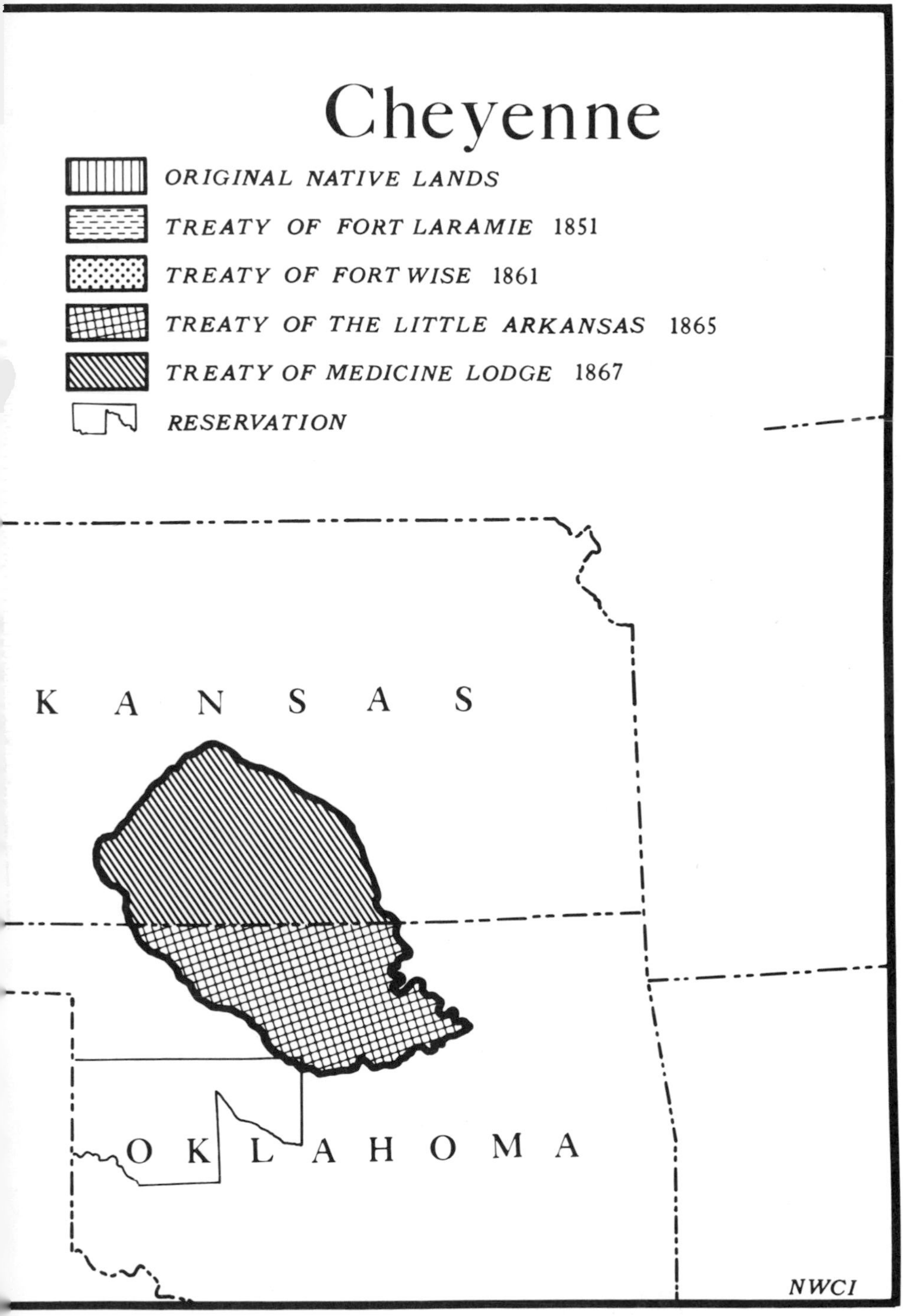
Cheyenne
ORIGINAL NATIVE LANDS
TREATY OF FORT LARAMIE 1851
TREATY OF FORT WISE 1861
TREATY OF THE LITTLE ARKANSAS 1865
TREATY OF MEDICINE LODGE 1867
RESERVATION
KANSAS
OKLAHOMA
NWCI

read children should be happy has sent me here to know your wants that he may supply them.

Children. Your great father the Chief of the white people intends to build a house and fill it with such things as you may want and exchange with you for your skins & furs at a very low price. . . .

Children. Your Great father the Chief of all the white people has derected me [to] inform his red children to be at peace with each other, and with the white people who may come into your country under the protection of the Flag. . . [T]hose people who may visit you under the protection of that flag are good people and will do you no harm.

Children. If any one two or 3 of your great chiefs wishes to visit your great father and will go with me, he will send you back next Summer loaded with presents and some goods for the nation. You will then see with your own eyes and here with your own years what the white people can do for you. They do not speak with two tongues nor promise what they can't perform.*

After the meeting a Cheyenne chief invited Clark to his lodge, where Clark presented him with a small medal. The Indian would not accept it, for he "knew that the white people were all *medecine* and that he was afraid of the midal or anything that white people gave to him." Before the chief would accept the medal Clark had to persuade him that it was a token from one great chief to another. Evidently this chief had had little previous experience with white men. As he departed, Clark told the Cheyenne and another Mandan chief who had joined them that if they wished to be happy they had to shake off "all intimecy with the Seioux and unite themselves in a strong alliance."

The Cheyennes consequently moved onto the central plains primarily to cement an alliance with the Arapahos against the Teton Sioux. An equally important reason for their migration, however, was trade, for the tribe contained many of the more sophisticated traders among the northern Indians. As the Missouri Fur Company employee, John Luttig, stated, in his dealings he found the Cheyennes demanded twice as much for a prime beaver pelt as other tribes. The Cheyennes also acted as middlemen for the Arapahos and other tribes along the Arkansas River. They usually obtained trade items from the Missouri Indians who had bartered with the English and American traders. The chronicler of the Stephen H. Long expedition wrote that

*The chiefs stated that they would be happy to return with the expedition when they knew that an Arikara chief who accompanied some of the party back to St. Louis in 1804 was safe. The Arikara chief, unfortunately, had died in the fall of 1805 as he was returning to his people.

Courtesy Amon Carter Museum, Fort Worth, Texas

Plains Indian camp scene — drying meat

in July, 1820, the expedition encountered a large intertribal camp on the bank of the Arkansas, consisting of Cheyennes, Kiowas, Comanches, Kiowa-Apaches, Arapahos, and a few Shoshonis. No doubt the Cheyennes were trading.

The Cheyennes, however, were about to meet another breed of traders — white men who would eventually dominate their trade and thoroughly corrupt their way of life. With the opening of the Santa Fe trail in 1821, only a short time remained before the Cheyennes clashed with unruly Missourians. During the period the tribe had spread out in small bands from the Missouri River to the Arkansas. Their first encounters with the traders were especially lucrative. According to prominent Santa Fe trader Augustus Storrs, Cheyennes, Arapahos, Kiowas, Comanches, and Pawnees were attacking the traders. Since the Arapahos were more numerous than the Cheyennes, traders often referred to both tribes as Arapahos. This was the case in 1829 when the first military escort, four companies of the Sixth Infantry Regiment, accompanied the annual trade expedition. While waiting on the American side of the Arkansas River, the infantrymen were attacked by mounted warriors. The commander of the escort, Brevet Major Bennet Riley, reported that he thought the Indians were Kiowas, Arapahos, and Pawnees. The Cheyennes were surely there. While some Cheyennes were harassing the Santa Fe caravans, others in the north who lived near the mouth of the Teton River were signing a "treaty of friendship." During the summer of 1825 an infantry force under the command of Brigadier General Henry Atkins traveled from St. Louis up the Missouri River to make peace treaties with the Indians of the northern plains. On July 16 several bands of Cheyennes signed their first treaty with the United States government. None of the Indians recognized the significance of the treaty or understood its meaning. If they had understood they would not have signed, for in doing so they jeopardized their way of life and their traditions.

The treaty, signed by thirteen Cheyenne warriors, was a frank recognition of the supremacy of the Unites States. It stated in Article I:

> It is admitted by the Chayenne tribe of Indians, that they reside within the territorial limits of the United States, acknowledge their supremacy, and claim their protection, — The said tribe also admit the right of the United States to regulate all trade and intercourse with them.

Article II stipulated that the government would receive the Cheyennes under its protection, and "extend to them, from time to time, such benefits and acts of kindness as may be convenient, and seem just and proper to the President of the United States."

The remaining articles dealt with trade regulations and Indian-white relations, including procedure to follow when an Indian stole from or killed a white man. Article V stated that "[I]t shall be the duty of the said chiefs, upon complaint being made as aforesaid, to deliver up the person or persons whom the complaint is made, to the end that he or they may be punished, agreeably to the laws of the United States." The treaty went on to say that if a white man committed any "robbery, violence, or murder on a Cheyenne," he would receive the same treatment, which was a falsehood, intentional or not. White man's law was totally alien to the Cheyennes, for among them each man enforced his own legal code. If one Cheyenne killed another, the dead man's family avenged him. The other members of the band stayed out of the quarrel, and only rarely did a band banish one of its members. And white man's law would never be applied equally to both races, especially west of the Mississippi, for no jury would ever punish a white man for killing a "red savage."

Within a decade most of the Cheyennes living in the north moved to the central plains region. Although they were slowly being pushed from their lands by the Sioux, Chippewas, and Assiniboins, they had another reason for leaving — trade. At the same time a small group of American traders in the north were also being squeezed out of the fur trade along the upper Missouri and Yellowstone rivers.

Trading opportunities on the Arkansas were promising while competition with the American Fur Company and Rocky Mountain Fur Company was keen, so Charles Bent, his brother William, Ceran St. Vrain, and their partners shifted their operations farther south. In 1833 they began building Bent's Fort near the buffalo range on the Arkansas river. Their move turned out to be a fortunate one. By 1834 the trade was successful, for Kiowa, Comanche, Arapaho, and the Cheyenne bands led by Yellow Wolf, Little Robe, and Wolf Chief came regularly to Bent's Fort. Between 1835 and 1839 the partners expanded their operations and built Fort St. Vrain on a bend of the South Platte. In this way they were able to dominate trade with the Sioux and Cheyennes along the North and South Platte rivers. No longer did the remaining Cheyennes have a reason to stay in the north when trade was so readily accessible to them out of reach of their enemies.

As more Cheyennes reached the trading posts their trading skills seemed to vanish as they became increasingly addicted to trade whiskey. Bent and Company did not encourage the Indians to trade for whiskey, but as other traders from Missouri and Mexico began to lure the Indians away from the forts with "Taos Lightning" and "Pass Whiskey" (cheap rye spiced with tobacco and gunpowder), the men at the forts had no choice but to provide whiskey or lose trade. The whiskey trade meant tremendous profits. Jim Beckwourth, a trader who was called Yellow Crow by the Cheyennes, stated that if any man figured up the profits on a forty-gallon cask of whiskey, he would be "thunderstruck or rather whiskey struck." When this amount was traded to the Indians, he said, "four gallons of water were added to each gallon of alcohol," and in the resulting two-hundred gallons there were sixteen hundred pints. For each pint, said Beckwourth, "the trader gets a buffalo robe worth five dollars."

That whiskey adversely affected the Cheyennes is evident from descriptions made by explorers and traders before and after the Indians received large amounts of alcohol and began to realize the advantages of "high civilization." In 1825 Stephen Watts Kearney, at that time a major in General Atkinson's command, exclaimed that the Cheyennes were "decidedly the finest looking Indians" he had ever seen. Captain Lemuel Ford, a member of the Dodge expedition to the Rocky Mountains, wrote that the Cheyennes were "very neat" in their dress and "excelled" in their "beauty." He also observed that the females were "handsome . . . modest and their dress show[s] considerable taste." Another member of Dodge's expedition, Lieutenant Gaines P. Kingsbury, observed a village just after Mexican whiskey traders had departed. The Cheyennes are "very fond of whiskey," wrote Kingsbury and "will sell their horses, blankets, and everything else they possess for a drink. . . . In arranging the good things of this world in order of rank, they say that whiskey should stand first, then tobacco, third guns, forth, women." By the 1840s many braves were known to have become so addicted to whiskey that they sold their horses, food, clothing, and lodges, and even the services of their wives and daughters for alcohol. Conditions caused by ruthless traders became so bad that in 1844 George Bent persuaded the Cheyenne chiefs to send a man to St. Louis and "personally urge action" against those "insidious devils" from both sides of the boundary who were threatening the very life of the tribe. This mission, undertaken by a man whom the whites called Slim Face, had no effect whatever. The white men could not understand this Cheyenne dilemma. The Cheyennes, who were once a "stout, bold, athletic set of people" had within a decade become a tribe of drunkards.

During the 1840s the Cheyenne way of life deteriorated further as more and more white men penetrated the Far West. Until then the Indians had been corrupted only by traders and occasional explorers. But with the rapid settling of Oregon, the beginning of the Mexican War, and later the California Gold Rush, more travelers crossed Cheyenne hunting grounds, killing off the small game, changing the migration habits of the buffalo herds, and infecting the Indians with unfamiliar diseases.

As early as 1846 Cheyenne chief Yellow Wolf (O-cum-who-wast) perceived that his people's way of life was

Courtesy National Park Service

Cheyenne camp, 1879

changing rapidly. On August 29 he visited Lieutenant James W. Abert, who, sick with fever, had been left at Bent's Fort by General Kearney's Army of the West. Abert's journal gives a remarkable insight into Yellow Wolf's fears concerning his people. The chief was a man of considerable influence and "enlarged views," and gifted with more "foresight than any other man in the tribe." He was clearly disturbed by the decline in the number of his people and of the once abundant buffalo. He observed that before many years the beasts would disappear and that to survive the Indians had to adopt the habits of the white men. He proposed building a structure similar to Bent's Fort to protect his tribe from enemies. He also wanted his people to become farmers and cattlemen. He admitted, however, that giving up old habits would be difficult but that during the transition

Courtesy National Archives

Stump Horn and family (Southern Cheyenne); home and horse-drawn travois.

the squaws and old men could "remain at home cultivating the ground and being safely secured in their fort."

Yellow Wolf's fears were well-founded. In seventeen years his tribe's lodges had been reduced by half, and the trend seemed irreversible. The year before, 1845, many Cheyennes had caught measles or whooping cough. An even greater calamity, however, was that they were slowly starving; they had not seen a single buffalo herd in 1845, and the next year was little better. No buffalo had been found from January to the first of August, and the one herd they found was small. Abert implied that the whites had begun to wipe out the buffalo from the Southern Plains. This was not actually the case in 1846 with buffalo, but it was with small game. The whites had merely built roads and caused the herds to migrate farther north.* If Yellow Wolf could have foreseen the future, he would have known that worse was yet to come. Besides bringing miners through the

*Abert also stated: "As the people of the United States have been, and are, the great cause of the diminution of the quantity of game, by continually traveling through the country, where the animals breed; by killing many of them, and by the immense numbers that they induce the Indians to destroy for their robes, it seems but fair that the United States should assist these Cheyenne."

area, the 1849 gold rush to California brought the ravages of cholera to the plains, and the Cheyennes were again reduced. Comparing them with the Pawnees and some bands of Sioux, the Cheyennes were not as hard hit because they were farther from the main trails. More than eleven hundred Pawnees died that year.

Among the Plains tribes the Cheyennes had committed fewer depredations than others and were, according to Yellow Wolf, more deserving of government assistance. "We have not robbed or stolen from you, and you take no notice of us," the chief stated, "nor do you make us any presents, while you are continually doing benefits to the Pawnees, who both killed and rob your people, and who are our enemies." By this simple statement Yellow Wolf pointed out one of the paradoxes of government policy, that of helping its enemies and taking its friends for granted. Inconsistency was characteristic of the United States government in its dealings with the American Indians.

Yellow Wolf did not understand the ramifications of asking the United States government to help the Cheyennes. Little did he realize that government involvement was synonymous with a bewildering bureaucracy, red tape, conflicting interests between the newly created Interior Department and the War Department and, above all, the secondary status to which his tribe would be relegated.

In November, 1846, "Broken Hand" Thomas Fitzpatrick was appointed agent for the Upper Platte and Arkansas river country. The new agent's tasks were to establish good relations with "his wards," to stop them from committing atrocities along the Santa Fe trail, to control Indian-white trade, and to keep the tribes at peace with one another. At Bent's Fort, Yellow Wolf repeated to Fitzpatrick the request he had made to Abert the year before and also volunteered the services of Cheyenne braves to help stop the Comanches from raiding on the trail to Santa Fe. The agent refused this offer, saying that the government had more than enough soldiers to control the raiders — obviously an exaggeration.

To keep peace between the whites and the Indians and to prevent the emigrants and whiskey peddlers from taking advantage of the tribesmen after the tragic cholera epidemic of 1849, Fitzpatrick believed that a treaty was desperately needed. He

Courtesy Library of Congress

Thomas "Broken Hand" Fitzpatrick, noted scout and Indian agent proposed to the superintendent in St. Louis that the Cheyennes, Arapahos, Sioux, Crows, Assiniboins, Gros-Ventre Mandans, and Arikaras be called to Fort Laramie. There a treaty should be negotiated with these tribes, "stipulating for the right of way through their country, and the use of grass and game, "paying the natives with "small annuities in useful articles of merchandise and agricultural implements, and instruction." This time his superiors listened and agreed. One superintendent wrote that "we can never whip them into friendship," that a treaty could do no harm, and the expense would be less than a six-month war. In March, 1850, the Senate unanimously approved a bill appropriating funds for the proposed treaty. The House, however, was in the middle of a debate leading to the Compromise of 1850 and did not act. Not until February, 1851, did Congress appropriate one hundred thousand dollars for concluding the treaty. The original figure proposed had been two hundred thousand dollars.

The Treaty of Fort Laramie was concluded on September 17, 1851. The first article contained the provision that the tribes agreed to abstain from "all hostilities whatever against each other, to maintain good faith and friendship in all mutual intercourse, and to make an effective and lasting peace." The second article recognized the government's right to build roads and military posts in the region; in return, the third article committed the government to protecting the Indians from white depredations. Article five delineated the boundaries of each tribe.

> The territory of the Cheyennes and Arapahoes, commencing at the Red Bute, or the place where the road leaves the north fork of the Platte River to its source; thence along the main range of the Rocky Mountains to the headwaters of the Arkansas River; thence down the Arkansas River to the crossing of the Santa Fe road; thence in a northwesterly direction to the forks of the Platte River, and thence up the Platte River to the place of beginning.
>
> It is, however, understood that, in making this recognition and acknowledgment, the aforesaid Indian nations do not hereby abandon or prejudice any rights or claims they may have to other lands; and further, that they do not surrender the privilege of hunting, fishing, or passing over any of the tracts of country heretofore described.

"In consideration of the treaty stipulations, and for damages which have or may occur," the government agreed to pay an annual stipend of fifty thousand dollars for a period of fifty years.

The payment would not be in cash but would consist of provisions, merchandise, domestic animals, and farming implements.

No doubt fifty years seemed like a long time to Yellow Wolf and the other Cheyenne chiefs. It also seemed like a long time to Senators who were reluctant to part with fifty thousand dollars of government revenues annually. As a result they cut the period to ten years when approving the treaty in 1852. Some Senators no doubt believed that they were being exceedingly generous. The Cheyennes, however, had not been told that the Senate had the right to alter a treaty that they had already signed. In August 1853, nevertheless, Fitzpatrick, by presenting more gifts than usual, induced some of the bewildered Cheyennes to ratify the amended treaty. The Indian superintendents were not overly alarmed at the Senate's stinginess. As one wrote, "this modification . . . I think very proper, as the condition of these wandering hordes will be entirely changed" during the next few years. What the superintendent probably meant subjectively was that the "hordes" would be so subdued, starved, and dependent by that time that the stipends could safely be reduced. If the trend in Indian-government relations in the Eastern states during the 1820s and 1830s continued, the Western Indians would be forced to sell their lands in order to survive in the white man's world.*

By setting definite boundaries for the tribes in the Fort Laramie treaty, the government had instituted a policy which had already proved successful with Eastern Indians. This policy was simply one of dividing and conquering. As long as the natives were able to roam at will throughout the West, the government could not exercise any meaningful control. But with each tribe occupying specific lands and agents distributing annuities only at designated locations within these lands, the government was able to institute controls. Whenever the Indians got out of hand or the United States needed additional tracts of assigned land, agents would be able to bribe or cajole the Indians into granting the wish without upsetting other tribes. In this way the government could whittle away Indian domain and have to

*A prominent Friend of the Indian, Helen Hunt Jackson, observed in her classic book, *A Century of Dishonor* that: "A dollar apiece a year 'in goods, animals, etc., those Indians had been promised that they should have for fifty years. It must have been patent to the meanest intellect that this was little to pay each year to any one man from whom we were taking away . . . his means of support.' But, unluckily for the Indians, there were fifty thousand of them. It entered into some thrifty Congressman's head to multiply fifty by fifty, and the aggregate terrified everybody."

Courtesy National Archives

Chief Powder Face, Arapaho, 1868-74

Courtesy Smithsonian Institution

Cheyenne camp, 1895; drying meat

deal with only one tribe at a time. It would be much easier than trying to wrest territory from the combined tribes. In case of conflict it would also be easier to fight one tribe at a time. So reasoned government officials.

The next years were difficult for the Cheyennes. Although they attempted to observe the Treaty of Fort Laramie, they were becoming impoverished. Agent Fitzpatrick wrote in 1853 that when he arrived to have the Cheyennes amend the treaty and to present the annuities, the Cheyennes, Arapahos, and many of the Sioux were actually starving. They were, he continued, "in abject want of food half the year, and their reliance for that scanty supply, in the rapid decrease of the buffalo," was "fast disappearing." He also observed that their women were "pinched with want and their children constantly [cried] with hunger." The one course that remained open to the Indians, wrote Fitzpatrick, was "simply to make such modification in the 'intercourse' laws as will invite . . . traders among them, and open the whole Indian

Territory for settlement." To Fitzpatrick trade was the only "civilizer" of the Indians. It taught them "the value of other things besides the spoils of the chase," and offered them "other pursuits and excitements than those of war." Evidently the agent did not wish to preserve their culture. If the lands had been completely opened to settlement and trade, the Cheyennes would have lost all tribal affiliations and surely would have been swindled out of all their land. As it turned out, this was what very nearly happened.

Conditions continued to worsen. During the hunting season Cheyenne braves were driven off the Platte trails by emigrants, and their game was disappearing. There were enough incidents between the whites and various bands to keep the Indians in an almost constant state of turmoil. In the summer of 1856 a small war party of Cheyennes from the South Platte region, out to retaliate against Pawnee raiders, came across a mail wagon on the North Platte road. Two warriors rode toward the wagon to beg for tobacco. Terrified, the mail carrier fired at the Indians, and they returned the fire, wounding him. The damage had been done. Although the chiefs within the party stopped their men from continuing their fire, flogged them, and apologized to the wounded mail carrier, he reported the "attack" to the army at Fort Kearney. The next day an army patrol caught up with the war party and killed six. Now throughly exasperated, the Cheyennes retaliated by attacking an emigrant train, killing three men and a child and capturing a woman whom they later killed. Within the next week war parties attacked several other emigrant trains. To restore peace Cheyenne chiefs ordered the killing of all members of war parties who violated the treaty with the white men in the future.

Every violation committed, whether by Indians or whites, made the situation on the Plains increasingly unpleasant for the Cheyennes. As a result of the "Grattan Massacre" in 1854 and Colonel "hornet" Harney's retaliatory actions against the Sioux, the Cheyennes and Arapahos also suffered. As their agent, John W. Whitfield, who had replaced Fitzpatrick in 1854, explained after hearing of the affair, every tribe from Texas to Oregon should receive a "gentle drubbing." Besides "pacifying" the Sioux, Harney also made certain demands of the Cheyennes located near Fort Laramie. In effect, therefore, he made demands against the entire tribe. Bands were still shifting easily throughout the region in search of game. Harney ordered the tribe to make peace with the Pawnees, hunt only in their own country, and withdraw completely from the Platte trails. If the Cheyennes did not comply, Harney bluntly warned them, he would make war and "sweep them from the face of the earth."

Because of Harney's threat and other evidences of hostility and unrest, the Cheyennes were uncertain concerning their relations with the United States. They tried to follow the path of least resistance, but their positive attitude did not convince the army. The commander at Fort Laramie, Major William Hoffman, called them "an unruly race, . . . and I have little confidence in their promises of good conduct unless they are kept in dread of immediate punishment for their misdemeanors." The same attitude was also displayed when the Cheyennes received no guns with their annuities. This disturbed them to such a degree, according to their friend William Bent, that he had a difficult time keeping them from going on the warpath. How else could they kill game or defend themselves against other tribes which had received their yearly ration of firearms?

By 1856-1857 Cheyenne braves were becoming aggressive and chiefs were having a difficult time keeping them from joining war parties intent on avenging themselves against the whites whom they held responsible for all of their problems. Already the army had sent an expedition to chastise the tribe and, although the expedition was only partially successful, it caused the chiefs of the bands on the Arkansas and South Platte rivers to consider breaking ties with the Cheyennes on the North Platte. In late October, 1857, four principle chiefs of the southern bands met with William Bent. White Antelope, High-Back Wolf, Tall Bear, and Starved Bear told their friend that the Cheyennes on the Arkansas and South Platte had committed fewer depredations than other Plains Indians. They admitted, however, that some of the young braves had on occasion joined the northern Cheyenne and Sioux bands in their raids. What the chiefs wanted from Bent was for him to use his influence with the Indian superintendents, explain the situation to them, and get them their annuities for the year. Bent realized that what the chiefs had said was basically true and came to their aid. As a result of subsequent communications, both the superintendent

Courtesy National Archives

Arapaho camp with buffalo meat drying, near Fort Dodge, Kansas

and the agent agreed that the Southern Cheyennes had already been sufficiently punished by the army and that new agreements of friendship should be made.

Before any positive action could be taken concerning the Cheyennes and Arapahos in the south, men from Kansas, Missouri, and "yondersiders" converged on the Colorado country looking for gold. By the fall of 1858 hundreds of miners had fanned out along Cherry Creek and had established the twin towns of Denver and Aurora. The next year thousands of other adventurers joined the rush. Because of the tremendous influx of whites into the Cheyenne and Arapaho domain, the Indians had an increasingly difficult time surviving on the limited game of the area. As more men arrived and staked out ranches and farms, they changed the migrations of the buffalo again, and the Indians began to beg food from the miners in order to live. The Indians were generally friendly to the newcomers. One Arapaho chief,

Little Raven, even visited Denver, learned to eat with a knife and fork, and raved over the white men's cigars and liquor.

With such a heavy influx of settlers, politicians who were anxious to impress their constituents began demanding a land cession from the Cheyennes and Arapahos. In 1860, even before a land treaty was seriously contemplated, the government disregarded the terms of the Treaty of Fort Laramie and established the Territory of Colorado. Only then did it attempt to negotiate for new tribal boundaries.

Many of the Cheyennes and Arapahos were ready for a new treaty that would protect them from white intruders. They were even willing to give up part of their vast domain for a more restricted reservation if it would be free from interference. They understood, however, that they would retain their freedom to hunt the buffalo. When invited to gather at Fort Wise to discuss a new agreement, some of the Arapaho and Cheyenne chiefs readily accepted.

The invitation, issued late in 1860, to assemble in January, 1861, did not allow the chiefs on the Arkansas time to notify others who were hunting on the northern plains. When the treaty was signed, therefore, only six of the forty-four chiefs were present; for that reason many Cheyennes and Arapahos questioned the treaty's validity. The chiefs present at Fort Wise had, in fact, told the white commissioners that more of their absent tribesmen should be present before the treaty was concluded. To this suggestion the officials stated that the others could sign later.

On February 18, 1861, only four Arapaho and six Cheyenne chiefs made their marks on the Treaty of Fort Wise. What they had been told the agreement included and what was actually in it were quite different. Their understanding was that, although they would live on their reservation, they still had the right to hunt buffalo on the plains. According to what they signed, however, this was not the case. Article One stated:

> The chiefs and delegates of said Arapahoe and Cheyenne tribes of Indians do hereby cede and relinquish to the United States all lands now owned, possessed, or claimed by them, wherever situated, except a tract to be reserved for the use of said tribes located within the following described boundaries, to wit; Beginning at the mouth of the Sandy Fork of the Arkansas River and extending westwardly along the said river to the mouth of the Purgatory River to the northern boundary of the Territory of New Mexico; thence west along said boundary to a point where a line drawn due south from a point on the

Arkansas River, five miles east of the mouth of the Huerfano River, would intersect said northern boundary of New Mexico; thence due north from that point on said boundary of the Sandy Fork to the place of the beginning.

The Arapahoe and Cheyennes, being desirous of promoting settled habits of industry and enterprise among themselves, by abolishing the tenure in common by which they now hold their lands, and by assigning limited quantities thereof in severalty to the individual members of the respective tribes, to be cultivated and improved for their individual use and benefit, it is hereby agreed and stipulated that the tract of country contained within the boundary above described shall be set apart and retained by them for the purposes aforesaid.

The rest of Article One described how the new reservation would be divided between the two tribes.

Article Two stated that part of the land for each tribe was to be divided into forty acre plots and given "to each member of said tribes without distinction of age or sex" and to include wherever possible some timber and grass land. It also stipulated that two different sections of one hundred and sixty acres would be set aside, one for the Indian agent and the other for the establishment and support of schools. All other lands and water were to be owned in common by the tribe occupying that portion of the reservation. Any increase in the tribe's numbers, or for any reason approved by the agent, would allow the common lands to be distributed and assigned "in such manner as the Secretary of the Interior may prescribe and direct." Finally, Article Two declared that the area would be called the "Reservation of the Arapahoe and Cheyenne of the Upper Arkansas." All laws which had been passed or would be passed by Congress "regulating trade and commerce . . . shall have full force and effect" over the Indians "and no white person except as shall be in the employment of the United States" would be allowed "to reside or go on any portion of said reservation without the written permission of the superintendent of the central superintendency, or the agent of the tribes."

The third article stipulated that the tribes could not sell, lease, or otherwise dispose of their land except to the United States government or members of the respective bands, and only according to provisions established by the Secretary of the Interior. The reservation would be exempt from taxation "until otherwise provided by Congress." In short, the Indians could sell or lease their land only to the government; and the United States reserved the right to tax them in the future.

For this huge cession the Cheyennes were promised what the government officials considered fair terms. Articles Four and Five dealt with the "stipulations" for the Indians. Each tribe was to be paid thirty thousand dollars a year in annuities for the next fifteen years or a total of four hundred fifty thousand dollars. During the first five years the government also promised to spend five thousand per year on the development of mills and a mechanic shop and employees to teach the Cheyennes how to run them. At the "discretion of the President of the United States," however, these annuities could be discontinued entirely should said Indians fail to make "reasonable and satisfactory" efforts to advance and improve their position. In that case such other provision shall be made for them as the President and Congress may judge to be "suitable and proper."

Overall the Treaty of Fort Wise contained much of the same phraseology found in other Indian treaties of this period. The government promised protection in return for good behavior, and all Cheyennes and Arapahos were to be included in the treaty. The terms of the Laramie treaty concerning remaining annuities were still in effect, but other parts of that treaty could be changed "in such manner and to whatever effect" would "be necessary and expedient" for the best interests of the Indians involved. There was also a provision allowing the government to build roads on the reservation where necessary.

Under the terms of this treaty the Cheyennes were now officially reservation Indians, and they could either abide by reservation regulations or lose their benefits. Although they did not realize it at the time, the document was a bad treaty. Land in severalty was an unknown concept, for individual land ownership was alien to their culture. Actually neither the reservation lands nor the four hundred fifty thousand dollars in the annuities was theirs. They could not sell or lease the land, and officials dictated how their money was to be spent. But they could not have handled land and money if they had been given the opportunity. The point was that the government did not handle the land and money in their interest. The promised annuities were not paid regularly, and the goods brought were often inferior.

The Reservation consisted of nothing but dry, sandy, barren, almost gameless land, so desolate that whites would not consider taking it. Even experienced farmers would have had difficulty growing crops on the Cheyenne land. Yet they, who had recently been nomadic hunters, were supposed to support themselves on this "abundant land."

Even if their reservation had been managed efficiently and the tribe had been maintained by regular government aid, the Cheyennes would have had a difficult time adjusting to the demands listed in the treaty. The government, however, had more pressing problems than the Cheyennes for the next five years — preserving the Federal Union. It did not, therefore, seriously attempt to keep the treaty's provisions; neither did it regulate trade nor keep whites out of the reservation. No mills or mechanic shops were built. And even if the government had wanted to provide the promised annuities, it could not have done so. The Indians were left in a state of limbo, yet they were supposed to live on their new reservation without the assistance promised them.

With troops moving east from the frontier forts, the Cheyennes and other Plains Indians were left somewhat to their own devices. Some again began raiding wagon trains, farms, and ranches. Whether Cheyennes were greatly involved in the raids of 1861 is not known, but settlers claimed that they were among the raiders, and it is likely that some were. The most prominent of the Cheyenne war societies, the Dog Soldiers, had refused to abide by the treaty, and other young braves resented being forced to adopt the white man's "way of life."

The Treaty of Fort Wise had left the Indians sullen and resentful, and by 1862 many of them refused to reside on the reservation. Cheyenne bands roamed their old hunting grounds and occasionally attacked overland stagecoaches and outlying settlements. The situation became so bad that Governor John Evans of the Colorado Territory ordered the Cheyennes to return to the reservation or be treated as hostiles. After three successive failures to obtain troops from the army, he began preparing the Colorado militia under the command of a recent evangelical preacher, John M. Chivington, to take care of the Indian problem. At this time Evans was under pressure from the residents of the territory who resented the annuities that supported the Indians during the winter, enabling them to plunder the rest of the year. The residents were anxious for the militia to crush the natives in Colorado before the government ordered it to fight Confederates. If the militia must fight, it should fight for the people of Colorado. Evans probably would have followed the same policy even if he had not been under pressure. As early as 1862 he allegedly conspired with Chivington and Agent Samuel G. Colley of the Cheyennes and Arapahos to rid the entire territory of all Indians.

Fearing retaliation from the militia, and on the advice of William Bent and Major Edward W. Wynkoop, in 1864 Black Kettle decided to submit to Evan's order to return to the reservation. But submitting was not easy. Black Kettle's lodges were still in the north, and reaching the reservation without encountering the militia was difficult. Persuading Evans to agree to stop hostilities was another problem. Finally, after Evans hedged for weeks, Wynkoop was able to arrange a meeting at Camp Weld between Black Kettle and other Cheyenne chiefs and Evans and Chivington. After the council was arranged Evans was said to have exclaimed, "But what shall I do with the Third Colorado Regiment, if I make peace? They have been raised to kill Indians and they must kill Indians." But if he desired to, Evans could not conclude peace. He had asked Major General Samuel R. Curtis, commanding officer of the Department of Kansas, if he could make a peace treaty. Curtis had wired back, "I want no peace until the Indians have suffered more. . . . No peace is to be made without my directions." The resulting meeting at Camp Weld on September 24, 1864, had no real objective. Evans was in no position to conclude a peace.

The Indians, desiring an end to the war, returned to their reservation and camped near Fort Lyon. There Wynkoop promised the Cheyennes protection and issued them rations. These unauthorized actions cost the major his command. On November 2 Major Scott J. Anthony became the commanding officer at the fort, and shortly thereafter he ordered the Cheyennes to leave the vicinity and camp twenty-five miles away on Sand Creek, where they would be safe "until his superiors had indicated their plans." After the Cheyennes left the fort thinking they were safe from attack, Major Anthony informed his superiors that there was a band within forty miles and that he would "try to keep the Indians quiet until such a time as he received reinforcements."

The reinforcements came November 26 in the form of Chivington's six-hundred man militia regiment. Greeting the ex-preacher with enthusiasm, Anthony told him that his own command would gladly assist the Colorado regiments in attacking the camp. Other officers disapproved, because an attack would violate the pledge of safety given by both Wynkoop and Anthony. To these remarks Chivington cried "Damn any man who sympathizes with Indians. I have come to kill Indians and believe it right and honorable to use any means under God's heaven to kill Indians."

At eight o'clock the night of November 28 some seven hundred soldiers marched from Fort Lyon to Sand Creek. At daybreak the next morning they attacked the camp and began slaughtering the unsuspecting Indians. Robert Bent, forced by Chivington to act as guide for the expedition, gave the following testimony. As the troopers came near the camp "I saw the American flag waving and heard Black Kettle tell the Indians to stand around the flag, and there they huddled . . . . I also saw a white flag raised." These flags were in such a position, continued Bent, that the troopers saw them. As the men began firing, the Indians ran for cover. The camp was predominantly one of women and children, with only about sixty men there, for the rest were away hunting. "There seemed," Bent related, "to be indiscriminate slaughter of men, women, and children. There were some thirty or forty squaws collected in a hole for protection; they sent out a little girl about six years old with a white flag on a stick, she had proceeded but a few steps when she was shot and killed. All the squaws in that hole were afterwards killed. . . . Everyone I saw dead was scalped. I saw one squaw cut open with an unborn child . . . lying by her side. . . . I saw quite a number of infants in arms killed with their mothers."

After the Sand Creek Massacre, some of Chivington's subordinates wanted to follow up the attack and strike the larger Cheyenne and Arapaho camps in the Smoky Hills of Kansas before those bands heard what had happened in Colorado. "The massacre was a terrible one," Major Anthony wrote "and such a one as each of the hostile tribes on the plains richly deserve. I think one such visitation to each hostile tribe would forever put an end to the Indian war on the plains." The major regretted "exceedingly that this punishment could not have fallen upon some other band."

The war on the Plains intensified. Black Kettle and the others who escaped the Chivington Massacre joined the Cheyennes, Arapahos, and Sioux camping in the Smoky Hills. The Cheyennes spread the story of the brutal slaying and passed the pipe. Sioux and Cheyenne bands smoked the pipe and joined the war. A combined war party of two thousand Cheyennes, Arapahos, and Sioux spread a path of desolation along the South Platte trail. They attacked Julesburg, Colorado, looting and burning the town, daring the soldiers in the nearby fort to stop them. These Indians raided up and down the Platte route, stopping all communications and causing severe food shortages in many communities, especially Denver.

Returning to their camps in the Big Timber region on the Republican river, the Indians had to decide how to avoid the army expeditions being assembled against them. Most of the Cheyennes and Arapahos from the south decided to join their Sioux allies and northern Cheyenne kinsmen in the Powder River country, but Black Kettle refused to go north. About four hundred Indians — mostly old men, women, and badly-wounded braves — agreed to follow him back to the Arkansas. Little Raven's band of Arapahos accompanied the Cheyennes south.

Without his knowledge Black Kettle had risen in prominence among government officials who were attempting to halt the Indian uprising and to settle land claims in Colorado. Settlers were encroaching on the lands guaranteed the Indians in the Fort Wise treaty. Black Kettle, fearful of future massacres, appeared ready to conclude another treaty.

While Black Kettle and Little Raven led their bands south, the treaty commissioners gathered at the mouth of the Little Arkansas River near present Wichita, Kansas. On October 11 the Indians arrived to discuss a new treaty. In the negotiations that followed Black Kettle, who was now looked upon almost as an outcast by the majority of Cheyennes, was skeptical about any new agreement. How could he sign away the Cheyenne lands when he represented only eighty lodges? The rest of the tribe was in the Powder River country and surely would not recognize the agreement. Little Raven suffered from even more doubts and

Courtesy Smithsonian Institution

Interior of Sun Dance Lodge, Cheyenne, about 1903

stated that it would be hard to leave the country God had given them. "Our friends are buried there. . . . [At Sand Creek] White Antelope and many other chiefs lie there; our women and children lie there. . . . I do not feel disposed to go right off to a new country and leave them." Little Raven and Black Kettle nevertheless agreed to move.

On October 14, 1865, the Treaty of the Little Arkansas was signed. Article One contained nothing original for these Indians. There was to be perpetual peace, all hostile acts were to be submitted to arbitration, and members of the tribe who committed depredations were to be surrendered and "punished according to the laws of the United States." In Article Two the Cheyennes and Arapahos abandoned all claims to their former lands:

> The United States hereby agree that the district of country embraced within the following limits, or such portion of the same as may hereafter be designated by the President of the United States for that purpose, viz: commencing at the mouth of the Red Creek or Red Fork of the Arkansas River; thence up said creek or fork to its source; thence westwardly to a point on the Cimarone River, opposite the mouth of Buffalo Creek; thence due north to the Arkansas River ; thence down the same to the beginning, shall be, and is hereby, set apart for the absolute and undisturbed use and occupation of the tribes who are parties to this treaty, and of such other friendly tribes as they may from time to time agree to admit among them . . . .

The same article also provided that the Cheyennes and Arapahos would not be required to settle on this land until "such time as the United States shall have extinguished all claims of title thereto on the part of other Indians, so that the Indian parties hereto may live thereon at peace with all other tribes." This article stated that the Cheyennes and Arapahos agreed to accept this new land as their permanent home and that "they would not go from said country for hunting or other purposes without the consent in writing of their agent or other authorized person."

According to the treaty the tribes were, until moved to their new reservation, free "to reside upon and range at pleasure throughout the unsettled portions of that country they claim as originally theirs." They were also to receive annuities, and blood relatives were to receive patents of land in "fee simple" from their former reservation in Colorado.

The Treaty of the Little Arkansas contained a provision which at the time was unusual. The United States actually apologized for the Chivington Massacre:

> The United States being desirous to express its condemnation of, and, as far as may be, repudiate the gross and wanton outrages perpetrated against certain bands of Cheyenne and Arapahoe Indians, on the twenty-ninth day of November, A.D. 1864, at Sand Creek, in Colorado Territory, while the said Indians were at peace by lawful authority being promised and induced to seek. . . .

To make reparations for this "gross and wanton outrage," the government offered additional lands to the chiefs and survivors.

Realizing that the number of Cheyennes and Arapahos present was only a minority, the commissioners made an additional demand on the signees. They promised to "use their utmost endeavor to induce that portion of the respective tribes not now present to unite with them and accede to the . . . beneficial provisions of this treaty." In signing the treaty, the chiefs agreed to abrogate all former ones. Three days later, October 17, the chiefs signed an amendment to the treaty which declared that the Cheyennes, Arapahos, and Kiowa-Apaches were to be confederated for efficiency in matters relating to Indian control. This is just another example of how the government has used convenience as an excuse to limit freedom.

The Treaty of the Little Arkansas was another calamity for the Cheyennes and Arapahos. Before they could settle on their new reservation, the land had first to be taken from other tribes. The two tribes gave up their marginal lands in Colorado in exchange for the panhandle region of Indian Territory, where the little water to be found was so brackish that horses would not drink it. And the treaty commission had the audacity to offer equally useless acreage as compensation for the wanton massacre at Sand Creek. Perhaps the worst stipulation of all was that which required the Indians to secure written consent of the agent before leaving the reservation. This provision made them totally dependent on the government, for they could no longer supplement their meager, often rotten rations with game. If they had to rely on their agents and government rations, they would be starving most of the time. As usual the government promised more than it was willing to produce. The Treaty of the Little Arkansas was really a treaty of futility geared to end hostilities. Majorities of both tribes refused to accept the provisions, and the treaty did not protect the bands of Black Kettle and Little Raven.

Courtesy National Archives

Little Raven, Arapaho chief, 1868-74

All that the treaty actually accomplished was to deprive the Cheyennes and Arapahos of their lands in Colorado.

Before the Cheyennes signed another treaty their ranks were further diminished. In the spring of 1866 a large number of those remaining in the northern country decided to head south for the summer to see their relatives and to hunt. When they reached the Smoky Hills of Kansas, they found only a few young Cheyennes and Arapahos who had left their bands against the wishes of their chiefs. Only then did they learn of the new treaty which surrendered the land in Colorado. Having tasted freedom in the north, the Cheyennes had no respect for a chief who would sign away their lands. And because they had not signed it, they declared the treaty invalid. Even when Major Wynkoop traveled to their lodges and attempted to persuade them to accept the Little Arkansas Treaty before the army was sent to force them out of Kansas, the Cheyenne chiefs curtly told him that they would rather die on the land they claimed than be starved to death by the government. They promised Wynkoop, however, that they would keep their young men from raiding and as far away from army units as possible.

That summer, as more Cheyennes heard of the Sioux and Northern Cheyenne successes in protecting their Powder River country from the white invasion, some braves dreamed that they, too, could force the whites out of their hunting grounds. Uniting under their Dog Soldier war leader, Roman Nose, the Cheyennes issued an ultimatum to the new stagecoach company then establishing stations throughout the heart of their buffalo range. In the autumn Roman Nose and a small delegation visited Fort Wallace and told the Overland Stage Company agent to cease all operations or be wiped out. Before the Cheyennes were able to make good their threats, however, early snow storms halted the stage runs, and the Indians had only the satisfaction of attacking relay stations and capturing a few horses.

The Overland stage line was only one of the Cheyennes' problems. An Indian agent, I.C. Taylor, who operated out of Fort Zarah, was a serious threat to the Indians. Drunk most of the time and incompetent, Taylor did his best to undermine Major Wynkoop's efforts to pacify the Cheyennes in Kansas. Wynkoop held councils with the chiefs, including some of the leaders of the Dog Soldiers, in an attempt to keep the peace; at the same

Courtesy Amon Carter Museum, Fort Worth

Yellow Bear and Little Wolf, Northern Arapahos

Courtesy Amon Carter Museum, Fort Worth

Spotted Horse, Northern Cheyenne

time Taylor complained to his superiors that Wynkoop was undermining his authority with the Indians. Later the agent tried to convince his superiors that the only way to maintain peace was for the army to wage a campaign of annihilation against the Dog Soldiers. In this way, he reasoned, the Cheyennes would be forced on to their reservation. In October Taylor claimed that he had persuaded the Dog Soldiers to leave the Smoky Hills and settle with the reservation Indians. This statement, although a figment of the drunken agent's imagination, was accepted temporarily by both the Indian superintendent and General Winfield Scott Hancock.

General Hancock itched to punish the Indians for their raids and to move them out of the way of progress, and he prepared for a spring campaign. In the meantime, he attempted to persuade the Cheyennes to join the remnant of the tribe south of the Arkansas River. On April 12, 1867, several chiefs acquiesced to the general's wishes and appeared at Fort Larned. Spoiling for a fight, however, Hancock treated his visitors harshly. Instead of waiting until the next day for a conference, he ordered one that same evening, although the Indians had a fear of night meetings. That night he told them that they would either obey him or he would treat them as hostiles and destroy them. The white men, Hancock observed, were converging on the Plains from both the East and West; nothing could stop them. "They require room and cannot help it," he said. He told the sullen delegation that he was displeased that so few chiefs had attended the conference, and he was most displeased that Roman Nose had not come. He promised to visit these errant chiefs at their camp. The chiefs explained that they understood this meeting was for chiefs only, and Roman Nose was only a war leader. They added that for Hancock and the army to visit the combined camp of Sioux and Cheyennes would be a mistake, because many of the Cheyennes were survivors of the Chivington Massacre and were afraid of all soldiers. They would run away from any show of force whether peaceful or not. Major Wynkoop agreed.

Hancock was persistent. He understood exactly what the Cheyennes told him, and he visualized an opportunity to provoke the conflict he had already decided on. His command included Lieutenant Colonel George A. Custer and part of the Seventh Cavalry, and Custer was as eager for battle as Hancock.

They approached in so threatening a manner that the Indians fled their camp, and Hancock ordered Custer to force them to return while the infantry waited near the deserted camp. When Custer reported that he had found evidence of Indian depredations, Hancock had the excuse he needed, even though Custer admitted that neither he nor his scouts were certain that the Cheyennes had committed the raids. Hancock brushed aside their doubts and ordered the camp burned.

Their possessions lost, the Cheyennes raided ranches all along the Kansas frontier. Hancock had precipitated the conflict but was unable to do more than that. Custer had worn out his command's horses chasing the Oglalas and trying to provoke a fight. Meanwhile Hancock received orders from the East to halt all offensive warfare. A new Indian policy was being worked out for the tribes by well-meaning but naive Eastern reformers. This was the so-called Peace Policy of President Ulysses S. Grant.

Pressured by the Friends of the Indian and other Eastern reformers, the government tried again to establish peace with the Western Indians. Plans were made for two major conclaves — one with the Indians of the northern plains and another with those of the southern plains. Trusted Indian agents went among the Southern Plains tribes to persuade them to assemble in Medicine Lodge Valley, about sixty miles south of Fort Larned, Kansas. The chiefs were promised gifts and supplies in generous quantities. To this often repeated promise one old Cheyenne warily observed, "A dog would rush to eat provisions."

In October, 1867, the Arapahos, Kiowas, Comanches, Kiowa-Apaches, and Black Kettle's Cheyenne band arrived in the valley and waited for the commissioners. When the peace delegation arrived, no other Cheyennes were present — only two minor Cheyenne chiefs attended the talks. Black Kettle himself was absent, for he had been forced to leave the talks to hold council with the other Cheyenne chiefs and Dog Soldier leaders. If he did not join them in the council, they warned him, they would kill all of his horses. The Cheyenne chiefs and Dog Soldiers no doubt feared that Black Kettle would sign another bad treaty. When the time came for the Cheyennes to answer the commissioners, one of the chiefs present stated that he could not speak for his people because many of them were absent.

On October 21, the Kiowas and Comanches signed their

treaty, and a week later the Cheyennes arrived and also signed the Treaty of Medicine Lodge Creek. All but a few of the articles in the treaty were similar to those of the treaties of Fort Wise and the Little Arkansas. The Cheyennes relinquished lands granted them at the Little Arkansas in exchange for the following:

> The United States agrees that the following district of country to wit: commencing at the point where the Arkansas River crosses the 37th parallel of north latitude, hence west on said parallel — the line being the southern boundary of the State of Kansas — to the Cimarone River, (sometimes called the Red Fork of the Arkansas River), thence down said Cimarone River, in the middle of the main channel thereof, to the Arkansas; thence up the Arkansas River, in the middle of the main channel thereof, to the place of beginning, shall be and the same is hereby set apart for the absolute and undisturbed use and occupation of the Indians herein named, and for such other friendly tribes or individual Indians, as from time to time they may be willing, with the consent of the United States, to admit among them. . . .

The Cheyennes and Arapahos could hunt buffalo only as far as the Arkansas River, and then only with their agent's permission. Another new provision was that all children between the ages of six and sixteen would attend school, and that the government would furnish a building and provide a teacher "competent to teach the elementary branches of an English education." A physician, blacksmith, resident agent, and other personnel would be maintained at government expense on the reservation for a period of not less than ten years to help the Indians adjust to their new mode of life. Article Ten dealt with annuities. In lieu of money the government promised the Indians annuity gifts of clothing and other supplies for thirty years. Every male over fourteen was to receive "a suit of good substantial woolen clothing, consisting of coat, pantaloons, flannel shirt, hat, and a pair of home-made socks." Each female over twelve was to be given a "flannel skirt, or the goods necessary to make it, a pair of woolen hose, twelve yards of calico, and twelve yards of cotton domestics. Children under the ages mentioned were to receive flannel and cotton goods as may be needed to make each a suit . . . together with a pair of woolen hose for each." In addition to these gifts the government agreed to spend twenty thousand dollars annually for whatever the Secretary of the Interior might indicate to be "proper."

No doubt the commissioners and the government believed

that by dressing the Indians in white man's clothing, giving them the rudimentary elements of the white's way of life, and instructing their children in the white man's tongue, they would quickly become indoctrinated. In any event they would not stand in the way of the white man's progress. But this new treaty, like so many of its predecessors, was merely a justification for future military operations. Some of the Cheyennes had been bullied and cajoled into signing an unworkable agreement, but their chiefs' pleas that the Smoky Hills be owned jointly by both races had been rejected by the commissioners. The Dog Soldiers' war leaders, including Roman Nose, had refused to sign and they were not, therefore, bound by the treaty. Another war would be required to destroy the Cheyennes' way of life.

Soon enough government agents saw convincing evidence that the Cheyennes were unhappy with the Medicine Lodge Treaty. Although it had been signed by fourteen chiefs, Roman Nose commanded the allegiance of a large number of the warriors in every band, and in May, 1868, these warriors began slipping away to join the war leader. The agents had failed to deliver specified annuities, including rifles and ammunition, until the Indians threatened them. Those Indians who remained at peace were treated almost as hostiles. Only grudgingly did agents give them clothing annuities of the cheapest quality. No physician or teacher had arrived. The government, in other words, had not met its treaty commitments.

During the summer months Indian depredations aroused the countryside from Kansas to Texas. The most publicized incident was the attack on Major George A. Forsyth's command by a combined force of Cheyennes, Arapahos, and Sioux. In the engagement Roman Nose was killed which aroused the Cheyennes to even more furious activity. General Phillip S. Sheridan, knowing that the Indian ponies were too weak for hard use and that the Indians ceased all warlike activity during the winter months, planned a winter campaign. Sheridan devised a large-scale pincer movement, sending one force eastward from Fort Bascom, New Mexico, and another southeast from Fort Lyon. The third and largest contingent, including eleven companies of Custer's Seventh Cavalry, would move south from Fort Hays, Kansas.

While Sheridan was assembling his main command, Black

Kettle established his band's winter camp in the Washita Valley, where he was joined by many warriors who had drifted south after the battle with Forsyth's command. Other bands also set up camps above and below them in the valley. In November, hearing rumors that the army was marching south to punish all treaty violators, Black Kettle, accompanied by another Cheyenne and two Arapaho chiefs, traveled to Fort Cobb to inform General Hazen that his band and those of the Arapahos wanted peace. The fort commander coldly warned them not to come to Fort Cobb or to join any of the friendly Kiowa or Comanche bands. Hazen later told General William T.Sherman that he had felt no responsibility for what might happen to Black Kettle's band, and he did not consider it proper to offer the Cheyennes peace while Sheridan was marching to punish them.

Returning to his camp on November 26, Black Kettle had little time for rest. The next morning at dawn he heard a woman's scream and then Custer's regimental band playing "Garryowen." For the second time the army had surrounded the chief's camp. In the initial charge both Black Kettle and his wife were killed. Although Custer had orders to kill only men and to capture women and children, his troops made no such distinction. Between eighteen and forty women and children were killed and only between nine and twenty warriors — losses not as severe as at Sand Creek, but another massacre of women and children. After shooting the entire pony herd Custer beat a hasty retreat, abandoning a patrol sent after the Indians to its fate. Other Cheyenne and Arapaho bands were appearing, and his position had become untenable.

Sheridan was well pleased with Custer's limited success, for he was convinced that Black Kettle's band was guilty of more depredations than any other group of Cheyennes. The battle of the Washita, however, had not completely satisfied Sheridan. His command moved through the valley killing Indians wherever it found them. While leading his troops down the Washita river Sheridan realized that the Indians' resistance was finally broken. Every day he saw evidence of their disorganized flight, for the ground was littered with abandoned jerky, buffalo robes, and cooking utensils. Near an abandoned village his force discovered the remains of hundreds of ponies that had been shot by the Indians to keep them from being captured by the troops. The scant grazing and cold weather had made these animals too weak to be driven in the hurried exodus. In his memoirs Sheridan wrote that "the wholesale slaughter" was the "most cheering indication that our campaign would be ultimately successful, and we all prayed for a least a couple of months more of cold weather and plenty of snow."

After the Washita campaign, survivors of Black Kettle's band under Little Robe and several bands of Arapahos arrived at Fort Cobb seeking peace, but General Sheridan told them bluntly that they could not "make peace now" and then" commence killing whites in the spring." If they were not ready to make a complete peace, they could leave the fort, and "we will fight this thing out." He also informed them that he would not release any prisoners taken by Custer at the Battle of the Washita until all the bands of both tribes surrendered. When Sheridan finished delivering his stern message, Little Robe said only, "It is for you to say what we have to do."

Many Cheyenne bands were slow to accept Sheridan's harsh terms. Some of the warriors stated that they would rather die as free men than to waste away as prisoners of the whites. Once again the tribe was divided as it had been after Sand Creek. Those chiefs who were determined to continue fighting berated Little Robe for surrendering. Little Robe, on the other hand, wanted his women and children released, and he urged the other bands to submit to Sheridan. There was no hope of escaping the horse soldiers on their grain-fed horses, for the Indian ponies were already worn out from too many quick retreats and the lack of decent forage. The bedraggled group of die-hards was being hunted down by Custer's cavalry and detachments from forts Bascom and Lyons. The Cheyennes still might have evaded the troops for a time, even on their worn-out ponies, if it had not been for their hated enemies, the Pawnees, who eagerly helped the army track them down.

During the years between 1869 and 1873, the Cheyenne way of life was in a state of transition. The tribe had been decimated, and many of its ablest leaders had been killed. Once a proud and powerful people, they had been cowed into a frustrating, semisedentary existence. They were still strong enough to resist settling on the arid reservation granted them by the Medicine Lodge Treaty, but submissive enough to accept the government

Courtesy Amon Carter Museum, Fort Worth

Feather Wolf, Cheyenne

Courtesy Amon Carter Museum, Fort Worth

Arapaho boy, Weensizeneet

rations offered them. At times they displayed a spirit characteristic of their former independence, for when they found buffalo below the Arkansas, they lived exclusively by the chase. But when supplies ran low they relied on their agent for rations, which consisted of a pound of meat and eight ounces of flour and ground corn daily. The Cheyennes were outwardly peaceful, for their fighting days seemed to have ended.

Another conflict, however, was necessary to subdue them completely. The reasons for this last war were many. During the years of relative peace, white men had again taken advantage of the Cheyennes. Article Two of the Medicine Lodge Treaty stated that "no persons" except government employees "shall ever be permitted to pass over, settle on, or reside in the territory." As on previous occasions, however, unauthorized traders and whiskey dealers traded for buffalo robes and Indian rations, and when these two commodities were exhausted they traded for ponies. The chiefs asked that the most notorious of the unlawful traders be kept off the reservation, but neither the agent nor the army was able to comply with the request. The army apprehended several traders, but a Missouri court refused to convict them.

Other causes of irritation were the poor-quality rations which were often late in arriving. On more than one occasion, furthermore, the agent had withheld annuities from the Indians as a means of punishment for minor infractions, such as refusing to send their children to a Quaker school. The government decided to build another road through the territory, which the Cheyennes naturally resented, and the army was pressuring them to settle on a permanent reservation and stop their wandering. In 1873 the government suggested that the tribe accept a permanent, separate reservation carved out of the lands originally granted at the Treaty of Medicine Lodge Creek. They would share this reserve, not with the Arapahos, but with their Northern Cheyenne kinsmen. (The Indians' agent wanted to separate the tribes to eliminate the Cheyennes' influence on the Arapahos. The Arapahos stayed on their lands, sent their children to the reservation school, and caused far less trouble.) This ploy came to nothing, for the Northern Cheyennes refused to move south, and the Senate took no action on the proposed treaty.

The Cheyennes had faced similar situations before. But the

Courtesy National Park Service

Cheyenne family — chief American Horse with his wives and children, 1891.

indiscriminate killing of the buffalo, the mainstay of their previous way of life, was something else. White hidehunters killed the animals in tremendous numbers and left the carcasses to rot. An estimated seven million, five hundred thousand buffalo were killed for their hides alone between 1872 and 1874. To the Cheyennes this wanton slaughter was the final insult.

Courtesy Amon Carter Museum, Fort Worth

Arapaho warrior

Because of the scarcity of buffalo on the Southern Plains, more Cheyennes than usual came to the agency for rations in the spring of 1874. Not anticipating this increase, the agent had not requisitioned enough supplies. The Indians, now hungry and grumbling over not being able to supplement their rations with buffalo meat, needed only a small incident to spark an uprising. A band of white rustlers stole forty-three ponies from Chief Little Robe's herd. A small party, including the chief's son, tried but failed to recover the stock. Frustrated, they retaliated by slaughtering a herd of cattle on the Kansas border. While returning to the agency, they met a cavalry detachment, and in the skirmish that followed Little Robe's son was badly wounded.

Cheyenne retaliation was immediate. War parties were organized to kill all hide-hunters encountered, and one attacked a mail party and a small detachment of the Sixth Cavalry between Camp Supply and Fort Dodge. Soon the Cheyennes were smoking war pipes with the Kiowas and Comanches, and war had come again to the Southern Plains. By the end of June most of the tribe was on the warpath, for of the nearly two thousand Cheyennes, only two hundred eighty remained peacefully near the agency. For the last time they were a united people.

The war of 1874-1875, like all the other Indian attempts to protect their way of life, was futile. Neither the Cheyennes, Comanches, nor the bands of Kiowas, Arapahos, and Kiowa-Apaches had a chance against the six army columns sent against them. By February, 1875, the survivors were returned to their agencies. General Sheridan, now the Commanding Officer of the Division of the Missouri, treated them even more harshly than before. All of the Cheyennes' weapons were taken from them; all of their ponies and mules were killed. Then the men were forced to line up while the agent, army officers, and civilians picked out the so-called "ringleaders" of the uprising. Thirty-two Cheyennes were found guilty and sentenced to be imprisoned at Fort Marion, Florida, where they would never again be able to influence their people. Only thirty reached their destination, for one was shot for refusing to be shackled and another was killed near Houston, Florida.

In 1875 the remaining Cheyennes began to accept the painful fact that their old way of life was gone forever. Their pony herds, the main symbol of their wealth and social position, had been

Courtesy Godfrey Family Photographs

Enemies meet — chief Two Moons (Cheyenne) and Goes Ahead (Crow), 1911

Courtesy National Archives

Council of Cheyennes and Arapahos at Seger Colony, Oklahoma, 1900

slaughtered, and many of their friends had been killed. They no longer could roam the plains and hunt the buffalo. Their children were being taught new values and a new language, and white missionaries were insisting that they accept an alien religion. Many men felt that they had lost their honor and the respect of their families. But their fate was simply that of many other tribes, and none would avoid it in the end. The Cheyennes had been enveloped and overwhelmed by white Americans in seventy-one years.

In 1875 few if any Cheyennes still living had witnessed the signing of the first treaty of friendship in 1825. If there were one or two old men who had, they probably could not comprehend how their tribe had been robbed at the treaty table as well as beaten on the battlefield. How had their lands been stolen from them? How had their tribe been split? How had most of their war

Courtesy Amon Carter Museum, Fort Worth

The son of Ute chief Ouray who was captured and raised by Arapahos

Courtesy Smithsonian Institution

Arapaho participants in the Ghost Dance, about 1893

chiefs, braves, and even their women and children been killed? Why were they no longer a proud, free people? The answer was that the Cheyennes, like every other Indian tribe, had been the victims of white promises, treaties, and greed for land. By using threats, bribes, punitive measures, and lies, the whites had forced the Cheyennes to give up their lands and way of life. First they had signed a treaty of friendship. Next they were tricked into accepting definite boundaries. And finally they were allotted small reservations. For giving up their tribal lands they were promised a total of nearly two million dollars, but of this amount, they received only a fraction. Nor was this all, for despite their concessions, despite the government's promises, they were ultimately dispossessed of all their lands and forcibly moved to Indian Territory, land they had never wanted or claimed. The government, always in the name of progress, would break yet another treaty.

Courtesy Amon Carter Museum, Fort Worth

Arapaho chief Sharp Nose and family

Courtesy National Archives

Dull Knife, Northern Cheyenne chief who took part in the Battle of the Little Big Horn.

Courtesy Amon Carter Museum, Fort Worth

Chief Washakie in Shoshone camp

SUGGESTED READINGS

Berthrong, Donald J. *The Southern Cheyennes.* Norman: University of Oklahoma Press, 1963.

Brown, Dee Alexander. *Bury My Heart at Wounded Knee: An Indian History of the American West.* New York: Holt, Rinehart and Winston, 1970.

Carriker, Robert C. *Fort Supply Indian Territory: Frontier Outpost on the Plains.* Norman: University of Oklahoma Press, 1970.

Grinnell, George Bird. *The Fighting Cheyennes.* Norman: University of Oklahoma Press, 1966.

Jackson, Helen Hunt. *A Century of Dishonor: The Early Crusade for Indian Reform.* New York: Harper & Row, Publishers, 1965.

Lavender, David. *Bent's Fort.* Gloucester Mass.: Peter Smith, 1968.

Leckie, William H. *The Military Conquest of the Southern Plains.* Norman: University of Oklahoma Press, 1963

Seger, John H. *Early Days Among the Cheyenne and Arapahoe Indians.* Norman: University of Oklahoma Press, 1956.

John Stands In Timber and Margot Liberty. *Cheyenne Memoirs.* New Haven: Yale University Press, 1967.

Courtesy Amon Carter Museum, Fort Worth

Group of Shoshone women and children

Courtesy Amon Carter Museum, Fort Worth

Shoshone woman carrying papoose

Courtesy Amon Carter Museum, Fort Worth

Shoshone warrior Moragootch

Courtesy Smithsonian Institution

Shoshone chief Washakie, about 1882

Courtesy National Archives

Skin painting, pictorial history of Shoshone chief Washakie's combats

"The Comanchees are in stature rather low, and in person often approaching to corpulency. In their movements they are heavy and ungraceful; and on their feet, one of the most unattractive and slovenly looking races of Indians that I have ever seen; but the moment they mount their horses, they seem at once metamorphosed, and surprise the spectator with the ease and elegance of their movements . . . , the moment he lays his hand upon his horse, his face even becomes handsome, and he gracefully flies away like a different being."

George Catlin, *North American Indians.*

CHAPTER 5

Treaties with the Comanches

Valerie Sherer Mathes

THE WORDS ARE those of George Catlin, the pioneer painter who worked among the Plains Indians in the 1830s. The horse indeed transformed the Comanches, as it had other Plains Indians, into swift knights of the Plains.

The Comanches had acquired the horse by the time of their arrival on the southern Plains and soon became of all the Plains Indians the richest in horses. The Kwahadi band of Comanches, with an estimated population in 1867 of less than two thousand, were reputed to own fifteen thousand head of horses. The wealth of each Comanche warrior was measured by his horse herd, and when he died, his best horse was often killed in order that he be well mounted in the afterlife. Obtaining horses by raiding Texas, New Mexico and northern Mexico, by purchase or by capturing wild mustangs, the Comanches traded many animals to other Plains tribes to the north.

The Comanches, like other Indians of the Plains, depended upon the buffalo for their livelihood; as the horse was the vehicle, the buffalo was the fuel that sustained the Plains Indian. Comanches in quest of buffalo traveled in bands ranging in size from a single family to a camp of kinsmen to a larger group of several hundred people. A dozen or so Comanche bands are identifiable historically. During the 19th century the more important included the Penateka or "honey eaters," who had preceded the main Comanche exodus as they moved onto the Plains. The middle Comanche bands included the Nokoni or "wanderers," the Kotsoteka or "the buffalo eaters," the Tanima

VALERIE SHERER MATHES was born July 1, 1941 in Toledo, Ohio. She attended the University of New Mexico where she received both B.A. and M.A. degrees with a major in Western History and a minor in Ethnology. (B.A. 1963; M.A., 1965). She has been teaching United States History at City College of San Francisco since the fall of 1967 and since 1969 has been teaching History of the Indians of the United States.

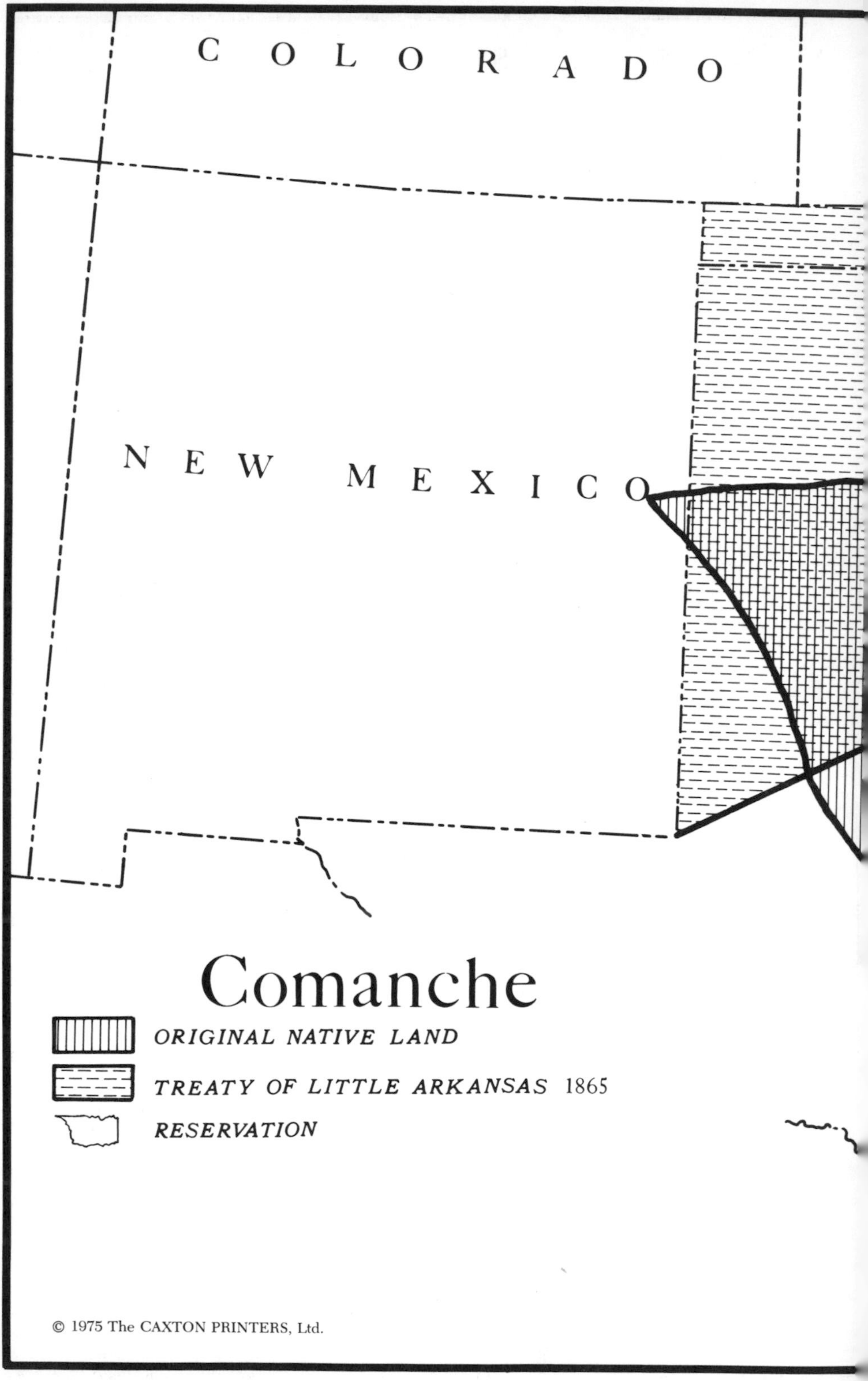
COLORADO
NEW MEXICO
Comanche
ORIGINAL NATIVE LAND
TREATY OF LITTLE ARKANSAS 1865
RESERVATION

A N S A S
MO.
OKLA.
ARKANSAS
TEXAS
LA.
NWCI

Comache feats of horsemanship.

or "liver eaters" and the Tenawa or "down-stream." The northern Comanches were the Yamparika or "yap eaters" (the yap was a potato-like root). Another important Comanche band which made the Llano Estacado of Texas and New Mexico its home was the Kwahadi (or Antelope) band.

The Comanches, members of the Shoshonean linguistic family, originated in the Rocky Mountains of Wyoming and moved to western Kansas and eastern Colorado in the early decades of the 1700s. Comanchería, the new home of the Comanches, continued to grow as the Indians dispersed, and by the 1800s included southeastern Colorado, southwestern Kansas, western Oklahoma, northwestern Texas, and eastern New Mexico. The most extreme geographical feature of Comanchería was the Llano Estacado or Staked Plains — the largest tract of nearly level land in the United States. The lack of water and of landmarks in this vast area often discouraged pursuit, and prior to their final defeat in the 1870s, many Comanche bands had found temporary refuge in the Llano Estacado.

Comanchería was surrounded by various Plains tribes, some hostile and some friendly, and was shared with the Kiowas and their allies, the Kiowa-Apaches. The Kiowas and Kiowa-Apaches became allied with the northern Comanche bands in 1790, when peace was finally achieved after many years of war. As the Comanches moved south onto the Plains, they encroached on the hunting grounds of other Plains tribes, making warfare inevitable. On the extreme northwest of Comanchería were the Utes, kinsmen of the Comanches but also hereditary enemies. Recent research by Marvin Opler has revealed that the word Comanche, in the Ute Language, means enemy, and between 1726 and 1786 the Comanches and Utes were warring continually. On the northwest of Comanchería and along the Arkansas River were the Cheyennes and Arapahos, who moved into Comanchería around the year 1820. War commenced soon after, and the Comanches were defeated in 1838, leaving the Cheyennes and Arapahos in possession of northern Comanchería. To the northeast were the Pawnees, and to the east and northeast were the Osage. During most of the 19th century both tribes were at war with the Comanches. To the southeast were the Cherokees and Creeks of Indian Territory, who were often called upon as mediators in the Plains wars. Also to the southeast were the various Caddoan peoples who were forced into Comanchería by the pressure of white settlements and who became allied with the Comanches. Along the western border were various Apache bands, who were at war with the Comanches until the end of the 19th century.

Just as the Comanches checked the expansion of some Plains tribes, they temporarily halted French expansion to the southwest as well as Spanish advance to the northeast. Although the French and Comanches soon became allies, the Spanish and Comanche generally remained enemies. In 1762, with the transfer of the Louisiana territory to Spain, the Marqués de Rubí reorganized Spanish defenses and recommended peace with the Comanches in order to gain them as allies against the continually raiding Apaches. To implement this policy the Spanish built a village for the Comanches on the Arkansas River in 1787. Al-

Courtesy Amon Carter Museum, Fort Worth

Ute camp

Courtesy Amon Carter Museum, Fort Worth

Ute warrior

Courtesy Amon Carter Museum, Fort Worth

Ute women and child

Courtesy National Archives

Pawnee lodges at Loup, Nebraska, 1873

though unable to make sedentary Indians of the Comanches, the Spanish were successful in obtaining peace between them and the settlements of New Mexico, partially because of the village on the Arkansas and partially because of the lucrative trade with the *comancheros* of New Mexico. Peace for the Texas and Mexican frontiers, however, was not as easily obtained. The Spanish had established a mission on the San Sabá River in Texas for their Apache allies. In March, 1758, a large party of Comanches attacked and destroyed the mission as well as the punitive expedition that was immediately dispatched. Spanish extension into Comanchería was thus halted, and from then on, Comanche raids on Texas settlements became chronic.

The Comanches' first contact with white invaders of their land came in 1724 when Bourgmont, a French trader, visited one of their Kansas villages. English-speaking traders contacted the Comanches within the first two decades of the 1800s, but the first meeting with federal officials took place in 1834 when the Dragoon Expedition, commanded by Colonel Henry Dodge, was ordered to proceed to the Plains to establish peace. Around 1832 there had been an increase in wars between Plains tribes,

Courtesy Amon Carter Museum, Fort Worth

Pawnees, Night Chief and Man Who Left His Enemies Lying in the Water.

Courtesy Amon Carter Museum, Fort Worth

Pawnee war and hunting scenes on a buffalo hide

Comanche meeting the Dragoons.

as well as against intruding Eastern Indians who had been dispossessed by the continual white encroachment upon their land. These dispossessed Indians competed with the Comanches, not only for land, but also for the gradually disappearing buffalo. The hostilities forced the federal government to seek peace, and in 1832 and again in 1833 unsuccessful expeditions were sent to the Plains. In 1834 the Dragoon Expedition was finally able to negotiate the first of five treaties signed between 1835 and 1867 with the Comanches. This expedition initially visited a large Comanche camp and then proceeded to the Wichita village on the North Fork of the Red river, where a council was held with the Wichita and the Comanche chiefs who were visiting in the village. Colonel Dodge encouraged the Indians to send delegates to a council to be held at Fort Gibson the following September. The Comanches did not attend the Fort Gibson council, however, and another meeting was scheduled for Camp Holmes on the Canadian River in August, 1835, with the Comanches and the Wichitas. Since the resulting treaty was signed only by leaders of the northern Comanche bands, not all of the Comanches were obliged to comply with its provisions. In the treaty the Indians consented to allow traffic to pass unharmed through their land to New Mexico, to share their hunting grounds with the Eastern tribes, to cease attacks along the Santa Fe Trail and to establish perpetual peace between themselves and the Indians of Indian Territory. Restitution was to be made by both Indians and whites of any property taken during raids. These provisions were soon ignored by the Indians, partially because no annuity goods were provided to remind them yearly of their concessions. The treaty did provide for presents, which the Indians were to receive immediately upon signing.

Comanche-white relations worsened with the settlement of Texas, when the Comanches' major enemy became the Anglo-American settlers in Texas. Early Anglo-American trading contacts with the Comanches were friendly, and the initial contact with Anglo settlers was also peaceful, since the settlers did not receive grants of land inside Comanchería. It was not until the latter part of the 1830s that the Texans began to dispossess the Comanches of their best hunting grounds. From then on the Indians continually attacked the Texas settlements for the next half-century. The southern Comanche Penateka band was the one usually at war with the Texas settlements, since the northernmost bands seldom traveled that far south. During the Texas war of independence, most of the southern Comanches remained quiet. In May, 1836, however, some northern Comanches and their Kiowa allies made one of their rare attacks on the Texas frontier, bringing immediate retaliation.

When Sam Houston became the first president of the Republic of Texas in 1836, he attempted to conciliate the Comanches and other Texas Indians and to regulate Indian trade. As a young man Houston lived among the Western Cherokees, married a Cherokee woman, and was adopted into the tribe. But when Mirabeau Bonaparte Lamar became president in December, 1838, he undertook a policy of extermination.

It was not surprising that the Comanches, who had lived for years by raiding Mexican settlements, would transfer their attention to the nearer Texas frontier. Both Indians and white settlers provoked hostilities, and as the settlers pushed into Comanchería, they represented a tempting prey. Several fruitless peace councils were held in 1838, but they had scarcely closed when hostilities were renewed. By 1840 the Comanches were tired of war, and in March of that year sixty-five Comanche men, women and children, arrived at San Antonio to attend a conference. During the conference Texas authorities informed the chiefs and warriors that they were to be held hostages until all white prisoners were returned. The Indians attempted to escape but thirty-five were killed, while the remainder were recaptured. On learning of this treachery, the Comanches took up the hatchet, torturing and killing all the white hostages they held and then retaliating against the whole Texas frontier.

When Houston became president of the Republic of Texas again in 1841, he restored his policy of peace and sent out scouts to ask the Indians to meet him for peace conferences. The more docile Texas Indians complied with his request, but not the majority of the Comanches. Not until 1844 was Houston successful in getting the southern Comanches to attend a council. In that year the southern Comanches and smaller Texas tribes met at Tehuacana Creek and entered into a mutual pledge of friendship with the republic. Texas agreed to appoint Indian agents, to establish trading houses among the Indians, and to give presents to the tribes. When peace was finally secured, the Indians were to receive powder, lead, and guns for hunting. Houston proposed that an Indian-white boundary be delineated, but the Comanches rejected this proposal. The Indians agreed to attend a general council each year but although these councils were called regularly to reacquaint them with the treaty provisions, they did not always attend.

"The Treaty of Peace, Friendship, and Commerce Between the Republic of Texas and the Comanche, Keechi, Waco, Caddo, Anadahkah, Ionie, Delaware, Shawnee, Cherokee, Lepan, and Tahuahkano Tribes of Indians" was signed on October 9, 1844, and ratified on January 24, 1845, becoming one of the few Indian treaties formally ratified by the Texas Senate. This treaty, which bound only a part of the Penateka Comanches, was signed by some of their chiefs, including Buffalo Hump and Old Owl. Other Comanche bands continued their traditional attacks on

Courtesy Amon Carter Museum, Fort Worth

Gray Leggings, Penetaka Comanche

Mexico, and on their way to and from the border, they attacked Texas ranches and settlements. Houston's policies unfortunately had not brought peace to the Texas frontier. When Texas entered the Union in 1845, she retained control of her public lands but transferred her Indian problems to the federal government. In 1846 the federal government's representatives met with the Penateka Comanches and other Texas Indians at Tehuacana Creek (Council Springs) on the Brazos. In Article 10 of the treaty the signatory tribes agreed forever "to remain, at peace with the United States," and agreed that "all animosities for past offenses" were to be forgotten and forgiven. In Article 11, furthermore, the Indians agreed "to remain friendly with such tribes as are now at peace with the United States." They also agreed to accept the jurisdiction of the United States, to trade only with licensed traders, to give up white and Negro prisoners, to surrender murderers and robbers on demand, to restore stolen horses, to cooperate with agents, and to stop the liquor trade. In return the government agreed to establish trading houses, to furnish blacksmiths and teachers, to give the Indians gifts valued at ten thousand dollars, and to prohibit whites from going among the Indians, except when carrying a pass from the President of the United States. Since the federal government had no legal right to prevent the citizens of the State of Texas from going among the Indians, the Senate struck out this provision, one of many promises broken by the government over the years. This council, though attended only by the Penatekas, was the largest gathering of the southern Comanches ever held. Shortly after the signing of this treaty, a number of Comanche chiefs, including the Penateka chief Santa Ana, who until his death urged his people to keep peace, were escorted to Washington to be shown the power and wealth of the nation.

The Comanches were not pleased with the treaty, for by the terms of Texas' annexation, she retained ownership of her public lands, and the federal government could not guarantee the Indians permanent rights to any of their lands. The Senate adjourned, furthermore, without ratifying this new treaty, and therefore no money was appropriated for the purchase of the promised presents. Robert S. Neighbors, the Texas Indian agent to the Tonkawas and Lipan Apaches, was assigned the awkward task of meeting with the Indians and explaining the government's failure to meet its treaty obligations. Fortunately for Neighbors, local traders furnished presents on credit.

The Texas frontier east of San Antonio enjoyed relative peace in 1847, despite the immigration of German colonists into Comanchería. Peace was attributed largely to the work of Robert S. Neighbors, who was appointed special agent for the Indians of Texas on March 20, 1847, and who served until 1849. Acting on the theory that an Indian agent should maintain close relations with his charges, Neighbors visited and counseled Indians in their villages, praising them for their compliance with treaties or reprimanding them when they broke treaty promises. During the winter and spring of 1847-1848 Neighbors established contact with some of the northern Comanche bands and held councils with some chiefs of the Penateka band and members of the Tenawa, Nokoni and Kotsoteka bands. He was aided in his peace efforts by the Texas Rangers, who had been organized in 1835.

The whites brought a means of destruction that was more deadly than they or the Indians at first realized. Smallpox broke out in Comanche villages in 1848, and the next year an epidemic of cholera killed a number of the survivors, including southern Comanche chiefs. At a council called to select new chiefs, the Penatekas agreed that continued warfare with the United States would surely cause their total destruction. The new chiefs accordingly proceeded to Fredericksburg to inform the army that they were friendly.

With Neighbors' removal for political reasons, the Comanches' situation worsened, particularly because the new agent was elderly and could not visit the Indians in their villages. And Congress still had not provided funds to purchase the presents promised in the 1846 treaty. In December, 1850, however, the agent was able to persuade a number of the Penatekas to sign a new agreement which was actually an enlargement of their former treaty promises. This agreement was never submitted to the Senate because it was regarded as a special agreement under the terms of the general treaty of 1846. In it, however, the Comanches made a substantial concession by agreeing not to go south of the Llano river without the consent of an army officer. But this provision did not prevent white settlers from entering Indian lands. The Indians had also been assured in the treaty that the government would establish trading houses and agencies for them, give them presents, and negotiate a permanent boundary. The new agreement resulted in the return of a number of Indian hostages, but it did not end the border warfare.

With the discovery of gold in California, miners crossed Comanche land and were soon followed by settlers whose presence required the army to build several forts for their protection in the 1850s. The continual passage of emigrant trains and gold-seekers drove away the game, and after 1850, the only region where buffalo could be found south of the Arkansas valley was in Comanchería. Soon there would not be enough game for the Plains Indians; during the 1870s, white buffalo hunters would kill an estimated five million four hundred thousand buffalo. When their food supply disappeared, the Comanches had no choice but to steal from the passing emigrant trains or the Texas and Mexican settlements. New Mexico was also attacked by Comanche raiders, and by 1855 these incursions had pushed the New Mexican settlements south. Ironically, the Indians found that the white settlers in Texas and New Mexico were a good market for the horses and goods which they stole in raids elsewhere.

The northern bands, seeing their southern kinsmen receiving presents under terms of treaties with the federal government, in 1848 expressed to Agent Neighbors their desire to enter into a treaty with the United States. Thomas Fitzpatrick, United States Indian agent for the Upper Platte and Arkansas rivers, was the first agent to establish regular communications with both the northern Comanches and the Kiowas. In the spring of 1851, he met with members of both tribes as well as Kiowa-Apaches, Arapahos, and Cheyennes at Fort Sumner (later renamed Fort Atkinson). Fitzpatrick proposed a general council at Fort Laramie on the Platte river, but the Comanches, Kiowas, and Kiowa-Apaches refused to attend because it was so far from their home. In August, 1852, Congress appropriated twenty thousand dollars for the purchase of presents to be used in negotiating a new Indian treaty. In July, 1853, Fitzpatrick negotiated a treaty with the Yamparika band of Comanches, the Kiowa-Apaches, and Kiowas at Fort Atkinson. The Indians agreed that "peace, friendship, and amity shall hereafter exist between [them and] the United States." They also agreed to the right of the United States to lay out roads through their hunting grounds, to build

Courtesy National Archives

Milky Way, Penetaka Comanche, 1872

forts along the Santa Fe Trail, and to protect emigrants passing through Comanchería. They further agreed to make restitution for any injuries inflicted on United States citizens. They promised not to raid into Mexico, but they refused to give up the Mexican prisoners they were holding. They agreed, however, to return any captives taken after the treaty was signed. In return the Indians would receive annuities in goods worth eighteen thousand dollars for ten years, and for an additional five years if the president deemed it necessary. Furthermore Article 7 stated that:

> The United States do moreover bind themselves, in consideration of the covenants contained in the preceding articles of this treaty, to protect and defend the Indian tribes, parties hereto, against the committal of any depredations upon them, and in their territories, by the people of the United States, for and during the term for which this treaty shall be in force, and to compensate them for any injuries that may result therefrom.

Again, only part of the Comanches signed the treaty. The government did not build the roads, nor because of white encroachment, could it protect the Indians, although it did issue supplies. And the Indian raids continued in violation of their treaty concessions. Since the presents continued to be given out despite Comanche attacks on the Texas frontier, the Indians brazenly stole horses in Texas in June and went to the Arkansas river to accept their annuities in July. One year after the treaty was signed the Indians denied they had agreed to stay out of Mexico; and several weeks after receiving their first annuity goods, several hundred Comanches went to Mexico on a raid.

The Treaty of Fort Atkinson temporarily disturbed the Comanche-Osage relations. The Osages had been traditional enemies of the Comanches, but in 1843 both sides buried the hatchet and entered into mutual trade. The Osages traded guns, ammunition, and other items to the Comanches for horses, mules, and white prisoners. After signing the treaty the Comanches received as annuities most of the items they usually obtained from the Osages. Failing to persuade the Comanches to cease using the annuity goods, the Osages went to war against them, with hostilities lasting until 1858, when peace was finally restored.

The poverty and misery of the Texas Indians, owing to the continued introduction of liquor and the never-ending en-

Courtesy Godfrey Family Photographs

Kicking Bird, Kiowa warrior

croachment of settlers, became so bad that it was necessary to establish a reservation for them. In February, 1854, the Texas legislature authorized the federal government to survey and create two reservations. The Comanche Reserve (or the Upper Reserve) was located on the Clear Fork of the Brazos and was assigned to the Penatekas, while the Lower Reserve was assigned to the Caddo and allied tribes. During the existence of the Comanche Reserve, only about four hundred of the estimated one thousand to one thousand two hundred Penateka moved there, while the rest joined the Yamparika and Kotsoteka Comanches and the Kiowas in the North. These Comanches and Kiowas not only continued their frontier raids but also tried to entice the reservation Indians away.

The Texas Indian reservations were assigned resident agents, and Robert Neighbors was selected to supervise all Texas Indians. An interpreter, a farmer, and a teacher were also hired for each of the reservations. In January, 1856, four companies of cavalry had been assigned to the Comanche Reserve to protect the Indians and keep them at peace. By 1858 the reservation Comanches were making progress toward becoming civilized. They had planted crops and their children were attending school.

Consigning the Texas Indians to reservations did not stop the raids upon the Texas frontier since many bands of southern and northern Comanches refused to settle on their reservations. After 1856, the raids increased. In December, 1857, Agent Neighbors estimated that five hundred horses, worth thousands of dollars, had been stolen from the Brazos and Colorado valleys, and three citizens had been killed. During 1858 the Comanche raids on the Texas counties were fiercer than ever; reports of murders came from as far east as Denton County and as far south as Lampasas County. Angered by the attacks, the people of Texas charged that thefts and murders had been perpetrated by the reservation Indians, and their attitude toward all Indians became more hostile than ever. Neighbors realized that the peaceful Indians on the reservations would not be allowed to remain in Texas as long as the raids by the northern Comanche bands continued, and he furnished Indian scouts from the friendly tribes to aid in stopping Comanche raids. For many years he had tried to persuade the government to create a reservation for the northern Co-

Courtesy Amon Carter Museum, Fort Worth

White Horse, Kiowa warrior, d. 1874

manche bands, and in 1858 a strip of land west of the 98th meridian was finally set aside. But the northern bands resisted being placed on a reservation. The raids continued, and both Texas Rangers and United States Army troops were sent in pursuit of the Comanche raiders. Several times during 1858, various Comanche bands north of the Red river were defeated in battles.

The Texas settlers, convinced that the reservation Indians were guilty of taking part in the raids, demanded their removal. A few reservation Indians may have participated occasionally, but many of the rumors were exaggerated. The Department of the Interior received many complaints, nevertheless, and in May a party of two hundred fifty Texans invaded the Lower Reserve but were turned back by determined army resistance. Neighbors worked frantically to obtain authority from Washington to remove the Indians from Texas for their own safety. On June 11, 1859, the Department of the Interior consented to the removal, and in the following month the Indians from both reserves were on the way to their new home in the upper valley of the Washita, in the Leased District of Indian Territory (present-day Oklahoma). The Leased District, west of the 98th meridian, had been leased in 1855 to the federal government by the Choctaws and Chickasaws to accommodate any Indians the government wished to place there. The hundreds of Indians from the Lower Reserve and the three hundred eighty-four Penateka Comanches from the Comanche Reserve were escorted by the militia to their new home one hundred seventy miles away. These Texas refugees were settled among the Wichita and the Wichita agency was built on Leeper Creek. Several weeks later, Fort Cobb was established on the Washita river to protect the Leased District.

By 1859 the northern and middle Comanches were being squeezed from all sides and began to concentrate between the Arkansas and Canadian rivers. Attacked by the Texans on the south, encroached upon by the civilized Indians on the east and pressed by white emigration from the north and northeast, many Comanches sought refuge in the Llano Estacado. Thus surrounded by aggressors on all sides and weakened by disease and hunger, some Comanche families huddled around the agency on the Arkansas river while the young warriors raided the frontier from the Red river to Corpus Christi. The removal of the reserva-

Courtesy Amon Carter Museum, Fort Worth

Wichitas on horseback

tion Comanches had not made an appreciable effect upon continued raids as those Indians had not been the major participants.

With the opening of the Civil War, Indian Territory was surrounded by the Confederate Army and its agents. The Indians of the Territory negotiated treaties with Confederate Indian Commissioner, Albert Pike. Two Confederate treaties with the Comanches were signed at the Wichita agency on August 12 and 13, 1861. One treaty was negotiated with the Penateka Comanches and other Indians from the Leased District, and the second was negotiated with the "Comanches of the Prairies and Staked Plain," which included the Nokoni, Yamparika, Kotsoteka bands and the remnants of the Tanimas.

These Confederate treaties, similar to those negotiated with the federal government, required that each side give up its prisoners — the Comanches would be paid for the return of theirs. They promised provisions, and an agency was to be established among them. The Confederate Government asked that the Comanches settle down on their reservation and become self-sufficient. The Penateka Comanches, already on the reservation, were well cared for by their agent, Mathew Leeper, but the hostile bands only occasionally visited the agency to trade or request gifts. In 1862 the agency was attacked by Delawares and Shawnees who were sympathetic to the Union, and relations between the Confederacy and the Comanches collapsed. Many of the Penatekas fled to the Wichita Mountains for safety. Despite the loss of the agency, Comanche raids decreased temporarily after the negotiation of the treaty.

Desiring to gain the Plains Indians' allegiance, in August, 1861, the federal government negotiated an agreement with the Comanches and Kiowas to suspend hostilities against the Indians on or before September 1, 1862, and promised that a permanent treaty would be negotiated at a later date. By the winter of 1861-1862, therefore, there were probably as many Comanches acknowledging the sovereignty of the United States and gathering at Fort Wise for issuance of food as there were allied with the Confederacy at Fort Cobb.

In May, 1861, the Comanches living near the New Mexico settlements entered into a truce with the federal government in which they agreed to stop attacks on the lives and property of Americans in New Mexico, Kansas, and Texas. The Indians also agreed to punish any warriors who might violate this agreement and to return to Fort Union or any other place that might be designated for trade. Neither side honored the truce, and no permanent treaty was ever negotiated.

A United States Indian agent obtained permission to take Comanche, Kiowa, Arapaho, Cheyenne, and Kiowa-Apache chiefs to Washington, where in 1863 they signed a treaty to make perpetual the agreement signed at Fort Atkinson in 1853. In return, the government was to furnish the tribes with twenty-five thousand dollars in annuity goods. Although the annuity goods were furnished, this treaty was never ratified by the Senate.

During 1864 Comanches, Kiowas, Kiowa-Apaches, and northern Plains Indians, including Cheyennes, formed an alliance, and made many raids along the trails to Denver and along the Arkansas river. Although these attacks were largely the work of the Cheyennes and their allies, the Comanches and Kiowas were active along the Arkansas river and Santa Fe Trail. In November, 1864, the same month that Colonel John Chivington attacked Black Kettle's peaceful Cheyenne camp at Sand Creek, the commander of the United States forces in New Mexico sent a punitive expedition under Christopher (Kit) Carson against the

Courtesy Amon Carter Museum, Fort Worth

Lone Wolf, famous Kiowa war chief

southern Plains Indians. On November 24 Carson and his volunteers, aided by Ute and Jicarilla Apache scouts, attacked the main Kiowa camp near Adobe Walls on the Canadian River. Overwhelmed by large numbers, Carson and his men withdrew.

The Kiowa and Comanche agent, Jesse H. Leavenworth, from his base at Fort Riley, continually worked to secure peace. By appealing to Washington, he was able to call a temporary halt to military action against the Indians, and by early August, 1865, he persuaded the Kiowas and Comanches to attend a council at the mouth of the Little Arkansas river. The Indians agreed not only to cease their attacks on travelers on the Santa Fe Trail and other roads but to meet with peace commissioners in October.

Large numbers of Kiowa-Apaches, Kiowas, and Comanches as well as Cheyennes and Arapahos attended the October conference, at which time the Kiowa-Apaches severed their traditional alliance with the Kiowas and Comanches and formed a union with the Cheyennes and Arapahos. On October 18 a peace treaty between the United States and the Kiowas and Comanches was signed, though it was not ratified until May 22, 1866. The purpose of the treaty was to move the Indians onto a reservation south of the Arkansas river, thus keeping them from the heavily traveled routes through the Plains. The Comanches and Kiowas were promised "absolute and undisturbed use and occupation" of western New Mexico, what is now the Panhandle of Texas, Oklahoma west of the Cimarron river, and north to the Kansas-Colorado border. Only military officers, Indian agents and government officials were allowed to enter or reside in the designated area. The Indians agreed to the building of military roads and military posts in their new reservation. They also promised to cease raids on frontier settlements and on travelers along the Santa Fe Trail. For these concessions they were entitled to receive annuities biannually for the next forty years. Article 6 of the treaty read:

> The Indians parties to this treaty expressly covenant and agree that they will use their utmost endeavors to induce that portion of the respective tribes not now present to unite with them and accede to the provisions of this treaty, which union and accession shall be evidenced and made binding on all parties whenever such absentees shall have participated in the beneficial provisions of this treaty.

But like the previous Comanche treaties, this one, too, was inef-

Courtesy National Archives

Kicking Bird, Kiowa chief, 1868-74

fective because only six of the nine Comanche bands were present. Those who were present found it impossible to comply with Article 6, for they could not persuade their absent tribesmen to accede to the treaty provisions. Immediately following the Treaty of the Little Arkansas, however, traffic moved unmolested over the Santa Fe, Smoky Hill, and Platte trails.

With the Civil War over, and while Texas was going through military reconstruction, the army could not protect the Texas frontier from Indian raids. On learning of this situation, the Indians increased their raids. On August 5, 1867, the Texas governor reported that since the close of the war Indians had killed one hundred sixty-two people, taken forty-three prisoners, and wounded twenty-four others. Two special Indian agents, sent to investigate the Indian situation along the Arkansas river frontier, reported in 1866 that both Comanches and Kiowas were violating the Treaty of the Little Arkansas and that neither tribe had come to receive the annuities. One reason for this, the agents pointed out, was that the annuity goods were of inferior quality. Failure of the federal government to carry out its part of the Treaty of the Little Arkansas, together with a military campaign against the Cheyennes and Sioux on the northern Plains, caused another period of warfare in which the Comanches were major participants.

These continued hostilities caused Congress to create a Joint Special Committee on the Conditions of the Indian Tribes in 1865, and in January, 1867, the committee presented its five hundred page report. Graft and ineptitude in the Indian Bureau were exposed, and evidence was presented indicating that Indian wars were often caused by aggression by lawless whites. Following the report, a Peace Commission of four civilians and three generals was appointed and authorized to bring the Indian chiefs together to negotiate a more effective and permanent peace.

The commissioners met with more than five thousand southern Plains Indians at Medicine Lodge Creek, seventy miles south of Fort Larned, Kansas, in October, 1867. General William Tecumseh Sherman, who was one of the commissioners, ordered the Department of the Missouri to make fifty thousand rations (one hundred fifty thousand meals) available to the attending Indians, and additional food was purchased from Peace Com-

Courtesy Smithsonian Institution

Broken Leg, Kiowa woman, 1898

mission funds. The commissioners opened the conference by referring to reports that the Indians had been violating their treaties. The Indians were then encouraged to present their side and to point out their own grievances against the whites. The Kiowas were the first to speak, followed by Ten Bears of the Yamparika Comanches. Ten Bears' oration excerpted below is one of the finest examples of Indian speeches that have ever been recorded.

My people have never first drawn a bow or fired a gun against the whites. There has been trouble on the line between us, and my young men have danced the war dance. But it was not begun by us. It was you who sent out the first soldier, and it was we who sent out the second. . . .

You said that you wanted to put us upon a reservation, to build us houses and to make us Medicine Lodges. I do not want them. I was born upon the prairie, where the wind blew free, and there was nothing to break the light of the sun. I was born where there were no enclosures, and where everything drew a free breath. I want to die there, and not within walls. I know every stream and every wood between the Rio Grande and the Arkansas. I have hunted and lived over that country. I lived like my fathers before me, and like them, I lived happily.

When I was at Washington, the Great Father told me that all the Comanche land was ours, and that no one should hinder us in living upon it. So why do you ask us to leave the rivers, and the sun, and the wind, and live in houses? Do not ask us to give up the buffalo for the sheep. . . . If the Texans had kept out of my country, there might have been peace. But that which you now say we must live on is too small. . . .

The white man has the country which we loved and we only wish to wander on the prairie until we die. . . . I want no blood upon my land to stain the grass. I want it all clear and pure, and I wish it so, that all who go through among my people may find peace when they come in and leave it when they go out.

Another Comanche orator was Silver Brooch, a Penateka who said that because his band was shrinking it would join the Kwahadi band in the spring if the government did not keep its promises to the Indians. When the government had failed to provide money for reservation buildings promised in the treaty, the resulting attacks should not have surprised anyone who heard Silver Brooch's threat. The treaty, which was signed by the Kiowas and Comanches on October 21, 1867, was the last treaty negotiated with the southern Plains tribes.

Article 1. From this day forward all war between the parties to this agreement shall forever cease.

The Government of the United States desires peace, and its honor is here pledged to keep it. The Indians desire peace, and they now pledge their honor to maintain it. If bad men among the whites, or among other people subject to the authority of the United States, shall commit any wrong upon the person or property of the Indians, the United States will, upon proof made to the agent and forwarded to the Commissioner of Indian Affairs at Washington City, proceed at once to cause the offender to be arrested and punished according to the laws of the United States, and also re-imburse the injured person for the loss sustained. . . .

The same provision applied to any Indian who committed depredations against United States citizens. The Indians were to turn over any warrior involved in raids, and the injured party was to be reimbursed from the annuity money.

In Article 4 the government agreed to construct at its own expense a number of buildings on the reservation, including a warehouse and an agency headquarters. Articles 13 and 14 specified that the government would supply the Indians annually with a farmer, blacksmith, physician, teacher, carpenter, miller, and engineer, and buildings for them were also to be constructed. The Indians pledged themselves to compel their children between six and sixteen to attend the school which was to be erected. Article 15 authorized the construction of a seven hundred fifty dollar house on the reservation for Silver Brooch, who had been farming on the reservation previous to the treaty. By the summer of 1868, however, no money had been appropriated to fulfill treaty provisions, and not even Silver Brooch's house was built. This was one of the treaty promises Silver Brooch referred to when he threatened to join the Kwahadi if the government did not keep its pledges.

The Kiowas and Comanches agreed to surrender all of the land granted in 1865 with the exception of a tract in southwestern Oklahoma between the Washita and Red rivers, about three million acres — a small area compared to the once vast Comanchería. In 1866 the government carved this reservation out of the Chickasaw and Choctaw lands in Oklahoma as punishment for their allegiance to the Confederate States during the Civil War.

Annuities for the signatories were to be issued on the 15th of October every year and were to include:

For each male person over fourteen years of age, a suit of good substantial woollen clothing, consisting of coat, pantaloons, flannel shirt, hat, and a pair of home made socks. For each female over twelve years of age, a flannel skirt, or

> the goods necessary to make it, a pair of woollen hose, and twelve yards of calico, and twelve yards of "domestic."
>
> For the boys and girls under the ages named, such flannel and cotton goods as may be needed, to make each a suit as aforesaid, together with a pair of woollen hose for each. . . .

In addition to the clothing, twenty-five thousand dollars was set aside for the next thirty years to be used by the Secretary of the Interior to purchase whatever articles the Indians might need.

This treaty emphasized encouraging the Indians to become farmers. Article 6 provided that any head of a family who wanted to begin farming would have the privilege of selecting three hundred twenty acres which would "cease to be held in common" by the tribe and would be "held in the exclusive possession of the person selecting it, and of his family so long as he or they may continue to cultivate it." In order to be eligible for treaty benefits, the Indians could not live anywhere except on the reservation. A clause in Article 11, however, allowed the Indians the right to hunt buffalo south of the Arkansas river "so long as the buffalo may range thereon in such numbers as to justify the chase." This provision made the treaty ambiguous, for the Indians were denied the right to make permanent homes outside the reservation but could spend the major part of a year following the buffalo off the reservation and still comply with the treaty terms. This hunting clause obviously weakened the attempt to convert the Indians to farmers.

The Senate finally ratified the treaty in the summer of 1868, but frontier raids increased while Congress debated the appropriation of annuity funds. It was not until July 20, 1868, that five hundred thousand dollars was appropriated to implement the treaty provisions. (Since the beginning of United States' Indian policy, Indian tribes had been treated as separate nations and treaties were required to regulate Indian-government relations. The Senate, which had the sole power of ratifying Indian treaties, often failed, owing to political contingencies, to ratify treaties within a reasonable length of time. Some treaties, furthermore, such as the Little Arkansas Treaty of 1865, were radically changed by the Senate, and the revised versions were rarely returned to the Indians for approval. Although ratification took nearly a year, the treaty of Medicine Lodge Creek was not altered appreciably.)

The Penateka, Nokoni, Kotsoteka and Yamparika bands had attended the conference at Medicine Lodge Creek, but about one-third of the Comanches, including the powerful Kwahadis, were not represented. Ten Bears signed the final document binding only his band to its provisions, but many Kiowa and Comanche chiefs did not sign. Many Comanche and Kiowa warriors resumed their plunder of settlements of Texas and Indian Territory during the winter of 1867-1868.

As provided in the treaty, the Comanches, Kiowas, and Kiowa-Apaches were to assemble promptly on their assigned lands, and in April, 1868, Jesse Henry Leavenworth established the agency headquarters near old Fort Cobb. When the Indians arrived, they expected to receive their annuities immediately, but Congress had not yet appropriated the money. The promised troops were not there to protect the agency, furthermore, and soon hundreds of Indians were gathered around it demanding food and presents. Without soldiers, food, or presents, it was almost impossible for Leavenworth to manage the Indians. Failing to receive their promised goods, some of the Comanches, including the Yamparikas, left the reservation and moved to the upper Arkansas river accompanied by Kiowas. The situation became even more explosive when the Cheyennes, aided by some Arapahos and Sioux, again took up the hatchet, and there was a danger that the Comanches and Kiowas would join them. It was essential, therefore, to return the Indians to their reservations and keep them away from the warring Cheyennes and Sioux. During the winter of 1868 the Kiowas, Kiowa-Apaches, and Comanches gradually moved onto their reservation, where they received the desperately needed food and long overdue annuities. While the southern Plains Indians remained at their agency, the government launched a campaign against the Cheyennes and Arapahos which in December resulted in the attack on the Upper Washita camp of the Cheyenne chief Black Kettle. This successful winter campaign of the Washita drove many of the remaining southern Plains bands onto their reservation.

In 1869 a new Kiowa, Comanche, and Kiowa-Apache agency was built a few miles from Fort Sill, which had been constructed in the same year in the middle of the Kiowa and Comanche reservation. With the southern Plains tribes back on their reservation, their control reverted to the Indian Bureau. Because of the report of the Peace Commission, demands for reforms began to appear, and in October, 1868, the Indian Peace Commission recommended the appointment of new Indian agents nominated by various religious organizations. The Quakers responded most enthusiastically. On July 1, 1869, Quaker Indian agent Lawrie Tatum arrived at Fort Sill to take over as agent to the Comanches, Kiowas, and Kiowa-Apaches. About one thousand five hundred of the estimated two thousand four hundred sixteen Comanches were living off the reservation when Agent Tatum took over. Tatum believed that kindness and honesty would solve the Indian problem. He was opposed to the use of military force and forbade the use of troops on the reservation. From the beginning he found, however, that soldiers were needed to control the Indians, particularly on the days when annuities were issued.

After the 1870 Kiowa Sun Dance, small parties of Kiowa-Apaches, Kiowas, and Comanches dispersed in all directions, remaining off the reservation and harrassing the Texas frontier until winter. When the Kiowas began raiding Fort Sill's horse herd, Tatum assigned guards and attempted to pacify the Indians by withholding half of their rations. By the summer of 1871 the peace policy was abandoned. Rations were denied families of those who went on raids, and the army was again allowed to enter Indian Territory in pursuit of raiders and to recover stolen property. Agent Tatum also requested the army to bring in the Kwahadis, who had never been on the reservation, by force if necessary. In late September Colonel Ranald S. MacKenzie of the Fourth Cavalry was sent to drive the Kwahadi onto the reservation. On October 3 the command moved out, guided by Tonkawa scouts. For two months MacKenzie unsuccessfully pursued the Kwahadis, who were ably led by Chief Quanah Parker.

(Quanah Parker's mother, Cynthia Ann Parker, was one of the many white captives taken during the Plains wars. She was nine years old when, on May 19, 1836, her family was attacked at Parker, Texas by a party of Comanches and Kiowas. Although the other women captives taken that day were eventually returned or escaped, Cynthia Ann remained for many years with the Comanches. By the time she was fifteen, she had married a young Kwahadi chief. On December 19, 1860, the Texas Rangers

Courtesy Amon Carter Museum, Fort Worth

Kiowa chief Satanta, who killed himself in a Texas prison, 1874

Courtesy Amon Carter Museum, Fort Worth

Satank, one of the greatest Kiowa warriors, about 1870

Courtesy Amon Carter Museum, Fort Worth

Big Tree, Kiowa warrior and chief

attacked the Kwahadi camp, taking Cynthia Ann and her infant daughter, Prairie Flower, back to her white family. Cynthia Ann, fully acculturized because of her many years with the Comanches, desired only to return to her husband and his people. Several times she stole horses and raced off across the prairie but was always recaptured by the Rangers. Both Cynthia Ann and her child died shortly after their return to her family. Her son Quanah, born about 1845, had escaped the Rangers in 1860 and remained with the Comanches. Quanah became one of the most famous of all Comanche leaders. After surrendering his people in 1875 he set about helping them to make the best of the new situation. He encouraged agriculture and education among his people, and in 1886 was appointed a judge of the Court of Indian Offenses and served on it until 1898.)

During the winter of 1871-1872 the Comanches remained quiet, and all but the Kwahadis came in for their rations. With the arrival of spring, 1872, however, they renewed their raids, and the army was called on again. Colonel MacKenzie was ordered to pursue the elusive Kwahadis, and during the summer of 1872 he and his command marched across the Llano Estacado. Although he did not find any Indians there, he dispelled the myth that troops could not operate in that desert-like area. In September, 1872, MacKenzie discovered and attacked a large Kwahadi village on McClellan Creek, taking thousands of Indian ponies and one hundred twenty women and children captive. The captives were held temporarily at Fort Concho until June, 1873, when they were sent to Fort Sill.

Severely disturbed by their numerous problems — disease, hunger, land encroachment and wars with the army — the Comanches were receptive to the appearance of a young messiah, a Comanche named Isatai, who claimed he had supernatural powers to cure the sick and make the white men's guns harmless. Isatai announced that the Comanches should give their own dance, a medicine dance, probably modeled after the Kiowa Sun Dance. In May, 1874, every Comanche band was represented at the gathering. Two days later the Comanches, joined by other northern Plains Indians, headed for Adobe Walls, an old trading post on the Canadian River that was still the headquarters for the hated buffalo hunters. At daybreak on June 27 the Comanches, led by Quanah Parker, attacked. The prophet Isatai, who had

Courtesy Amon Carter Museum, Fort Worth

Quanah Parker, Comanche chief (son of Cynthia Ann Parker), who helped Comanches adjust to reservation life.

promised immunity from bullets, found that his medicine was not strong enough that day, and a number of Comanches fell dead or wounded. The discouraged Indians gave up and withdrew.

Since the southern Plains Indians continued to raid Kansas, Colorado, New Mexico, and Texas, during 1874 orders were issued for all friendly Indians to camp near specified posts by the summer to avoid being considered hostile. Many Kiowas and most of the Comanches refused to comply with this order. Troops were sent into Comanche and Kiowa country from all sides to drive the Indians onto the reservation or to kill them. The Indians fled before the converging troops into the recesses of Palo Duro Canyon in the heart of the Llano Estacado. On September 27, 1874, Colonel MacKenzie discovered hundreds of tepees along the bottom of the canyon. In the ensuing battle the soldiers destroyed more than one thousand four hundred Indian ponies and hundreds of tepees, and the Indians, now without their mounts and winter supply of food, were all but defeated. As the winter grew more severe, bands of Indians struggled to the reservation to surrender. In April Quanah Parker and his Kwahadi band capitulated at Fort Sill. The Comanches never again took part in a major war, although in June, 1879, they made their last minor raid on a ranch south of Big Spring. With the almost total annihilation of the buffalo, the strength of the army, and the loss of most of their ponies, the knights of the southern Plains gave up and succumbed to reservation life.

SUGGESTED READINGS

Brown, Dee. *Bury My Heart at Wounded Knee.* New York: Holt Reinhart and Winston, 1970.

Berlandier, Jean Louis. *The Indians of Texas in 1830.* Washington: Smithsonian Institution Press, 1969.

Jones, Douglas C. *The Treaty of Medicine Lodge: The Story of the Great Treaty Council as Told by Eyewitnesses.* Norman: University of Oklahoma Press, 1966.

Leckie, William H. *The Military Conquest of the Southern Plains.* Norman: University of Oklahoma Press, 1963.

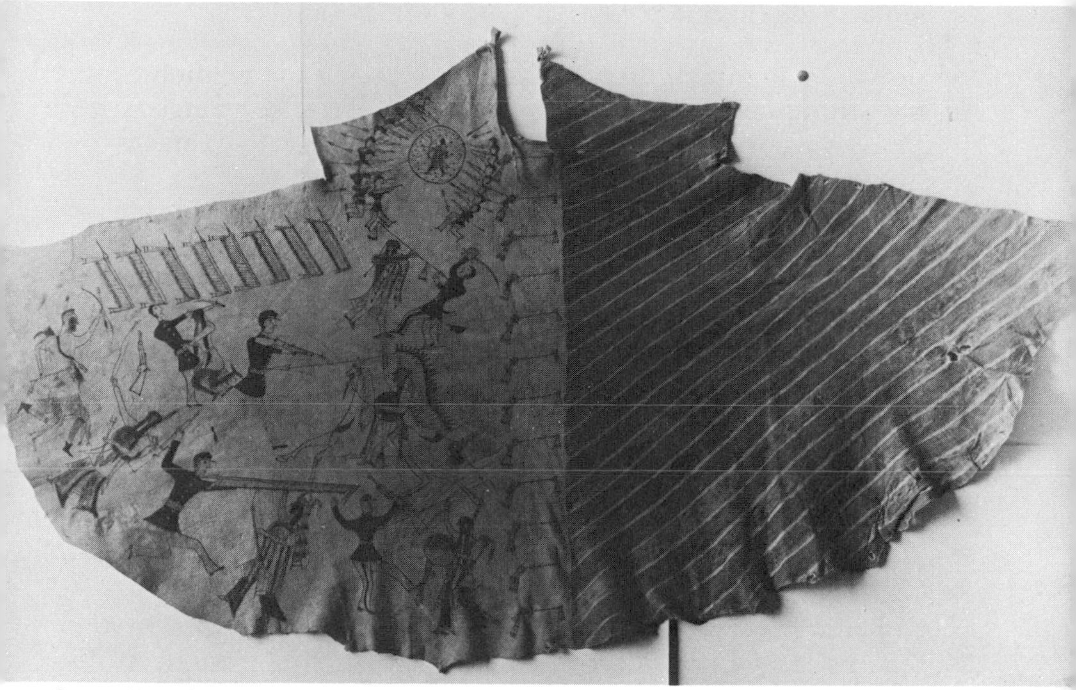

Courtesy National Archives

Tipi with battle scene between Kiowas and soldiers, about 1895

Lehmann, Herman. *Nine Years Among the Indians 1870-1879: The Story of the Captivity and Life of a Texan Among the Indians.* Austin: Von Boeckmann-Jones Company, Printers, 1927.

Newcomb, W. W. *The Indians of Texas from Prehistoric to Modern Times.* Austin: University of Texas Press, 1961.

Nye, Wilbur Sturtevant. *Plains Indians Raiders: The Final Phases of Warfare from the Arkansas to the Red River.* Norman: University of Oklahoma Press, 1968.

Richardson, Rupert Norval. *The Comanche Barrier to South Plains Settlement.* Glendale: The Arthur H. Clark Company, 1933.

Vestal, Stanley. *Warpath and Council Fire: The Plains Indians' Struggle for Survival in War and in Diplomacy, 1851-1891.* New York: Random House, 1948.

Wallace, Ernest and E. Adamson Hoebel. *The Comanches; Lords of the South Plains.* Norman: University of Oklahoma Press, 1969.

Webb, Walter Prescott. *The Texas Rangers: A Century of Frontier Defense.* Austin: University of Texas Press, 1965.

Courtesy Amon Carter Museum, Fort Worth

Comanche beef issue, 1891

The history of treaty-making with the Sioux is the history of treaty-making with all Indians. The treaties were made for the accommodation of the whites, and broken when they interfered with the money-getters. . . . That the Indian has not always discriminated between the innocent and the guilty in taking his revenge is certain. . . . If his sense of justice had led him to fine discrimination in these matters the red man would long ago have made an attack on the nation's Capitol.

McLaughlin, *My Friend the Indian*, p. 289.

CHAPTER 6

Treaties with the Teton Sioux

Donald E. Worcester

THE TETON or Western Sioux (Lakota) were composed of a number of tribal groups: Brulés, Oglalas, Hunkpapas, Minneconjou, and Sans Arcs as well as some smaller bands. Sioux was a corruption of a Chippewa word for "adder," their term for their enemy. The Sioux called themselves Dakota or Lakota, meaning "The Allies." The Tetons were numerous and powerful, and if they had been genuine allies they could have defended their lands much more effectively. But alliances were completely unknown to them, although the Brulés and Oglalas occasionally got together to badger the Pawnees. These raids were usually the final events of celebrations, such as the Sun Dance, rather than purposeful campaigns. Against the whites they united only once for a few months, and then only because the army went to attack them in their last refuge. It was a memorable occasion, nevertheless, for it culminated on the sultry afternoon of June 25, 1876, on the Little Bighorn. The bands split up immediately afterward, for the victory came too late.

The absence of cooperation for defense of tribal lands made it easy for the whites to encroach on them. In 1848 the flood of emigrants along the Platte river to Oregon and California used up all of the grass and drove away the game. By the following year the Brulés, whose hunting grounds were along both sides of the Platte, retaliated. Because of their attacks on wagon trains, the government built Fort Kearney at Grand Island on the South Platte and converted the old American Fur Company trading

---

Donald E. Worcester was born in Tempe, Arizona, on April 29, 1915, and grew up on ranches there and in southern California. In 1947 he received his Ph.D. degree at the University of California, Berkeley. Since that time he has taught at the University of Florida (1947-63) and Texas Christian University (1963 —) except for a year as Visiting Professor at the University of Madrid. He has published more than twenty-five articles on Indians, horses, and Latin America, and fifteen books. His most recent book is *Brazil: From Colony to World Power* (New York: Scribner's, 1973). He is presently writing a history of the Western Apaches and lives on a small ranch near Aledo, Texas, and raises Arabian horses. He was president of Western Writers of America, 1973-74, and of the Western History Association, 1974-75.

Courtesy National Archives

Teton Sioux horse races in front of Fort Pierre, S.D. Painting by Karl Bodner, 1833-34.

post on Laramie fork into Fort Laramie. The Brulés and Cheyennes struck back in anger at this intrusion.

That summer a cholera epidemic spread throughout the Mississippi Valley, and travelers brought the dread disease to the Brulés and Oglalas, who were both hard hit, and the Cheyennes probably lost half of their number. Smallpox followed in the wake of the cholera.

When the diseases finally abated, the young men demanded vengeance, for they were convinced that the whites had spread the sickness among them by magic. They began attacking travelers on the Overland Trail. In the summer of 1851 Indian Superintendent D. D. Mitchell called a council of the Sioux, Cheyennes, Arapahos, Crows, Assiniboines, Gros-Ventre Mandans, and Arikaras to negotiate a treaty. The 1851 Treaty of Fort Laramie contained in its first article a provision that peace was to be observed among all the tribes.

Article 2. The aforesaid nations do hereby recognize the right of the United States government to establish roads, military and other posts, within their respective territories.

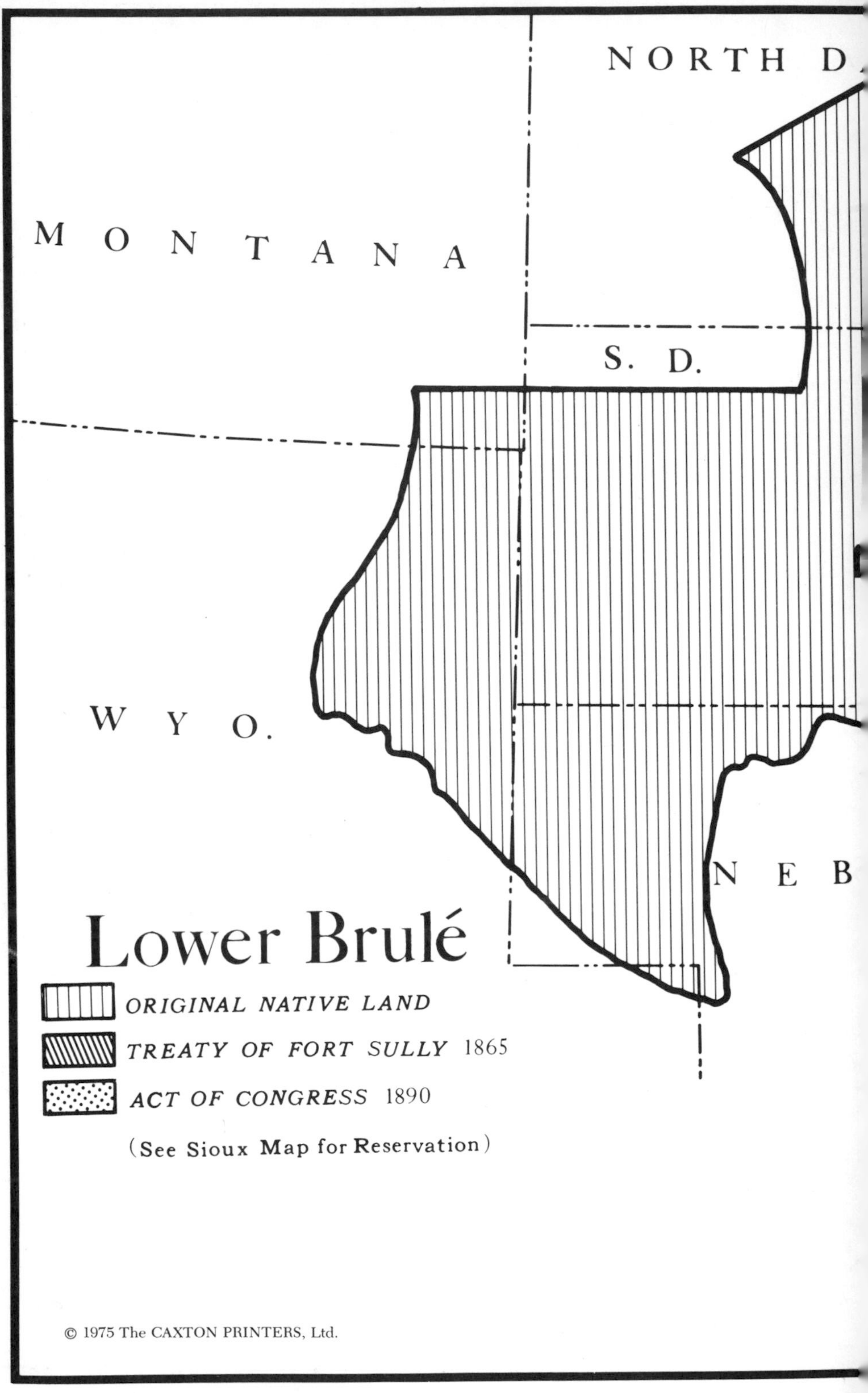
NORTH D
MONTANA
S. D.
WYO.
NEB
Lower Brulé
ORIGINAL NATIVE LAND
TREATY OF FORT SULLY 1865
ACT OF CONGRESS 1890
(See Sioux Map for Reservation)

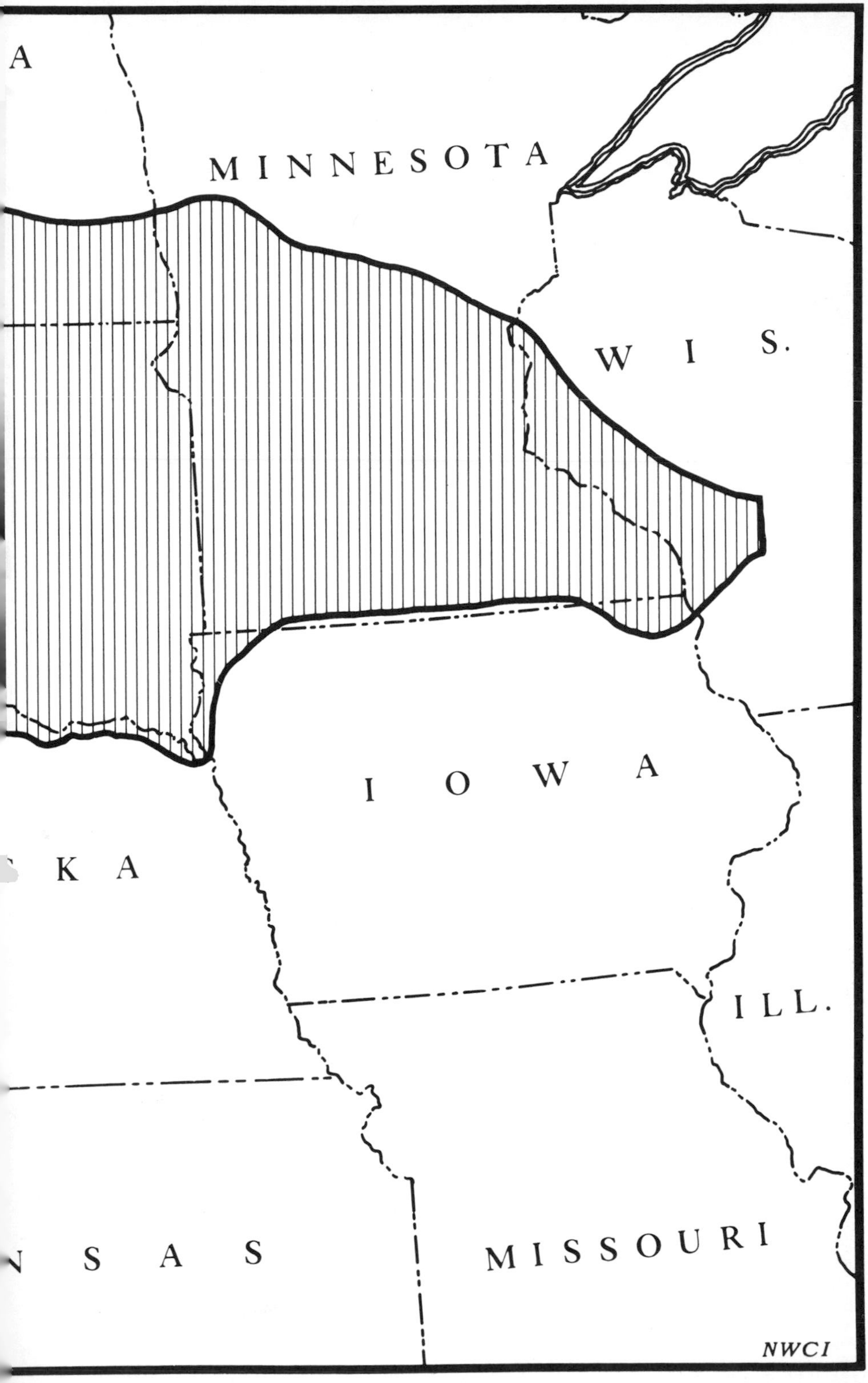

A
MINNESOTA
WIS.
IOWA
KA
ILL.
NSAS
MISSOURI
NWCI

Courtesy Amon Carter Museum, Fort Worth

Sioux preparing for Sun Dance (the only photographs ever taken of a Sioux Sun Dance lodge).

Article 3. In consideration of the rights and privileges acknowledged in the preceding article, the United States bind themselves to protect the aforesaid Indian nations against the commission of all depredations by the said United States, after ratification of this treaty.

Article 4. The aforesaid Indians do hereby agree and bind themselves to make restitution or satisfaction for any wrongs committed . . . by any band or individual of their people, on the people of the United States, whilst lawfully residing in or passing through their respective territories.

Article 5. The aforesaid Indians do hereby recognize and acknowledge the following tracts of country, included within the metes and boundaries hereinafter designated, as their respective territories, viz:

The territory of the Sioux or Dacotah Nation, commencing the mouth of the White Earth River, on the Missouri River; hence in a southwesterly direction to the north fork of the Platte River to a point known as the Red Bute, or where the road leaves the river; thence along the range of mountains known as the Black Hills, to the head-waters of the Heart River to its mouth; and thence down the Missouri River to the place of beginning.

The original treaty included a government promise to provide fifty thousand dollars annually in provisions, merchandise, domestic animals, and agricultural implements for a period of fifty years. The Senate reduced the term to ten years, to be extended five more at the discretion of the president. The Indians presumably were to agree to this change.

For the first time the powerful Tetons, who earlier had driven the Cheyennes from the Black Hills, were, by the treaty, limited to a particular territory. They were happily unaware of the implications of the treaty concerning boundaries, however, and in the next few years drove the Crows from their hunting grounds along the Powder and Bighorn rivers in Wyoming and Montana.

Some of the Sioux, known as the "Laramie Loafers," settled down to live in the vicinity of Fort Laramie, while others continued to roam widely and came to the fort only in late summer when the annuity gifts were to be distributed. Regarding themselves as independent as ever, they did not react favorably to the attempts of brash young army officers to order them around. In 1853 Lieutenant Hugh B. Fleming was sent to arrest a Minneconju, and he marched a small detachment into the center of a big Teton camp. The astonished Indians ran for their weapons

Courtesy Amon Carter Museum, Fort Worth

Sioux Sun Dance lodge

Courtesy Amon Carter Museum, Fort Worth

Three Bears, Oglala warrior

Courtesy National Park Service

Sioux drying buffalo meat, near Fort Laramie, Wyoming

and war ponies. Someone fired a shot, and the troops fired a volley, killing three or four Minneconjus, then hastily retreated.

Even the most friendly of the Tetons were infuriated at this unprovoked attack, but Indian agent Thomas Fitzpatrick, a veteran Indian trader, persuaded the chiefs to keep the fragile peace. Presumably at the same time he also induced them to accept the Senate amendment to the Treaty of 1851 that changed the annuity payments from fifty to ten or fifteen years. The Indians claimed later that they knew nothing about this change, and it does not seem to have been an appropriate time to have informed them of so drastic a cut.

In August of 1854 the Tetons were camped near Fort Laramie again, awaiting the distribution of the annuity gifts. Many emigrant trains were moving past the fort to the west. One day a Minneconju in the Brulé camp of Brave Bear killed an ox. According to one account, the animal had been adandoned as lame, but two men came back to recover it and discovered that it had been killed. Another account had the Minneconju killing the ox while a man was leading it. At any rate, the emigrants complained to Lieutenant Fleming, who was still irritated over his difficulties of the previous year.

Brave Bear rode to the fort and offered to let the Indian agent pay for the ox from the annuity gifts. The officers refused this offer. The Minneconju must be arrested. According to Lieutenant Fleming, this was only one of many "outrages," and if it went unpunished he was sure there would be others. The Treaty of 1851 said nothing about arrests. In case of an offense by an Indian, the chief should give satisfaction. Brave Bear tried to do so, but was refused.

Lieutenant J. L. Grattan, fresh from West Point, was eager for action. Grattan was what the civilian packers called a "shavetail," the name they gave to untrained pack mules. In order to identify these mules, which blundered around and got into trouble instead of getting into line at the ringing of a bell, the packers shaved their tails. The experienced mules (and officers) were called "bell sharp."

Grattan set out for the Brulé camp with two non-coms, twenty-seven men, two field pieces, and the post interpreter, who was drunk and who hated the Sioux. Teton chiefs rode up and urged him to let the agent take care of the matter, and once

Courtesy Smithsonian Institution

Slow Bull, Oglala Sioux warrior, participating in the Hunka ceremony

more Brave Bear offered ponies to pay for the ox. Grattan brushed them aside. He formed his men in line of battle across a creek from the Brulé camp. The astonished Brulé warriors hastily strung their bows, mounted their war ponies, and hid in the willows along the creek.

Brave Bear went back and forth between the troops and the camp, trying desperately to preserve the peace. The Minneconju refused to submit to arrest, and Grattan refused payment for the ox. There is no way of knowing who fired the first shot, but the troops fired a volley, and shot from the field pieces tore through the tepees. Brave Bear, caught in the line of fire, fell mortally wounded. Spotted Tail and other Brulé warriors dashed out of the willows and killed every soldier. Then, worried at this attack over what they regarded as a trifling matter, they put the war back in the bag and went off for their fall hunt. Later in the fall Spotted Tail, Long Chin, Red Leaf, and two other Brulé warriors attacked a government mail wagon and killed the two drivers and a passenger.

In 1855 Brigadier General W.S. Harney, a veteran of the Seminole War, was sent to punish the Brulés. Harney had nothing but contempt for Indians and he regarded promises made them as mere jokes. He assembled a large force of infantry and dragoons at Fort Leavenworth in eastern Kansas. In the meantime, Thomas S. Twiss, an ex-army officer, had replaced Fitzpatrick as Indian agent at Fort Laramie. He sent runners to all of the Teton tribes. Move south of the Platte and come to Fort Laramie at once, he ordered. Once there he would protect them, but if they remained away, the army would attack them. The men who had robbed the mail wagon were murderers and would be treated as such. The Tetons, who ordinarily thought over such requests a long time before acting, hurried to the fort. Twiss now had skillfully isolated the Brulés where they could be attacked without the possibility of help from other bands. It was a clever maneuver on his part.

Little Thunder, who had succeeded Brave Bear as Brulé chief, was camped with his band on Bluewater creek near Ash Hollow, where the Oregon Trail followed the south bank of the Platte. The Brulés had been warned that troops were coming, but they had killed some buffalo and were waiting for the meat to dry. They remained in camp, with no scouts out, as was typical of

Courtesy Smithsonian Institution

Miniconjou warrior Kicking Bear wearing shirt trimmed with human scalps, 1896.

them, unaware that Harney had sent his dragoons to attack the camp from above while the infantry marched upstream.

Surprised at daybreak, Spotted Tail and others came out with a white flag to parley and give the women and children time to escape. Harney was willing to talk, but the troops kept moving. The Brulés fled in panic, abandoning their possessions and many of their ponies. Of the two hundred fifty Brulés in camp, eighty-six were killed and seventy women and children were captured. Spotted Tail's wife and daughter were among the prisoners.

Harney sent the captives down river and marched on to Fort Laramie, where he instructed the friendly chiefs to come to council. He brusquely ordered them to deliver to Fort Laramie the "murderers" who had robbed the mail wagon, or he would return the following year and punish them again.

The Tetons called Harney "The Hornet." He marched boldly through the heart of the Teton country and dared the hostiles to try his sting again. There were no takers.

The Brulés were terrified by Harney's crushing victory at the Bluewater. They regarded the loss of a single man as a calamity, and in their terms the Bluewater attack was the worst disaster the Tetons had suffered in the memory of man. Stunned and frightened, they did not know what to expect next.

The Brulés now begged Spotted Tail and the others who had attacked the mail wagon to go to Fort Laramie and surrender to save the rest of the band. Ordinarily they would have regarded these warriors as heroes, but now they urged them to sacrifice themselves. It took great courage for Spotted Tail, Red Leaf, and Long Chin to surrender, for the traders had warned them that Harney would take them to Kansas and hang them. Each man dressed in his finest war costume, mounted his best pony, and rode slowly toward the fort chanting his death song. Spotted Tail asked only to see his wife and child before he died.

The three Brulés were taken by army ambulance to Fort Leavenworth in heavily populated eastern Kansas. They were astonished to see thousands upon thousands of white men, for they had assumed that the whites were no more numerous than any Indian tribe. To Spotted Tail this was convincing evidence that it was foolish to fight the whites. Although Harney had intended them to be hanged, in January, 1856, they were par-

Courtesy Amon Carter Museum, Fort Worth

Spotted Tail, noted Brulé Sioux chief

doned. Spotted Tail was determined to avoid war with the whites at all costs thereafter.

The Oglalas and Brulés continued hunting south of the Platte and became associated with the Southern Cheyennes, who also roamed this region. The Platte area was heavily traveled, and game was scarce there. The Treaty of 1851 had recognized the Powder River and Bighorn regions as Crow hunting grounds, but the Hunkpapas and Minneconjus raided the Crows constantly, and after 1855, the Oglalas moved north of the Platte and joined in the attacks on the Crows.

The Crows were also at war with the powerful Blackfeet of Montana, and they were gradually pushed out of their best hunting grounds. Because of the war with the Tetons it became almost impossible for Indian agents to get the annuity goods to the Crows. In 1854 the Crows had gone to Fort Union at the mouth of the Yellowstone River, but they had suffered a severe defeat on the return journey. The next year they received no annuity goods. In 1856 they were persuaded to come in again, though they were fearful of smallpox as well as the Tetons. Their fears were justified, for smallpox spread among them, and the following year they again refused to come.

The Treaty of 1851 called for the tribes to cease warring on one another. Agent Twiss did not report the fact that the Tetons were constantly raiding the Crows and usurping their hunting grounds. Since there was so much trouble delivering annuity goods to the Crows, however, Twiss agreed to take care of the Crow goods at his agency, which was in the heart of Teton country — country where no Crow dared set foot. In 1860 the Indian Bureau shipped the Crows' supplies to Twiss. Presumably he took care of them, for they never reached the Crows.

In 1856 General Harney had drawn up a new treaty with the Tetons. They had accepted it, but it was rejected by the Senate. The Tetons were not familiar with concepts such as "advice and consent," and they considered the treaty to be in force. No one bothered to tell them that it was not.

The next year the Tetons held a great council near the Black Hills. Most of the talk was about white encroachments. They agreed to resist further intrusions by the whites, but they did not develop any overall plan for united action. There were thousands of Teton warriors, and it seemed to them that no

Courtesy National Park Service

Burial of a Crow chief; painting by J. H. Sharp about 1905

Courtesy National Park Service

Crow chief Plenty Coups

Courtesy National Park Service

Crow camp on Little Big Horn River; painting by J. H. Sharp

people, not even the whites, could defeat them. Spotted Tail, who had different thoughts on the subject, was unable to convince anyone that it was hopeless to fight the whites.

In the 1850s a stream of settlers flowed into the lands along the Missouri in Kansas, Nebraska, Iowa, and Dakota. As the available lands filled, the newcomers made repeated attempts to get title to Indian lands, and they frequently suggested that all of the Indians be sent to Indian Territory. The Pawnees and other tribes who were already surrounded by whites were even worse off than the Tetons. The latter were aware of the conditions along the Missouri, which made them all the more determined to resist the white advance.

When the Civil War began, most of the troops marched eastward, leaving only a small force at each post. In 1862 the Minnesota Sioux fought a bloody war, blaming the whites for encroaching on Santee land. Many of the Santees appeared suddenly in the Teton country, loaded with loot and full of talk about victories. Soon it became clear that they were seeking a refuge,

Courtesy Smithsonian Institution

Crow warriors Poor Elk, Black Foot, Long Ears, He Shows His Face, and Old Onion, 1871.

for troops were on their trail, and these troops made no distinction between Santees and Tetons.

In 1862 the Tetons were still friendly, but the situation was becoming explosive, and it called for tact, not heavy-handed treatment. Volunteer troops began replacing the regular forces in the military posts. Ignorant of Indians and their ways, these troops were anxious for an Indian war so they could demonstrate their supposed superiority. The Indians between the Platte and the Arkansas were especially nervous, for they had been told that a "paper" which their chiefs had signed in 1860 had given away their lands. The Cheyennes had been guaranteed the whole region that is now the State of Colorado, but when gold was discovered, the whites poured in by the thousands. The resentful Cheyennes began raiding the mining settlements, and in 1864 Colonel H.M. Chivington was sent out with the Colorado

Courtesy Smithsonian Institution

Crow warrior undergoing self-torture by pulling against thongs tied to skewers through the flesh of his chest.

Volunteers to punish the raiders. He could not find any large band, but he did manage to stir up the Indians along the Platte. His attack on Black Kettle's friendly camp at Sand Creek is a well-known atrocity story and needs no re-telling here.

The survivors sent pipe-bearers to all Cheyenne and Teton camps, and when the war-pipe was passed around, even Spotted Tail could not keep his people from joining the Cheyennes. Teton and Cheyenne war parties cut off all travel along the Overland Trail, and soon the freight companies were demanding that the government subdue the Plains tribes.

When the Civil War ended, there were plenty of troops available. The army sent three cavalry columns into the Powder river country to build two forts and to thrash the Indians. The troops were mostly Civil War veterans but inexperienced in Indian fighting; they did not know how to fight Indians or to get along peaceably with them.

General Patrick E. Connor commanded the expedition. At the head of the Powder river he built Camp Connor, later renamed Fort Reno, and left two companies of ex-Confederate troops to hold it. Connor marched all over the country looking for hostile Tetons to whip, but he found only a camp of friendly Arapahos under a chief named Medicine Man. On the frontier when it came to punishing Indians, one was as good as another. Connor accepted this code and soundly thrashed the astonished Arapahos. Otherwise the Great Powder river campaign of 1865 was a dismal and costly failure, for the Indians ran off hundreds of cavalry horses and pack mules and drove the other two columns out of their hunting grounds. The Sioux cut off communications with Fort Connor, so that the troops were barely able to survive the winter.

In 1865 a peace commission was sent to the Tetons, headed by General S.R. Curtis, whose order to Colonel Chivington to punish Cheyennes had initiated the current troubles. Newton Edmunds, a Dakota politician, was Curtis' main adviser. With a steamboat load of gifts, they went up the Missouri, where they held council with the peaceful "stay-around-the-fort" chiefs and got them to sign the treaty. The peace policy was thereby inaugurated among the friendly Tetons along the Missouri. Government officials assumed that all of the Tetons had signed, for the commissioners compiled a list of ten thousand three hundred

Courtesy Amon Carter Museum, Fort Worth

Sioux warrior, Grizzly Bear's Nose

"hostiles," implying that they had agreed to the treaty, although the commission had not seen a single one of them. The commissioners announced that they had made peace with the bands that had been at war, yet in the hostile camps there were at least eighteen thousand Tetons who knew nothing of any peace. The treaty specified that the Tetons would permit the building of a railroad and military posts on their lands. No Indians, not even those who signed the treaty, were told of this stipulation.

Similar treaties were signed by the tribes of the southern plains, and in the East it was assumed that the whole region west of the Mississippi was now at peace. While the treaty was being signed, however, the hostile Tetons were celebrating their success in liberating Connor's cavalry horses. As usual they climaxed their celebrations by sending raiding parties down to the Platte.

News of these raids surprised government officials, and it finally occurred to someone that peace had been made only with Indians who were already peaceful. A copy of the treaty was sent to Fort Laramie with instructions to the commander to persuade the hostile chiefs to come to the fort and sign it. The commander, Colonel Henry E. Maynadier, asked Big Mouth and some friendly Oglalas to carry a message to the bands in the Powder river and Bighorn regions. In January, 1866, Swift Bear and his Brulé Corn Band approached the fort. The Corn Band was friendly, and Swift Bear and Standing Elk willingly signed the treaty.

In March Spotted Tail, who had not wanted to go to war against the whites, sent a message to the fort that his daughter had died, and before her death had asked to be buried near Fort Laramie. Colonel Maynadier agreed, and when Spotted Tail and his band arrived, the colonel showed him every courtesy. Spotted Tail spoke bitterly of the mistreatment by the troops that had forced the friendly bands to join the hostiles. He also signed the treaty, and from this time on maintained peaceful relations with the whites.

The Senate quickly ratified the treaty, and the government announced that peace had been made with all of the Tetons. The Bozeman Trail to the Montana goldfields, which followed the Powder river, was now believed to be safe for travel. Yet the majority of the Tetons were still camping in that region, and they

Courtesy Amon Carter Museum, Fort Worth

Two Strikes, Brulé Sioux warrior

Courtesy Amon Carter Museum, Fort Worth

Charge-on-the-Hawk, Brulé Sioux warrior

Courtesy Amon Carter Museum, Fort Worth

Brulé Sioux chief Spotted Tail with wife and daughter

had never considered signing any treaty. None of the white men or halfbreeds at Fort Laramie would risk his life by daring to enter the Powder river country, but many gold-seekers, happily ignorant of the real situation, prepared to take the Bozeman Trail.

By late spring it was clear to all that the hostiles remained far away and had no intention of coming to Fort Laramie or of signing the treaty. E.B. Taylor, head of the Indian Bureau, traveled to the fort and named himself and Colonel Maynadier as commissioners to treat with the hostile Tetons. Taylor had orders to put the peace policy into effect with them, and he was determined to do so whether or not they wanted it. The men at Fort Laramie, who knew the Tetons well, tried to convince him that it was a time for caution, but he charged ahead as if he knew what he was doing.

Taylor sent messengers to the hostile camps asking the chiefs to come to the fort for a council. He sweetened the request with a promise of all manner of gifts for them, including rifles and powder. The offer of guns was tempting, and in June many of the hostiles, including Red Cloud and Man-Afraid-of-His-Horses, camped near the fort. Taylor immediately demanded that they sign the treaty.

These were not friendly "stay-around-the-fort" chiefs who were accustomed to taking orders from white men. They insisted that the treaty be read to them. When they heard the mention of a road to be built through their lands, they grew angry. Taylor blandly told them that the road was the one already in use along the Platte, although he knew very well that it was the Bozeman Trail, for the government had already announced that it was open and safe for travel. The Tetons were determined that this, their best remaining hunting ground, was not to be ruined by whites.

While the council was going on a large body of infantry with a wagon train arrived at Fort Laramie. A chief of the Corn Band visited the camp and talked to Colonel Henry B. Carrington. Where were the soldiers going? They were on their way, Carrington told him, to build forts to guard the new road to Montana. The chief hurried to spread the news.

In the council Red Cloud angrily denounced Taylor as a liar. The hostile Tetons seized their rifles and broke camp. They sent

Courtesy Amon Carter Museum, Fort Worth

Red Cloud, famous Oglala chief

back a grim warning to Carrington — anyone who comes into their country will die. As a reminder they stuck a pole in the trail and tied a bit of red cloth and a lock of hair to it. Anyone who knew the Plains Indian sign language would understand the message — turn back or die!

On his return to Washington Taylor said nothing about the incident that had broken up the council. Most of the chiefs had signed the treaty, he reported. There was one who refused — Red Cloud — but Taylor dismissed him as a minor chief of a small band called Bad Faces. Man-Afraid-of-His-Horses had also refused to sign, and he was regarded by his own people as favoring peace with the whites. Taylor neglected to mention him.

The plan to build the forts on the Bozeman Trail had been decided on soon after the Tetons had presumably signed the treaty. In keeping with the peace policy Carrington had only seven hundred infantry and no cavalry, and he was marching into the same region where General Connor, with three thousand cavalry, had failed. The Indians who had resisted Connor's force were still there, and more resentful than ever.

Colonel Carrington had been chosen to head the expedition in line with the peace policy. His orders were to build two forts and to organize patrols, and this was all that was expected of him, for he was not a fighting man. He was convinced, as were many Easterners who did not know them, that the Tetons would remain peaceful as long as they were not molested, and he was careful to avoid any trouble with them.

Men who knew the Tetons expected the worst, and they were astonished that wagon trains of settlers were allowed to take the Bozeman Trail. Even though the Tetons harrassed these people, killed some, and ran off their animals, for a time others were allowed to follow them. The official attitude was that there were only a few trouble-makers, and if the troops did not retaliate against them, they would soon abandon their hostility.

At Fort Reno, Carrington found several wagon trains waiting for him to provide a military escort. Carrington merely instructed them to organize and to keep together. They went on without an escort.

At Piney Fork, Carrington selected the site for Fort Phil Kearney and began work on it. Later he sent two companies on to

Courtesy National Park Service

Oglala Sioux burial

the Bighorn to build Fort C. F. Smith. The wagon trains kept coming, even though they were attacked all along the trail. Carrington still could not provide escorts.

The Cheyennes sent a message to Carrington. Did he come in peace or to make war? Carrington replied that he had not come to fight, and some of the Cheyenne chiefs came to the fort for a talk. They warned him that the Sioux were determined to keep the whites out of their lands.

Even though Carrington's troops were attacked any time they left the fort, it was clear that he did not intend to retaliate, and he did not even request a substantial increase in the number of troops. Crows and Cheyennes both offered to serve as scouts against the Tetons, but Carrington sent for Omahas and Winnebagoes from eastern Nebraska, Indians who knew nothing about the Teton country but who were not likely to cause trouble.

In December the number of Tetons around the fort increased, and they constantly harassed the loggers and the troops that guarded them. When a large body of Indians attacked the loggers, Carrington sent Captain William Fetterman and eighty-one men to the rescue. Fetterman had constantly criticized Carrington for his refusal to retaliate against the Indians, and though he had explicit orders not to go past Lodge Trail Ridge, Fetterman foolishly followed a decoy party and led his men into a perfect trap. Not one escaped.

The "Fetterman massacre" shocked the nation, and heads must fall. Carrington was immediately relieved of his command, and charges and counter-charges flew. The forts were secure, and the army could easily have sent in enough troops to subdue the Indians. But public pressure demanded peace. There was to be no military offensive against the peace-loving Indians.

In February of 1867 a new commission came to Fort Laramie to negotiate with the Tetons. It was composed of J. C. Sanborn, General Alfred Sully, and an Indian trader named G. P. Beauvais. The commissioners sent messages and waited. In June Man-Afraid-of-His-Horses and Iron Shell bluntly told them to abandon the forts on the Powder and Bighorn rivers, and then they would talk peace.

In order to keep the friendly Indians at peace, the government sent General W. S. Hancock, late of the Army of the Potomac, to persuade them to remain peaceable. Hancock's idea of accomplishing his peaceful mission was to put on a display of military strength that would overawe the tribes. But he overdid it, for he marched toward the Teton and Cheyenne camps in so threatening a manner the Indians adandoned their belongings and fled.

To Hancock's simple mind this was evidence of hostility, and he knew what to do about that. He ordered the deserted camps burned. The Indians, having lost everything, now began raiding ranches and settlements. This was additional proof of their hostility, and Hancock quickly recognized it as such. He sent George Armstrong Custer and the Seventh Cavalry Regiment after them. Custer, who was anxious for a fight, followed the Oglalas when they went to hunt buffalo, and of course, made

Courtesy Amon Carter Museum, Fort Worth

Lone Wolf, Oglala Sioux warrior

hunting impossible. The Oglalas had few guns, so they were unable to do much more than make a few minor attacks, but their hatred for "Long Hair" Custer grew. In this way Hancock's "peace mission" began a new Indian war.

Another commission was sent to treat with the Tetons and Cheyennes. It included N. G. Taylor of the peace policy, J. B. Sanborn, and the "Hornet" — General W. S. Harney. Harney's presence was an unsubtle reminder of the Bluewater disaster to the Brulés in 1855. The commission reached Fort Laramie in September, 1867, but there were no hostile Tetons there. They sent word that they would probably come next year. While Taylor stood by wringing his hands, Harney and Sanborn grimly asked Sherman how many troops would be needed to give the hostiles a thorough whipping. Sherman, who was committed to upholding the peace policy, replied that not enough troops could be spared from duty in the South. And a war against the Teton Sioux, he said, would be costly.

The continuing uncertain conditions made travel on the Bozeman Trail perilous, except for army supply trains, and civilian travel ceased. The garrisons in the two forts were able to defend themselves but nothing more. When a supply of new breech-loading rifles arrived, however, their rapid fire gave the troops an advantage. A short time later Captain J. N. Powell and a detail of twenty-six men were guarding the woodcutters when a large Sioux war party attacked them. The heavy wagon boxes were arranged to serve as a fort, and in the "Wagon Box" fight the soldiers and woodcutters held off a large number of angry Teton warriors. The significance of the battle, other than in proving the effectiveness of the new guns, was that it finally convinced officials that the Indian troubles were not caused by a small group of renegade Tetons. The government was faced with the choice of accepting peace on the Tetons' terms or sending enough troops to run them out of the Powder river country. Again it followed the advice of the advocates of peace, which was to give in to Teton demands until the Union Pacific Railroad was completed, although the connection between the two was clear only to those who knew nothing of the Teton region.

At any rate, because of the peace policy and its ardent supporters, the government agreed to abandon the two forts and to close the Bozeman Trail. Red Cloud claimed a rare victory. Much has

Courtesy Amon Carter Museum, Fort Worth

White Hawk, Oglala warrior

been made of this Indian victory over the government, but it was, in fact, a victory for the Eastern peace policy advocates as much as for Red Cloud. There were plenty of troops available to crush the Teton and Cheyenne hostiles, but the army was not permitted to beef up its forces for a campaign in the Powder river country.

A new treaty was drawn to replace that of 1865. The Powder river and Bighorn river region was acknowledged as unceded Indian territory closed to whites. When the troops marched out of forts C. F. Smith and Phil Kearny for the last time, the jubilant warriors burned them to the ground then rode down the trail to Fort Laramie. In November, 1868, Red Cloud and other hostile chiefs signed the treaty, which means that they touched the pen while their names were being written.

The Sioux Treaty of 1868 contained a number of provisions that would cause difficulties in the future. Article 2 states:

> The United States agrees that the following district of country, to wit, viz: commencing on the east bank of the Missouri River where the forty-sixth parallel of north latitude crosses the same, thence along low-water mark down the east bank to a point opposite where the northern line of the State of Nebraska strikes the river, thence west across said river, and along the northern line of Nebraska to the one hundred and fourth degree of longitude west from Greenwich, thence north on said meridian to a point where the forty-sixth parallel of north latitude intercepts the same, thence due east along said parallel to place of beginning; and, in addition thereto, all existing reservations on the east bank of said river shall be, and the same is, set apart for the absolute and undisturbed use and occupation of the Indians herein named, and for such friendly tribes or individual Indians as from time to time may be willing, with the consent of the United States, to admit amongst them; and the United States now solemnly agrees that no person except those herein designated and authorized so to do, and except such officers, agents, and employees of the Government as may be authorized to enter upon Indian reservations in discharge of duties enjoined by law, shall ever be permitted to pass over, settle upon, or reside in the territory described in this article, or in such territory as may be added to this reservation for the use of said Indians, and henceforth will and do hereby relinquish all claims or right in and to portion of the United States or territories, except such as embraced within the limits aforesaid, and except as hereinafter provided.
>
> Article 6. If any individual belonging to said tribes of Indians, or legally incorporated with them, being the head of a family, shall desire to commence farming, he shall have the privilege to select, in the presence and with the assistance of the agent, then in charge, a tract of land within said reservation, not exceeding three hundred and twenty acres in extent. . . .

Courtesy Amon Carter Museum, Fort Worth

Ear-of-Corn, Oglala wife of Lone Wolf

Courtesy National Park Service

Treaty of 1868, Fort Laramie, Wyoming. The Indians are Packs-His-Drum, Old-Man-Afraid-of-His-Horses, and Red Bear.

The government agreed to provide schools and a teacher for each thirty children between the ages of six and sixteen. It would also provide one pound of meat and one of flour per day for each Indian for four years. On their part, the tribes had to agree to permit the construction of railroads and military posts being established on their lands.

Article 12. No treaty for the cession of any portion or part of the reservation herein described which may be held in common shall be any validity or force as against the said Indians, *unless executed and signed by a least three-fourths of all the adult male Indians*, occupying or interested in the same; and no cession by the tribe shall be understood or construed in such manner as to deprive, without his consent, any individual member of the tribe of his rights to any tract of land selected by him, as provided in article 6 of this treaty.

Article 16. The United States hereby agrees and stipulates that the country north of the North Platte River and east of the summits of the Big Horn Mountains shall be held and considered to be unceded Indian territory, and also stipulates and agrees that no white person or persons shall be permitted to settle upon or occupy any portion of the same; or without the consent of the

Courtesy National Park Service

Council negotiating Treaty of 1868, Fort Laramie, Wyoming.

Indians first had [been] obtained, to pass through the same: and it is further agreed by the United States that within ninety days after the conclusion of peace with all the lands of the Sioux Nation, the military posts now established in the territory in this article named shall be abandoned, and that the road leading to them and by them to the settlements in the Territory of Montana shall be closed.

The last article abrogated and annulled all earlier treaties and agreements in so far as such treaties and agreements obligated the United States to furnish money, clothing, or other articles to these Indians.

The chiefs who joined Red Cloud in signing the treaty were not aware of all that it stipulated, for they had been told only that it concerned peace and trade. When they learned that they had agreed to leave the Platte and go to live near the Missouri, they were furious. Now they were to be forced to move to a region they detested, and troops with Pawnee scouts drove hunting parties out of their old hunting grounds south of the Platte. Red Cloud must have wondered what had happened to his "victory."

A new commission came to Fort Laramie. Without asking its purpose the Tetons declared that their chiefs were not to sign any more papers — they had been cheated too often already. The commissioners were loaded with presents, but no guns. The issue to be decided was where the Brulé and Oglala agencies were to be located. Neither Red Cloud nor Spotted Tail was willing to leave the Platte, so no agreement was reached.

What kind of war is it, where if we kill the enemy it is death and if he kills us it is a massacre?

Wendell Phillips

CHAPTER 7

The Friends of the Indian and the Peace Policy

Donald E. Worcester

THE FRIENDS of the Indian, a group of Eastern reformers, were delighted when the government agreed to abandon the military posts on the Bozeman Trail, and Red Cloud vowed to abandon the warpath. Yet by the fall of that year the Cheyennes were at war because of treaty violations, and it soon became clear that the peace commission had failed. Other reformers now became concerned over the issue of Indian rights. Colonel Edward Wynkoop, who resigned as agent to the Cheyennes and Arapahos because of the army's attacks on them, declared that there could be no real hope for the Indians until public sympathies were aroused for the Indian "as they have been for the African." Public sympathies were aroused, and the movement for Indian rights was launched.

Concern for Indian rights was not new. From the late 17th century on, the Quakers had been concerned about the mistreatment of the Indians, and other voices were raised occasionally in protest against blatant acts of the government or frontier people. Before the Civil War, however, the anti-slavery crusade attracted most of the humanitarians and reformers, and only a few of them took up the defense of Indian rights. Two of these were men who had experience with Indians — Episcopal Bishop Henry B. Whipple and John Beeson of Oregon. Beeson's protests against abuse of Indians in the Northwest aroused the ire of his Oregon neighbors. When they burned his home and took potshots at him from ambush, he concluded that Oregonians did not appreciate Indian rights' enthusiasts, so he left hastily for the East to carry on his fight where opposition was less forcefully expressed. Both Beeson and Whipple conferred with President Abraham Lincoln concerning the need for revising Indian policy. "If we get through this war and I live," Lincoln replied to Whipple, "this Indian system will be reformed." In 1862 and the following year he urged Congress to reorganize the Indian Bureau, but Congress took only limited action affecting the Mission Indians of California and no others.

When the Civil War ended, many anti-slavery reformers, principally Republicans, were gradually attracted to the cause of the red men. Although these Friends of the Indian were from many walks of life, most of them were immediately convinced that their red brothers' salvation was to become Christian farmers. Most of them were pacifists by nature and abhorred the cruder forms of violence.

Henry Ward Beecher and Wendell Phillips were two energetic reformers who became interested in Indian rights after the Civil War, although their interests were many and varied. Both were articulate, and when they spoke people listened. Phillips was increasingly drawn into the battle for Indian rights after 1868, and he pursued this cause the rest of his life.

A joint committee of Congress investigated the causes of the Sioux and Cheyenne hostilities of 1864-65, and reported to Congress in January, 1867. The committee blamed the troubles on lawless whites and recommended a more peaceful policy toward the Indians. The Red Cloud War and the "Fetterman Massacre" on the Bozeman Trail soon aroused wide public interest. After the congressional committee's report appeared, Lydia Maria Child wrote an impassioned pamphlet, "An Appeal for the Indians." She urged ministers, Quakers, and congressmen to use their influence to obtain justice for all the tribes. Peter Cooper responded, and in May, 1868, called a meeting at Cooper's Union which resulted in creation of an organization to promote the "protection and elevation of the Indians" and to aid the government in preventing frontier wars. The privately organized U.S. Indian Commission, which included Cooper and Beecher as well as other prominent reformers, began sending memorials to Congress blasting "fraudulent treaties" and the "insatiable lust and avarice of unscrupulous men." Bewildered by these outbursts, Congress amended the Indian Appropriation Act, so that for the next two years General Sherman would have control of distributing supplies to the Indians.

Wendell Phillips and other humanitarians, who had an in-

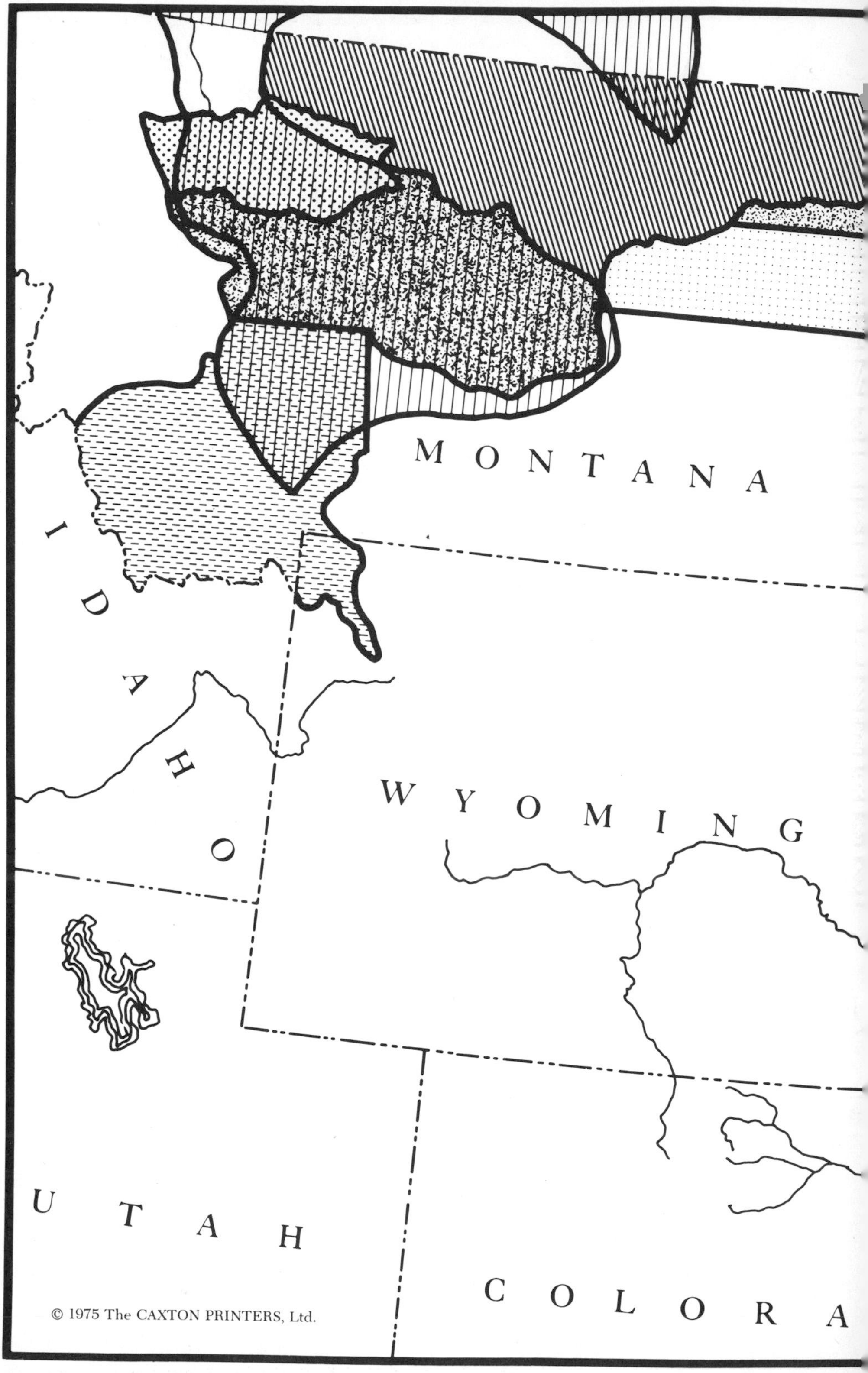
MONTANA
IDAHO
WYOMING
UTAH
COLORA
© 1975 The CAXTON PRINTERS, Ltd.

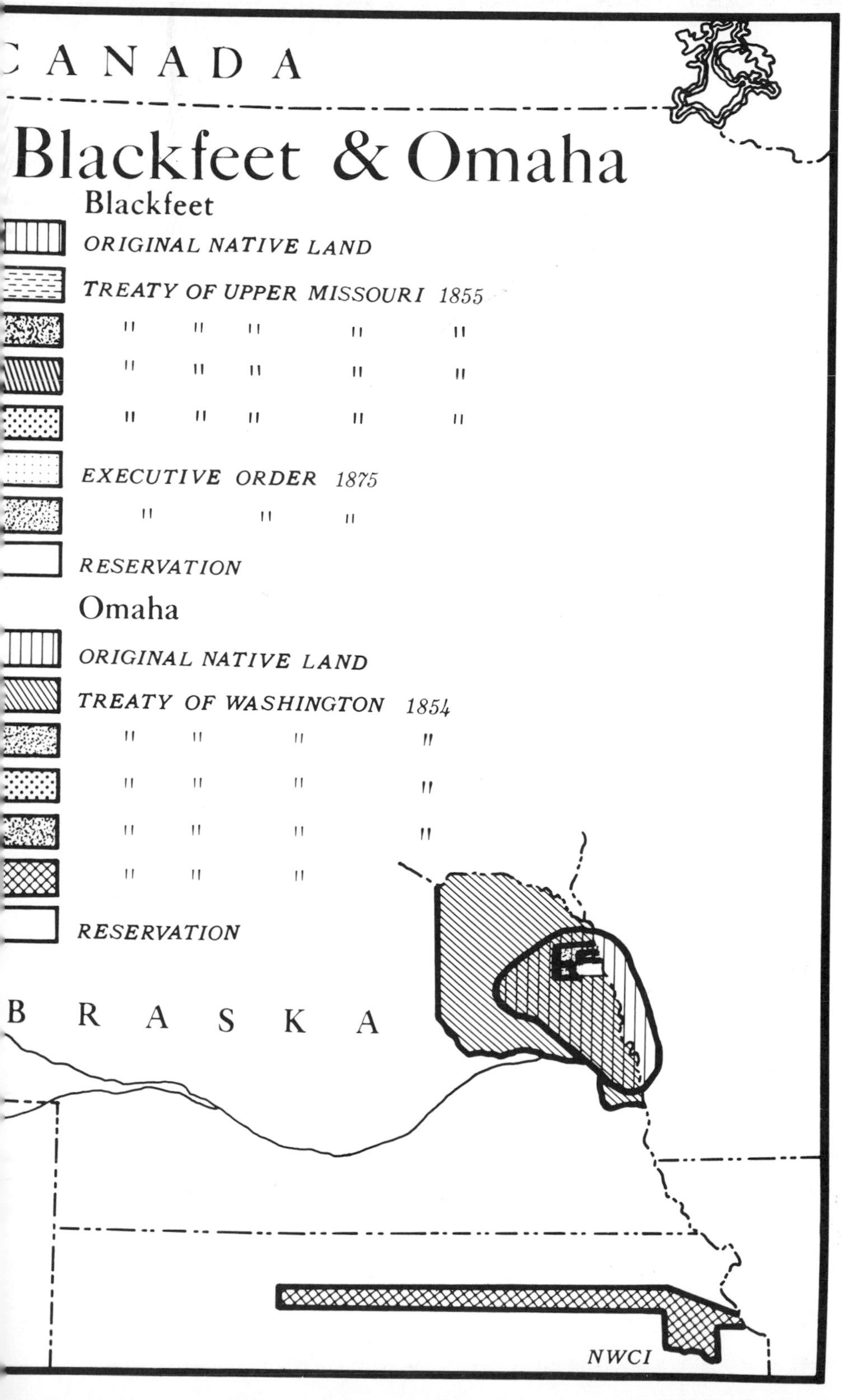
C A N A D A
Blackfeet & Omaha
Blackfeet
ORIGINAL NATIVE LAND
TREATY OF UPPER MISSOURI 1855
" " " " "
" " " " "
" " " " "
EXECUTIVE ORDER 1875
" " "
RESERVATION
Omaha
ORIGINAL NATIVE LAND
TREATY OF WASHINGTON 1854
" " " "
" " " "
" " " "
" " "
RESERVATION
B R A S K A
NWCI

herent distaste for the military, were discouraged when Ulysses S. Grant was elected president, but Grant announced that "All Indians disposed to peace will find the new policy a peace-policy," and they took heart. Grant added that he had great faith in the "humane Quaker plan." His policy followed closely many suggestions Quakers had made, and some Quakers also helped in working out the policy. The result was that Grant's "Peace policy" was often referred to, not necessarily in flattery, as the "Quaker Plan."

Grant's sincerity was reflected in his appointment of Ely S. Parker as Commissioner of Indian Affairs. Parker, who had served as Grant's aide, and who had drafted the terms for Lee's surrender, was a Seneca Indian who as a youth had determined to make a success of the white man's way of life. He had, with difficulty, obtained an education as civil engineer, only to find that Indian civil engineers were not in demand anywhere. By chance he became acquainted with ex-army officer Grant, and the two became friends. When the Civil War began and Grant returned to the army, he managed to overcome army resistance and obtained a commission for Parker.

As Indian Commissioner, Parker called on the Quakers for a list of their members who would be suitable as Indian agents. Grant had decided to carry out his peace policy by using some army officers in the Indian service, though he reserved two superintendencies and seven agencies for the Quakers. Unlike the various groups of Indian rights enthusiasts, who wanted to change the Indians' way of life instantly, the Quakers were convinced that educating and "civilizing" the Indians must be a slow, long-term process that could not be rushed through in four years.

By 1868 the various humanitarian groups, old and new, were in general agreement concerning Indian policy. They agreed that Indians, whether they consented or not, should be confined to reservations and educated, Christianized, and assimilated. Indians must also take up farming. There were some mild objections to these inflexible goals. The Universal Peace Union protested against removing the tribes without their consent and without fair compensation for their lands. The Union also urged amending the Constitution to give Indians citizenship, since the

Senate had excluded them from coverage under the 14th Amendment. But these were only small matters of disagreement.

In 1869 the Friends of the Indian devised plans for a Board of Indian Commissioners to guard all Indian funds. It was to be composed of "ten persons eminent for intelligence and philanthropy," which ruled out everyone except the leaders of the Indian rights crusade. They presented the plan to Congress, and it became law. President Grant dutifully nominated the full board from among the leaders of the Friends of the Indian, for although Ely Parker wanted Indians included on the Board, the humanitarians did not know of any who met their qualifications, and they gave Grant a list to choose from. The chairman of this group of high priests was a Philadelphia merchant named William Welsh, who soon resigned in anger. Indian Commissioner Parker quite properly had refused to turn over control of Indian funds to the Board. The law creating the Board had given it the power to investigate and recommend, nothing more. But to Board chairman Welsh that was a flimsy excuse.

The Board did have the right to travel at government expense, and it took full advantage of this privilege to gather information that could be used against Parker. Welsh accused Parker of wrong-doing on thirteen occasions. Among the misdeeds Welsh listed was that Parker had failed to consult the Board. Part of the problem was that to a man the brethren were convinced that the major step in "civilizing" the Indians was converting them to Christianity. Parker had expressed some sympathy for Indians who preferred to cling to their own religious views, for which Welsh damned him as a "heathen" unfit for his office. He had "exceeded his authority" when Congress failed to pass the Indian Appropriation act in time and he received many warnings that the Indians were starving and on the verge of violence. Parker had purchased supplies on credit and shipped them by rapid transportation at a cost higher than that allowed in the contract. By this action he ended unnecessary suffering and averted a senseless Indian war. A House committee cleared Parker on all counts.

When newspapers attacked the Friends of the Indian for bungling, they quickly blamed their troubles on the "Indian Ring," presumably composed of the men who had contracts for supplying the Indians. There were, in fact, a substantial number of scoundrels who were defrauding both the Indians and the government, but they were "rugged individualists," and there is no evidence that they were organized. The system for supplying the Indians with food and clothing provided many opportunities for large and small pilfering, and too many men, from contractors to agents, could not resist the temptation to enrich themselves at the expense of the Indians. One of Welsh's most persistent charges was that the "Indian Ring" controlled the Interior Department and Ely Parker.

Late in January, 1870, accounts of a massacre of Piegans (Blackfeet) in Montana reached the East. A cavalry force under Colonel E. M. Baker had been sent out to punish some Indians who had stolen horses and had run across a Piegan camp in which there were mostly women and children and old men. Even though these were not the horse thieves he sought, Baker naturally attacked the surprised Indians, and his troops fought well. By the time the "battle" was over they had killed one hundred seventy-three of the enemy. The victory was made less glorious to some when a count of the dead revealed that all but fifteen were women, children, and old men. Fifty of the dead were under twelve years of age.

News of Baker's "victory," coming soon after the peace policy had been announced, was not well received by the Eastern press or by Congress. In the House Aaron Sargent (R., California) moved to amend the army's appropriation bill, so that any time a similar incident occurred, funds would be automatically cut off. Grant urged Congress to provide sufficient funds to carry out treaty obligations, and the amendment was defeated.

The army was badly discredited by the Piegan affair, its admission that many of the dead were women and children, and that it had released more than one hundred women and children when the temperature was 40° below zero because it had insufficient food for them, Wendell Phillips remarked caustically that "I only know the names of three savages upon the Plains — Colonel Baker, General Custer, and at the head of all General Sherman." By the spring of 1870 there was a growing demand that the army's activities be curtailed and that church control be extended over all of the agencies, since the Quakers had proved successful as Indian agents. William Welsh, who was not a Quaker, recommended that the Quakers be given charge of the

Courtesy National Park Service

Blackfoot camp, 1879

whole Indian service because "There is a devotion to this cause in the Society of Friends that I do not find as marked in any other religious body."

In June of 1870 Red Cloud and Spotted Tail again went to Washington. The trip was intended to put them in a good humor for negotiations over the relocation of their agencies. For the first time they learned that the Treaty of 1868 had limited their territory drastically. Red Cloud was angry and wanted to return immediately to his people, but he was taken by way of New York City, where he spoke at Cooper Union. Red Cloud was at his best. In concluding he said, "The riches that we have in this world, Secretary [of the Interior] Cox said truly, we cannot take with us to the next world. Then I wish to know why Commissioners are sent to us who do nothing but rob us and get the riches

Courtesy National Archives

Blackfoot chief Curley Bear, 1903

Courtesy Smithsonian Institution

Piegan Blackfeet, Spotted Eagle, Chief Elk, and Bull Child, taking part in Medicine Lodge ceremony. All three are blowing eaglebone whistles.

of this world away." *The Nation*, commenting on the emotional effect of Red Cloud's talk on the audience, compared it to "nothing so much as the public recital of a fugitive slave in former years." The Massachussetts Indian Commission was founded the same month to campaign for Indian rights. Public sympathy for Indians had been aroused by the Piegan massacre, and it was considerably increased by Red Cloud and the other Sioux in New York City.

Not all Americans agreed with the Friends of the Indian that frontier people were all inhumane and callous. James M. Ashley of Ohio became governor of Montana Territory in 1868 and became familiar with frontier conditions. He soon regarded the Indians as the aggressors and the settlers as innocent victims. Ashley, who had been an anti-slavery leader before the Civil War, should logically have joined the Friends of the Indian, but he had learned something of frontier conditions, while they had not. Attacks on the settlers by Eastern humanitarians, such as Wendell Phillips, aroused Ashley to reply. In the October 1, 1870, issue of *The National Standard* he blasted the Indians in a way that made his constituents rejoice. But editor Aaron Powell was not amused, and he wrote a reply to Ashley. He feared, he said, that the "western atmosphere" had affected Ashley's political views and very possibly made him "unsuitable" for his present office. Evidently Powell was more convincing than Ashley, for the latter was soon replaced by a confirmed and trusted advocate of the peace policy.

The Friends of the Indian knew nothing at all about Indians, but they were certain that they understood the "Indian problem" better than anyone else, and they did not entertain notions to the contrary. They were inspired by a spirit of chivalry, which meant essentially that they were prone to interfere in other people's affairs. The brethern became convinced that the chiefs were obstacles to progress, and so must be destroyed. Congress, taken in by their impressive if meaningless arguments, passed an act that did away with the chiefs' authority and with tribal organization, though it violated many treaties in the process. The Sioux were especially dependent on their tribal organization and on their chiefs, for it was the only system they knew.

Fortunately for the Sioux, they were unaware of the various absurd plans the brethren concocted for them. One was an elabo-

Courtesy National Archives

Red Cloud delegation: Red Dog, Little Wound, John Bridgeman (interpreter), Red Cloud, American Horse, and Red Shirt. Oglala Sioux, 1876.

rate scheme to scatter them widely over the East, with each state receiving its quota. Happily for the Sioux, neither President Grant nor Secretary of the Interior Carl Schurz would listen to this monstrous plan.

The Friends of the Indian were convinced that all men involved in the business of providing for the Indians were dishonest. There is no doubt that there was much fraud, but all agents were by no means dishonest or ineffective. The freighters were the worst offenders. They were paid per one hundred pounds per one hundred miles. They could not always falsify weights, but no one had any idea of the mileage from one place to another in the Teton country, and here was where the best opportunities for fraud lay. An odometer was attached to the wheel of one wagon to measure the distance actually traveled. At night one wagon boss had the wheel raised and spun a few hundred miles, but the distance he submitted was so outrageously exaggerated that the army was ordered to determine the distance.

Because of the growing demand that other churches become involved in Indian affairs, Grant instructed Ely Parker to explain his policy to other denominations, so that they as well as the Quakers could nominate agents from their congregations. Congress passed an act which assigned the selection of agents to various churches, and it fell to the Episcopalians to provide an agent for the Oglalas. By 1872 thirteen different denominations were in charge of seventy-three agencies. The new policy was not much of an improvement, sad to say, for one of the church-selected agents, who attended church twice on Sundays and twice more during the week, and in between times spent hours conferring with ministers, was indicted on thirty-two counts of fraud, larceny, forgery, and similar misdeeds. For eight years the churches chose the most pious of men to serve the government and the Indians in a spirit of true Christianity, only to discover that these men were not proof against temptation. Carl Schurz moved gradually to eliminate the churches from the process of selecting agents, and the churches were relieved to be able to give the responsibility back to the government.

The new agents did not always get on well with their wards. Red Cloud constantly complained of his agent no matter who the agent was. Spotted Tail simply took charge of his agent and issued orders from the agent's office. Red Cloud and Spotted Tail both resisted the effort to move their agencies from the Platte until their rations were cut off. The Oglalas' Episcopal agent was virtually confined to the stockade around his headquarters, for if he rode out he was surrounded by menacing warriors who demanded to know where he was going. In 1872 the new Oglala agent, Dr. J. W. Daniels, tried to persuade the Oglalas to move to White river, near the Missouri. Red Cloud refused. Another trip to Washington distracted him, and while he was away the Oglalas were moved. Spotted Tail's Brulé agency was located on the White river, two hundred twenty-five miles west of the Missouri. The only way to deliver rations was by opening a wagon road from Fort Laramie. Spotted Tail warned that if the wagon train crossed the Platte to the north it meant war. The Brulé goods were delivered to the Red Cloud agency, and the Brulés got them there.

Courtesy Amon Carter Museum, Fort Worth

Crow Agency buildings, Yellowstone River, 1871

Each winter the "non-treaty" Sioux, a polite term used to designate the "hostiles" while the peace policy was in effect, came to the agencies to be fed during the winter months and to replenish their supply of ammunition. The Friends of the Indian were at the apex of their power. In February, 1874, while the Board of Indian Commissioners was announcing that the peace policy was an "unqualified success," the agents to the Brulés and Oglalas were calling for troops to be stationed at their agencies, which suggested that the "success" of the peace policy was somewhat less than "unqualified." The Commissioners sent Bishop Hare to investigate the two suspect agents. He recognized the dangers and agreed that troops should be stationed at both agencies. The Friends of the Indian bitterly attacked the bishop for his defection from the cause, but he was undisturbed by the clamor. He warned President Grant that if he allowed Custer to march into the Black Hills as planned white men would follow, and the Tetons would surely take the warpath. The expedition was a blatant violation of the Treaty of 1868, and rumors of its coming had the Tetons in a frenzy.

By 1874 both Congress and the public were becoming disenchanted with the peace policy, so the War Department allowed the Black Hills expedition to march. Presumably Custer's pur-

Courtesy Amon Carter Museum, Fort Worth

Sioux shooting steers at beef issue, Pine Ridge, S.D.

pose was to survey routes and sites for military posts. In 1859-60, however, Captain W. F. Raynolds had made an excellent survey of the Black Hills which provided all of the information needed. Custer took a number of "scientists" (gold miners) with him, and his report was concerned more with gold than with routes. He could not wait until his command returned to Fort Abraham Lincoln to announce the good news. He sent "Lonesome" Charlie Reynolds on a dangerous journey through Teton country with the terse message — gold in the Black Hills!

Western newspapers carried the story far and wide and parties of miners were quickly organized and on their way to the Hills. The army was charged with keeping unauthorized whites out of Indian lands. The troops stopped some parties and removed others, but by the spring of 1875 there were too many miners for the army to check unless reinforcements were sent.

The Tetons were furious. To restrain them, since it could not restrain the whites who were invading Sioux lands by the hundreds, the army built a post near Red Cloud agency. Again there were rumors that the Tetons would be sent to Indian Territory,

Courtesy Amon Carter Museum, Fort Worth

Sioux skinning a steer after beef issue, Pine Ridge Agency, S.D.

and these rumors intensified their rage. At Red Cloud agency Dr. J. J. Savile wanted to put up a flagpole. The chiefs told him bluntly that they wanted no flagpole — it reminded them of the army. Savile blithely ignored them and went ahead with his plan. The angry Oglalas rushed in and chopped his flagpole into firewood. Savile was so frightened he sent a frantic call for troops.

The commander at Camp Robinson sent Lieutenant Emmet Crawford and twenty-six men to see what the trouble was about. Crawford saw an enormous throng of Indians surging around the stockade while others dashed up from all directions. At the same time the Indians discovered the troops and surrounded them menacingly. Young-Man-Afraid-of-His-Horses and other friendly Oglalas rescued the helpless soldiers and got them into the stockade, while enraged warriors tried to set fire to it. Man-Afraid-of-His-Horses and Red Cloud tried to calm their people, but the "non-treaty Sioux" tore down their tepees and headed for the Powder river country in an ugly mood.

When calm was restored, agent Savile announced to the Oglalas that they must be counted, and he added that there would be no more rations until the count was completed. Being counted was mysterious and frightening, but many of the Oglalas came in at once, and the others reluctantly followed. The count proved that there were nine thousand of them at the agency, although earlier estimates had placed the number no higher than six thousand five hundred.

The winter of 1874 was one of great suffering at the agencies, for the fall steamer bringing supplies was delayed and frozen in all winter, far from its destination. Crowds of starving Indians surrounded the forts, begging for food, yet the Secretary of the Interior refused to let the army supply rations, because that would mean acknowledging his staff's inefficiency. Better the Indians should starve than make such an admission. The Tetons became desperate.

In 1875 the Indian Homestead Act allowed Indians who gave up their tribal way of life to acquire land under the homestead law that previously applied only to whites. This law, which had very little effect on the Indians, was simply another reflection of the misguided conviction that Indians should adopt the whites' concept of private property.

In the spring of 1875 the Indian Bureau brought a number of chiefs to Washington to convince them that they must sell the Black Hills, but they refused to act without consulting their people. They were sent back to the agencies to await a special commission that would arrive in the autumn. Before returning to his agency Red Cloud demanded a new agent — not a "praying" one or an army officer. He wanted, he said, a rich agent who would not be tempted to steal from the Indians. The Friends of the Indian looked at Red Cloud and shook their heads in sorrow. He was a great disappointment. In 1870 they had convinced themselves that he would, by some unexplained miracle, become a good make-believe Christian farmer in their own image. Here he was, still resisting all they were trying to do for him and his people. Lesser men would have become discouraged, but not the brethren.

In September the commission to convince the Tetons that, for their own good, they should part with the Black Hills, arrived at Camp Robinson. The Secretary of the Interior instructed the commissioners to represent the Indians as well as the govern-

Chief
Man Afraid
Horses and his Tepee taken at
e Agency S. D. Jan 17th 1891

Courtesy National Archives

Young-Man-Afraid-of-His-Horses at Pine Ridge Agency, 1891

ment, and while performing this delicate balancing act, to persuade them to give up the Powder river and the Bighorn river country as well. Part of the purchase price would be used to pay for food and clothing supplied them. When the commissioners arrived at Chadron Creek, a considerable distance from Camp Robinson, they found twenty thousand Tetons awaiting them. The warriors were quarrelling violently among themselves, and the prospects for a profitable meeting with them were slim indeed.

The Treaty of 1868 had specified that in any future land cession, three-fourths of the adult males must approve it for it to be valid. The commissioners rode up in an army ambulance with an escort of cavalry, expecting to line up the Sioux for their signatures. Brulé and Oglala warriors, dressed and painted and mounted on war ponies, dashed menacingly around the cavalrymen as if eager for battle. As the commissioners stepped out of the ambulance, Little Big Man, brandishing a Winchester carbine in his right hand and holding several cartridges between the fingers of his left hand, whipped his pony into a run toward the frightened commissioners, shouting that he was going to kill them for trying to steal Teton lands. The army officers hustled the commissioners into the ambulance, and the cavalry surrounded it. Spotted Tail and Man-Afraid-of-His-Horses and their trusted Brulé and Oglala warriors closed in around the cavalry and escorted them and the ashen-faced commissioners to safety, while thousands of angry warriors crowded around them. It was a close call, for one random shot could have started a furious battle.

When they got safely back to Camp Robinson and their courage returned, the commissioners sent for twenty of the leading chiefs. There was no more silly talk about getting the consent of three-fourths of that ill-mannered bunch of savages. Spotted Tail asked the commissioners to put their offer in writing. They offered four hundred thousand dollars a year for mining rights in the Black Hills or six million dollars to purchase the region. The chiefs rejected both offers. Some thought that settled the matter.

This time the fragile peace was shattered beyond repair. The view from Washington was that a pack of shiftless, greedy aborigines was standing in the way of American progress. The government had politely asked them to step aside, and they had stubbornly refused. Now it was time to teach them humility and obedience. Late in November, 1875, President Grant, the secretaries of War and the Interior, and the Commissioner of Indian Affairs conferred. Reflecting on the militant mood of Congress and the nation, they agreed to jettison the peace policy.

A terse command went out to all of the agencies — tell the hostiles to return to the agencies by the end of January, or the army would drive them back. Some officials were sure that the order would also frighten the Tetons into giving up the Black Hills and Powder river country, but the army was more optimistic. Having been held back for eight years by the peace policy, the army ordered three columns of cavalry and infantry prepared to march against the Tetons in the spring. Officers who knew the Teton country were aware that the order was a simple declaration of war, for the Indians could not possibly comply with it even if they were disposed to do so. Because of the peace policy, the hostiles were not likely to show much concern over the order.

Courtesy Amon Carter Museum, Fort Worth

Sioux chief American Horse

The order to the hostiles reached the agencies shortly before Christmas. Runners set out in severe winter weather. Because of the hard going, some of them did not reach the hostile camps before the period of grace had expired. It made no difference. Without waiting to learn if the hostiles had complied or were trying to comply, the army launched its campaign. On March 1, General George Crook marched his command north from Fort Fetterman in Wyoming.

Thousands of hostiles were wintering at the agencies as usual, and they learned that the army was preparing to attack their friends in the distant camps. As soon as the weather improved, hundreds of them headed for the Powder river country. In May Generals Terry and Custer marched from Fort Abraham Lincoln, near Bismarck, while General Gibbon started down the Yellowstone from Montana. The stage was set for Crook's defeat on the Rosebud a week before disaster struck the Seventh Cavalry Regiment on the Little Bighorn. In place of the sporadic individual combats of earlier days, the Sioux and their allies adopted new tactics, the attack in overwhelming numbers. This new manner of attack was responsible for the defeat of both Crook and Custer. But the Tetons were never able to remain united, and for them the sun was already setting.

After the battle the various bands scattered, and troops dogged their trails until they surrendered or returned to the agencies. Sitting Bull led his band across the border to "Grandmother's Land" — Canada — but eventually most of them returned to the agencies and surrendered, although descendants of others still live in Canada.

The Northern Cheyennes, who had taken part in the defeat of Custer, were surprised and attacked in winter camp, and they lost everything they owned. When the Cheyenne Little Chief surrendered to General Nelson A. Miles in January, 1877, he exclaimed, "We are weak, compared with you and your forces; we are out of ammunition; we cannot make a rifle, a round of ammunition, or a knife; in fact we are at the mercy of those who are taking possession of our country; your terms are harsh and cruel, but we are going to accept them and place ourselves at your mercy."

News of Custer's shocking defeat convinced the nation that a serious war was on. The army had claimed all along that it could

Courtesy Godfrey Family Photographs

War chief Gall, Hunkpapa Sioux who took part in the defeat of Custer

Courtesy National Park Service

Sioux warrior, Rain-in-the-Face, who became famous owing to Longfellow's poem, "The Revenge of Rain-in-the-Face." He fought against Custer.

Crow Scout Curley.

Curley

Photo From Life By

David F. Barry

Photographer of

NOTED INDIANS

Superior, Wisconsin

GENERAL CUSTER'S Crow Indian scout, the only person who escaped from the Custer fight. Curley was of the Crow Indian tribe. He made for the timber and headed for the Big Horn river where he joined General Terry and informed him that General Custer and his soldiers had all been killed by the Sioux. Curley didn't wait to see the finish of that battle which lasted about 35 minutes. Curley simply guessed the result that he had reported to General Terry. Seeing the thousands of Sioux Indians, he decided what the result would be and never stopped to see that awful slaughter.

On the tenth anniversary, June 25, 1886, Chief Gall at the Battle Field told Curley, "if he had not sneaked away, he would not be there today."

Curley died a few years ago at the Crow Agency in Montana.

D. F. BARRY

Crow scout Curley by David F. Barry, Photographer

handle the hostiles with no great difficulty. Now there was a frantic search for a scapegoat. The army tried first to blame the Indian Office for giving false reports and for allowing the hostiles to leave the agencies. The truth was that army officers stationed at posts near the agencies were well aware that the hostiles were leaving in large numbers. Overconfident, the army had looked forward to a successful Indian war with expectation.

The Indians who remained at the agencies were worried. The government had taken the Black Hills, which had been promised them forever, and then started a war for no apparent reason. After nearly a decade of the peace policy this was frightening, for they could not imagine what the government intended to do next. There were the usual threats that their rations would be cut off, and that they would be moved to Indian Territory.

The oft-repeated threat to cut off rations to the Tetons was not simply to scare them, for Congress was out of patience and took no action on the appropriation bill for feeding them. The Indians, because of their willfulness, deserved punishment. Starvation would make them more amenable to losing the Black Hills and the hunting grounds to the west. For the record, of course, Congress wanted the matter handled in an outwardly legal manner.

In July the army demanded that the agencies be transferred from the Indian Office to the War Department, and the transfer was made. Army officers now became agents. This move also frightened the Sioux, for they knew that the army itched for an excuse to avenge Custer's defeat.

In August Congress passed the appropriation bill but stipulated that this was the last food for the Tetons until they ceded the lands it demanded. Congress also appropriated money for yet another commission to persuade the chiefs to sign the new agreement, and peace policy leaders were named to serve on it. The so-called agreement was simply that the Tetons were to give up their lands without protest.

The new council began with Bishop Whipple's sincere prayer for the indians, which, considering the commissioners' intentions, gave the meeting an unintended sardonic air from the outset. Then the commissioners informed the chiefs that for their own good they must move to the Missouri river or to Indian Territory, and they must relinquish their claims to the Black

Courtesy Amon Carter Museum, Fort Worth

Sitting Bull addressing council at Fort Yates.

Hills, Powder river, and Bighorn hunting grounds. The Secretary of the Interior had suspected that the Tetons might not recognize the many advantages to them in signing the agreement, and for this reason he had named Assistant Attorney-General Gaylord to the commission. When Bishop Whipple concluded his prayer Gaylord added an "amen" which was simply a blunt warning that if they did not sign they would surely starve.

Spotted Tail stalked out of the council in anger, but Standing Elk replied to Gaylord. "Your words are like a man knocking me on the head with a club," he said. "What you have said has put great fear into us. Whatever we do, wherever we go, we are expected to say Yes!Yes! Yes!—and when we don't agree at once to what you ask of us in council, you always say, You won't get anything to eat! You won't get anything to eat!"

The commissioners neglected to mention the Treaty of 1868, and the Tetons apparently had forgotten its provisions concerning acceptance of land cessions by three-fourths of the adult males. Now the government was willing to accept an "agreement" that a few chiefs had been bullied into signing. Later a Dakota lawyer would make the inspired suggestion that since in 1876 the government had violated the Treaty of 1868, it had established a precedent and could violate the treaty any time it was convenient to do so!

At the council one warrior had expressed fear that the army would seize all of the guns and ponies. The commissioners assured him that his fears were nonsense, that no Indian property would be taken from them. But General Sheridan was convinced that the agency Indians needed a lesson in humility, and the way to provide that was to take their guns and ponies and make them camp close to the agency headquarters where it would be easy to keep watch over them. Red Cloud refused to move his camp from Chadron Creek. He awoke one morning to find his camp surrounded by cavalry and hated Pawnee scouts and his pony herd gone. He and others had to lay down their arms and begin the long walk to the agency.

The troops drove the ponies, more than seven hundred of them, to Fort Laramie and sold them for less than five dollars each. Many of these animals had been given to Oglalas the previous year in payment for giving up their right to hunt in Nebraska. At that time the same animals were valued at one hundred twenty dollars a head.

In 1877 Congress ordered the Brulé and Oglala supplies delivered at the Missouri river, with the usual blunt warning that there would be no more until they moved there. General Crook was furious, for he had informed the Indian Bureau in unmistakable language that the Tetons hated the Missouri region and were determined not to move there. Crook secretly asked T. H. Tibbles, a one-time scout and genuine friend of the Indians, to warn Spotted Tail to refuse to discuss moving and to make some threatening gesture that would intimidate the men from Washington. Tibbles gave this advice to the Brulé chief.

The new commissioners arrived in May, with the Reverend Alfred Riggs as interpreter. The Brulés came to the council in war paint, and they listened stolidly as the bald-headed commissioner told them how much better off they would be if they lived near the Missouri. The government, he said, would send them horses, wagons, plows, and cattle.

Spotted Tail rose to reply. "I have made many treaties with the men who come from Washington," he said. "Never has one of these been kept. All the men who come from Washington are liars, but the worst liars among them are the bald-headed ones. You're a bald-headed old liar! This last treaty must be kept." He waved a copy of the treaty. "If everything here is not on wheels

Courtesy Amon Carter Museum, Fort Worth

Omaha village

and moving inside of ten days, I shall turn my young men loose, and they will make a desert of all the country between here and the Platte."

The commissioners turned pale and hastily departed. The Indian Bureau brought Red Cloud and Spotted Tail to Washington once more, to put them in a more pliant mood. The two chiefs conferred with President Rutherford B. Hayes, who promised them that if they would move to the Missouri for the winter, in the spring they could choose sites for their agencies. The Secretary of the Interior's report for 1878 stated that "The Indians were found to be quite determined to move westward, and the promise of the Government in that respect was faithfully kept."

To make room for the Brulés the government callously dispossessed the much-abused Poncas of their reservation, homes, and farms, and carted them off to Indian Territory. By error the Ponca land had been consigned to the Sioux in 1868, so the Poncas were the losers. Conditions on the trip and in Indian Territory were so bad that within a year the Poncas had been reduced from seven hundred ten to four hundred thirty. When Chief Standing Bear's last son died, he and a small group loaded the body on a wagon and headed north. They found a temporary refuge among their relatives, the Omahas, near Decatur, Nebraska. The War Department ordered General Crook to arrest

Courtesy Amon Carter Museum, Fort Worth

Betsy Dick, noted Omaha woman

them and return them to Indian Territory. Again Crook called on T. H. Tibbles, this time to lead the battle to save Standing Bear and to recover the Ponca lands.

Tibbles secured the aid of a brilliant young Omaha lawyer, John L. Webster, in seeking a writ of habeas corpus for Standing Bear. Before Judge Dundy's court reached a decision, Standing Bear spoke. He held out his hand. "That hand is not the color of yours," he said, "but if I pierce it I shall feel pain. The blood that

Courtesy Smithsonian Institution

Omaha, Joseph La Flesche (seated, second from left) and others in council, about 1883-1884.

will flow from mine is the same color as yours. I am a man. The same God made us both."

He spoke of his struggles to return to his own land and the graves of his ancestors. "But a man bars the passage. He is a thousand times more powerful than I. Behind him I see soldiers as numerous as leaves of the trees. They will obey that man's orders. I too must obey his orders. If he says that I cannot pass, I cannot. The long struggle will have been in vain. My wife and child and I must return and sink beneath the flood. We are weak and faint and sick. I cannot fight."

Judge Dundy wiped the tears from his eyes while General Crook covered his face with his hands. Judge Dundy declared that an Indian is a person within the laws of the United States and therefore had the right to appeal to the courts. With a shout everyone in the room rose to his feet. Crook rushed to grasp Standing Bear's hand, and the others quickly followed. This was,

Courtesy Smithsonian Institution

Omaha earth lodge, 1890s

for all Indians, a momentous decision, but it took Tibbles two years of constant compaigning before the president finally appointed a committee composed of Generals Crook and Miles and others to investigate the Poncas. Their report induced Congress to pass a law on March 3, 1881, giving individual Poncas the right to choose the land they preferred and reimbursing them for their losses. Among those who supported a petition for returning the Poncas to their lands was Senator Henry M. Teller of Colorado, who would later serve as Secretary of the Interior. Tibbles was penniless and exhausted, but when the Boston Committee asked him to draft a severalty bill to allot land to individual Indians, he complied. He believed that his draft was the basis for the famous Dawes Severalty Act of 1887.

By 1880 there were a number of organizations dedicated to settling the "Indian problem." Among them were the Indian Rights Association, the Indian Humanitarian Association, the Indian Defense Association, the Boston Indian Citizenship Committee and several others. The leaders of these societies held closed meetings each year to decide on the Indian policy

Courtesy National Archives

Indian delegation with agents on White House grounds, before 1877

they would persuade Congress to follow. When Congress opened, a large group of Friends of the Indian met in Washington in the parlor of the Riggs House. This was a public meeting to announce plans and policies, and members of Congress and occasionally the head of the Indian Bureau and even Cabinet members were invited to attend. Anyone who was bold enough to disagree with the brethren was eased out and not asked to return.

Retired minister Dr. T. A. Bland was one of those who recognized nonsense when he heard it and said so, and was quickly ostracized. He organized an Indian rights association of his own and began writing for *The Council Fire,* which was founded in Washington in 1878. In its pages he carried on a campaign of opposition to the policies of the powerful Friends of the Indian. Bland visited Spotted Tail, Red Cloud, and other chiefs and acquired first-hand information as to what the Indians wanted and needed. The orthodox groups were not at all interested in what the Indians might think was best for them. To the leaders of these groups their own views were all that mattered. How could Indians know as well as they what was good for them?

The yearly meetings in Riggs House were conducted in a

thoroughly religious atmosphere. Those present enjoyed nothing more than when they could sit and sniffle softly while some Indian boy sang well-known hymns in his native language. This and many similar activities of the Friends of the Indian were certainly not injurious to the Indians. The danger came when the brethren devised their Indian policy for the coming year. Because these high priests of Indian rights were influential men, few of the Indian Bureau officials dared oppose them openly. Congress, too, was usually amenable to their wishes, for they maintained a permanent secretary in Washington, and C. C. Pointer knew influential men in government and how to convince them. One of the pioneer lobbyists in America, he was as effective in defeating bills sponsored by Indian rights groups other than his own as he was in persuading Congress to pass the bills he presented.

When Grover Cleveland was elected president, the Friends of the Indians descended on the new Secretary of the Interior, L. Q. C. Lamar of Mississippi. They spouted the usual nonsense about the evils of tribal organization. Lamar, an ex-Confederate officer, replied coolly but with finality. "Gentlemen," he said, "the tribe is the Indian's natural political condition, and he should by no means be removed from that condition until he is fitted for a higher one." This statement temporarily ended the government's policy of destroying the chiefs' authority and the tribal organization.

The brethren next turned their ire against the squawmen living on the reservations. Since these men had married according to Indian custom, they were wallowing in sin. Some agents and commissioners also hated the squawmen, for they read newspapers and kept the chiefs informed as to what was being planned in Washington. They were, in fact, extremely helpful to the tribes in their painful adjustment to reservation life, and they had been urged to remain with the Indians for that purpose. In 1883 the Dawes commission learned the truth about the squawmen and their halfbreed children. Most of them had farms, and they were ever willing to serve without pay in any project to improve conditions for their tribe.

In 1883 A. K. Smiley, a member of the Board of Indian Commissioners, invited other board members to the Mountain House at Lake Mohonk, New York. Smiley and his wife, who were

Chief Two Strike
Chief Crow Dog
Chief High Hawk
Leaders of The Hostile Indians
at Pine Ridge Agcy S.D.
During the late Sioux War

Courtesy Amon Carter Museum, Fort Worth

George Bartlett with Sioux chiefs Two Strikes, Crow Dog, and High Hawk, Pine Ridge.

Quakers, owned and operated the hotel, and they made their guests so comfortable that they were loath to leave. After several delightful days of talking about Indian welfare and nothing else, Smiley suggested that the meeting be an annual event. His guests gladly agreed. Thus were born the famed Lake Mohonk Conferences. Each year in summer or early autumn, the Smileys played host to a select group of visitors. It was at these affairs that high-minded and thoroughly Christian men and women, who were totally uninformed about Indians, designed government Indian policy. In this fashion a small but vocal and articulate group of reformers brought the Indian question to the forefront. In 1864 Indian problems were seldom mentioned in the press. Twenty years later, thanks to efforts of the Friends of the Indian, they had become the greatest domestic issue facing America.

The Friends of the Indian occasionally and accidentally did something that was actually beneficial for the Indians, but not often. They equated their great interest in Indian affairs with deep understanding. Few congressmen were much better in-

Courtesy Amon Carter Museum, Fort Worth

Sioux chief Gall and son, possibly at Carlisle Indian School

Courtesy Amon Carter Museum, Fort Worth

Daughters of Sioux chief Gall

formed concerning Indians, and they allowed themselves to be charmed into unwise actions by the moving nonsense the brethren inflicted on them. One important example was when Congress, dazzled by the Friends' logic, passed a bill outlawing tribal organization and chieftains. In doing so, it violated scores of treaties and did irreparable harm to many tribes which were clinging desperately to what was left of their past way of life.

At the Lake Mohonk conference of 1885 the delegates agreed on an all-out crusade to root "Indianism" out of the Indians. Their plan for disposing of "surplus" Indian lands, forcing the Indians to farm, and giving them education and citizenship seemed so excellent that it could not be allowed to fail simply because the Indians refused to see the beauty in it.

The brethren had other improvements in mind for the Indians. After Crow Dog murdered Spotted Tail in 1881, he was convicted and sentenced to hang. The Supreme Court, however, ruled that the courts had no jurisdiction over Indians on reservations, and Crow Dog was set free. The brethren were astonished and irate at this decision, and they determined to set up Indian courts with Indian judges, so that wrongdoers would not go unpunished. Congress created the courts as desired, but the Sioux continued to rely on tribal custom for settling disputes within the tribe. Among the Indian agents, only McLaughlin was enthusiastic about the plan. He set up an Indian court at Standing Rock. The only problem — how to assess fines — was solved by obliging the culprits to pay them in weapons. Most of the offenders were members of Sitting Bull's hostiles, who lorded it over the tamer reservation Indians. As a result the latter were greatly amused when the Indian judge fined Sitting Bull one Winchester and two tomahawks. Before long the Standing Rock court had collected an impressive arsenal, and since most of the weapons were taken from Sitting Bull's band, the Hunkpapas were generally satisfied with the court and its penalties. At the Cheyenne River agency, where Captain Schwan had established a tradition of strict discipline characteristic of the Prussian army, the penalties were assessed in days at hard labor, and the Cheyenne River Sioux were much less enthusiastic about the court than were those at Standing Rock.

The Tetons were now broken and defenseless, at the mercy of the government and its advisers. The Friends of the Indian

Courtesy National Archives

Sioux Indian police, Pine Ridge Agency, 1882

were in the ascendant, and saw their way clear at last to carry out their plans by methods which could not fail. They had tried to give the Tetons the satisfying life of hard work and farming, and had met nothing but bull-headed resistance. This had convinced them that their gentle methods were a waste of time. They had learned their mistake, and now they grimly agreed how to correct it. It was time for the Tetons to be taught a much-needed, though certainly painful, lesson in obedience.

The riches of that we have in this world, Secretary Cox said truly, we cannot take with us to the next world. Then I wish to know why commissioners are sent out to us who do nothing but rob us and get the riches of this world away from us?

Red Cloud

CHAPTER 8

THE SIOUX LAND GRAB

Donald E. Worcester

IN 1878 RED CLOUD and Spotted Tail were able to locate their agencies where they wanted them, at Pine Ridge and Rosebud. Although the Tetons had lost the Black Hills and the Powder river-Bighorn lands, they still held the right of perpetual occupancy of the Great Sioux Reserve. As in the past, however, treaty guarantees were slender reeds to lean on, even in fair weather, and in Indian treaties "perpetual" had come to mean something considerably less than forever. The rest of South Dakota had filled up with whites, who now cast jealous eyes across the Missouri at the 35,000 square miles of Sioux lands. Again they raised demands that the Tetons be sent to Indian Territory. Congress had never forgiven the Sioux for fighting to save their hunting grounds, and some congressmen were willing to remove them from their reservations. The Friends of the Indian, somewhat subdued by the popular hostility toward the Tetons, said nothing or agreed that it would be a good idea to move them to Indian Territory.

In 1882 R. F. Pettigrew, delegate to Congress from Dakota Territory, suggested to Secretary of the Interior Henry M. Teller that he inquire to see if the Tetons would sell some of their land. Teller was a westerner, and although as a congressman he had supported the Poncas and opposed a severalty act because he knew that the Indians preferred tribal to private ownership of land, as Secretary of the Interior his views of Indians rights to land had become those of the Dakota land-boomers. He appointed a commission to make inquiry: Newton Edmunds, a Dakota politician, Judge Peter C. Shannon, chief justice of the Dakota Supreme Court and a typical frontier jurist, and James H. Teller of Ohio, whose only qualification was that his brother was

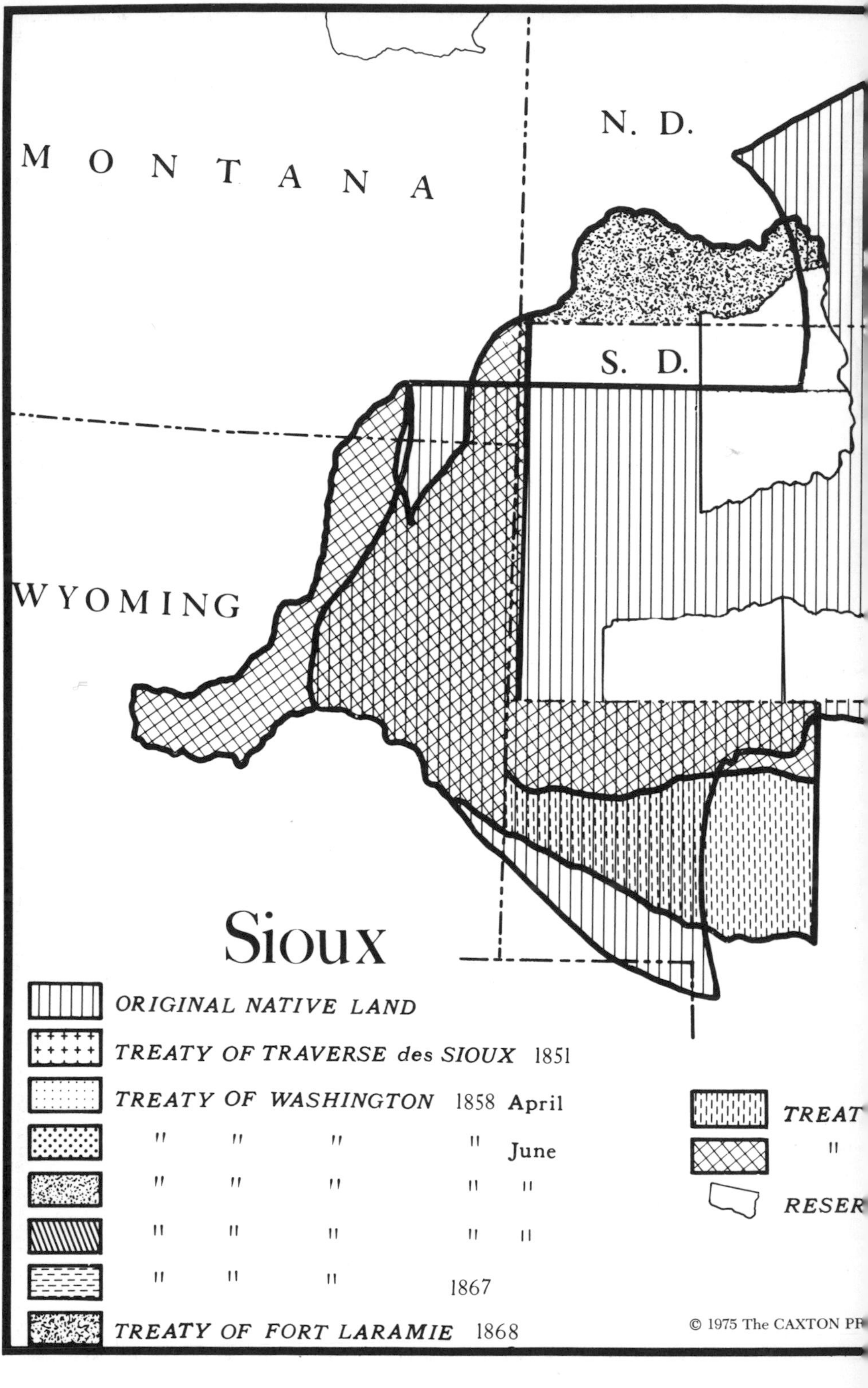
N. D.
MONTANA
S. D.
WYOMING
Sioux
ORIGINAL NATIVE LAND
TREATY OF TRAVERSE des SIOUX 1851
TREATY OF WASHINGTON 1858 April
" " " " June
" " " " "
" " " " "
" " " 1867
TREATY OF FORT LARAMIE 1868
TREAT
"
RESER
© 1975 The CAXTON PR

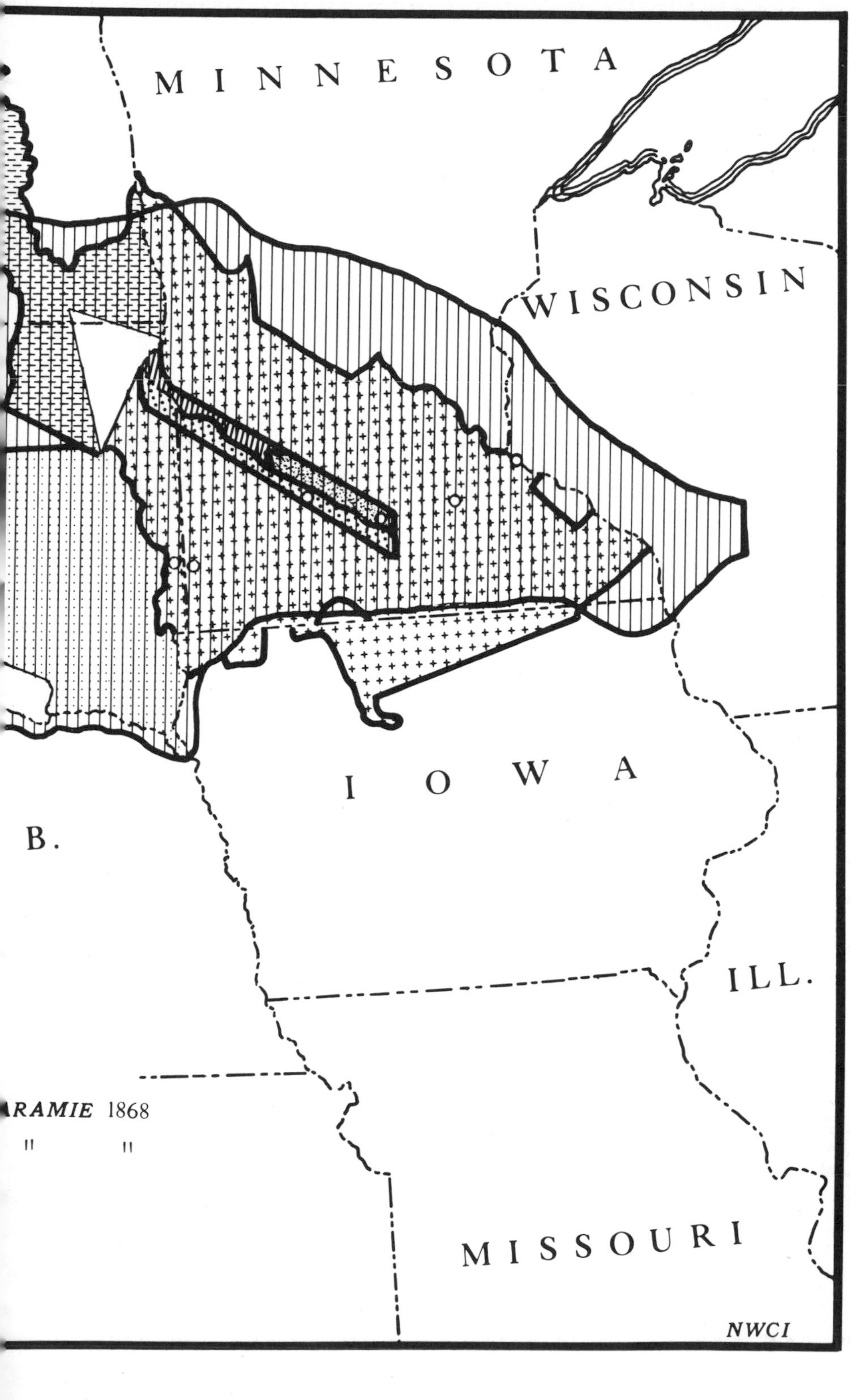

MINNESOTA
WISCONSIN
IOWA
B.
ILL.
RAMIE 1868
" "
MISSOURI
NWCI

Courtesy Amon Carter Museum, Fort Worth

Tepee, cabin, and family of Sioux Indian policeman, Pine Ridge Agency, 1886.

the Secretary of the Interior. This commission's only duty was to ask the Tetons if they were willing to sell any of their land.

Edmunds ignored the instructions from the outset, and his sole aim was to force the Tetons to give up half of their land, the choicer half that the land-boomers craved. To make sure that he had a reliable interpreter, he hired the Reverend Samuel D. Hinman, an old friend who was fluent in the Sioux language. Hinman had served as interpreter for the commission in 1868 and as a member of the commission of 1876. He had played an active role in badgering the Poncas into accepting removal to Indian Territory, so Edmunds had no fear that moral scruples would undermine Hinman's effectiveness. He worded the so-called agreement in such a deceptive way that the Tetons could not tell that they were expected to give up any of their land. They had come, Edmunds told the Sioux, to lay out six agencies so that the Indians could claim these areas as their own. He spoke in glowing terms of the splendid new reservations they would receive, neglecting to add that these would be carved out of land they already owned. Then the government would, in its generosity, give them twenty-five thousand cows and one thousand bulls. The land was worth no less than seven million dollars, the

Courtesy Amon Carter Museum, Fort Worth

Pine Ridge Agency, South Dakota, 1886

cattle about one million. There would, of course, be some papers, to be signed, papers, he did not add, that would cost them fourteen thousand square miles of land.

Edmunds also ignored the stipulation of the Treaty of 1868 that no land cession could be made unless three-fourths of the adult males approved and sought only a few chiefs and head men. Hinman bullied Red Cloud and other Oglalas into signing by the threat that they would be shipped to Indian Territory if they refused. Stories soon appeared in newspapers with glowing descriptions of the Teton lands soon to be opened to settlement. The squawmen informed the chiefs that a land grab was in the making, and the Oglalas quickly repudiated the "agreement."

When he learned of Edmunds' activities, Episcopal Bishop W. H. Hare, a genuine friend of the Indians, wrote to influential friends in the East protesting the manner of dealing with theTetons. Several missionaries also informed friends and officials of the distasteful affair. The Friends of the Indian were now aroused, and Congress became suspicious. When Congress convened in December there were a number of men demanding to know what the Secretary of the Interior and his commission were doing with regard to the Sioux reservations.

A Senate resolution requested the Secretary to produce all papers concerning the so-called agreement with the Sioux. Teller stalled and wired Edmunds to complete his work at Lower Brulé and Crow Creek agencies immediately so that the Indians could be moved under the pretext that they were agreeable. Edmunds anticipated no trouble, but the Brulés stubbornly refused to move. Captain William G. Dougherty, who had served as their agent while the army had been in charge of the reservations, and Episcopal missionary H. Burt had advised them to stand fast. Despite all of Edmunds' threats, the Indians grimly refused to be stampeded into signing or moving.

Commissioner Shannon now came up with a solution. He added two amendments to the agreement which made it possible to take over Lower Brulé without Indian approval. J. H. Teller hurried East with what Edmunds called a "complete agreement" with the Sioux, although not a single Indian had signed it. Secretary Teller and President Arthur quickly approved the document, but on the advice of his legal counsel, who considered them improper, Arthur removed the two amendments. The "agreement" was then taken to the Senate for its approval.

In the meantime Reverend Hinman and Judge Shannon were still hammering away at the Lower Brulés. The Indians wanted to sell hides to raise money enough to send their chiefs to Washington. Shannon and Hinman wired J. H. Teller to ask his brother to issue an order banning the sale of hides, and the order was issued. The commissioners had almost reached the nadir of dirty dealing.

J. H. Teller was soon back from Washington with another order from the Secretary of the Interior to the Lower Brulés. It stated that enough signatures had been obtained at the other agencies to put the land agreement into effect at Lower Brulé without their approval. They were informed that they must move or troops would be sent to remove them forcibly. If the chiefs signed, they would be paid for property left behind. If they refused, they would get nothing, and they could be moved wherever and whenever the government chose. Teller had no authority to carry out these underhanded threats, but the Indians had no way of knowing that. Still they refused to sign.

The Dakota newspapers joined the battle, announcing that President Arthur would shortly abolish the Crow Creek reserva-

Courtesy National Park Service

Army camp at Rosebud Agency

tion and open the land to settlement. A crowd of land-boomers massed on the edge of Crow Creek agency, ready to dash in and claim the best parts. The commissioners, learning that the Crow Creek Indians were terrified by the reports, hurried there and began bullying them again. Land-boomers now rushed onto the reservation and began to stake out claims. Pretending that President Arthur had signed an order to open Crow Creek for settlement, they demanded that the Indians leave. The commissioners listed the names of the chiefs as if they had signed, declared their work finished, and so informed Secretary Teller. He approved the agreement and sent it to Arthur, who passed it to the Senate for approval.

The so-called agreement had only three hundred eighty-four Sioux names on it, presumably chiefs and headmen. Shannon's legal mind now produced his bizarre excuse for not getting the signatures of three-fourths of the adult males — in 1876 the government had violated the Treaty of 1868, and having established the precedent, was free to violate it again. The Senate took no action while the uproar increased in intensity, and those behind the land grab became worried. The Indian Rights Association declared that the government's seizure of the Black Hills in 1876 had been a shameful action, but it was certainly no legal precedent for other treaty violations.

Senator Henry L. Dawes of Massachusetts, spokesman of the

Courtesy Library of Congress

Senator Henry L. Dawes of Massachusetts, author of the Dawes Act

Courtesy National Archives

Crow prisoners, Crow Agency, Montana, 1887

Friends of the Indian in the Senate, led the fight to send Edmunds' fake agreement back to the Sioux. On March 3 the Senate ordered the Interior Department to return the land agreement to the agencies for approval by three-fourths of the adult males. Secretary Teller reappointed the same trusty three to the new commission to secure the needed approval. So anxious was Secretary Teller to get his job done before the new Congress convened that he kept President Arthur waiting in a Senate anteroom until two o'clock in the morning to sign the agreement as soon as the Senate passed on it. But the president waited in vain.

Because of his fluency in the Tetons' language, the Reverend Hinman was sent to the agencies to secure the necessary signatures. At Pine Ridge, Red Cloud was still opposed, but he allowed Hinman to visit the camps. Hinman secured some "signatures," but it was soon learned that these were of small boys who

Courtesy William C. Brown Photographs

Indian veterans, Crow Agency Park, 1926

touched the pen while he wrote their names. When questioned on this unusual practice, Hinman declared that he had done it to please the fathers, but he intended to remove the names, and he seemed wounded when no one believed him. What he had done was to ask the fathers to let their sons sign, saying that only the ones who signed could remain on the reservation. Even though he was caught in devious dealings, Hinman continued to collect the names of young boys, using every possible threat from cutting off food to shipping them to Indian Territory, and promising everything desired to those who would sign. Claiming that he had the signatures of three-fourths of the adult males at Pine Ridge, he went on to Standing Rock.

At Standing Rock Hinman was in for an unpleasant surprise. The chiefs refused to talk to him because another man, Senator Dawes, was coming to see them. Hinman knew the game was up, for the Sioux were not weakening, and the protest against the

Courtesy Smithsonian Institution

Camp at Grand River, Standing Rock Agency, N.D., showing log cabin, tepee, and small sweat lodge.

commission was too shrill to be ignored. The Indian Rights Association demanded a full investigation of the attempted land grab, and the Senate again ordered Secretary Teller to produce all of the documents sent or received by the commission, including letters and telegrams.

The Senate appointed a select committee to examine the affairs of the Crow and Sioux tribes with regard to proposals to reduce the size of their reservations. Senator Dawes was named chairman, and Dawes had a genuine if occasionally misguided interest in the welfare of the Indians. But Dawes knew little of western affairs, and neither Secretary Teller nor Edmunds seemed concerned over his appointment.

In July Senator Dawes wrote Teller that Bishop Hare had informed him the Edmunds commission was not dealing honestly with the Sioux and had threatened them. Earlier Dawes had looked into the record of Hinman's role in helping to frighten the Poncas into giving up their lands in Nebraska and moving to Indian Territory. He had been shocked at what he learned.

The message to Teller was a polite warning that Dawes meant business. Teller sent a copy to Edmunds. Edmunds wrote to all of the Sioux agents innocently inquiring if any member of his commission had threatened the Indians. All replied that the answer was no. Some were indignant that anyone would even question the honesty of the commission.

Armed with these letters, Edmunds waited confidently at Bismarck for Dawes' arrival, certain that he could win over the Senator before he ever talked to any Indians. But Dawes entered Dakota Territory by way of the Northern Pacific and went straight to the agencies and began taking testimony. The Edmunds commission panicked.

Secretary Teller wrote Dawes, urging him to talk to Edmunds before visiting the agencies. "I suppose you are aware," he said, "that a great number of people in that vicinity do not want the Indians to part with any portion of their land, and in fact they would much rather have them remain wild Indians than have them become civilized; and in some cases those who profess the most love for the Indians are the ones who for selfish purposes prefer the Indians to remain Indians."

The "selfish" men he referred to were Bishop William Hare, Bishop H. B. Whipple, the Reverend T. L. Riggs, missionary at Rosebud, the Reverend H. Burt, Crow Creek, and the Reverend Luke Walker, a fullblood Sioux missionary and teacher at Lower Brulé. These men did not disapprove of the sale of surplus reservation lands, but they were opposed to cheating the Indians. Bishop Hare had urged Teller to send a new commission with terms that were fair to the Indians, in which case he and the missionaries would help secure the signatures. Teller did not reply.

The Dawes commission visited every reservation and then went to Omaha and asked the Edmunds commission to present its case. The commission denied all charges, then introduced an orator from Dakota who tried to charm the committee into believing that the agreement had been properly approved by the Sioux. The senators listened, unsmiling. The truth was that the Edmunds commission, even with the help of the Secretary of the

Courtesy Amon Carter museum, Fort Worth

Sioux ready for the "Grass Dance" at Pine Ridge Reservation, watched by the Eighth Cavalry and Third Infantry.

Interior, had failed in its attempt to cheat the Sioux out of half their remaining lands. It had united the Indians and made them suspicious of any future attempt to reach an agreement, even an honest one. In a way, this was as significant for the Indians as Red Cloud's victory had been in 1868. But like Red Cloud's victory, it was short lived, for what had failed as a dishonest effort to dispossess the Tetons of half of their lands would now become the goal of honest, earnest, men.

The Friends of the Indian now resumed their well-intentioned plan to make over the Sioux warriors into imitation Christian farmers. At first they had been blindly certain that this could be accomplished in four years, but in 1883 Senator Dawes informed them that very few families raised enough food to support themselves, and not many even tried to farm. The brethren were mightily vexed at this news. If the Indians were too unenlightened to see what was good for them, they must be forced to accept it by any means possible. Like all self-righteous men, they were convinced that only they knew the basic truths, in particular what was good for the Indians. Their voices became shrill.

Bursting with desire to help their red brothers, in spite of themselves, the Friends of the Indian solved the sticky problem of how (for their own good!) the Sioux could be settled on land and kept from wandering. It was simple — take away half of their land, and they would have no place to go. The frontier politicos and land-boomers heard this sagacious plan, and their hearts filled with joy and expectation.

The brethren also figured out a way to make absolutely certain that the Sioux applied themselves to farming — cut off their rations and let them work or starve. And if they still refused to send their children to school so they could become "civilized," let the Indian police round them up, put the obstinate fathers in jail, and cut off rations for the families. The well-fed Friends of the Indian justified the idea of starving the Sioux into obedience as quite proper and thoroughly Christian. They quoted St. Paul as saying "He who will not work shall not eat."

In 1885 the Friends launched this new crusade to dispose of "surplus" reservation lands and to force the Indians to work and to allow their children to be educated. A few worried about the danger of applying too much pressure — others felt that it was a good time to stamp out Indianism entirely, and they demanded action. The Dakota land-boomers and the Friends of the Indian were now united for the common goal of reducing the Sioux reservations. Among those who favored turning the Indians loose among the whites to sink or swim was Captain R. H. Pratt of Carlisle Indian School. When someone pointed out a flaw in this plan — the Indians would surely sink — Pratt smiled and cheerfully agreed. But how could that be considered a flaw? After all, a few might survive, if any of them deserved to, which he doubted.

The fact that their plans necessitated open violation of treaties without number bothered the brethren not at all. Senator Dawes reminded them that in 1879-81 they had crusaded in defense of treaties. The Sioux land title, he told them, "is a title-deed as perfect as yours, and to talk of taking that land from them without their consent for their own good is the same as talking of taking away our neighbor's title to his home for his own good."

The brethren saw absolutely no logic or merit in Dawes' argument, and they began to suspect his judgment. They went on without him, marching into Secretary of the Interior Lamar's office with a plan for violating the treaties and destroying the

Courtesy National Park Service

Sioux chief John Grass

reservations for the benefit of the Indians. Lamar told them in plain and forceful language that he would not allow the Indians to be uprooted and flung into conditions for which they were unprepared. No one policy, he said, could be applied to all Indians, and what they suggested was less merciful than a war of extermination. "Those that are ready I will push on," he concluded; "those who are not I will protect." He had nothing more to say about the matter.

Senator Dawes was no longer comfortable in his role of spokesman for the Friends of the Indian, especially because of their attempts to interfere in governmental policy making. They were also too eager to have coercive measures included in every part of the bill he was writing. His bill called for allotting one hundred sixty acres of land as well as citizenship to each Indian head of family. A colleague pointed out that his bill, if it became law, could be used to destroy the Indians.

This thought troubled Senator Dawes, but it did not prevent him from introducing his bill in the Senate. His Sioux land-purchase bill would enable the Dakota land-boomers to grab as much of the Sioux lands as the underhanded Edmunds commission could have provided. But Dawes was determined to produce a law, and he could not hold back simply because his law might be used for purposes other than those he intended. The Dawes bill was stalled in Congress until the Cleveland administration needed Republican support for other measures.

The General Allotment (Dawes) Act became law on February 8, 1887. It was a brutally coercive law, with starvation the first of its sanctions, and it gave the government the right to violate treaties. The brethren were ecstatic over what they termed the "Indian Emancipation Act," a law that did more damage to the Indians and their way of life than any other ever enacted. Now the Sioux would be reduced to no more than a plot of land for each family, on which they must farm or starve. Their wandering days were over. The Dakota land-boomers also rejoiced, for Dawes provided them the opportunity to do legally what Edmunds had failed to accomplish dishonestly. The difference was that Edmunds was well aware that he was trying to rob the Sioux, while Dawes deluded himself into thinking that he was actually helping them. The Dawes Act was endorsed enthusiastically by

Courtesy Amon Carter Museum, Fort Worth

Beef issue at Standing Rock Agency, Hunkpapa Sioux

everyone but Secretary of the Interior Lamar, the Sioux, and the genuine friends of the Indians.

Secretary Lamar was suspicious of those who would aid the Indians by taking their lands and threatening them with starvation. When the Dawes bill became law he resigned, to be replaced by a man who was willing to cooperate with the Friends of the Indian. Experienced white farmers were finding it extremely difficult to succeed at farming in the Dakotas, and the Sioux knew nothing about farming. Some of them had, however, taken up cattle-raising with enthusiasm.

In 1876 the Cheyenne River Sioux had given up their ponies, which the army sold and used the proceeds to purchase six hundred cows and eight bulls. The Sioux were quick to learn cattle-raising, and by 1890 they were producing about one-fourth of the beef ration issued at Cheyenne River. Other Sioux had also acquired cattle, and during the severe winters of the 1880s, when many white cattlemen lost their entire herds, by constant effort the Sioux managed to keep their losses relatively low. If the Sioux were to succeed at cattle-raising, however, they needed more land, not less. But the Friends of the Indian were absolutely opposed to allowing the Sioux to develop a range cattle industry, because it would enable them to retain their cherished mobility. The brethren were determined that the Sioux should give up their nomadic ways and forget their former life.

In April, 1888, a Sioux bill passed which opened nine million acres of the Great Sioux Reserve for sale before any land was allotted to the Indians. Captain R. H. Pratt, head of the Carlisle Indian School, was chosen to take the Sioux Act to the Indians for their approval. Government officials and Friends of the Indian admired Pratt, so they took it for granted that the Sioux also admired him. But Pratt was an inflexible, hard-headed martinet, and to know him was not to love him — the Sioux called him the Mean-Man-with-the-Big-Nose. In the summer of 1888 he and the Reverend William J. Cleveland and John V. Wright traveled to Standing Rock agency and called for a council.

Chief Grass, who was one of the Sioux most friendly to the whites, went over the Treaty of 1868 point by point, showing how frequently it had been violated. He told the commissioners to return to Washington and tell the Great Father that when the government kept all of its promises the Sioux might be willing to talk, but not before.

Pratt was furious, for he could not stand opposition. You will vote, he shouted at the Sioux, and you will vote right. The *New York Tribune* described his methods as "bulldozing," which was an apt description. The council broke up for the day, for the Indians refused to be bulldozed into voting.

Pratt was also irritated by a reporter from Minneapolis, whose accounts of the proceedings reflected no admiration and much contempt for Pratt. On Pratt's orders the Indian police escorted the reporter across the Missouri, where he set up camp and kept informed on all that transpired. Newspapers were soon calling Pratt a bungler. Bull-headed as ever, he would listen to no one. The Sioux wanted to send their chiefs to Washington, but Pratt refused to allow it unless they signed the treaty first. For two weeks he cajoled and threatened. Then Chief Grass arose and said that the Indians had heard enough and were going back to their farms. Pratt mumbled and threatened, but the Sioux were gone.

After visiting other reservations with no greater success, Pratt wrote a bitter report. The treaties should be ignored, he said, and the Sioux lands should be taken from them with no further talk. The only real friend left to the Sioux was Dr. Bland of the Indian

Courtesy National Archives

Sioux camp at Pine Ridge, South Dakota, 1890

Rights Association, who opposed the sale and the plan to force the Indians to change their way of life suddenly and without preparation.

At the suggestion of the Friends of the Indian, the government now called delegations of chiefs to Washington. In Washington the chiefs poured forth a flood of complaints about unkept promises, but they refused to talk about land. As soon as they could, they returned to the reservations.

The Cleveland administration was puzzled. The Friends of the Indian had insisted that the chiefs' power be broken. Then they had suggested bringing the chiefs to Washington and treating them as official representatives of their tribes. The chiefs had come and gone and nothing had been accomplished. The Friends of the Indian wanted to starve the Sioux into becoming farmers, but if the government met even half of the Sioux demands, none of them would have to work again for the rest of the century.

About the time the chiefs returned to their agencies, in November, 1888, Benjamin Harrison won the presidential election, and he was a man the brethren could work with, for he knew even less about Indians than they did, and what happened to the Indians was of no concern to him. He appointed J. T. Morgan as

Indian Commissioner and told him to accept the views of the Indian welfare groups as official policy. Hooray!

Morgan stated his view of the Indian problem, after he had been well-coached by the brethren. His "longest established conviction," he said, was that the Indian reservation system was ridiculous and could not be allowed to continue. The Indians must be taught to live and work like whites and become absorbed by the white population. The Indian service, he continued, must be purged of "political appointees" and staffed with "dedicated men." Translated, this meant that the Democrats in the Indian service were "political appointees," who must be sacked and replaced by "dedicated men," meaning Republicans. The Friends of the Indian, who were largely of Republican persuasion, had strenuously objected to Cleveland's dismissal of Republicans from the Indian service, but now they looked on with approving smiles while Harrison purged the Democrats. In their joy over the thought of taking nine million acres from the Sioux they even forgot that they had once been enthusiastic promoters of civil service reform.

The brethren based their campaign at first on the fiction that the chiefs who had been brought to Washington had promised to persuade their people to accept the land grab. When they were quickly disabused of this fantasy, they planned an all-out drive to shatter Sioux opposition by whatever means were necessary, including starving them into submission.

The head of the new commission was General George Crook, who was appointed to convince the Sioux that the army was involved. Crook's presence gave the Sioux pause, for he was no blustering idiot like Captain Pratt. The word from Washington was that Crook had been appointed because he was a good friend of the Sioux. The Indians remembered him as "The Gray Fox," who had relentlessly harassed the hostiles until they surrendered, which in their eyes did not make him a "good friend." Yet Crook was sincere in his efforts to deal fairly and honestly with his old adversaries. The other members were Charles Foster, ex-governor of Ohio, and General William Warner. The commission had a contingency fund of twenty-five thousand dollars, which could be used as needed to win over some of the reluctant chiefs.

The commission reached Rosebud in May of 1889. This was

Courtesy Amon Carter Museum, Fort Worth

Sioux chiefs Kicking Bear, Young-Man-Afraid-of-His-Horses, and Standing Bear.

planting time, and many Brulés had finally been persuaded to plant small plots, even though their crops had been killed by drouth for two years in succession. The efforts to get them started farming seemed at last on the way to partial success, but at that critical juncture they were told to leave their farms and attend the council. The commissioners provided a feast, and by mid-June three-fourths of the adult males had been "persuaded" to sign. Dr. Bland of the Indian Rights Association had urged the Sioux not even to discuss a land cession. Bishop Hare declared that the commissioners had "carried persuasion to the verge of intimidation."

The same methods were not successful at Pine Ridge. An

Oglala, American Horse, made an impassioned speech against the land sale, and Crook noted wryly that he was "a better speaker than any of us." American Horse talked on and on, as if he were acquainted with the senatorial technique of filibustering.

Finally General Warner could stand it no longer, and he interrupted American Horse. He had heard of men being talked to death, he said, and now he knew that it was possible. American Horse waited until the Sioux stopped laughing and then continued.

When it was his turn to speak, Crook explained to the Sioux that if they signed they could keep half of their land, but if they refused they would lose it all. Even though this was not true, coming from Crook it was a serious threat. Crook knew that this was the best treaty the Sioux could hope to get, and that if they refused it they would simply lose their land. He was determined that they would accept it, for under the circumstances it was in their interest to do so. But the Oglalas were not stampeded into signing.

At Crow Creek and Lower Brulé the commission won easy victories, and soon had the necessary number of signatures, but in the meantime Crook had made many promises. Dr. Bland again charged the commission with using intimidation and bribery, but no one paid any attention to his accusations, for it seemed clear that the Sioux had simply heeded the wise council of their old friend General Crook. While the Sioux were trying to figure out how their decision to stand firmly against the sale had become a three-fourths vote in favor of it, the Friends of the Indian were joyfully anticipating carrying out the rest of their program for giving the Sioux a "better life."

The commissioners had made so many promises to the Sioux that it again seemed advisable to call the chiefs back to Washington and to reach some understanding with them before more complaints arose. General Crook, unlike Harney, was serious about the promises he had made, and he expected the government to honor them. At Rosebud and elsewhere he had signed written promises that the land agreement did not jeopardize their right to continue receiving food and clothing.

Crook's promises were only a few weeks old when Indian Commissioner Morgan ordered a cut of two million pounds of the beef ration at Rosebud, one million at Pine Ridge, and similar cuts at other agencies. Morgan had decided, he said, that there was "hocus pocus" at the agencies, that the lists of Indians were padded, and that the Indians were drawing rations for their ancestors. To upright civil servant Morgan it appeared that the government was being swindled, and since the presumed swindlers were Indians and not even Republicans, he self-righteously performed surgery in spite of anything anyone else had to say. But officials had long been quietly reducing Sioux rations, so that even before the cut they were receiving considerably less than the treaty had guaranteed them. When the Sioux had found that their protests were unheeded, they had stopped reporting deaths, and in this way lessened the injury somewhat.

Crook felt that his honor was at stake, for he had promised no cut in rations if the Sioux signed. He protested to Morgan that beef was their main food, and the reduction of beef ration would surely cause intense suffering. Their crops had failed the past two years, and they had been ordered away from their farms at planting time. The truth was, as Crook knew, that they were already suffering from malnutrition before the cuts were ordered. Starving them did not seem to him the most likely way to make them become self-supporting.

Morgan was unmoved. There was no way to restore the beef ration, he untruthfully declared, except by act of Congress. When the Ghost Dance troubles erupted, however, Morgan had no difficulty in restoring the beef ration, but by then, of course, the damage had been done. Crook had no choice but to accept Morgan's promise that he would ask Congress to increase the beef ration, but when he told the Sioux chiefs they simply gave up. None of them had any faith in Congress.

Congress did nothing to aid the starving Sioux. It was a winter of extreme cold, hunger, and despondency for the Sioux, and it was not much better — perhaps even worse — for many white homesteaders. The drouth of 1889 was the worst so far, and faced with starvation, many of them abandoned their parched lands and left the territory. Land prices fell and farm mortgage companies failed.

The cut in beef rations had stunned the Sioux, for it convinced them that they did not know what they had signed away, and that the government would not honor General Crook's prom-

Courtesy Amon Carter Museum, Fort Worth

Sioux watching Ghost Dance, 1890

ises. Bishop Hare hoped that, because of their despondency, it would now be possible to lead them gently into a new life, but efforts to induce them to change merely added to their gloominess. Once they recovered from the shock, they attacked the squawmen and halfbreeds and the church-going fullbloods. Somehow these men must have betrayed the tribe.

In the fall of 1889 economy-minded Commissioner Morgan allowed the purchase of trail herds from Texas for the beef ration, although the contract called for northern ranch cattle. The trail cattle reached the agencies in poor condition, and they became skin and bones as winter came on. The issuance of poor cattle in the place of fat ones reduced the amount of beef to the Sioux by more than half what the treaty specified.

In February, 1890, President Harrison announced that the Sioux had accepted the land agreement. Without making the survey or the allotments to the Indians called for in the so-called agreement, Harrison opened nine million acres to settlement. General Crook died in March, and together these two events killed any lingering hopes the Sioux might have had.

At this blackest moment in their history, when they were starving and epidemics of measles and influenza and whooping

Courtesy National Archives

Big Foot's band of Minneconju Sioux at a dance, Cheyenne River Agency, 1890.

cough were killing hundreds of their children, hope came suddenly from an unexpected source. They learned of the Ghost Dance that the Paiute prophet Wovoka was teaching other tribes, and they sent a delegation to Nevada to investigate. If they performed the dance regularly, he told them, one day soon the earth would tremble and the whites would be washed away. The dead Indians would return, and with them the buffalo herds. But the Indians must be peaceful, he warned them.

The Sioux, especially the former hostiles, were given an exhilarating feeling of optimism, and they embraced the Ghost Dance with the desperation of drowning men. It occurred to them that if the whites were going to be swept away anyway, they might as well help a few of them on their journey. For the hungry and resentful Sioux, killing a few whites would have had a substantial therapeutic value. As they thought of this delightful possibility, Ghost Dance shirts appeared among them, shirts of skin or cloth that presumably had magical powers to stop bullets. And even though the believers tried hard to convince the doubters that the shirts were indeed bullet-proof, many Sioux remained unconvinced. Some fanatics persuaded a warrior named Porcupine to put on his shirt and let them demonstrate. He did, and was laid up for six weeks with a bullet in the thigh. This demonstration reaffirmed the convictions of many and raised doubts in all those who had witnessed the experiment. But elsewhere many Sioux still believed absolutely in the magical powers of the shirts, and their faith paved the way for tragedy. Their faith is not surprising, for they had always believed that it was supernatural powers that enabled their buffalo-hide shields to stop arrows.

In 1889 the Harrison administration had introduced a policy that was felicitously called "home rule" for the Indians. "Home rule" meant to the Sioux simply that the selection of agents for their reservations was turned over to Senator R. F. Pettigrew, whose suggestion to Secretary Teller had led to the Edmunds commission. And so, at a time when experienced agents were needed as never before, all but one of them were replaced by "deserving" but inexperienced Dakota Republicans. The new agent at Pine Ridge, where the Indians had become defiant and unmanageable, was a timid young man named D. R. Royer. The Sioux quickly sized him up and gave him a new name — "Young-Man-Afraid-of-Indians." Within a week Royer was bleating to the Indian Office that the Indians were out of control and calling for troops. One reason for the Indians' growing defiance was their lingering confidence in the Ghost shirts' ability to stop bullets.

The House delayed passage of the Sioux Appropriation Act for the fiscal year 1891 until August 19, 1890, seven weeks after the new fiscal year had begun. As a result it was impossible to get clothing and food to the agencies until well into the winter, which added considerably to the suffering.

As the Sioux became more and more hopeful that the Ghost Dance would liberate them, the agents' authority vanished at all of the reservations, and the chiefs were again the leaders of their people. Most of the agents now agreed that troops were needed, but the Indian Office and the brethren were reluctant to admit that all of their talk of "progress" had been empty, and they refused to allow the War Department to help. Agent Royer continued sending a steady stream of telegrams to the Indian Office pleading for troops at his agency. His terror finally overcame him, and one day he dashed to the nearest fort and declared that

Courtesy National Park Service

Sitting Bull, who appeared in Buffalo Bill's Wild West Show.

the Indians were up in arms. Troops accompanied him back to the agency and remained there.

In November troops arrived at all of the agencies, but there was no panic. Red Cloud said glumly that they had taken his ponies before and probably would again, so he had the pony herds heavily guarded. General Nelson A. Miles, who earlier had discounted the talk of danger, now called it the most serious Indian crisis since Tecumseh's confederation, and sent more troops to the reservation headquarters. The people of the Dakotas, hearing rumors that seemed to imply an Indian war in the spring, were also calling for more troops.

Early in December, 1890, the Senate debated a request to provide one hundred thousand rifles for use by the citizens of Dakota. Senator Voorhees remarked that the trouble was clearly the result of hunger and suggested that it would be wiser to send one hundred thousand rations to the Sioux. Senator Dawes, who had represented the Friends of the Indian longer than he cared to remember, knew that the Sioux had been starved purposely and for their own good, but he did not care to hear the matter discussed.

When another Senator mentioned the government's failure to keep Crook's promises to the Sioux, Dawes replied testily that the promises had been kept. Although there was some danger in the present situation, he added, there could be no relief for the Sioux until they rejected the authority of chiefs like Red Cloud and Sitting Bull. These chiefs and others like them were the real obstacles to progress.

Senator Voorhees asked Dawes if he would say whether or not General Miles was correct in blaming the Sioux difficulties on hunger. Dawes replied with growing irritation that this was the first he had heard about the Sioux being hungry. They had been away from the agencies dancing and fighting, he said, and if they were hungry, it was because they had neglected their farms.

Voorhees looked at Dawes in surprise. Didn't Dawes, the leading Indian expert in Congress, know that the Sioux had been hungry for at least two years? Dawes angrily repeated that they were hungry because they left the agencies. At about this time many of the Ghost Dancers fled to the Badlands, convinced that the whites were trying to prohibit the dancing to prevent the

Paiute Wovoka's prophecy from coming true when the grass turned green in the spring.

General Miles stated publicly that the Sioux troubles were the result of the "forcing process," the government's attempt to make them become self-supporting at a time when they could not possibly grow crops because of the drouths. The Friends of the Indian and their man in the Senate were responsible for this policy. Miles added that coercing the Sioux into giving up half of their lands at such a time was another reason for the unrest. The same group claimed credit for the land deal.

At Standing Rock Sitting Bull encouraged the dancers to continue. In December, 1890, the Indian Office ordered agent McLaughlin to arrest him using Indian police and troops of the 8th Cavalry stationed at the agency. The attempted arrest turned into a bitter gun battle in which Sitting Bull and many others were killed. The rest of Sitting Bull's band fled to join the dancers who were still hiding in the Badlands. Most of them had been preparing to surrender, but the news of Sitting Bull's death frightened them and made them change their plans.

When the cold and hungry refugees finally came out of the Badlands, they were escorted toward Pine Ridge by eight troops of the Seventh Cavalry. Colonel George Forsyth received orders to disarm them and march them to the railroad at Gordon, Nebraska, where they presumably would be shipped to Indian Territory. They camped for the night at Wounded Knee Creek. Next morning Forsyth ordered the warriors to surrender their guns. Many of them wore their Ghost shirts, and now they ominously began chanting their death songs. The medicine man, Yellow Bird, reminded them that they were safe from bullets, then blew on an eagle-bone whistle and threw a handful of dirt in the air, the traditional Sioux signal to fight. Face to face with troops, the warriors drew their Winchesters from beneath their robes as the soldiers opened fire and the Hotchkiss guns poured shot into the tepees. Before the morning was over eighty-four men and boys, forty-four women, and eighteen children had been killed. A blizzard began, and it was three days before some of the wounded could be rescued. Custer and the Seventh Cavalry had been avenged.

A week later the Friends of the Indian met as usual in comfortable Riggs House in Washington to decide on Indian

Courtesy Amon Carter Museum, Fort Worth

Gathering up the dead after the Battle of Wounded Knee, 1890

policy for 1891. News arrived of the Wounded Knee disaster. Shocked at this interruption of their program, they searched angrily for someone to blame. Finally one of the brethren recovered his wits enough to suggest that Red Cloud and other old chiefs were the culprits, and all heartily agreed. Their optimism quickly returned. The Sioux had been taught a much-needed lesson. Now, while the Sioux were defeated and helpless, it would be easy to make them accept the "better life" the brethren had in store for them. Only Senator Dawes remained angry and resentful. While they had been searching for scapegoats, some low-minded individual among the brethren suggested that Congress was at fault! Swallowing rapidly, Dawes rose to reply to this insult.

He eased his conscience by pointing out that Congress had dutifully passed all of the necessary bills, though he forgot to add that it had passed some of them too late to prevent the Ghost Dance tragedy. He warned the brethren that Congress was in no mood to appropriate money for any more of their costly schemes.

Courtesy Amon Carter Museum, Fort Worth

Burial of Sioux killed at Wounded Knee, December 30, 1890

Congress was, in fact, considering leaving the Indians permanently under the War Department, which seemed more convenient than having to transfer control every time there was a crisis the Indian Bureau could not handle.

The Friends of the Indian patiently heard Dawes out, but they were not listening to anything he said. As soon as he finished speaking they passed a resolution approving a new Indian policy, demanding that the Ghost Dancers who had fled the agencies be arrested.

Instead, General Miles sent Sioux delegations to Washington, where they blamed the troubles on the cut in rations, the recurrent drouths, the taking of their lands in 1889, and the policy of starving them into becoming self-supporting. By the summer of 1891 things were back to normal at the agencies, for now the Indians were well-supplied with food. The Indian Office resumed its former ways. But the Friends of the Indian were no longer allowed to force their "Indian policy" on the govern-

Courtesy Smithsonian Institution

Sioux men in sweat lodge, Rosebud Reservation, 1898

Courtesy Amon Carter Museum, Fort Worth

Sioux camp, Pine Ridge Agency, 1891

Courtesy Smithsonian Institution

Chief Two Strikes addressing council of hostile and friendly Sioux chiefs at Pine Ridge Agency, January 17, 1891.

Courtesy Amon Carter Museum, Fort Worth

Sioux chiefs who counciled with General Miles to settle Indian war.

Courtesy National Archives

Council of Sioux chiefs and leaders at Pine Ridge Agency, 1891

ment, for their man in Congress was fed up with them. The Ghost Dance affair had cost the government one million two hundred thousand dollars, many times what providing the Sioux with adequate rations would have cost. This was, said James Mooney, who was sent to inquire into the Ghost Dance, a "significant commentary on the policy of breaking faith with Indians."

SUGGESTED READING

Robert G. Athearn, *William Tecumseh Sherman and the Settlement of the West.* Norman, 1956.

Royal B. Hassrick, *The Sioux: Life and Customs of a Warrior Society.* Norman, 1964.

George E. Hyde, *Red Cloud's Folk.* Norman, 1937, 1957.

———— *A Sioux Chronicle.* Norman, 1956.

———— *Spotted Tail's Folk. A History of the Brulé Sioux.* Norman, 1961.

Helen Hunt Jackson, *A Century of Dishonor.* New York, 1881, 1965.

Dorothy M. Johnson, *The Bloody Bozeman.* New York, 1971.

Oliver Knight, *Following the Indian Wars.* Norman, 1960.

Gordon MacGregor, *Warriors Without Weapons.* Chicago, 1946.

Robert W. Mardock, *The Reformers and the American Indian.* Columbia, Mo., 1971.

James McLaughlin, *My Friend, the Indian.* Boston, 1910.

Remi Nadeau, *Fort Laramie and the Sioux Indians.* Englewood Cliffs, 1967.

John G. Neihardt, *Black Elk Speaks.* Lincoln, 1961.

Thomas H. Tibbles, *Buckskin and Blanket Days.* Garden City, 1957.

Katharine C. Turner, *Red Men Calling on the Great White Father.* Norman, 1951.

Robert M. Utley, *The Last Days of the Sioux Nation.* New Haven, 1963.

Courtesy Smithsonian Institution

Sioux woman, wife of Left Hand, and daughter, 1904

Except the Negro, no race will lift up, at the judgment seat, such accusing hands against this nation as the Indian.

Wendell Phillips

Aside from the somewhat antiquated sentiments of eternal justice and the rights of man apart from man's power to enforce his rights, the quick extermination of the aborigines may be regarded as a blessing to both the red race and the white.

Hubert Howe Bancroft

CHAPTER 9

THE DISSIDENT CHIEF

R. Morris Day

OCTOBER 3, 1873, was a holiday for the citizens of Klamath County, Oregon, and Siskiyou County, California. Gathered on the open meadow just outside Fort Klamath, they waited in the early morning sun for the festivities to begin. At 9:30 A.M. the officer of the day walked to the guard-house, unlocked the cells and ordered the prisoners out: Captain Jack, Schonchin John, Black Jim, Boston Charley, Barncho and Slolux obeyed, climbed into the waiting wagon and sat down on four coffins. To the rumble of muffled drums, the team and wagon began the short journey to the meadow. From their perch on the coffins, the prisoners could see six freshly dug graves — "a new house for Jack," one of the diggers assured the curious Indians — as well as the stockade in which their families were confined. Just ahead they saw the heavy wooden gallows with six ropes dangling from the beam. At the foot of the scaffold Colonel Frank Wheaton ordered four of the prisoners to dismount. A blacksmith struck the shackles from their legs. Jack, followed by Schonchin John, Boston Charley and Black Jim, climbed the ladder and took his place beneath a noose. As soldiers adjusted the nooses, a settler in the crowd asked Jack what he would give him to exchange places. "Five hundred ponies and both my wives," Jack replied. The sentence of the court was read, followed by an executive order commuting the sentences of Barncho and Slolux to life imprisonment. The official ceremony was over; the trap dropped and the four Modocs went to their deaths as their relatives watched from the stockade.

R. MORRIS DAY received his Ph.D. from Texas Christian University in 1971 and is presently Associate Professor of History and Director of American Studies at East Tennessee State University. He has written research monographs on the British and American navies for the Institute of Behavioral Research; articles on American cultural and naval history; and a historical play portraying the Tennessee frontier.

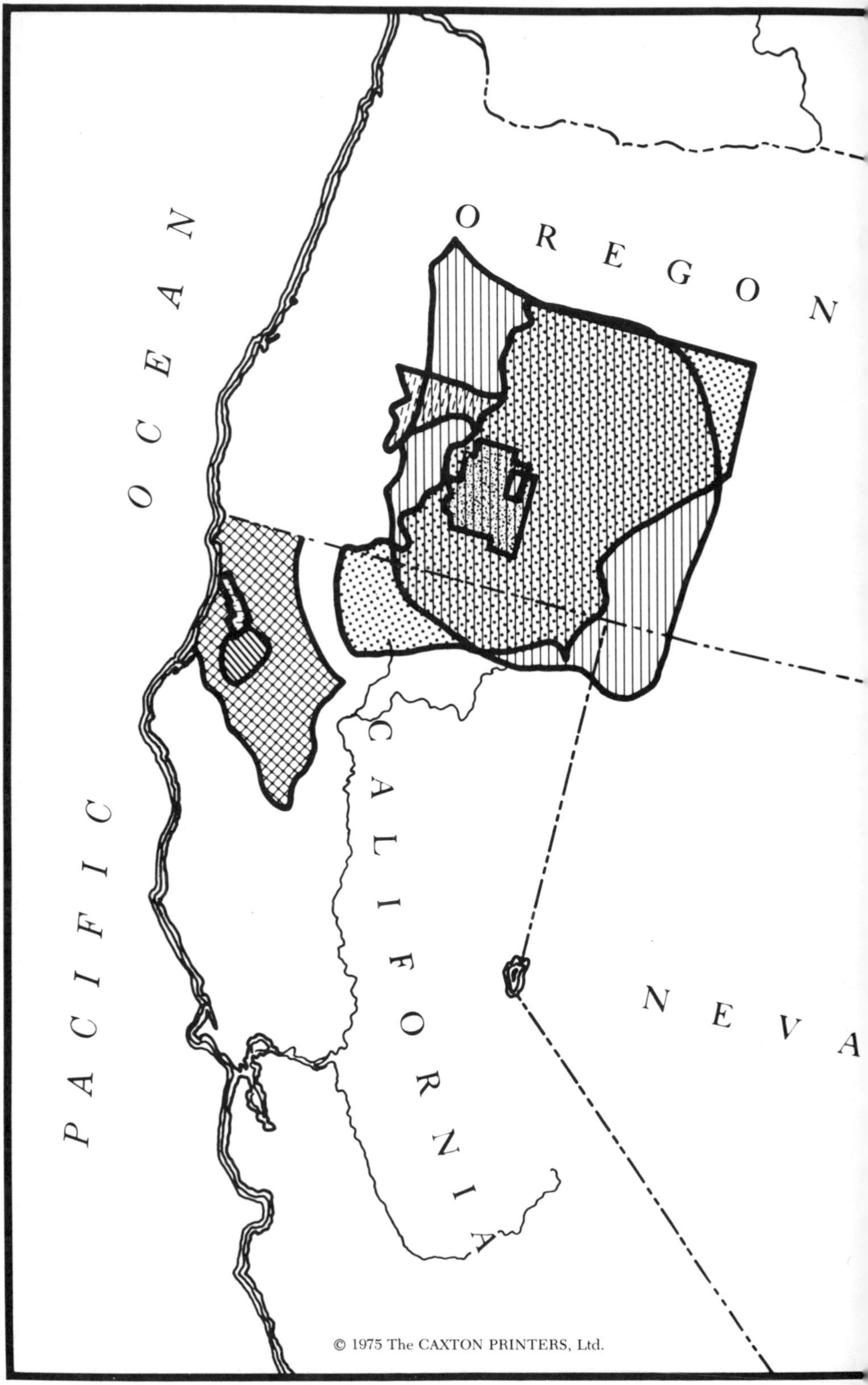
PACIFIC OCEAN
OREGON
CALIFORNIA
NEVA

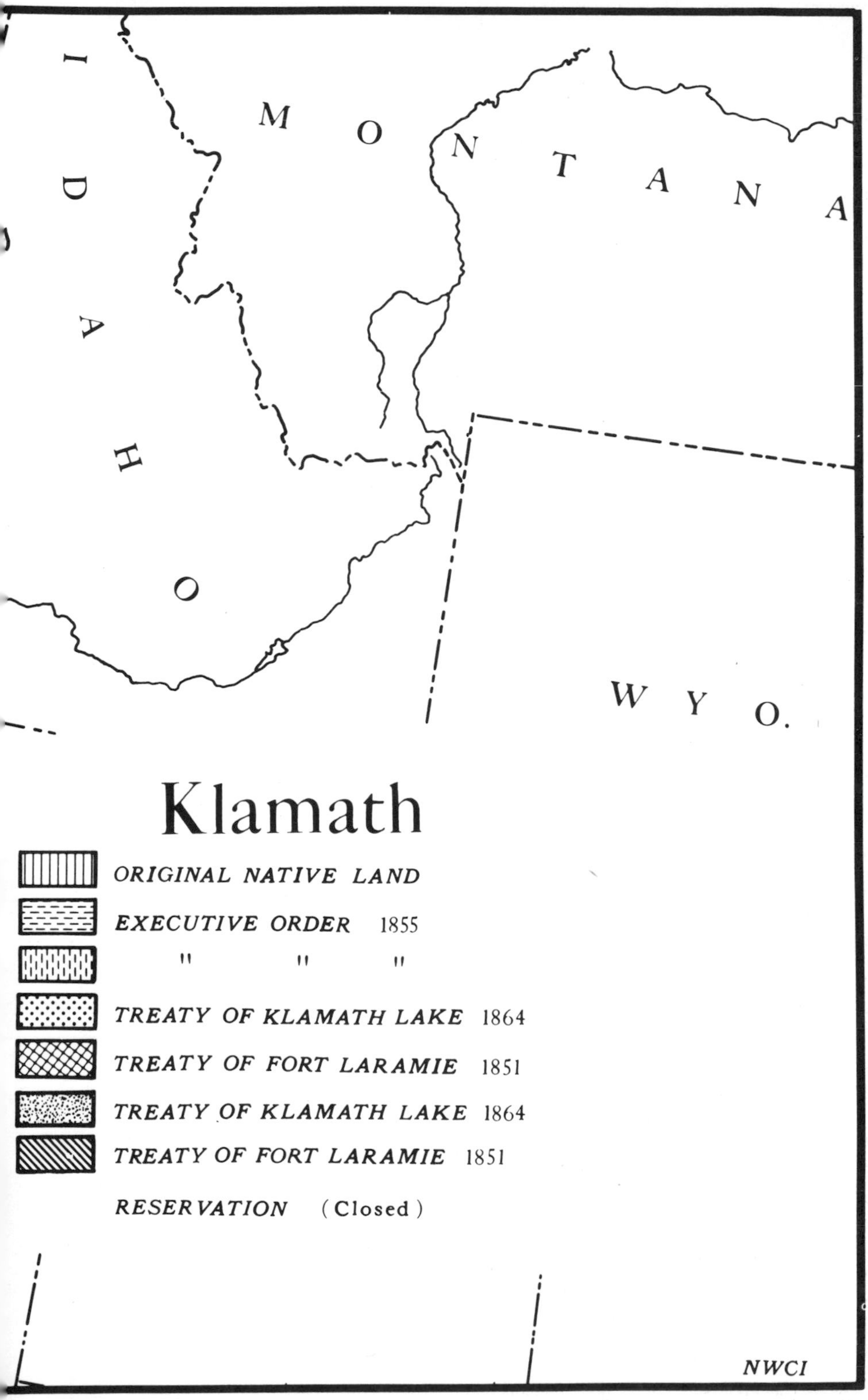

M O N T A N A
I D A H O
W Y O.
Klamath
ORIGINAL NATIVE LAND
EXECUTIVE ORDER 1855
" " "
TREATY OF KLAMATH LAKE 1864
TREATY OF FORT LARAMIE 1851
TREATY OF KLAMATH LAKE 1864
TREATY OF FORT LARAMIE 1851
RESERVATION (Closed)
NWCI

The Modoc-American conflict, which ended that autumn day on the gallows, began in the 1840s, the great decade of Manifest Destiny. Since roughly the time of Columbus, the Modocs had lived in southern Oregon and northern California, centered mainly around Klamath and Tule Lakes in the Lost River Basin. For a time they were on the periphery of white expansion: north of the Spanish thrust into California, south of the American settlements in the Oregon territory. Contacts with the whites were thus infrequent. But in 1846 this isolation abruptly ended, for John C. Frémont traveled through the area, exploring the region the United States was shortly to conquer, and two Willamette settlers, Jesse and Lindsay Applegate, surveyed a road which they hoped would provide an alternate route for the hazardous and difficult Oregon Trail, which ran across the Blue Mountains and through the Columbia Gorge.

Frémont and the Applegates were trail-blazers for settlers and miners who followed quickly on their heels. Emigrant wagons came first, driving off game and causing well-founded apprehension among the Modocs. In retaliation they struck back, one strategic ambush location on the shore of Tule Lake quickly earning the name Bloody Point. Legend magnified the conflict on both sides. For convenience, the whites added the various killings together and derived a single great massacre of an entire train at Bloody Point in 1852. When Ben Wright led a devastating attack on a Modoc village the same year, the Modocs remembered the circumstances quite differently. They had been invited to a feast under a flag of truce and ruthlessly shot; or, as a few believed, they had been liberally dosed with strychnine. The discovery of gold further exacerbated Modoc-American relations. By 1851 whites were prospecting in the Lost River region. If a miner was found murdered, the Indians were blamed; if an Indian, any Indian, was caught in the area, he was a likely candidate for the hanging tree. On the rough and crude frontier, white judicial policy many times resembled that of the old trapper, who on discovering that his traps had been stolen during the night, swore "that he would kill the first Indian he should meet, innocent or guilty" — and did.

Although sporadic raiding continued for over a decade, the bonds of civilization slowly tightened around the Modocs. Yreka City, a product of the mining boom of 1851, developed into a trading center for northern California. Adjusting to the mining town very quickly, especially its vices, the Modocs were soon buying whiskey and finding plenty of customers for their women, whom they were not reluctant to peddle. In 1863, however, the first settlers began staking claims in the Lost River Basin. Neither whiskey nor Modoc women interested them — only the prospect of a clear title to Modoc land. During the same year Major C. S. Drew built Fort Klamath and established a military garrison there, while Lincoln appointed a California lawyer, Elisha Steele, Indian Agent for the Yreka area.

If the whites and Indians were to live in any semblance of peace, some type of agreement or treaty defining the rights of each group was necessary. In 1864, surprisingly, Jack's band of Modocs made the first overture in this direction by asking Steele to draft a treaty for them. That Steele was their friend then, as well as years later when conditions were much gloomier, is not open to question. Naturally the Modocs would turn to him first. Why they did so at that time, however, has been disputed. The contemporary view was that the Modocs, conscious of their wicked crimes, went to their friend seeking advice on ways to avoid punishment. The modern view is that the Modocs were growing more and more apprehensive of white encroachment and therefore sought to retain as much of their land and as many of their rights as possible.

In any case, on St. Valentine's Day Steele and the Modocs signed a treaty. The Modocs agreed to refrain from such practices as murder, theft, prostitution, and drunkenness. Anyone who violated these provisions was to be handed over to the military at Fort Klamath. They were free to pursue occupations such as operating ferries and acting as guides. In regard to their lands, the treaty specified certain areas in which they were to reside, with the intention that these would become reservations. The Modocs agreed to obtain passes from the army in order to leave these areas; and Steele promised them protection during their visits to white settlements.

For numerous and complicated reasons, however, Steele's treaty was never ratified. Steele had made several powerful political enemies who were successful, after a prolonged struggle, in depriving him of office, and in 1864 he no longer had legal authority to negotiate a treaty. The Oregon settlers, moreover, disliked the treaty. Indian title to land had not been extinguished, nor were the Indians actually confined to a reservation. Rather they were left free "to perpetuate any peccadilloes which they were cunning enough to conceal." Finally, the Office of Indian Affairs had previously decided to make the Oregon Superintendency responsible for negotiating a treaty with the Modocs as well as the Klamaths. Ignoring Steele's treaty, the office secured an appropriation of twenty thousand dollars from Congress and proceeded with its plans to make a second treaty.

In the summer of 1864, therefore, J. W. P. Huntington, journalist, politician and Oregon Superintendent of Indian affairs, arrived in the Klamath country to arrange for a council meeting. The date was set for early October, and the area known as "Council Grove" near the Klamath Agency was designated as the location. Over a thousand Indians met with the government commissioners in October: some seven hundred Klamaths, over three hundred Modocs, and a small band of Paiutes whom the Oregonians called "Yahooskin Snakes." For a week whites and Modocs talked, with two local residents, Lindsay Applegate and W. C. McKay, acting as interpreters. Applegate was on excellent terms with all of the Indians represented, and without doubt he presented the government terms clearly.

Huntington's treaty provided for a permanent settlement between whites and Indians in the Lakes region. First, the Indians ceded all rights to their traditional lands to the United States. In turn, a tract of land north of Upper Klamath Lake was set aside as a reservation. While much of this land was considered unfit for settlement, the Indians were at least given access to the lake. All Indians covered by the treaty were to reside on this reservation, while whites, excepting public officials and employees, were forbidden access. The government reserved the right to locate other Indians on the reservation at a future date. In return for the cession the government agreed to pay the Indians eight thousand dollars annually for the first five years, five thousand dollars annually for the next five years, and three thousand dollars annually for the five years succeeding, payment to begin upon ratification. Second, to aid the Indians in adopting the white man's ways, a sum of thirty-five thousand dollars was allocated for the purchase of food, clothing, farming implements and teams. As soon as possible, mills, shops and a school-house

Courtesy Smithsonian Institution

Modoc Head Erect (also called Shacknasty Jim)

were to be erected, and resident farmers, craftsmen, and teachers were to instruct the Indians in both practical and book knowledge. Third, the Indians agreed to obey United States' laws. In particular, they were to stay sober, for as the treaty noted, "whisky is . . . the great source of evil [for] the noble Red men."

With varying degrees of reluctance, the Indians signed. Of the Indians, the Klamaths were by far the most willing. The reservation was, after all, located wholly on their land; they were giving up little and gaining much. They were, moreover, eager to cooperate with the whites, were in effect white men's Indians. According to Modoc myth, the Creator Kumush had predicted that the Klamaths would "be like women, easy to frighten." Schonchin, major chief of the Modocs, had more to lose but signed anyway. His band was located on the Sprague River, southeast of the reservation. In his prime he had led the attacks on emigrants which had earned the Modocs their reputation, but now, old and retired from the war-path, he was inclined to make the best of a less than perfect situation. "I thought," he later declared, that "if we killed all the white men we saw, that no more would come. We killed all we could; but they came more and more, like new grass in the spring. I looked around, and saw that many of our young men were dead, and could not come back to fight. My heart was sick. My people were few. I threw down my gun. I said, I will not fight again. I made friends with the white man. I am an old man; I cannot fight now. I want to die in peace." Jack was the most reluctant. Not only must he move from the Lost River country, but also he would have to pay deference to the recognized authority of Old Schonchin (so-called to distinguish him from his brother, Schonchin John, who died on the gallows with Jack). He signed, nevertheless, or at least he grasped the pen which made his mark under his Indian name, Keintpoos.

Whatever Jack's reasons for signing — and these he carried with him to the grave — he did not remain long on the reservation. Telling a local rancher, John A. Fairchild, that "the treaty was a lie," the dissident chief returned with his band to the Lost River country early in 1865. Perhaps, as one official sarcastically put it, Jack realized that "Reservation life was not healthy for royalty." Certainly he resented Old Schonchin's status. An advocate of peace and cooperation, the old Modoc received from the whites not only recognition as head chief but preferential treatment as well. Jack was recognized merely as a sub-chief. Nor did Jack like his neighbors on the reservation. Animosity had long existed between Klamath and Modoc, although, according to legend, the two had once belonged to the same group. At about the time of the American Revolution, however, the Modocs declared their independence and won the ensuing civil war. Klamath willingness to work for and with the whites compounded the mutual dislike and was especially offensive to Jack. Finally, under no circumstances could life on the reservation compare to the freedom of the Lost River region or the excitement of Yreka City. Jack and his followers had grown accustomed to both, and homesickness was a major factor in the decision to return.

The settlers in the region viewed Jack's return with consternation, and demanded his removal. In 1865 Captain McGreggor, commander at Fort Klamath, requested that the Modocs return to the reservation, but they refused. Lindsay Applegate, newly appointed sub-agent, made a second try the following year with the same results. And in 1867 Superintendent Huntington himself, in the Klamath area to distribute the first annuity goods provided for by the 1864 treaty, went down to Tule Lake in the hope of bringing Jack back. But Jack met him at Lost River, refused to return, refused any goods, and told Huntington that if he crossed the river, he "would fire on him." Although McGreggor, Applegate and Huntington all duly reported Jack's defiance to the authorities in Washington, no action was taken.

If Jack was aware of conditions on the Klamath Reservation, which he no doubt was, this could only confirm him in his decision. The promised government construction (saw-mills, flour-mills, etc.) had never begun, nor did any seem pending. But a comprehensive attempt to change the Indians' culture, their way of life, was well underway. The old hereditary chieftainships were abolished, and in their stead the agents substituted the democratic process. The elected chief, David Allen, or Allen David, as the Indians called him, soon earned Captain Jack's cordial hatred. A court system on the American model was instituted, replete with an Indian judge (the chief) and a sheriff. The agents waged a constant war against the native religion, singling out in particular the religious leaders known as shamans. One shaman was imprisoned for practicing "spiritual medicine" while others were fined. They were humiliated at every opportunity to demonstrate to the Indians that any claims of omnipotence were lies. When the shamans threatened ritual killings of the agents, the agents defied them, challenging them to do their worst. Nothing happened, and the shamans lost even more respect.

The Indians also claimed that they were being exploited by unscrupulous whites, especially military personnel from nearby Fort Klamath. Although Applegate had forbidden gambling, one captain told the gullible Indians that it was perfectly legal and relieved them of thirty-seven horses. The reservation lacked a store, and consequently the squaws traded at the fort commissary, paying for their goods through prostitution. On some occasions they even received change in the form of greenbacks. "Our women make us ashamed," David Allen protested, "they make us feel sick." Officers sometimes took the wife of an Indian willing or not, as did one, who failing in courtship, returned with armed soldiers and forcibly took her away. The double-standard was all too apparent to the Indians. "S'pose an Injun man, he see a white man's wife," complained one Indian cuckold. "He give presents; he win her heart; he talk to her sometime. He tell her, 'Come go with me.' She come. He take her away. White man come home. He no see his wife. He see him children cry. He get mad. He take a gun. He hunt'em. He find'em. He 'shoot'em, one Injun man."

Klamath Reservation and Captain Jack were, however, part of a larger scheme of things. There were many reservations with conditions approximating those of Klamath, and many chiefs like Jack, roaming free in the West and threatening the peace. Indeed to Easterners and Westerners alike — the former hoping to assimilate the Red men into civilization, the latter wanting to exterminate them — the Indian situation was like a tinderbox awaiting a spark. When newly elected President Ulysses S. Grant assumed office in 1869, therefore, he promised to pursue a policy toward the Indians that would lead to their "ultimate civilization and citizenship." Congress, "too busy to or too lazy to examine the Indian question," obligingly voted an appropriation of two million dollars to finance peace-making and provided for the president to appoint a ten-man commission to work jointly with the Secretary of the Interior in controlling the funds. Grant created the Board of Indian Commissioners in June, 1869, selecting men nominated by various religious denominations. The Board had full powers of inspection, could oversee the purchase of goods for Indians, and communicate any complaints against officials to the Indian Bureau or the Department of the Interior.

To achieve his aims, Grant could choose one of three policies. The first of these was the old method of allowing the Interior Department to be wholly responsible for administering Indian affairs. One official later called this the "civil service" policy, but actually it allowed the political party in power to use offices for patronage as a part of the general spoils system of the age. Such a system was vulnerable to abuse, for offices were rewards and must be lucrative for the appointees. Many agents were thus "feathering their own nests," rather than furthering the interest of their Indian wards. Indeed, "rapacious" and "rascally" became common adjectives to describe agents in the Eastern press.

The second method advocated was to turn the Indians over to the "tender care" of the War Department. General W. T. Sherman, the Western commander, favored this plan because he believed that Indians could be subdued only by force. The Army, therefore, should have full control. Grant liked the idea because he needed places for the large surplus of Union officers created by the ending of the Civil War. Despite evidence that military officers could be as corrupt as civilians, high-ranking officers in the West tended to blame civilians — officials as well as settlers — for causing the wars they had to fight. Without full responsibility they would not cooperate. At the conclusion of the Shoshone War in 1869, for example, the Indian superintendent in charge told the defeated Indians that they must reside on a reservation and that he would "use the military against [them] if [they] did not." They would not go. An appeal to Crook brought no aid. "I did not order them to go," he declared, "for the reason that I have their confidence that I will do . . . only what is best and right, both for themselves and the government."

The third method later became known as the "Quaker policy," named for its sponsors, the Society of Friends. "The ghost of Praise-God Barebone's Parliament has been reanimating the political dry bones around Washington," the *New York Tribune* reported in May, 1869. "The *habitues* of the Indian Office have been startled by the spectacle of white neckcloths, and broad-brimmed hats, and long brown coats, in their sanctuary, while snuff-colored apparitions, hugging antiquated umbrellas, mingle with the publicans and Sinners of that delectable locality." The "Friends" had indeed been lobbying in Washington. They wanted an independent Indian Bureau in which philanthropy and Christianity could be united to elevate the Indian as the combination had done, they believed, for the freemen in the south. Following an interview with Grant, however, they received the right to nominate superintendents and agents.

Assailed from three directions, Grant adopted all three policies, for he actually had little choice. He could not openly oppose religious interests. He could not totally neglect Congress, which had its eye on patronage. And he himself wished to promote army interests. When in 1870, Congress passed a law barring military officers from holding civil office, Grant simply turned the resulting vacancies over to Godly interests, causing a great scramble among the denominations — all except the Mormons, who realized the futility of making a request, and the Jews, who considered proselytizing unorthodox — to secure, if not a superintendency, at least an agency. Grant thus made a fragile peace with the religious groups by dividing up the reservations.

However well-intentioned, such a policy could lead only to confusion and bickering. Certainly this was the case in Oregon. To replace Huntington, who was a "Johnson man" in the first place, and a dying man in the second — "another wreck upon the shore of Time" as a result of intemperance — Grant selected Alfred B. Meacham. Although Meacham was later saved from having his head blown off only because the Modoc stripping him of his clothes did not want to get them dirty, he always posed as the Indian's friend. Probably he was, since the historian Hubert Howe Bancroft, who can always be trusted to represent the Westerner's view, sarcastically described him as "a man with a hobby. He believed that he knew all about the savage race, and how to control it." At any rate, shortly after Meacham's appointment, Grant adopted his three-fold policy. Oregon was assigned to the War Department. But Meacham had powerful friends in the state: they protested and a compromise was effected. As a Methodist layman, he qualified under the Quaker policy and could thus retain the superintendency. All agents except two, however, were to be appointed from the military. Captain O. C. Knapp, a Civil War hero, was assigned to the Klamath Reservation. Conflict was practically inevitable, for Meacham had a very low opinion of the army. On one occasion he declared that he would rather risk an attack than take along an escort, preferring the raids to the "presence of the soldiers." On another, he asserted that it would take twenty years to undo the effect of the military agents, for when they came "the Sabbath was soon disregarded; Christian and moral men . . . were compelled to resign."

During the summer and autumn of 1869 Meacham visited the reservations under his charge, attempting as best he could to improve conditions. At Klamath he faced an additional problem — Captain Jack. Believing that the Tule Lake Modocs could be returned without resorting to military force, Meacham dispatched a courier with the request that the Modocs meet him at Link River, a settlement half-way between Klamath Agency and Tule Lake. Jack replied that anyone wishing to see him must come to his country, and furthermore, that he was not in the mood to talk anyway. Despite this "insulting response," Meacham decided to go to the Lost River country and requested an army escort. At first the commander at Fort Klamath insisted that he had "no men to spare" because they were needed for "police duty." In reality, Meacham drily observed, this meant "that one half the soldiers were needed to guard the other half." (A few days earlier some soldiers had deserted, those sent after them deserted also, and all had to be captured and returned by the Klamath Indians). After some delay, however, a squad of soldiers was ordered to accompany the superintendent.

Meacham's party left Klamath Agency December 3. In addition to the soldiers and teamsters, he took along Knapp, I. D. Applegate, and McKay. When they reached Linkville they left the soldiers behind; they would still be close enough if an emergency arose, while far enough away not to alarm the Indians. On December 22, as the whites entered Modoc country, four warriors appeared and warned them to turn back. Meacham stubbornly pushed on, however, soon riding into the Indian camp. It was ominously silent, and no Indian was to be seen.

The ensuing talks were stormy. At first Jack permitted only Meacham to enter his lodge. But he refused to shake hands, smoke, or speak to the white man. The silence was broken when Scarfaced Charley delivered a tirade, the substance of which was "White man, go home!" Meacham held his ground, explaining that he was a "big chief" as well as their friend, and deserved a hearing. Jack then spoke for the first time. "I have nothing to say that you would like to hear," he declared. "All your people are liars and swindlers. I do not believe half that is told me." The ice was broken nevertheless and Jack agreed to talk with all the whites present, producing several letters written by local residents attesting to his good character and peaceful disposition.

The formal conference began with a feast, no Modoc eating until the whites had finished, in deference to memory of Ben Wright and his supposed attempt at poisoning them years ago. Through interpreter Frank Riddle, a squaw-man from Kentucky, Jack opened his arguments. First, he denied that he had been a party to the 1864 treaty. Meacham pointed out that Jack had made his mark — which was true — and had also accepted treaty goods from Huntington — which was doubtful. Jack then asked what part of the reservation was to be his, declaring that he would go if he could live near his friend, Link River Jack. Meacham agreed and began to feel relief when suddenly the shaman, Curly-Headed Doctor, rose and stated simply but firmly, "We won't go there." For the Modocs that ended the talks, and Jack started to leave. "Do not go," Meacham ordered. "We mean peace but we are ready for war .... You agreed to go with us, and you shall do it." Jack then asked what would happen "if he did not." Meacham "told him plainly that we would whip him until he was willing." Jack promised to make a decision in the morning.

Both sides, tense and suspicious of the other, withdrew for the night. The Modocs met in council. One party wanted to kill the whites immediately; Captain Jack and others dissented. As they debated this proposal, Curly-Headed Doctor "made medicine" but "failed therein, as Baal did Ahab," Meacham declared, the Methodist in him coming to the fore. Suspecting treachery, the whites inspected their arms and kept watch. Under the pretence of rounding up stray horses, they sent a messenger to Linkville with orders for the soldiers to come immediately. Tension mounted steadily as the night wore on.

Shortly after midnight the issue was unexpectedly decided.

Courtesy National Archives

Modoc Scar-Faced Charley, 1873

The debate was still going on in Jack's lodge, and Curly-Headed Doctor was making medicine accompanied by the chanting of an old woman, when the sound of horses' hooves on the frozen ground interrupted. Minutes later the troopers charged into camp at a full gallop with sabers clanking and sage-brush cracking. They were roaring drunk. Chaos ensued. Jack, the shaman, and a few others headed for the sage-brush. But the rest, confused and disorganized, were surrounded and disarmed. When daylight came, the Modocs began breaking camp and collecting their goods in preparation for the trip to the reservation. Hoping to persuade Jack to go also, Meacham sent the chief's sister, "Queen Mary," (an attractive woman whom Jack had sold as a mistress to at least five or six miners) to ask Jack to join them. The party set out for Klamath on the next day, Jack and the others joining it at Linkville. On December 28, 1869, Meacham triumphantly arrived at the agency with his wards.

Before leaving for Salem, Meacham hoped to insure that the Modocs would be contented on the reservation. A tract known as Modoc Point was set aside exclusively for them, and Meacham promised that when allotments of land were made in severalty (individual ownership) as provided for in the 1864 treaty, they could select sites from this land — in other words, they were the owners. He also explained the Modocs' rights to their Klamath neighbors and received the latter's promise that all would share equally in the timber on the slopes of the adjacent mountains.

To cement friendly relations between the Klamaths and Modocs, an impressive peace ceremony was held. A hatchet was laid in an open space. Allen David and Captain Jack then strode forward, each placing a pine bough on the hatchet. The sub-chiefs of both tribes followed suit. Allen David then made a speech, stressing that they were brothers and that they must live together peaceably under the white man's law, for "we cannot be Indians longer." Jack answered with a speech of his own. To the Klamaths he declared: "The blood is all washed from our hands. We are enemies no longer." To the whites he promised: "We will not throw away the white chief's words. I have planted a strong stake in the ground. I have tied myself with a strong rope. I will not dig up the stake. I will not break the rope."

Following the ceremony the Modocs were issued annuity goods (as payment for their lands under treaty). Jack and the sub-chiefs each received two pairs of blankets, the headmen one pair each, while every man, woman and child received one blanket. Each man received one woolen shirt and cloth for one pair of pants. Each woman and child was given one flannel dress pattern along with a supply of thread, needles and buttons. They were also issued a ration of flour and beef which formed the regular government supply.

With the Indians apparently contented, Meacham held a "big free talk" (informal conference) New Year's Eve. One old warrior, who had come into contact with a Methodist missionary years before, looked around him, saw Klamath and Modoc sitting together like brothers, and decided that this was the work of the Holy Spirit. "When I was a young man," he said, "I saw a white man on his knees telling the 'Holy Spirit' to come. Maybe the Great Spirit sent you Meacham with it." Indian and white together welcomed the new year, firing a pistol at the exact moment it arrived. Since the Indians failed to understand the significance, they were told that the "old year would die in the west, and another would be born in the east."

But this child-like tranquillity was short-lived. Jack and his Modocs went to work cutting and preparing timber for houses; seemingly, they were intent upon adhering to the treaty. But the Klamaths made life miserable for them. They taunted the prodigals for giving up their carefree days in the Lost River country and meekly coming to the reservation. The reservation was Klamath property, they claimed, and everything on it: the timber, the grass, even the fish in the lake. They demanded that the Modocs hand over a portion of the lumber they had finished as a tax for cutting timber. On occasion they drove Modoc women from the lake and prevented them from catching fish. The Modocs were constantly reminded that they were unwelcome intruders.

Although an extremely proud man, Jack held his temper. He relied upon Agent Knapp to enforce the Modocs' treaty rights and redress the grievances which they were suffering at the hands of the Klamaths. On three occasions, therefore, he visited the agent and requested aid. But Knapp was curt with Jack and never intervened; if the Modocs were having trouble, they could move to another location. They did — and the Klamaths followed, hurling the same abuse and making the same demands.

In April, 1870, moreover, Knapp declared the Modocs to be self-sufficient and stopped issuing them food.

Convinced that the Modocs could not live on the reservation in peace and that Knapp had no concern for their well-being, Jack decided to return to Lost River. In April he called a meeting of all the Modocs. So persuasive was he that even the Modocs of Old Schonchin's band resolved to go. In late April Jack and three hundred seventy-one Modocs (he had come in with less than fifty) quietly left Klamath Agency. Knapp blamed Lieutenant G. A. Goodale, commander at Fort Klamath, for allowing them to escape; Goodale blamed Knapp for provoking Jack into leaving. Neither made an attempt to return the Modocs.

Free of the reservation, Modoc solidarity quickly vanished. Old Schonchin, resenting Jack's authority, returned to Klamath. During the spring and summer of 1870 many families followed him. Another group, apprehensive lest Jack and Curly-Headed Doctor touch off a war with the whites, settled near Lower Klamath Lake. For them this was the best of both possible worlds: clear of reservation life as well as any trouble which might start at Lost River.

Those Modocs remaining with Jack quickly resumed their old habits. They frequented Yreka City and were evidently on good terms with the citizens there. In fact, Meacham later blamed the Indian women who plied their trade with the miners for giving Klamath Agency a bad reputation which was undeserved. The settlers in the Lost River Basin, however, were outraged. On one value both the "friends of the Indian" and the "enemies of the Indian" could agree — work. No single virtue was more American or more "civilized" to nineteenth-century men reared as they were under the Protestant ethic. "Why should immense regions — empires in extent — be rendered useless for human improvement, merely to perpetuate the vagabond propensities of savages?" the *New York Tribune* asked. Why, when they "could be better fed and clothed from the products of a single one of the large Illinois farms?" To be sure, whites were to blame for much of the trouble with the Indians, but "should the safety and comfort of . . . civilized settlers be jeopardized in an attempt to appease savages?" No better example, of course, of the "vagabond propensities of savages" could be found than in the behavior of Jack and his Modocs. After his

Courtesy National Archives

Captain Jack, Modoc subchief executed October 3, 1873

experience at Klamath, Jack no longer believed himself bound by the 1864 treaty. While the Modocs committed no violence, they made themselves a nuisance. They stole hay and turned their stock into hayfields to graze.They entered houses uninvited, whooped and yelled, rested on the beds, demanded free food. Jack tried to extort rent from the settlers, and some paid in order to keep the Indians away. To them Jack was comparable to a small-time hoodlum operating a "protection agency."

Appeals to the army for relief brought no response. An Apache war had begun in Arizona, and Crook and most of the troops had been sent there. The Department of the Columbia, which included the Modoc region, was reduced to an ineffectual force. Its commander, Civil War veteran, E. R. S. Canby, could only hope that peace would prevail. Only one infantry company remained at Fort Klamath, while the nearest supporting force — one infantry company and one troop of cavalry — was some one hundred miles distant at Camp Warner. For the moment, at least, Jack had little to fear from the army.

This uneasy yet peaceful state of affairs continued throughout 1870. Late in the next spring, however, Jack almost provoked a clash. His niece became sick, and the services of a shaman were needed. Since Curly-Headed Doctor was away stealing horses, Jack hired a Klamath shaman from the agency. The overconfident Klamath was so sure of his success that he accepted the fee in advance, which guaranteed a cure in Indian custom. But he failed, and Jack, in accordance with tribal law, killed him. The authorities promptly took notice of this violation of the 1864 treaty, and issued a warrant for Jack's arrest. Although Jack avoided apprehension, he quickly realized that he had made a mistake. In July he held an informal conference with some of the Yreka citizens who were sympathetic to the Modocs and told them that he would in no way disturb the peace. As a result, Jesse Applegate wrote Meacham that conciliation was still possible. The order for arrest should be suspended, and Jack's request for a small reservation in the Lost River area should be granted. If Meacham could come, the Modocs were willing to meet with him in council to settle all difficulties.

Deciding to "make one more effort for peace," Meacham secured the revocation of the arrest order, but his schedule prevented him from meeting with Jack. Instead, in August, 1871, he delegated his brother John, whom he had recently appointed to succeed Knapp as Agent at Klamath, as his personal representative. Meacham's instructions were simple. First, the Superintendent would try to persuade the officials in Washington to grant the Modocs a reservation in the Lost River country. Second, since this would take some time, the Indians must return to the Klamath Reservation. John was to do all in his power to protect them from harassment such as they had suffered previously. Third, if after a thorough investigation, Jack or any of his men were arrested, they were to be guaranteed a trial by jury under civil law. Fourth, and finally, if the Modocs complied, and Meacham failed to secure their reservation, he would allow them to go to the new Malheur Reservation, which would be ready for occupancy by autumn.

When John Meacham tried to set a date for the conference, however, he was rebuffed. Instead of negotiating, Jack went on a rent-collecting tour and allowed one of his men to lead a raid on the livestock of a wagon train traveling on the old emigrant road. Then he agreed to a talk, but only on condition that the parties of both sides consist of four men each. Meacham accepted, but when he and three other whites arrived at the council-site they found nearly thirty armed Modocs awaiting them. Under these circumstances real negotiations were impossible. As usual Curly-Headed Doctor and other hot-heads wanted to kill the four immediately. Vetoing this plan, Jack dictated his terms. The Modocs would not go to the reservation. They would, however, cease molesting the settlers. Meacham, whose party was badly outnumbered, could only give them permission to remain on Lost River until his brother Alfred could come to the Klamath area.

After this diplomatic fiasco, which was in effect the last serious effort to preserve the peace, both sides began to stiffen in their positions. A major factor as far as the Modocs were concerned was the religious revival known as the "Ghost Dance," which had begun in Nevada in 1869. The "Ghost Dance" religion was definitely anti-white in emphasis, a last desperate attempt of a threatened race to stave off extinction. Men, women and children danced so that Old Man Coyote would bring back the dead. Some, called the "dreamers," had actually been back to meet the dead. Once the dead had returned they would never die again — only the whites would be consumed. Spreading rapidly, the Ghost Dance reached the Modocs by 1872. A Walker River Paiute, Frank Spencer, took it to Klamath Reservation by 1871; in the spring of 1872, a reservation Modoc, Doctor George, introduced it to the Lost River Modocs. Curly-Headed Doctor became an enthusiastic convert, convinced that he could stop any white attack with a twisted-tule rope over which no white man could cross (he later tried this at the lava-bed fight, but it did not work). In its promise of a revival of numerical strength as well as invincibility in the face of white power, the Ghost Dance strengthened the Modoc resolve to fight, if necessary, to retain their homeland.

Jack's period of grace was fast running out; in Washington the War Department was becoming concerned over the possibility of a war and pressuring the Bureau of Indian Affairs to settle the matter. As a result, the Indian Commissioner rejected Meacham's request for a Lost River Reservation and in the spring of 1872, removed him from office, appointing in his stead an Oregon lawyer, T. B. Odeneal. The new superintendent was to return Jack to the reservation and thus solve the problem.

Odeneal apparently believed that force was the best remedy, but while he received permission to arrest Jack, both he and the army procrastinated. Neither kept the other informed, and during the summer nothing was accomplished. In November, however, Odeneal received orders from Washington to move the Modocs to the reservation — peaceably if possible, forcibly if necessary. He wrote Colonel Frank Wheaton, commander of the Lakes District, that he would hold a conference with Jack; if Jack persisted in his refusal, he would then send a request for troops, and Wheaton could send the necessary orders to Major John Green, the commander at Fort Klamath. Odeneal then sent Ivan Applegate (whom Jack thoroughly hated for having obtained the murder warrant in 1871) to request that Jack meet the new superintendent at Linkville. As might have been expected, Jack refused. He would not talk to anyone; he would not return to the reservation; instead he adhered to his 1864 treaty with Steele. Curly-Headed Doctor's followers made the standard proposal that Applegate be killed immediately in order to start the war, but after a heated debate, Jack again dampened their ardor.

Odeneal was greatly alarmed by Applegate's report. He de-

Courtesy Amon Carter Museum, Fort Worth

Cappolas (Boney Man), Modoc warrior

cided to act immediately in order to forestall war and requested troops from Major Green. Without waiting for orders from either of his superiors, Wheaton or Canby, Green complied and sent Captain James Jackson and some forty men to arrest Jack on November 28. The next day Jackson failed in the attempt to arrest Jack, and lost eight men either dead or wounded in the ensuing gunfight. The Modoc war had begun. With their superiors in complete ignorance of what was happening, Odeneal and Green thus touched off one of the most costly Indian wars in United States history. For over a year, Jack's little band defied the government; inflicting heavy casualties on the army, killing settlers, even assassinating Canby and other peace commissioners in 1873 (for which Jack and his cohorts were later hanged). Although in the end they were defeated, they provided powerful moral support to other tribes which must soon make the decision to resist or submit, in particular one band of Nez Percé. For its part, as subsequent events would reveal, the government learned nothing: neither to treat the Indians with justice nor to exterminate them ruthlessly the moment their land was desired. Either would have been more honest and humane than the policies followed.

BIBLIOGRAPHY

Fritz, Dr. Henry E. *The Movement for Indian Assimilation, 1860-1890.* Philadelphia: University of Pennsylvania Press, 1963.

Meacham, Hon. A. B. *Wigwam and War-Path; or the Royal Chief in Chains.* 2nd ed. Boston: John P. Dale and Company, 1875.

Murray, Keith A. *The Modocs and Their War.* Norman: University of Oklahoma Press, 1959.

Riddle, Jeff C. *The Indian History of the Modoc War and the Causes That Led to It.* Marnell and Company, 1914.

With justice, personal rights, and the protection of law, the Gospel will do for our Red brothers what it has done for other races — give to them homes, manhood and freedom.

H. B. Whipple, bishop of Minnesota

It was these Christian Nez Perces who made with the government a thief treaty. Sold to the government all of this land. Sold what did not belong to them. We got nothing for our country.

Yellow Wolf, Nez Perce warrior

CHAPTER 10

Thief Treaties and Lie-Talk Councils

R. Morris Day

AMONG THE INDIAN tribes of North America, the Nez Perces have occupied the place of honor in the American mind. Lewis and Clark, who explored the Northwest in 1805-1806, esteemed the Nez Perces (so-called by early French trappers in the area because they pierced their noses for ornamental purposes) above all other tribes they had encountered. Although critical of their stinginess, Clark nevertheless described them as the most hospitable Indians west of the Rocky Mountains. Lewis called them "affectionate people." Many years later, when a few small bands turned upon the invaders and fought a hopeless war to retain their freedom, they won the respect of whites, friend and foe alike. Helen Hunt Jackson, contemporary chronicler of Indian suffering, extolled them as the "richest, noblest, and most gentile" of the Northwest tribes. Their conqueror, General Nelson A. Miles, praised them as "the most intelligent that he [had] ever seen"; a people who if "justly treated . . . could be made loyal and useful" citizens. Even General O. O. Howard, whose role in the war was less than glorious, paid a grudging tribute to their military skill, comparing them to the Cossacks of the Russian steppes.

On the eve of the American conquest of the Pacific Northwest, the Nez Perces lived along the Snake River and its tributaries, the Grand Ronde, the Salmon, and the Clearwater. They were semi-nomadic, comparable to an Easterner who was rich enough "to have a winter house in New York, a house for the summer in Newport, and one for autumn in White Plains." Ignoring agriculture, they depended instead upon game and fish, roots and berries for their food. After the introduction of the horse, the Nez Perces perfected breeding techniques, building up large herds of Appaloosas. With their newly acquired mobility they hunted over wide expanses of territory and fought with their rivals, the Blackfeet to the north and the Snakes to the south. As in most primitive cultures, political authority was decentralized. A headman or war chief commanded more by example than by any abstract theory of power — similar to the German chieftains whom Tacitus described in *Germania*. No headman could compel compliance with his orders, and when he spoke in council he represented only his voluntary followers. Nez Perce religion was naturalistic as well as highly individualistic. In general they saw the earth as animate, as their "Great Mother" who provided them with the bounty of life. As a result, they were naturally reluctant to wound or molest the living Mother Earth. While they had shamans who could mediate between them and adverse forces such as the weather or disease, the Nez Perces exalted no organized priesthood. Instead, each Indian worked out his own relationship with a personal guardian spirit called his *Wyakin*. He sought his *Wyakin* much as the early monks sought God: after instruction he went alone into the wilderness to fast and wait. His *Wyakin* might appear as a yellow wolf, a wounded bear, or some other apparition of nature, and once found, could warn him in times of danger, assist him in difficulties, or punish him if ignored.

The Nez Perce culture was thus diametrically opposed to that of the Americans. Subscribers to the cult of progress, the latter sought to harness nature to their own ends. The whites were like grizzly bears, the Nez Perces like deer, Chief Joseph later declared. "We were contented to let things remain as the Great Spirit Chief made them. They were not; and would change the rivers and the mountains if they did not suit them." In the white scheme of things there was no room for either the reverence of nature or the tolerance of a religion so intimately connected with it. As General Miles rhapsodized when observing the Illinois countryside from his railway car, "where the smoke of their signal fires had curled toward the skies now stood the schoolhouse on the hill and the church-spire pointing to heaven." To enforce the acceptance of their culture, moreover, the Americans possessed a highly centralized political system based on a sophisticated theory of sovereignty. Ultimately that sovereignty was indivisible, as the Confederates were to be taught, and it was

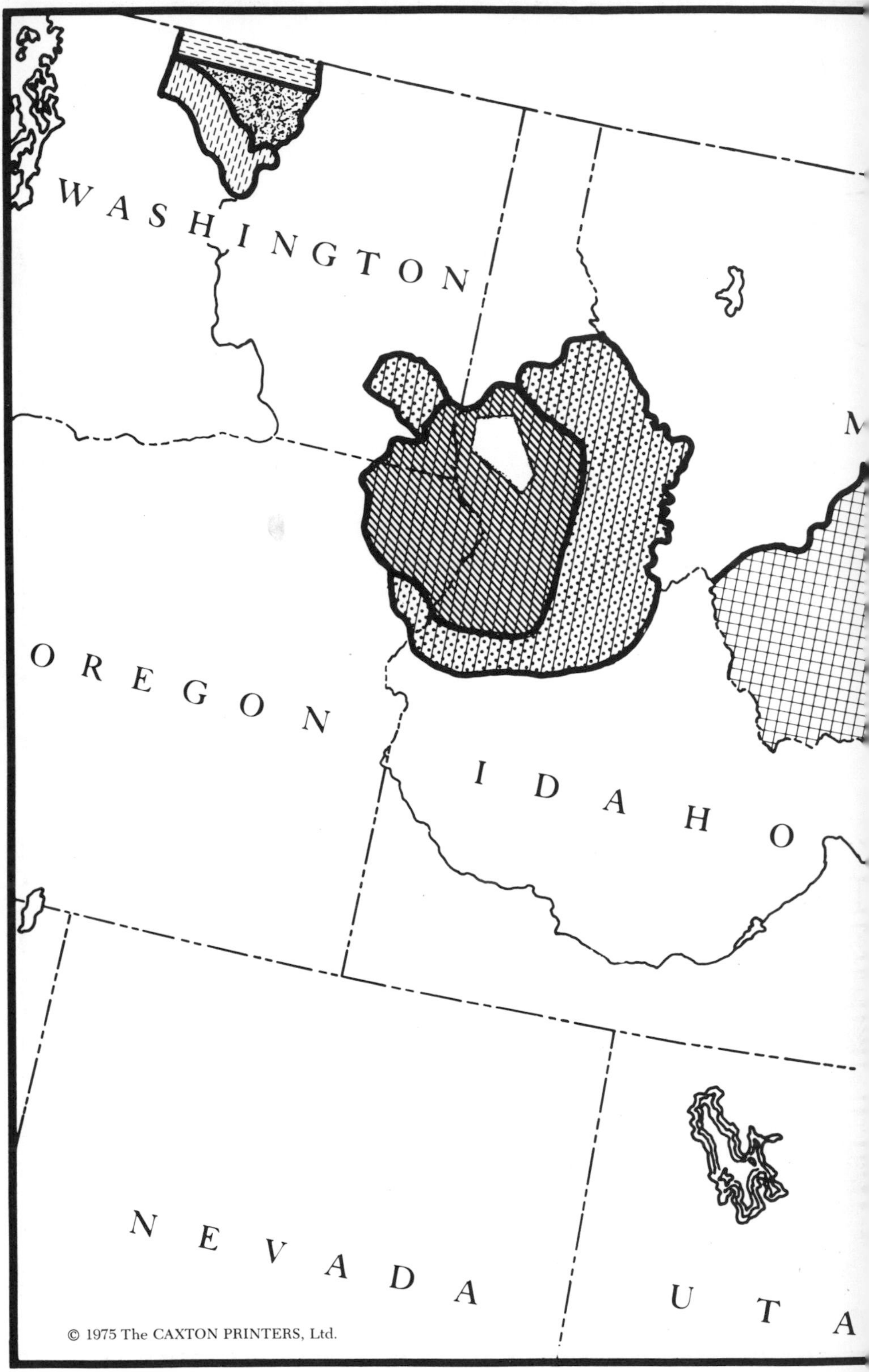
WASHINGTON
OREGON
IDAHO
NEVADA
UTA

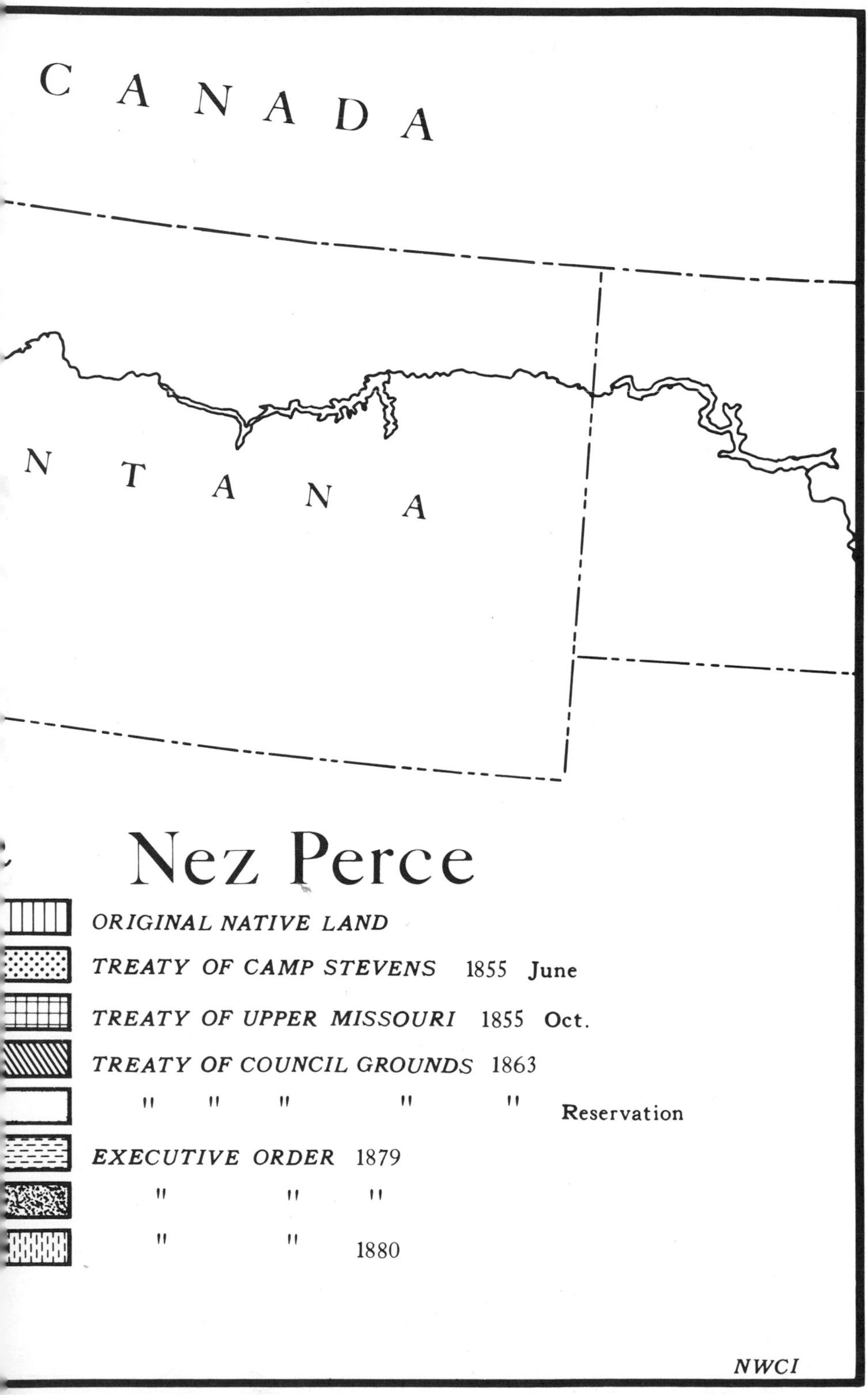
CANADA
NTANA
Nez Perce
ORIGINAL NATIVE LAND
TREATY OF CAMP STEVENS 1855 June
TREATY OF UPPER MISSOURI 1855 Oct.
TREATY OF COUNCIL GROUNDS 1863
" " " " " Reservation
EXECUTIVE ORDER 1879
" " "
" " 1880
NWCI

impersonal, as the Nez Perces were soon to learn. Between white and Indian there was an unbridgeable gulf in politics — one as great as that between a Roman Emperor and a German chieftain. Finally, neither side understood the way of life of the other. Excluding guns, liquor, plows, and other products of technology, the complex American culture was beyond the comprehension of the Nez Perces. The whites, on the other hand, believed they were the bearers of a superior civilization and laid the burden of change solely upon the Indians.

The inevitable cultural collision was, of course, in the future. From their mountainous rampart laying athwart the passage to the Northwest, the Nez Perces watched the white vanguard arrive with equanimity. During the first decades of the nineteenth century, the Hudson's Bay Company and John Jacob Astor's American Fur Company penetrated the area and built the first white settlements. Yet the traders posed only a slight threat to the Indians. Concerned exclusively with profit, they neither wanted land nor desired to change the Indian's way of life. Their effect was therefore minimal. They could never persuade the Nez Perces, for example, to become trappers despite the latter's desire to acquire white man's goods, especially firearms. On some occasions, to be sure, they made the Nez Perces painfully aware of the white man's ways. In 1813 John Clarke, an Astorian trader who had lost several prized possessions to pilfering Indians, taught the Nez Perces an object lesson on the sin of stealing. Catching an unfortunate Indian in the act of theft, he had the Indian's arms and legs bound, gave him a trial and promptly pronounced the death penalty. When a crude gallows had been constructed, Clarke summoned the other Indians and delivered a speech extolling the benefits which the whites bestowed and condemning the unsavory habits of the Indians. The formalities concluded, the poor Nez Perce dropped to his death — all in the time-honored manner of western civilized man.

Far more dangerous than the traders were the missionaries. Contact with the whites had acquainted the Nez Perces and other Indians with the powerful white God. Eager to share in the great and beneficial powers of this God, they sent a delegation to St. Louis in 1831 to request instructors in the new faith. Methodists, Presbyterians, and Roman Catholics responded. In 1834 Jason Lee led the initial Methodist expedition west. He was a man who could so easily "make the interests of God identical with his own" that he fitted perfectly an Indian Superintendent's description of the preacher who "had undoubtedly answered when someone else had been called of God to preach the Gospel." Ignoring the rugged domain of the Nez Perces, therefore, Lee and his followers pushed on to the fertile Willamette Valley. Once located, they waged a war of attrition against the Hudson's Bay claims, proselytized for new emigrants from the East, and agitated for a United States' colony to be planted in Oregon. They and their successors were to be highly successful in all three areas, and in the rush of empire-building conversion of the Indians was all but forgotten.

The task of ministering to the Nez Perces thus fell by default to the Presbyterians. Following an exploratory trip in 1835, the American Board sent Dr. Marcus Whitman and Reverend H.H. Spalding to the Northwest in 1836. Because of personal differences the two men could not work together, and so while Whitman settled at Waiilatpu, some twenty miles east of Fort Walla Walla in Cayuse country, Spalding turned back northeast to found Lapwai mission near the Clearwater in Nez Perce country. From the beginning Whitman had little success, but Spalding and his wife became real missionaries, converting many Nez Perces to both Christianity and agriculture.

Spalding also brought discord. Many of the Nez Perces resented the new religion. "Spalding call to Injuns," one Nez Perce declared, "Look up. See Jesus. See Jesus there. One hand pointin' Injuns to Jesus; other hand stealin' Injuns land. That religion," he concluded, "not good for Injun." The arrival of the Jesuit Peter De Smet in 1840 complicated the situation. To the Catholics, Protestant missionaries were "pretended ministers" who taught the Indians error; to the Protestants, the Catholic missionaries were Papists who might even be engaged in some conspiracy to take the West; while Jesuits were men, an otherwise rational John Adams had declared, who merited "eternal perdition on Earth and in Hell." In the middle were the Indians. As the fur trader Alexander Ross wrote, "Papists and Protestants" were "like rivals in trade, huddled together, working confusion" among their converts. When asked years later why he wanted neither schools nor churches built on the reservation, Joseph replied that "they will teach us to quarrel about God, as the Catholics and Protestants do". . .on our reservation. . ."and at other places. We do not want to learn that. We may quarrel with men sometimes about things on this earth, but we never quarrel about God. We do not want to learn that."

Nor did the Nez Perces enjoy being treated like ignorant juveniles. In his attempt to wield a firm hand, Spalding was fond of whipping and subjected even the chiefs to the lash. His whip cut deeper than he thought, as the following incident illustrates. Shortly after his arrival, Spalding sent a party east with a herd of horses to trade for cattle. Layman missionary William Gray was in charge and took with him three Nez Perces — Ellis, Blue Cloak, and The Hat — as well as several Flatheads. Along the way, however, and for unknown reasons, Ellis and Blue Cloak left Gray and returned home. Soon thereafter Gray and the remaining Indians walked into a Sioux trap, and when the latter offered the missionary his life if he would abandon his companions, he accepted. The Sioux then fell upon The Hat and the Flatheads, killing them to a man. Meanwhile Ellis and Blue Cloak arrived at Lapwai to face an angry Spalding. Unaware of the incident that was to make The Hat a martyr to white cowardice and duplicity, Spalding was determined to punish the two for returning without permission. When informed that each was to forfeit two horses and receive fifty lashes, Ellis disdainfully rode off, but Blue Cloak remained, apparently disbelieving the missionary's threats. Spalding then ordered a Nez Perce warrior to whip Blue Cloak. The warrior told Spalding to do it himself. "No," said the missionary, "I do not whip; I stand in the place of God, I command; God does not whip, he commands." "You are a liar," retorted the warrior, pointing to an image Spalding had made which showed God with a bundle of rods, preparing to whip two men for sin. "Whip him," ordered the warrior, "or if not, we will put you in his place and whip you." Spalding complied.

Certainly the Nez Perces also were both confused and resentful over the introduction of white laws and political concepts. The law-giver appeared in 1842 in the person of Dr. Elijah White. One of the original Methodist missionaries, White had quarreled with Jason Lee over mission work — misuse of funds and his fondness for Indian women, some observers reported — and had returned to the East in 1850. Through friends interested in acquiring Oregon for the United States, he secured an interview with the Secretary of War, J. C. Spencer. White hoped to receive an appointment as governor in Oregon, but in view of the delicate nature of Anglo-American relations, he succeeded only in obtaining the appointment as Indian sub-agent for the area. Returning to Oregon in 1842, he soon made little distinction between his commission as sub-agent and that of a governor.

The opportunity to exercise his new authority came in December, 1842. The Cayuses were causing trouble at Whitman's mission and there were rumors of a general Indian uprising. White immediately set out for Waiilatpu, but when he arrived, he could find no Cayuses with whom to treat. Pushing on to Lapwai, where it was reported that the Spaldings were having trouble (they were, but mainly as a result of feuds among the missionaries), he determined to solve any and all problems connected with the Nez Perces. Calling most of the principal headmen together, he promised them that the United States government would protect them from any invasions of their rights by white men. In return, despite the fact that the United States had as yet no jurisdiction whatsoever over Oregon, they must accept a code of laws.

Art. 1. Whoever wilfully takes a life shall be hung.

Art. 2. Whoever burns a dwelling-house shall be hung.

Art. 3. Whoever burns an out-building shall be imprisoned six months, receive fifty lashes, and pay all damages.

Art. 4. Whoever carelessly burns a house or any property shall pay damages.

Art. 5. If any one enter a dwelling without permission of the occupant, the chiefs shall punish him as they think proper. Public rooms are excepted.

Art. 6. If any one steal, he shall pay back twofold; and if it be the value of a beaver-skin or less, he shall receive twenty-five lashes; and if the value is over a beaver-skin, he shall pay back twofold, and receive fifty lashes.

Art. 7. If any one take a horse and ride it, without permission, or take any article and use it, without liberty, he shall pay for the use of it, and receive from twenty to fifty lashes, as the chief shall direct.

Art. 8. If any one enter a field and injure the crops, or throw down the fence, so that cattle or horses go in and do damage, he shall pay all damages, and receive twenty-five lashes for every offense.

Art. 9. Those only may keep dogs who travel or live among the game. If a dog kill a lamb, calf, or any domestic animal, the owner shall pay the damage, and kill the dog.

Art. 10. If an Indian raise a gun or other weapon against a white man, it shall be reported to the chiefs, and they shall punish him. If a white man do the same to an Indian, it shall be reported to Dr. White, and he shall punish or redress it.

Art. 11. If an Indian break these laws, he shall be punished by his chiefs; if a white man break them, he shall be reported to the agent, and punished at his instance.

The Nez Perces reluctantly accepted White's laws, but many no doubt had the same reservations which the Cayuse Yellow Serpent soon expressed. "Where are these laws from?" he asked. "Are they from God or from earth? I would that you might say they were from God. But I think they are from earth," the wise old warrior observed, "because, from what I know of white men, they did not honor these laws."

The laws, moreover, were only the first part of White's solution. The Nez Perce political organization must be tightened, he believed, in order to force the chiefs to accept more authority. Under the tradition system, a headman could rightly deny any responsibility for the actions of his own men. White demanded, therefore, that the Nez Perces select a supreme chief, something they had never done before. All of the other chiefs would have equal powers but would be subordinate to the high chief. Each would select a bodyguard of five men to enforce his lawful demands. After a confused debate among themselves, the Nez Perces elected Ellis as their supreme chief. Yet they never really recognized him as having full authority: the break with tradition was simply too great for them to comprehend the new order which White thought he was imposing. And Ellis, who quickly became egotistical and acted in a "haughty and over-bearing manner," insured that the Nez Perces would never adopt the new political scheme. White, however, naively assumed that centuries of tradition were blotted out by one single stroke of the pen and thus prepared the way for his countrymen to adopt the fiction that one chief could be responsible for all the nation.

The lack of any real means of enforcing their various decrees somewhat mitigated the destructive policies of Spalding and White. Those bands residing some distance from Lapwai were relatively unaffected, while even those near the mission itself, could refuse to obey if they chose. This era of haphazard, *laissez faire* relations with the whites, however, was rapidly drawing to a close. Two decades of white emigration had radically altered the political complexion of the Northwest. During the first half of the century, both the United States and Great Britain claimed the area and, in fact, had jointly occupied it. In 1846, however, both withdrew their extreme claims, the British bowing to the reality of numbers and the Americans to common sense. They set the boundary by treaty at the forty-ninth parallel, and in 1848 Congress organized the Oregon Territory. Then in 1853 the territory was divided, with the region north of the Columbia River line becoming the Territory of Washington.

What type of treatment could the Nez Perces and other Northwest tribes expect now that American authority was officially established? In the Organic Laws of Oregon, drawn up in 1845 in anticipation of achieving territorial status, the regulatory power of the Indians was defined in terms similar to those of the United States Constitution. An additional article guaranteed that the whites would always observe good faith toward the Indians. Tribal lands could never be taken without consent; property, rights, and liberties could never be disturbed; and force could never be used unless in a just and lawful cause.

Good intentions, however sincere, simply did not fit with reality. In 1847 some Cayuses murdered Whitman, his family, and several other whites. The killings threatened to touch off a general uprising in Eastern Oregon, for the Nez Perces clearly sympathized with the Cayuses. When the Oregonians announced that only those individuals directly responsible for the crime were to be punished, the Nez Perces were satisfied. As neutrals, however, they soon received a first-hand view of white justice. The Oregon Volunteers, although quickly crushing the Cayuses, failed to apprehend the guilty parties. Dropping any pretense of punishing individuals, the militia commander promised his men the Cayuse lands. With the governor's consent and without any legal sanction, these lands were opened to white settlement. Even after 1850 when the Indians responsible turned themselves in and were promptly hanged, the land-grab continued.

If the Cayuse war awakened the Nez Perces to their own danger, it was too late. The first governor of Washington Territory, I. I. Stevens, saw the Indians as impediments to progress in the Northwest. Indian title to lands must be extinguished, he told the legislature in January, 1854, in order to insure white ownership and open the way for a transcontinental railroad. His hopes of securing the railroad were frustrated by the Southern bloc in Congress, which had no intention of allowing a route that far north to be selected. With the Indians, however, Stevens was much more successful. To one tribe after the other he made promises he could not deliver, threatened when necessary, and on occasion, according to some sources, resorted to forgery whenever the first two methods failed. By the end of 1854 most of the western chiefs had affixed their marks to a treaty, and in the spring of 1855, Stevens was able to turn his attention to the tribes east of the Cascades. His agents arrived in April to arrange for a council with the Nez Perces and other tribes. Despite their misgivings, they agreed to the meeting; they could do little else than try to co-exist with the whites, for as the Cayuse war had shown, resistance was futile.

During the last week of May, therefore, the Walla Walla valley must have taken on the appearance of a gigantic, traveling carnival. Stevens and Joel Palmer, Superintendent of Indian Affairs in Oregon, arrived early with an escort of some fifty troops and began erecting tents and preparing the site for the reception of the Indians near the old Whitman mission. Soon thereafter the Indians, numbering several thousand, began to arrive. The Nez Perces made their entry with great pomp and circumstance, the warriors parading and performing feats of war and horsemanship. They hoped perhaps to convince the whites that they were a proud and powerful people. Other tribes, however, wore their distrust openly, refused presents, and made camp quietly and without fanfare.

The council began May 29, 1855. For several days Stevens hammered away at the Indians with one constant theme: the Indians must relinquish portions of their lands in order to provide for the needs of the whites. His promises changed constantly, however, as he sought to find something that the Indians would accept. He promised to give all tribes the trappings of white civilization such as mills and schools. He then promised that he would end the attacks upon them from the Blackfeet, Palmer joining with a promise to protect them also from evil white men. When these failed to elicit interest, Stevens threatened that if the Indians did not voluntarily give up part of their lands the more numerous whites would take it all. But the Indians were far less interested in hearing of either blessings or threats than in ascertaining exactly what they must give up. Their cool reception finally forced Stevens to get down to specifics. Showing the Indians maps, he proposed to set up two reservations: one in the Nez Perce country which included almost all of their traditional lands, the other in the Yakima country between the Columbia and Yakima rivers. Those Indians losing their lands were to move to either of the reservations.

The unhappy Indians attempted to delay in order to consider the terms, but Stevens increased the pressure. To those Indians in the Umatilla area who would have to move the greatest distance, he proposed a third reservation of their own. He increased the amount of payment to such a fantastic degree that the Yakimas' charge that they had been promised "a wagon-load of gold as much as six mules could pull over level ground" was not far from the truth. All those who had to move, he assured them, would not be forced to do so until Congress ratified the treaty. In dealing with the Nez Perces, Stevens could count on two factors to aid him. First, they were required to cede very little land and thus did not face the agonizing prospect of moving from their ancestral homes. Second, to overcome the resistance of those chiefs such as Looking Glass, who viewed any concessions with alarm, Stevens could count on the assistance of Chief Lawyer. Lawyer, so called because of his great ability to talk, was the leader of most of the Christian Nez Perces and was anxious to maintain smooth relations with the whites. If Lawyer could persuade the Nez Perces to sign, Stevens promised to uphold his authority as head chief as successor to Ellis, along with monetary rewards commensurate with his status.

When the treaties were brought out, therefore, the Nez Perces signed along with the other tribes. With the exception that they were confirmed in almost all of their lands, the 1855 treaty was typical of those made between the United States and the various Western tribes during this era. Reservation boundaries were described and set apart "for the exclusive use and benefit" of the Nez Perces; no whites could reside in the area without the permission of the Indians, the superintendent, and the agency. For Nez Perce cooperation — since they were not asked to make cessions — the United States was to pay them two

Courtesy National Archives

Looking Glass, Nez Perce chief, 1887

hundred thousand dollars, of which sixty thousand dollars was to be paid the first year after ratification and used as the president deemed necessary for their well-being. The remainder was to be paid annually over the next fifteen years. In addition, the government was to establish schools, shops, mills, and a hospital, to keep them repaired, and to provide skilled personnel to operate them for twenty years. To the head chief, moreover, the United States agreed to pay a salary of five hundred dollars annually, to build and furnish a comfortable house for him, and to plow and fence ten acres of land for his use. As usual the Nez Perces agreed to obey United States laws, maintain the peace, and prohibit the use of liquor on the reservation.

The immediate result of Stevens' diplomacy was war. He had promised those tribes which must move that they could remain on their lands until the treaties were ratified, which would be two to three years (they were ratified in 1859). The Indians, however, were quickly disillusioned as to the value of promises. The treaties were signed June 11, 1855; twelve days later Stevens and Palmer announced that the ceded territory was open to white settlement. The inevitable rush began; settlers hurried to stake out claims. At the same time gold was discovered in the Fort Colville area, and prospectors were soon swarming over it. East of the Cascades, practically every tribe except the Nez Perces went to war in a desperate, futile attempt to halt the white invasion.

Although furious, Stevens nevertheless realized that this was an opportunity to settle forever the Indian problem. Before the Washington assembly he declared that the Indians had given their consent by treaty to the cession of land. But they had acted treacherously and were in effect conspiring to destroy the white race. There will be no more treaties, he concluded, for "extermination should be the reward of their perfidy." The three-year war which followed all but fulfilled this objective. The whites murdered chiefs under flags of truce, hanged Indians without even the pretense of a trial, and burned the villages of any Indians who happened to be in their line of march. When the two territorial governments filed a claim for reimbursement for their military expenses in 1858, Horace Greeley sarcastically commented that "the enterprising territories of Oregon and Washington have handed into Congress their little bill for scalping Indians and violating squaws." Congress should certainly consider these claims, he said, sometime in the next century.

Despite pressure from the hostile tribes to join them in their campaign against the whites, the Nez Perces remained at peace. Some, while sympathizing with the hostiles, rightly feared that taking up arms would only provoke devastating reprisals. Others, especially those who followed Chief Lawyer, were determined to maintain friendly relations with the Americans whatever the cost. On occasion these "friendly" Nez Perces served as packers, scouts, auxilaries, and at least once formed a regular unit, blue uniforms and all, even though Colonel George Wright was just as quick to hang his allies on the charge of suspicion as he was the enemy. Actually the Nez Perces gained nothing from their attempt at appeasement. Friendliness was no guarantee that they would be safe from white encroachments, while the willingness of the Christian Nez Perces to fight for the Americans only widened the split between them and their non-Christian brethren. By standing aside while their neighbors were crushed, they simply insured that when their turn came they must stand alone.

That time was not far in the future; in fact, for most of the Nez Perces the day of reckoning was already at hand. As soon as the hostilities ceased in 1858, and despite the fact that the treaties of 1855 had not been ratified, settlers poured into the region east of the Cascades, occupying the lands ceded in 1855 and pressing ever closer to Nez Perce lands. Briefly in 1859 prospects for permanent peace seemed brighter. Congress finally ratified the Walla Walla Treaties. Many headmen were relieved that at last their title to the lands which they occupied had been confirmed — at least this is what the treaty provided and what the headmen, including Old Joseph, believed — while those who were willing and anxious to receive government annuities were hopeful that payment would now begin. American adherence to the treaty, however, lasted exactly one year. In 1860 gold was discovered on the Clearwater. The rush began, and by late 1861 miners were prospecting on Nez Perce lands. They appropriated land for claims and planned to appropriate more as soon as mining camps could be incorporated as towns, counties organized, and land-offices set up. The usual lawlessness which accompanied the mining frontier also aroused bitterness between Indian and white. Boise had over twenty murders in one year, while L. C. McWhorter has documented the cases of twenty-eight Nez Perces whom the whites murdered. Vigilance committees, moreover, occasionally hanged whites for the murder of other whites, but until 1873 no white was condemned to hang for the murder of an Indian, and even in that instance, no evidence exists that the sentence was executed.

Although in open defiance of the 1855 treaty, the Clearwater was rapidly becoming a white community. Agent A. J. Cain could not or would not stem the invasion. One man facing an army of determined miners would have been as laughable as it would have been tragic. In a similar situation in 1875 a reporter from the *St. Louis Dispatch* interviewed Ephraim Witcher, a miner locally known as "Buckskin." When asked what his chances were of entering the Black Hills to seek gold when the United States government had declared that it would protect the Sioux reservation, Buckskin replied that "The government means to do all that it says, but how can it prevent the inevitable? You can't dam a river, you can't stop twenty thousand western men . . . with a regiment or so of cavalry." The scent of gold "transforms men into crazy people," he declared, "wave follows wave, the tide is just like a stream that overflows its banks and deluges the whole country." If the miners cannot be stopped, what will the government do to preserve the peace? the reporter queried. "Rather than come into conflict with its own people," said Buckskin, it will buy the Indians out and then "throw open the reservation for settlement." If gold were found, Buckskin predicted, "then the fate of the reservation is settled."

Buckskin understood Indian affairs better — or at least was more honest in his appraisal — than the government officials, army officers, and Friends of the Indians *in toto*. In early April, 1861, Cain and his superior, Edward R. Geary, Superintendent of Indian Affairs for Oregon and Washington, (the superintendencies of Washington and Oregon had been united since 1857), bought out the Christian Nez Perces. By an agreement signed at Lapwai, Lawyer and his followers consented to the opening of the reservation area north of the Snake and Clearwater Rivers to the whites for mining purposes only. For this the Nez Perces, at least those who signed, were to receive fifty thousand dollars when the government approved the agreement, and whites were to be prohibited from mining south of the line along the South Fork of the Clearwater. Privately, Geary and Cain promised Lawyer that the annuities stipulated in the 1855 treaty, but which the government had failed to pay, would be forthcoming.

The miner's agreement, as it was called, was quickly broken. In October, 1861, Lewiston was laid out as a townsite and grew immediately to a population of over one thousand. For his connivance in allowing the agreement to be discarded, it was rumored that Lawyer received compensation. Strikes along the Salmon River quickly attracted miners southward, and by the end of the year the agreement was rendered worthless.

With the population growing so rapidly that territorial status for Idaho was already being considered, the whites could only attempt again to buy out the Nez Perces. Senator J. W. Nesmith of Oregon prepared the way in Congress. Before the Senate he listed the outrages perpetrated against the Nez Perces: whites had occupied their reservation; the government either failed to pay the annuities or else paid them in the form of worthless trinkets; and the miners were threatening and abusive toward their unwilling hosts. In order for the government to live up to its 1855 treaty obligations and for the protection of the Indians, they should be removed from their homeland to some remote area out of harm's way. Indeed, he declared, the Nez Perces themselves were anxious to be rid of their reservation and free from white intrusion. Nesmith's first statement for protection was warped logic at its best — violate the 1855 treaty totally in order to uphold it — and his second was either a deliberate lie or a misconceived notion. Congress accepted his interpretation of the situation, and in 1862 appropriated fifty thousand dollars for the negotiation of a new treaty with the Nez Perces.

Geary's successor in office, Calvin Hale, therefore, summoned the Nez Perces to meet with him in late May at Lapwai. When the headmen had assembled, Hale bluntly told them that they must cede most of their lands guaranteed them under the 1855 treaty and accept a much smaller reservation along the Clearwater. The harshness of this demand crystallized the division in the Nez Perce nation, which had begun with the arrival of the missionaries and widened thereafter with each fresh act of white aggression. Lawyer and his followers were willing to sign; after all, their lands were encompassed in the new reservation,

Courtesy National Archives

Nez Perce Agency, Idaho, 1879

and they were as determined as ever to be friends of the Americans. Another group, led by Big Thunder, would not agree to sign, even though their lands also lay within the projected boundaries. Opposition in this instance was against Lawyer's assumption, or presumption, that as head chief he spoke for the entire nation. Consequently Big Thunder announced formally in a tribal council that the Nez Perce nation was dissolved; that henceforth his people and Lawyer's were to be distinct peoples. Joseph, White Bird, and others of the non-Christian, anti-treaty faction, all of whom would be forced to give up their lands, observed the proceedings for a short time, then took their bands and went home. Why should they even discuss such a treaty of disinheritance? They had never accepted annuities, insisting that in 1855 they had simply signed a document guaranteeing them possession of their hereditary domain and thus required no payment for giving up nothing. Nor did they recognize Lawyer as head chief, or Elijah White's laws of 1842, upon which the head-chieftainship was based. That Lawyer could speak for them or sign away their lands was a ridiculous idea, unworthy of serious consideration.

On June 9, 1863, Lawyer signed away approximately ninety percent of the Nez Perce lands, including most of that belonging to Looking Glass's band, and all of Joseph's, White Bird's, and Toohoolhoolzote's. Despite the action of the anti-treaty headmen, he still persisted in viewing himself as head chief. Since such an assumption was a convenient fiction through which they hoped to make the treaty legally binding upon all Nez Perces, the government supported Lawyer's pretensions to the fullest degree possible.

By the terms of the treaty the Nez Perces accepted the small reservation and agreed to move there within one year after its ratification. For relinquishing these lands, the United States government promised to pay them two hundred sixty-two thousand dollars in addition to the sum stipulated (and largely unpaid) in the 1855 treaty, to be used as usual for the Indians' betterment: one hundred fifty thousand dollars for relocation expenses; fifty thousand dollars for agricultural implements; one hundred ten thousand dollars for a saw-mill and flouring-mill; fifty thousand dollars for education; and two thousand dollars for the erection of two churches. The privileges of the head chief were confirmed, and in addition two subordinate chiefs were to be elected. Like the head chief, their land would be plowed and fenced, a comfortable dwelling erected and furnished, and they themselves would receive a salary. All of the unfulfilled promises of 1855 were to be kept in the future and the hospital, schools and teachers provided. The government was to honor claims of those Nez Perces who had served with the Oregon Volunteers in 1856 and was to pay Timothy six hundred dollars for his "past service and faithfullness" to enable him to build a house.

Lawyer was repaid badly for his continued trust in the Americans. For several years Congress refused to ratify the treaty. Payment under the 1863 treaty could not be made until ratification, while intermittent funding of the 1855 treaty provisions never reached the Nez Perces. A succession of agents served at Lapwai, and each had one ability in common — stealing. One left with almost fifty thousand dollars, another with ten thousand dollars. By the time the Senate ratified the treaty in April, 1867, moreover, the government was anxious to take land near Lapwai for a military post. In response Lawyer received permission and funds to visit Washington to discuss amendments to the 1863 treaty.

Arriving in the spring of 1868, he and the three headmen who accompanied him were treated to a little sight-seeing and much whiskey. One headman died, apparently of typhoid, but according to the non-treaty Nez Perces, he had been pushed to his death from a window because of his refusal to agree to the amendments. As could be expected, the government got the land for the military post. In return, the Nez Perces were promised that additional twenty-acre lots off the reservation would be set aside if the agricultural lands on the reservation proved insufficient; that illegal lumber operations would be stopped; and that the Nez Perces would be reimbursed for the educational funds stolen by the agents.

Thereafter, conditions slowly improved for the treaty Nez Perces. In 1870, following Congress' prohibition of military officers serving as Indian Agents, President Grant's "peace policy," or "Quaker" policy, went into effect at the Lapwai reservation. At first the Nez Perces were awarded to the Catholics, but the Presbyterians protested so strenuously that they had come to the Nez Perces first that they acquired the reservation. John B. Monteith arrived in February, 1871, to take charge. Although he was honest, he set himself steadfastly to the task of assimilating the Indians into white culture: all Indian customs were deplorable and must be eradicated, all white customs were good and must be adopted and cherished — even long hair must go. As the most recent and most comprehensive historian of the Nez Perces, Alvin M. Josephy, Jr., has written, "Bereft of their own culture, their strength, self-respect, and dignity, they became a subjugated and lost people, a second-class minority in their own homeland."

The non-treaty Nez Perces living off the reservation viewed the plight of their Christian brothers with derision — their suffering was fit reward for their treachery. As Yellow Wolf later declared, "It was these Christian Nez Perces who made with the government a *thief* treaty. Sold to the government all of this land. Sold what did not belong to them. We got nothing for our country. None of our chiefs signed that land-stealing treaty. None was at that lie-talk council. Only Christian Indians and government." Or as Joseph put it, "Suppose a white man should come to me and say, 'Joseph I like your horses, and I want to buy them.' I say to him, 'No, my horses suit me, I will not sell them.' Then he goes to my neighbor, and says to him: 'Joseph has some good horses. I want to buy them, but he refuses to sell.' My neighbor answers, 'Pay me the money, and I will sell you Joseph's horses.' The white man returns to me, and says, 'Joseph, I have bought your horses, and you must let me have them.'"

In a desperate attempt to cling to their traditional values and customs, furthermore, many of the non-treaty Nez Perces were attracted to the Dreamer religious movement. Associated with the prophet Smoholla, the Dreamer faith stressed two major points. First, it rejected Christianity and reaffirmed with some elaborations the primitive religion of the Indians. The Dreamers, for example, could neither understand nor accept the conception of the Hereafter that the missionaries taught. That a God would inflict perpetual torture with the hottest fire on even a wicked man was beyond their comprehension. Opposed to this, the Dreamers visualized a Hereafter in which suffering was banished. Children and the more blameless adults were transported there immediately after death. A wicked man wandered in the wilderness, but "after a long, long time, maybe many snows, he finds himself. His mind and his heart feel differently. By and by he thinks, 'Where are my horses?' " Finding their tracks, he follows, mounts his best horse and is taken to the Spirit Land. Second, the Dreamers taught hope in stemming the white invasion. They believed that those Indians who had died previously would be resurrected and, united with those presently living, would conquer the whites and recover their lands. To what degree the Nez Perces embraced the Dreamer faith cannot be ascertained; but certainly the non-treaties must have found both religious and patriotic values congenial.

To the Americans, in any case, those Nez Perces living off the reservation were anti-treaty troublemakers, or worse, Dreamers who might be engaged in a conspiracy aginst the whites. Conflict could not long be postponed. The most exposed of the non-treaty lands was the Wallowa valley (Winding River) in which Joseph and his band lived. Surveyors entered the area in the late sixties

Courtesy Amon Carter Museum, Fort Worth

Chief Joseph, famed Nez Perce, who led his people in their final war

before the ratification of the 1863 treaty, and in the early seventies the first settlers spilled over from the neighboring Grande Ronde valley which had been open to settlement since 1855. Even as the first settlers appeared Old Joseph died, leaving the band under the care of his son of the same name, and admonishing him never to forget that "this country holds your father's body. Never sell the bones of your father and mother."

The settlers, however, already considered the land theirs and pressured the Indian officials to find a solution. As a result, Agent Monteith and T. B. Odeneal, Superintendent of Indian Affairs for Oregon, met with Joseph in March, 1873. During the talks which followed, Joseph so ably defended the legality of his position that both Monteith and Odeneal were inclined to agree with him. In their report to Washington, therefore, they argued that the Wallowa was indeed part of the Nez Perce reservation as the treaty of 1855 stipulated, and since Joseph had not signed the 1863 treaty, it was not binding upon him. They recommended that, while whites be allowed to settle in the lower valley, Joseph and his band should retain the upper. Agreeing substantially with these recommendations, the Secretary of the Interior prevailed upon President Grant to issue an executive order embodying the stipulations. Unfortunately, the boundaries were switched, thus calling for the whites and Indians to swap the areas in which each lived.

The Oregon politicians naturally opposed any settlement which allowed Joseph's band to retain any portion of the Wallowa valley. Governor Lafayette F. Grover summed up their views in several letters to high officials in Washington and in the army. Joseph and his band did not own the land, he said, for in adhering to the treaty of 1855 (which, it must be remembered, had included the Wallowa in the reservation), Joseph's Nez Perces had recognized that the reservation was owned in common by the tribe. Lawyer, therefore, was perfectly within his rights when, acting as head chief, he agreed to a restriction of that common land for the entire tribe. "Young Joseph," Grover continued, "does not object to going on the Reservation at this time;" and while a few "leading spirits" do object, the recent defeat of the "Modoc outlaws" would teach these a lesson. Indeed, Grover maintained, with the Modoc war ended, it would be less expensive to put Joseph's band on the Lapwai Reserva-

Courtesy Smithsonian Institution

Joseph Ratunda, Nez Perce, 1914

tion than to remove settlers and compensate them for their losses. "If this section of our State, which is now occupied by enterprising white families, should be removed to make a roaming ground for nomadic savages," he warned, "a very serious check will have been given to the growth of our frontier settlements, and to the spirit of our frontier people in their efforts to redeem the wilderness."

Confronted with the concerted protest of the Oregon politicians, Grant slowly gave way, and in 1874, officially rescinded the executive order of the previous year. Officials now had the problem of peaceably moving Jeseph's band on the reservation. Those on the scene, particularly General O. O. Howard, the Civil War veteran who had assumed the command of the Department of the Columbia in 1874, faced a perplexing situation: they could not have expected the Nez Perces to obey and leave their homeland, yet they dreaded the resort to force. Many Oregonians were aware, after all, of the justness of the Nez Perces' position, and that despite provocation from the whites, Joseph had held his warriors in check, thereby avoiding major incident. During the next two years, while the matter remained unresolved, Howard developed a formula for treating with the Nez Perces. The Government must pay for Joseph's lands, to be sure, since it was agreed that they had not been included in the 1863 treaty. If he refused to sell, however, this was open defiance of the authority of the United States, and force must then be used. So completely had Howard convinced himself of the validity of this position that when he later discussed the outbreak of the war, he declared that "its main cause lies back of ideas of rightful ownership, back of savage habits and instincts; it lies in the natural and persistent resistance of independent nations to the authority of other nations. Indian Joseph and his malcontents denied the jurisdiction of the United States over them."

To achieve his aims, Howard sought, and finally secured in 1876, the appointment of a federal commission to negotiate with the non-treaty bands for their removal to the reservation. If Joseph expected an impartial hearing, as he evidently did, he was doomed to quick disillusionment. Two of the commission members, Howard and his assistant adjutant general, Major Henry Claywood, were already decided on a course of action. The other three members, David H. Jerome, A. C. Barstow, and

William Stickney, were all Easterners and knew nothing about the Nez Perce problem except what they were told. And what they were told upon their arrival at Lapwai by Monteith (who reversed his position the moment his superiors in Washington did) and other Indian agents, was quite simple. All of the trouble was the result of Dreamer instigation. Suppress the Dreamers and move the non-treaty Indians onto the reservation where they could be converted to Christianity, and the problem would be solved.

When Joseph, the only non-treaty headman who bothered to come, arrived in November, 1876, the commissioners bluntly informed him that the treaty of 1863 was valid and would be enforced. He must give up his lands, for which the government, out of generosity, would make some compensation. Settlers were already in the area, the commissioners continued, and then with a refined sense of hypocrisy, declared that the Wallowa was too cold for Indians. Joseph's arguments were brushed aside, his request to remain in the valley denied. In their report, the commissioners recommended that any action necessary to stamp out the Dreamer faith, including transportation of the leaders and teachers to the Indian Territory, should be taken immediately. If the non-treaty Nez Perces refused to settle quietly on the reservation within "a reasonable time, in the judgment of the department, they should be placed [there] by force."

Time was fast running out for the non-treaties. Agent Monteith set April 1, 1877, as the deadline for their moving voluntarily to the reservation. Agreeing that spring was indeed sufficient time, Howard began making the necessary military preparations. In a last effort to ward off subjugation, therefore, the non-treaty headmen asked for a council. Perhaps to assuage any lingering doubts as to the justness of his position, Howard granted the request. The council was scheduled for early May, 1877.

If the Nez Perces held any hope of success they were grasping at an illusion. On the eve of the council Monteith formally requested military assistance, and troops began the march toward the Wallowa. When Joseph and the other non-treaties — Looking Glass, Toohoolhoolzote, and White Bird — arrived with their bands, it was simply to be told to obey. Howard adopted, furthermore, a condescending attitude toward the Nez Perces and treated them like naughty, ignorant children. This was the only way, he believed, to handle Indians. The result was disastrous. Toohoolhoolzote, evidently acting as spokesman for the non-treaties, asked Howard from what source he derived such great authority. According to the Indian version, Howard, who disliked the old chief and called him the "growler of growlers," told Toohoolhoolzote to "Shut up! . . . If you do not move, I will take the matter into my own hand, and make you suffer for your disobedience." Toohoolhoolzote exploded. "Who are you, that you ask us to talk, and then tell me I sha'n't talk? Are you the Great Spirit? Did you make the world? Did you make the sun? Did you make the river to run for us to drink? Did you make the grass to grow? Did you make all these things, that you talk to us as though we were boys?" Howard promptly arrested Toohoolhoolzote and sent him to the guardhouse. Rather than alleviating tension, the council had only made matters worse. One of the most prominent headmen was in jail, the others angered and confused.

Yet for the moment, peace was maintained. After a few days, Howard released Toohoolhoolzote and gave the Nez Perces thirty days in which to move onto the reservation. Returning home, the non-treaties began gathering their stock in order to comply. In late May Joseph's band, to the cheerful relief of the settlers, began moving into Idaho toward the reservation; the other bands were also on the move. On the Salmon they met, and with less than two weeks of freedom remaining, went into camp for the last time; as the men talked and brooded over their fate, resentment grew. Although the headmen advised moderation, some of the younger men were eager for war. "General Howard has shown us the rifle'," they declared, referring to the arrest of Toohoolhoolzote, and they boasted that they would start "his war" for him. In such a heated atmosphere it required little to touch off violence. During a war parade on June 13 the horse of a young warrior, Wahlilits, son of Eagle Robe who had been murdered by a white, accidently trampled some roots of Yellow Grizzly Bear's wife. "See what you do!" said Yellow Grizzly Bear sarcastically. "Playing brave, you ride over my woman's hard-worked food! If you so brave, why you not go kill the white men who killed your father?" Stung by the imputation against his manhood, Wahlilits and some of his youthful companions set out in search of the murderer, Larry Ott. Failing to find Ott, they killed Richard Devine, a settler who had been accused, along with two other whites, of having murdered a crippled Nez Perce some years previously.

Thus began the Nez Perce war, one of the most famous — and most costly — wars in frontier history. In the end, of course, the Nez Perces were defeated; in light of their pitiful strength as compared to that of the whites, defeat was inevitable. It was a tragic climax to a long series of injustices perpetrated against them. Their culture had been deliberately destroyed, their religion banned, their lands taken from them fraudulently. They had trusted in treaties — unaware that a treaty with the United States was a death-warrant.

BIBLIOGRAPHY

Burns, Robert Ignatius, S. J. *The Jesuits and the Indian Wars of the Northwest.* New Haven, Conn.: Yale University Press, 1966.

Howard, O. O. [Gen.] *Nez Perce Joseph: An Account of His Ancestors, His Lands, His Confederates, His Enemies, His Murders, His War, His Pursuit and Capture.* Boston: Lee and Shepard Publishers, 1881.

Chief Joseph. "An Indian's Views of Indian Affairs." *North American Review* (April, 1879), pp. 412-433.

Josephy, Alvin M., Jr. *The Nez Perce Indians and the Opening of the Northwest.* New Haven, Conn.: Yale University Press, 1965.

McWhorter, Lucullus V. *Hear Me, My Chiefs!* Ed. by Ruth Bordin. Caldwell, Idaho: The Caxton Printers Ltd., 1952.

———————————. *Yellow Wolf: His Own Story.* Caldwell, Idaho: Caxton Printers Ltd., 1940.

Miles, Nelson A. *Personal Recollections and Observations of General Nelson A. Miles.* New York: Da Capo Press, 1969.

"You are stronger than we. We have fought you so long as we had rifles and powder; but your weapons are better than ours. Give us weapons and turn us loose, and we will fight you again; but we are worn out; we have no more heart, we have no provisions, no means to leave; your troops are everywhere; our springs and waterholes are either occupied or overlooked by your young men. You have driven us from our last and best stronghold, and we have no more heart. Do with us as may seem good to you, but do not forget we are men and braves."

Chief Cadete

CHAPTER 11

The Apaches

Sandra L. Myres

EL GRAN APACHERÍA — when the Spaniards first arrived in 1540 it extended from the Pecos River in the east to the Colorado in the west and from the San Francisco Mountains of New Mexico to northern Chihuahua. It was a harsh land of deserts and mountains, little vegetation and less water, sparsely covered with cacti, mesquites and small brushy plants; a land of extreme climate, cold nights and hot days, scorched by the siroccos and summer heat, frozen by blue northers and winter snows. Its thin and sandy soils, thrown up in strange formations as though left over from the Creation and dumped here in some last, huge wasteheap, were covered by rocks and boulders, sometimes piled into rugged mountains or hidden beneath the black lava beds of long forgotten volcanic overflows. Yet in all its harshness it was, and is, a place of great beauty — the clouds chase their shadows across the plains, the evening sunsets turn the mountains blue, purple, rose and orange; the minerals beneath the surface tint the land with every color and hue. In its desolate and open spaces the land presents an awesomeness, a majesty, that is both frightening and exhilarating to the soul of man.

Here dwelt the Tinde, The People, called by the Europeans Apaches (from the Zuñi word for enemy). The Tinde were an Athapaskan-speaking people who many years earlier, long before the historical memory of man, moved southward and came at last to the Apachería, scattered their camps from one end to the other and claimed the land as their own.

SANDRA L. MYRES, was born Columbus, Ohio, May 17, 1933, and was educated in public schools in Ohio, Tennessee, West Virginia, Washington and Texas. She received her Ph.D. in history at Texas Christian University in 1967. Her publications include *S.D. Myres: Saddlemaker* (Kerrville, Texas: 1961); *Force Without Fanfare* (TCU Press, Fort Worth: 1968); *The Ranch in Spanish Texas, 1690-1800* (University of Texas at El Paso Press: 1969); *One Man, One Vote: Gerrymandering vs. Reapportionment* (Steck-Vaughn, Austin: 1970); and *Essays on the American West* (University of Texas Press, Austin: 1969). She is currently completing a book length manuscript on the Texas Indians entitled *Immigrants in Their Own Land* to be published next year by Alfred A. Knopf.

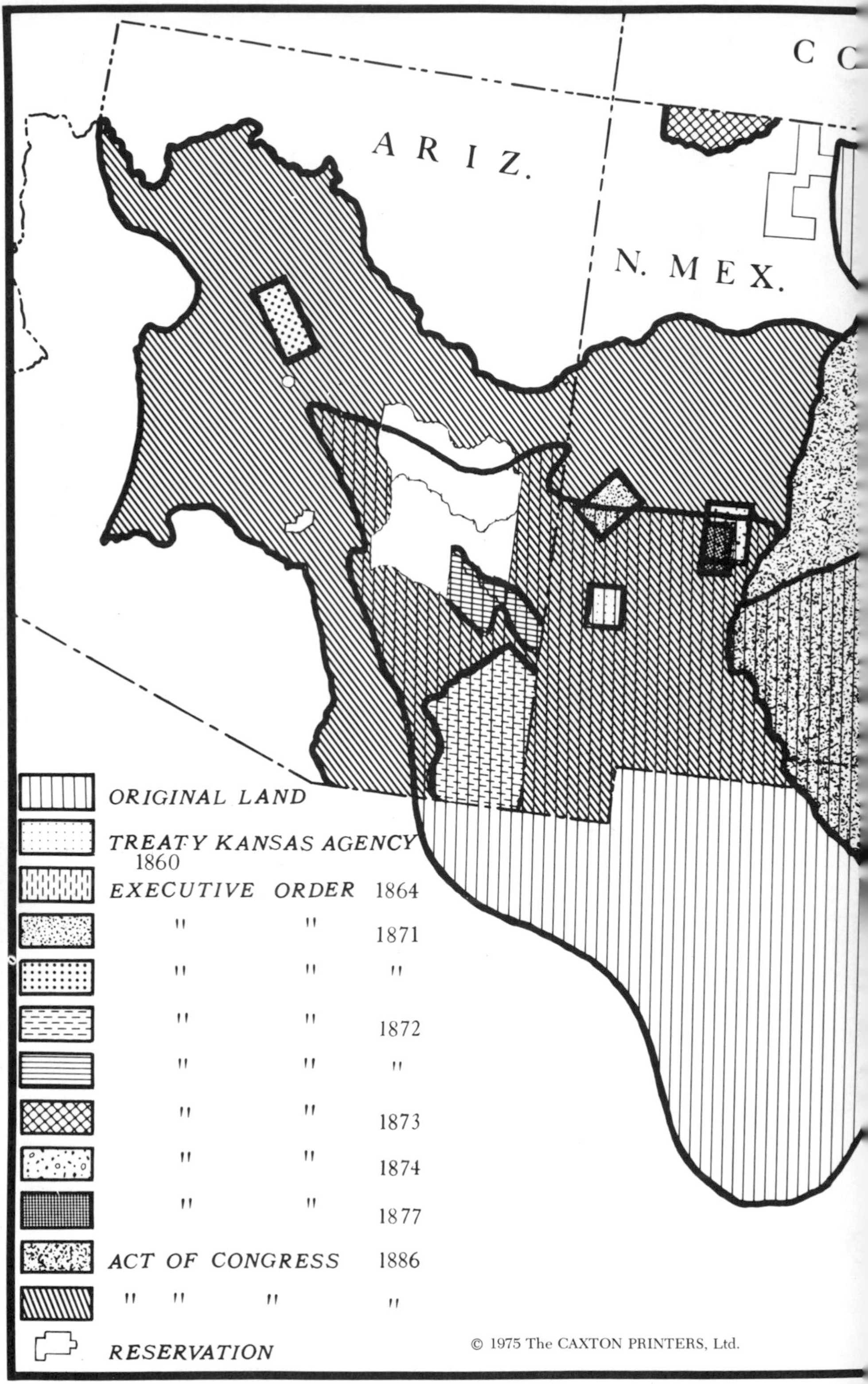
ARIZ.
N. MEX.
C C
ORIGINAL LAND
TREATY KANSAS AGENCY 1860
EXECUTIVE ORDER 1864
" " 1871
" " "
" " 1872
" " "
" " 1873
" " 1874
" " 1877
ACT OF CONGRESS 1886
" " " "
RESERVATION
© 1975 The CAXTON PRINTERS, Ltd.

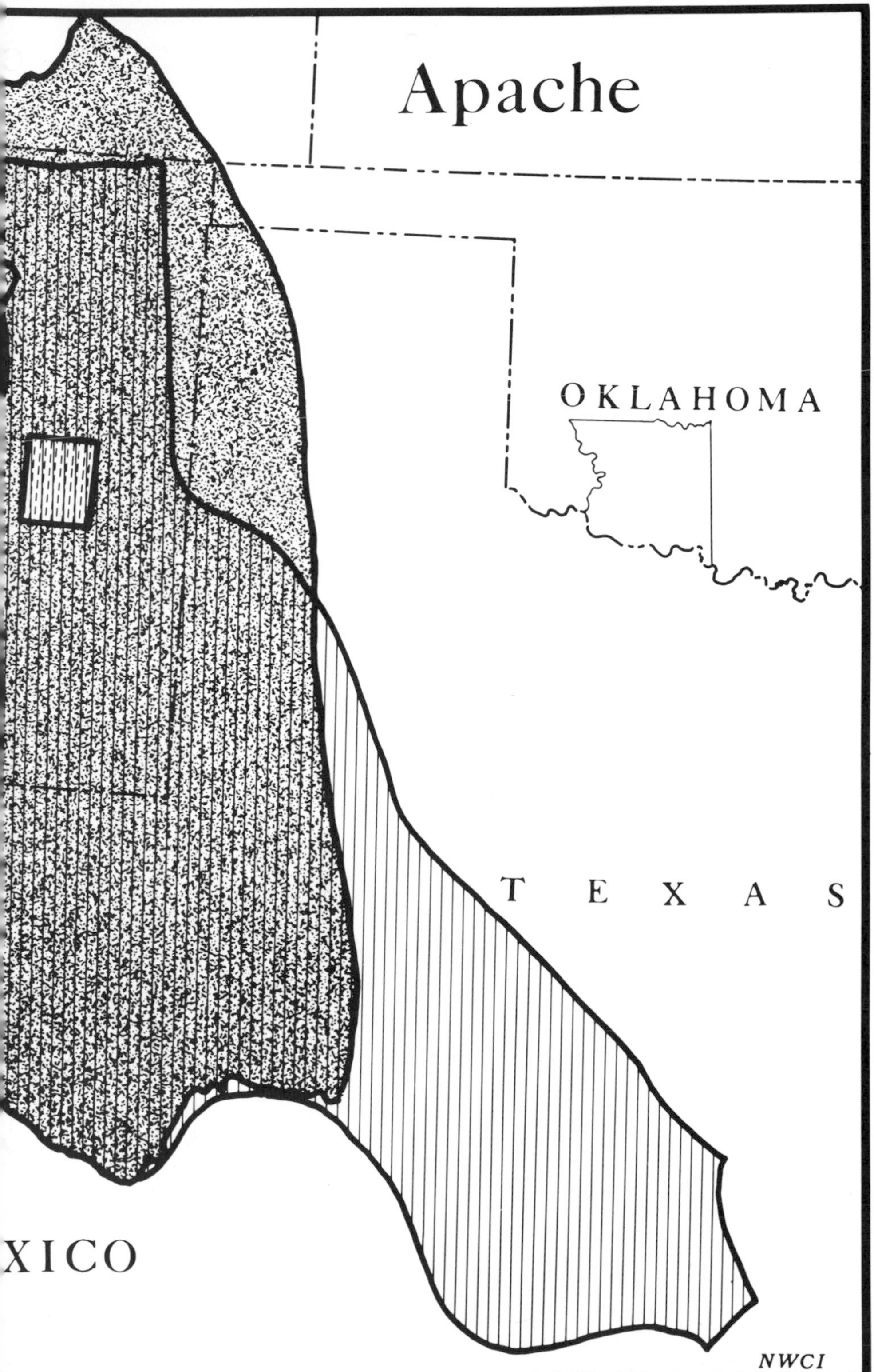
Apache
OKLAHOMA
TEXAS
XICO
NWCI

Anthropologists and ethnohistorians disagree as to just where the Apaches came from and exactly when they arrived in the Southwest, although most are agreed that the historic Apaches were descendants of the last immigrants to cross the Bering Straits. Some investigators contend that the Tinde emerged from the older Southwestern cultures about 1000 A.D., but most scholars maintain that they began migrating southward from the McKenzie Basin of Canada at about that date, moved along the Rocky Mountains and finally arrived in the Southwestern desert and plains regions between 1200 and 1500 A.D. Certainly by the seventeenth century, at the very latest, the Apaches had gained a stronghold from the Arkansas River southward through northwestern Texas, New Mexico and Arizona and had entered upon a Golden Age of conquest and domination. By the time the Spaniards arrived in the Apachería, the Tinde, never tightly organized, were divided into innumerable small bands usually designated by the Europeans under some descriptive or geographic name. To the west were the Mimbreños, the Navajos, the Gileños, the Chiricahuas and the Tonto Basin Apaches while to the east roamed the Faraones, the Mescaleros, Llaneros, Jicarillas and Lipanes.

Until the arrival of the Europeans, the Tinde followed a free and satisfying way of life well adapted to the land they inhabited. To the People, the harsh yet bitterly beautiful land yielded a meager but sufficient living. They were a proud and fiercely independent folk, who cared little for prolonged contacts with their fellow human beings. They survived by hunting in small groups, and though they preferred large game — deer, antelope, buffalo and later, after the arrival of the Spaniards, horses and mules as well — they could and did supplement this fare with smaller animals such as rabbits, fieldmice, the succulent rattlesnake and desert insects. Although they were avid hunters, the Apaches were careful never to exhaust all the resources of an area, so that they need not wander too far in search of meat, and they supplemented their protein-rich diet with desert plants and foodstuffs gathered from the seemingly barren land. The saguaro cactus, the fruit of the prickly pear, piñon nuts, mescal from the ubiquitous agave, various native grasses, all gave them sustenance.

From time to time various groups planted maize, squash and

beans in small patches along the rivers and streams, but so successful were the Tinde in wresting a living from the semi-arid land that they apparently never felt compelled to settle down to an entirely sedentary, agricultural existence. They preferred instead to cultivate their little garden plots when and where the mood and season fitted their fancy and to devote most of their time to the free and restless wandering that nurtured their proudly independent souls.

All in all, the Apaches were entranced by the "luxuries" of the Southwestern area and made the region their permanent home. Like most Amerind groups, the Apaches did not always get along with their neighbors. As they migrated into the Southwest, they attempted to displace the peoples they encountered, or at least those which seemed to stand in their way. The Navajo and other western groups warred against the Pueblo tribes in New Mexico, and the eastern bands fought with the Caddoan peoples for dominance on the Texas plains and prairies. Most of the time the Apaches won. They looted and raided the Pueblo towns, pushed the Wichitas and Pawnees eastward from the plains and quickly gained military domination over the Apachería.

Despite their talent for warfare and conquest, the Apaches were not constantly engaged in battle. Between raids and skirmishes to control hunting grounds and water holes, they engaged in peaceful contacts and trade with their new neighbors. Through such encounters, the Apaches acquired a number of cultural traits from the older inhabitants of the region. Apache society was highly flexible and open to new ideas, and the Tinde quickly adapted to several regional and geographic patterns and borrowed skills, tools, ceremonies and other culture traits which seemed attractive or practical to them.

Although related by language and general lifestyle, the various Apache groups differed somewhat in culture. Most of the western desert peoples lived in "wickiups"—temporary conical brush and thatch dwellings; while the eastern groups adopted the portable hide "tepee" common to the Plains tribes. The Kiowa and Lipan Apaches spent most of the year hunting, while other groups subsisted on a combination of hunting, planting and gathering. The eastern Jicarilla and some of the western bands,

Courtesy National Archives

Apache ranchería or camp

especially the Gileños and Tontos, were the most agriculturally inclined and practiced irrigation as well as dry farming methods.

Dress and costume, too, varied from place to place and from time to time. Costume and its decoration reflected the strong individuality of the Tinde, and rarely did any two of them dress alike. The usual items of clothing — breechcloth and shirt for the men and skirt and overblouse for the women — came in many styles and hues, supplemented with a wide variety of decorative devices and jewelry, including deer hooves, shells, fish spines, various plants and herbs, feathers and skins. The only generally common element of dress was the tough, stout hightopped moccasin with turned up toes made of undressed deer, or, later, cowhides. This eminently practical footwear was well adapted to the Apaches' environment and way of life. Among the rag-tag odds and ends of clothing only the sturdy, boot-like moccasin stood out as a uniform item.

Arts and crafts also reflected great variety. Apache women were master craftsmen in the making of the elaborate and beautiful baskets which served as their dishes, storage jars and water casks; but here, too, the patterns, weaves and materials incorporated reflected a high degree of individuality.

Individualism and independence characterized not only the material culture of The People but their political and social relationships as well. Most of the year the Tinde lived and traveled in small local bands consisting of six to eight families united to other similar groups through an exogamous, matrilineal clan system. Polygamy was the usual practice, but all wives must be of a different clan than their husbands; men frequently took their sisters-in-law to wife. Among most Apache groups, social practice dictated the wedding of a widowed clanswoman by either an immediate relative or clan brother of a deceased warrior, but customs varied.

There was no tribal government, only a loose system of band "chieftains" who were choosen principally for their skills in war or hunting and who were easily replaced or ignored when it suited the fancy of the band members. Occasionally, particularly in time of war or for raids on neighboring folk, several bands might unite under a single leader, but such confederations were at best temporary conveniences. A battle fought by united Amerinds could be won, but once the immediate fruits of victory were theirs, Apache alliances usually fell apart and the white man triumphed. Had they been able to coalesce against the encroachments of the Europeans, they might have won not only battles but the war as well and driven the invaders from their land. But this the Apaches were rarely able to do. To the Tinde, love of liberty was stronger than ties of kinship, individual desire transcended social or military necessity. Always Apache affairs were subject to the fierce individualism and love of liberty which eventually cost them their freedom.

The Apaches had a highly developed ethical and moral sense, but it differed significantly from that of European society. The Apache lived by his wits and courage in a hostile environment, and he valued and cultivated those traits which enabled him to survive in an inhospitable land. Apache society was a warrior society; they enjoyed battle and cultivated in their young men and women the skills which would be most helpful in their rarely peaceful, always difficult world. The "perfect man," from the standpoint of the Tinde, was a stealthy, cunning thief who could slide silently into an enemy camp and make off with one or more essential items without getting caught in the process. To the Apaches, deceit was a trait to be cultivated, and justice and revenge were synonymous ideas. This is not to say that the Tinde lacked a code of conduct, but their codes were so very different from those of Europeans — Spaniards, Frenchmen or Anglos — that most white men looked upon the Apaches as cruel, treacherous and vicious, not to be trusted in the society of "honest" men.

On the other hand, the Tinde found little to admire in the white man's ways and took a perverse pleasure in laughing at the peccadillos of the *Pinda Lick-o-yi,* the white eyes. A strong, vigorous people, the Apaches mocked any sign of physical weakness, and they viewed most Europeans as poor specimens. The Tinde could sustain themselves on little food or water and travel long distances on foot or horseback. The European with his large supplies of food, water and equipment, unable to live off the land, seemed an object for pity and derision. The Tinde did not respect or understand the white man, nor did they particularly want to. They were a highly flexible and pragmatic people (even in the days before Will James), and they wished only to take or borrow those items of European culture which they found useful and reject the rest.

Such was not to be. The arrival of the first Europeans in the Southwest made radical changes in Apache lifeways. The Spaniards sought to settle The People in villages and missions, teach them new skills, utilize their labor, destroy or replace old mores, bring an end to polygamy, raiding and "useless" nomadic wandering. Such tampering was by no means selectively practiced against the Tinde. Across the length and breadth of two continents, the European invaders imposed their system of religion, government and thought upon the inhabitants. One by one the native peoples were conquered, missionized, converted, exploited. From north to south and east to west the Europeans overran the land of once great tribes, displaced the game, resettled the people, plowed and broke the land and despoiled the countryside with towns and cities.

Not all the Amerinds succumbed easily to the wave of invasion and conquest. Some fought back. Of them all, the Tinde fought the hardest and longest to hold their place and waged a long, almost unceasing battle for their right to live on their own land in their own way. From 1540 to 1886 they took on all comers — other Amerinds, Spaniards, Frenchmen, Anglos — giving way only slowly to the inexorable pressures of overwhelming popula-

Courtesy Amon Carter Museum, Fort Worth

Wife and child of Geronimo, Apache warrior

tion and technology. Finally all that was left of the once great Apachería were a few arid reservations, confining and forbidding places grudgingly parceled out for Apache homes but controlled by the Great White Fathers in Washington. But before the end came the Tinde fought desperately, with every means at their command, to preserve something of the old ways. When fighting seemed futile, the Tinde entered into one agreement after another, signed treaty after treaty in an effort to retain something of their way of life. For over three hundred years they nearly succeeded.

Although the first contacts between Apaches and Spaniards were few and generally peaceful, these early cordial relationships did not last long. As the Spaniards extended their conquest northward, they severed pre-existing relationships between native peoples, introduced new social and political values and set in motion a complex process of cultural change and destruction.

Throughout the first years of northern conquest and expansion, the Spaniards were less concerned with the Apaches than with other nomadic inhabitants of the area such as the Sumas, Janos, Chinarras and Jocomes. In fact, during the sixteenth and early seventeenth century there is little mention in Spanish documents of Apache groups, at least by the names with which we are familiar. From 1599 to 1680 the *conquistadores* concentrated their missionizing and settlement efforts on the sedentary Pueblan peoples and left the Apaches pretty much to their own devices. Not until the Great Pueblo Revolt of 1680 and the establishment of the presidio at Janos in 1685 did Apaches and Spaniards come to the close contacts which soon led to trouble.

Despite the lack of direct association before the seventeenth century, the arrival of the Europeans in the Apachería had a revolutionary impact on Tinde life. The Spaniards introduced the first livestock into the region, and these animals — horses, mules, goats, sheep and cattle — quickly became a highly prized and marketable commodity among not only the Apaches but other tribes as well. The Apaches and other Amerinds took to the horse much as a later generation of Americans embraced Henry Ford's marvelous motor car. For the people of the plains, the horse provided a new mode of transportation for both hunting and warfare, intensified their nomadic habits and increased their mobility and martial skills. Among the more sedentary tribes, the

Courtesy Amon Carter Museum, Fort Worth

Loco, famous Warm Springs Apache war leader

introduction of livestock turned them more and more to a raiding economy and culture, to what Edward Spicer has described, in his book *Cycles of Conquest*, as a "predatory, parasitic way of life."

At first the Tinde obtained their supplies of horses, cattle and sheep from neighboring tribes, but as the demand for livestock increased — first as food and later as items for trade and as symbols of wealth — the Apaches extended their raids into Spanish controlled territory. By the early eighteenth century the Navajos had decimated the horse and sheep herds of New Mexico while their Athapaskan cousins, the western and eastern Apaches, attacked deep into Mexico and hit towns and outposts with alarming regularity. Spanish ranches, farms and presidios throughout the northern provinces of New Spain became the prime, albeit involuntary, suppliers of livestock for the Indian trade, and the Tinde quickly became the acknowledged leaders in this new economic enterprise.

Another element in the increasingly unfriendly encounters between Spaniards and Apaches was the slave trade. The Spaniards needed laborers for their ranches, farms, mines and workshops, and despite royal decrees prohibiting enslavement of Indians, the frontiersmen of New Spain found ways to circumvent the law. Beginning in the late seventeenth century, the Spaniards launched expeditions deep into the Apachería to "recruit" a native labor force and sent captive Apaches — men, women and children — southward to end their days in misery in the mines of Sonora and Durango, on the haciendas of the northern provinces or in the woolen mills at Ensenillas. The Tinde retaliated and took prisoners of their own to be kept as servants or sold or traded to other tribes. Often captives became pawns in negotiations between Amerinds and Europeans. The Spaniards frequently held women and children as hostages in an attempt to force Apache warriors to halt their raids, and the Tinde soon began to do the same. Throughout the entire period of Spanish-Apache contact, the two sides kept up a fairly constant exchange of hostages and prisoners, a trade which led to a good deal of racial mixture (especially in the case of women captives) but did little to improve race relations.

Despite later bloody Apache raids accompanied by rape, scalping and murder, the Tinde at first preferred to capture

Courtesy National Archives

San Juan, Mescalero Apache chief

rather than kill. It was to their advantage that the Spaniards continue to live in order to furnish the Apaches with livestock and captives. Just as they had previously carefully husbanded game resources, so the Tinde made some attempt to maintain their sources of supply in the Spanish settlements, ranchos and haciendas. But as relations became increasingly bitter between the two peoples, subtle changes occurred on both sides.

For a while the Tinde had things their own way. The Spainards seemed incapable of mounting any effective defense against the hit-and-run guerrilla tactics of the Apache raiders. By 1750 the Tinde had ravaged the countryside along a line from the Sonora River south of Arispe to the mining and ranching districts on the middle Moctezuma and upper Yaqui rivers. During the next decade, the Spaniards abandoned the Sonoran capital of San Juan Bautista and retreated southward, leaving the whole San Pedro Valley to the Apaches. To the east, bands of Mescaleros and Jicarillas, joined by fugitives from the Pueblos, raided and plundered from Santa Fé to Chihuahua, attacked Paso del Norte and turned the Camino Real into the *Jornada del Muerto*.

Throughout the late seventeenth and early eighteenth centuries, the Spaniards attempted to control the Apaches through a vacillating policy of peace and war. The government offered gifts and bribes as an inducement to end raids and tried to settle the Tinde and other nomadic peoples in missions, pueblos or near presidial garrisons, where they could teach them European ways and the Christian religion and bring them into the structure of Spanish society as laborers and herdsmen. The *Reglamento de 1729*, issued by the Marqués de Casa-Fuerte, Viceroy of New Spain, prohibited attacks on the Apaches or other Amerinds "until all effort to pacify them by persuasion has failed," and required that whenever the Indians asked for peace, officials must accept the offer. But what the viceroy ordered from Mexico City or the king decreed from Spain, did not always coincide with the desires of frontier dwellers, Spaniards or Apaches. In the northern provinces life went on as before. The Tinde continued to raid, take captives and enjoy a new golden age of conquest, while frustrated presidial commanders and harassed settlers sent out punitive expeditions, violated the laws against enslavement and longed for more troops and a hardline government program.

Courtesy Amon Carter Museum, Fort Worth

Chato, Chiricahua Apache, a former hostile who became a scout for the Army.

Part of the reason for the Spaniards' failure to deal effectively with The People was that they never completely understood the fragmented nature of Apache politics. The Spaniards attempted to treat with the various Tindean bands as they had with the more sophisticated and highly organized tribes of central Mexico, but such policies achieved little success. Given the lack of Tinde unity, an agreement negotiated with one band had no effect on any other group, even if they knew of it — which they rarely did. And, just as the Spaniards misinterpreted the nature of Apache "politics," so the Tinde misunderstood the Europeans and continued to believe that Spanish "government" was similar to their own, where agreements and treaties could be binding only between the actual contracting parties.

Furthermore, the Spaniards, for all their elaborate bureaucracy, lacked coordination in regard to Indian affairs. Spanish policy, at least in the northern provinces, was almost completely decentralized. Each commander was empowered to act on his own authority in dealing with the Amerinds, and difficulties of communication made it impossible for Spaniards in one area to know what was going on elsewhere. One provincial governor might negotiate a truce with an Apache band, only to have the agreement violated by a neighboring official.

This lack of communication and centralized policy worked to the advantage of the Tinde, who often made peace in one province while they continued to raid in another. For example, a treaty made in good faith between the Llanero band of El Calvo and the Spanish governor of Texas had no effect on El Calvo's attitude toward the Spaniards in New Mexico. He might bargain for peace in Texas and leave his women and children within the protection of a nearby presidio, where they would be fed and cared for while he and his men went off raiding in the neighboring province. On their return the Apaches bartered or sold their purloined livestock and captives and continued on their way, safe from pursuit and happy in the knowledge that they had not broken their agreement with Texas officials. If a commander in one area became discouraged by such cavalier treatment, the Tinde simply gathered up their people, moved to another province and began the cycle over again.

Such actions on the part of the Tinde have usually been cited as examples of Apache shrewdness in playing off one frontier official against another. To some extent this is true, for the Tinde quickly learned how easy it was to play such games with the foolish white men. Nonetheless, what the Spaniards considered perfidy the Apaches interpreted as liberty, and their action reflected not so much a breach of faith as the Tindes' failure to understand European diplomacy and political morality. Both sides thought they were right, and both pursued the dictates of their own ethical standards and long established cultural patterns. As Max Moorhead so succinctly stated it in *The Apache Frontier*:

> There were heroes and villains aplenty on both sides. For all his faults, the Spaniard was struggling to extend civilization; and, for all his virtues, the Apache was struggling to preserve his way of life, however limited.

Whatever the case, Apache policy was generally the more successful. Up to a point it triumphed over that of the Europeans. More than any other native Americans, with the possible exception of the Comanches, the Tinde resisted Spanish attempts at conquest and domination and remained in at least partial control of their homeland.

Finally the Spaniards had had enough and decided to undertake a complete reorganization. In 1766 the Marqués de Rubí, acting on orders from the *Visitador-General* of New Spain, José de Gálvez, carried out a three-year inspection tour of Spain's northern provinces from eastern Texas to Altar in western Sonora. On his return Rubí submitted a plan for the restructuring of the frontier defenses. According to the Marqués, the Apaches were a "perfidious, brutal and vile nation" who had proved "treacherous to all Spanish offers of peace and protection." Only when the northern borderlands were free of Apaches would they be safe for Spanish civilization. He therefore recommended that the Spaniards end all treaties and agreements with the Apaches and instead apply the old principle of divide and conquer, turning one Indian group against another and utilizing Indian mercenaries to carry on an all-out war of extermination against the Tinde.

Fortunately for the Apaches, Rubí's recommendations did not receive complete approval. Although the King and the Council of the Indies agreed that the Apaches represented the greatest single threat to the peace and security of the realm, still the King preferred to temper harshness with humanitarianism. Thus the *Reglamento de 1772*, although based on Rubí's report and providing for the all-out war which the Marqués suggested, also required gentle and humane treatment for prisoners and those hostiles who were willing to surrender themselves and settle peacefully under the watchful eye of Spanish authorities.

Rubí also advised, and the King agreed, that in order to bring an end to the Tinde practice of playing off one frontier official against another, a unified military command should be instituted under a *commandant general* who would have virtually viceregal powers within the northern provinces, which would be combined into a new politico-military jurisdiction known as the *Provincias Internas*.

During the 1770s the Spaniards vigorously prosecuted the new war policy. They built a new line of presidios and sent military expeditions into every corner of the Apachería. Throughout the *Provincias*, the Commandant General, Teodoro de Croix, and his chief aides, governors Juan Bautista de Anza of New Mexico and Juan de Ugalde of Coahuila, attacked Tinde camps, negotiated treaties with the Comanches, Utes and Wichitas — Tinde enemies of long standing — and at the same time attempted to stir up trouble between various Apache groups.

At last the Apaches' lack of tribal structure and their long standing enmity with neighboring tribes worked to the Spaniards' advantage. In 1779 Ugalde persuaded the Mescaleros to attack the Lipanes in his province, while later the same year the Spaniards renewed their treaties with the Lipanes and used them as auxiliaries against the Mescaleros. At the same time the Spaniards continued their alliance with the Comanches and encouraged all of the Apaches' enemies to keep up their pressure on the Tinde. In 1785, while nominally at peace with the Lipanes, that most Christian Governor Domingo Cabello of Texas concluded a new agreement with the Comanches which allowed them passage across Texas for the purpose of attacking the Lipanes and Mescaleros in Coahuila.

Despite these successes, the Crown was hard pressed to provide adequate money and troops for a protracted war. In 1786 the Viceroy of Mexico, Bernardo de Gálvez, proposed a new two-part plan based on both continued military engagements and a pacification program designed to undermine the Apaches' culture and make them dependent upon Spanish largess for their subsistence and survival. The government, Gálvez believed, should make peace with each separate band of Apaches and force their compliance with the terms of the treaties by making them settle near presidios or towns where they would be given food, firearms adequate for hunting but not for war and large supplies of liquor and trade goods.

It was a cynical, expensive plan, but it worked. In 1790 the Lipanes, caught between the invading Comanches from the north and the Spanish advance from the south, presented themselves at San Fernando de Austria in Coahuila and agreed to the provisions outlined by the Spaniards. In the Mescalero country a combination of Spanish and Comanche forces defeated band after band of the Tinde and forced them to sue for peace, while further west, Gálvez' "pacification by dependency" policy lured bands of Apaches to the vicinity of Tubac and Tucson, where they settled down and eventually became known as Mansos, tame Apaches.

For the next twenty-five years a general peace prevailed throughout the Apachería. The pacification program eroded Apache culture, and the Tinde grew accustomed to European trade goods, handouts and liquor. The Spanish population increased, new settlements appeared, ranches and farms flourished. Had it not been for the Mexican Revolution, the Apaches might have remained quiescent, victims of liquor, disease and cultural disintegration.

But with the outbreak of the wars for independence in Mexico, government policy on the frontiers broke down. Royal troops were no longer available to maintain the garrisons; the flow of gifts and subsidies to the Apaches ceased. As food supplies dwindled and more and more men went southward to join the revolutionary armies, the Tinde drifted away from the presidios and towns and returned to their old ways. After 1824 Mexican national leaders, hardpressed by internal revolts and attempts to establish a stable government, were unable to take decisive action. Various western bands again struck at Sonora and Chihuahua, while in the east the war between Mexico and Texas left the field open for the Lipanes and Mescaleros to renew their attacks on outlying ranches and villages. By 1848 the northern frontier had reverted to its former state. Much of Sonora was depopulated, Fronteras and Tubac were abandoned, and Apache war parties penetrated south as far as Ures and Hermosillo.

But now a new element had been added to Tinde warfare. In addition to driving off livestock and taking captives, the Apaches, for the first time, began to take a heavy toll in scalps and lives. The old "joyful raider," carefully husbanding the resources of the region, had disappeared, and in his place stood a militant, bitter warrior, one who no longer had any trust in nor respect for his foes. The Tinde seemed determined to follow the Spaniards' example and carry out a war of extermination against their enemies. Mexican officials reported that between 1820 and 1835 Apaches killed more than five thousand whites and forced four thousand more to flee the northern provinces.

Frightened and harassed, frontier officials turned to desperate measures. The governments of Sonora and Chihuahua offered bounties of up to one hundred and fifty pesos for Apache scalps and enlisted the aid of "Norteamericano" mercenaries in their efforts to stem the growing tide of Apache warfare. At Santa Rita del Cobre, a small mining village in southern New Mexico, a group of Mexican and Anglo scalp hunters invited Juan José's peaceful band to a great feast and then, at the height of the festivities, shot into the crowd of men, women and children with a fully loaded howitzer well primed with bullets, nails, pieces of chain, slugs and stones. Over four hundred Apaches lost their lives in the ensuing slaughter.

Despite such tactics, the Mexicans seemed incapable of stopping the Tinde, who were now thoroughly reassertive. In retaliation for the massacre at Santa Rita, the Apache war leader Mangas Coloradas and his Warm Springs Mimbreños cut off the tiny settlement, forced its inhabitants to flee and then ambushed and massacred almost every citizen. Other bands rose to the challenge, and within a few years the Tinde again dominated most of the Apachería.

But changes had taken place. Despite the seeming Apache victory, their way of life had been radically altered by the centuries of conflict and inter-relationships with the Europeans. Along the eastern fringes of the mountains and out on the plains of Texas the once proud Lipanes, decimated by centuries of war against Spaniards, Comanches and Mexicans, were split into two separate groups, both doomed to eventual extinction. Further to the west the Mescalero, Chiricahua and other groups, greatly reduced in numbers, had become increasingly dependent upon the Europeans. Steel knives, copper kettles, firearms and ammunition, and livestock to replace the fast declining supply of game were now essential to the Tindes' lifestyle. The old ways were gone forever. Within a few years new intruders — the Anglo-Americans — came to the Apachería. They soon proved to be an even more implacable and less easily defeated enemy than the Spaniards or Mexicans.

The first contacts between the Tinde and the Anglos came in the eastern regions of the Apachería, in the lands remaining to the Lipanes. Here the Spanish policy of the late eighteenth century had been noticeably successful, and the Tinde had settled down to a fairly peaceful existence. One group, the Lipanes de Abajo or Lower Lipanes, lived between San Antonio and Laredo on the northern side of the Río Grande, while another group, the Lipanes de Arriba or Upper Lipanes, roamed the Mexican side of the river.

During the first years of Anglo colonization, the Lower Lipanes, neighbors of the Austin settlements, remained peaceful. Under their principal chief, Flacco the Elder, they espoused the Texan cause during the war with Mexico; some of them even received commissions in the Texan army. Once independence was accomplished, President Sam Houston, blood brother to the Cherokees and sympathetic to the Amerinds, arranged for treaties with a number of Texas tribes, including the Apaches.

Nonetheless, as W. W. Newcomb points out in *The Indians of Texas from Prehistoric to Modern Times*:

> Treaties between Texas and its Indians were never taken very seriously by any of the signatories. Texans hoped to gain concessions from treaties, but gave little or nothing themselves, and they knew whatever promises they made would likely be broken.

The Texas Congress refused to ratify Houston's agreements, and when Mirabeau B. Lamar became President of the Republic, he repudiated Houston's program and instituted plans for the extermination or total expulsion of all Indians within the borders of Texas. According to Lamar, who reflected the attitude of most

Anglos, "The white man and the red man cannot dwell in harmony together."

Most Texans believed that if you had met one "redskin" you had met them all, and this soon led to misunderstanding and bloodshed. Peaceful Lipan bands were frequently blamed for raids carried out by Comanches or Kiowas, while the Lipanes, rapidly acclimated to Anglo duplicity, were not above raiding and stealing and blaming it on their Amerind kinsmen. Generally, however, the Texas Lipanes tried to maintain friendly relations with the Anglos. In 1844 the Lipanes, along with representatives of several other tribes, participated in a peace conference on the Clear Fork of the Brazos and signed a new treaty with the government of the Republic. Then in 1845 Texas became part of the United States, treaties made by the Republic were abrogated, new ones had to be negotiated, and the trend of future Anglo-Apache relations became apparent.

In 1845 the United States government was attempting to work out a satisfactory solution to its "Indian problem." The Anglos had made little attempt to Europeanize or Christianize the Amerinds: most frontiersmen believed "the only good Indian is a dead Indian." In order to end disputes between settlers who wanted the Amerinds' lands and equally militant redmen who were determined to defend their territories, the United States worked out a system of segregation and isolation based on the creation of what Chief Justice John Marshall termed "dependent domestic nations." Within the areas set aside for them, the Amerinds retained legal possession of the land, and although they had none of the privileges of regular citizenship, they were allowed to manage their own affairs with little government assistance or interference.

It soon became apparent, however, that isolation and the creation of separate Indian enclaves within the United States could not continue. As land became scarce, whites were increasingly reluctant to see territory set aside for Indian "hunting preserves," and as game disappeared and Anglo settlers intruded on their lands the Indians became less and less capable of supporting and protecting themselves. In 1830 Congress passed an Indian Removal Bill which provided for the transfer, with or without tribal consent, of the Amerinds east of the Mississippi to lands in the newly acquired Louisiana Territory. Still this did not solve "The Problem" for long. In 1849 management of Indian affairs passed from the War Department to the newly created Indian Bureau of the Department of the Interior, and the concept of "Indian reservations" under the charge of civilian agents replaced that of simple isolation and removal. Land was still to be set aside for the Indians, but the government now agreed to furnish them with supplies, tools, seed and livestock so that, although they remained isolated from their white neighbors, they might eventually become self-supporting.

The new policy was soon applied to the Apaches. In 1845 the United States government established two reservations for the Texas Indians; and the Lipanes, along with the Tonkawas, Anadarkos, Caddos and several other tribes, took up residence at the Brazos Agency south of Fort Belknap. But this did not satisfy area settlers. Although the reservation Apaches began farming and stockraising and even supplied scouts for the army, the Anglos were determined to have the region to themselves. Ranchers and farmers continually complained that their herds were being raided and that their lives and property would not be safe until the Indians were removed. They considered any red man fair game, attacked Indian cattle herds and threatened to destroy the reservations. Had it not been for the protests and protection of the Indian agent, Robert S. Neighbors, whites might have massacred the entire reservation population. In 1859, in order to "protect" the Indians from their neighbors, the government closed the Texas reservations and moved the Lipanes and their kinsmen north into Indian Territory and resettled them near Fort Cobb.

Some of the Lipanes resisted both reservations and removal and fled to the Mescaleros or moved south of the Río Grande. However, as they were soon to learn, they were but prolonging the inevitable. The events in Texas foreshadowed what was to take place throughout the Apachería. Already, far to the west in New Mexico and Arizona, the Tinde were learning that the new pale-eyes were even less trustworthy than the Spaniards or Mexicans.

The arrival of the first United States troops in the Southwest during the Mexican War seemed, at first, to portend a new period of peace. Despite earlier, and not always pleasant, contacts with Anglo trappers, traders, miners and scalphunters, the Tinde were inclined to welcome the newcomers. The Apaches even hoped that the "Americanos" might become allies in the long-standing war against the hated Mexicans. Were not the Anglos also enemies of the nation to the south? Had they not, like The People, defeated the Mexicans in open warfare?

What the Tinde did not know was that the Anglos viewed Apaches and Mexicans in a very different context. If the Anglos had little respect for the Mexicans, they had even less for the Apaches, whom they saw as a savage, barbaric race to be contained, controlled or exterminated. The United States government had no intention of joining the Apaches or any other Amerinds in making war on "civilized" peoples, not even Mexicans. Far from it! The Treaty of Guadalupe Hidalgo contained a clause (number eleven) which provided that the United States would restrain Indian raids into Mexico, make it illegal to own captives or property taken from Mexico by Indian raiders, rescue and deliver up all captives and attempt to enforce the security of the border between the two countries in laws governing Indian removals. This made no sense to the Tinde, who saw no reason why they should be bound by an agreement in which they had no part. Even more incomprehensible was the idea, vaguely explained to various Apache leaders, that the Anglos now considered themselves the conquerors of the Apachería by virtue of the Anglo defeat of the Mexicans. Strange logic indeed! The Mexicans had not conquered the Apachería, quite the contrary, hence how could the Anglos claim to have done so?

Still, the Tinde preferred to bide their time and attempt to negotiate with the newcomers. General Stephen Watts Kearney and Kit Carson, surveying the territory between the Río Grande and Colorado River in 1846, found the Mimbreños, Chiricahuas and Pinaleños wary but willing to discuss terms to allow Anglos to cross their lands or even settle in the Apachería providing they paid for the privilege. To the east, near the Sierra Blanca, the Jicarillas and Mescaleros met in council and sent a message to the governor of New Mexico stating that they would give up their Mexican captives and make peace. In September, 1850, a group of Mescaleros visited El Paso where they received food, kind treatment and encouragement to return. In April, 1851, Governor James S. Calhoun of New Mexico (who was also the U.S. Indian agent for the new Territory) succeeded in reaching agreements with several Jicarilla and Mescalero chiefs. A year later John Greiner, who succeeded Calhoun as agent for New Mexico, reported to Washington that a number of Mescaleros and Jicarillas had visited Santa Fé and signed a treaty of peace and friendship. Furthermore, he ended triumphantly, "For the last four months there has scarcely been a complaint of Indian depredation. . . ."

Despite their inability to stop raids across the border into Mexico, the Anglos managed to come to terms with various bands of Mimbreños, Gileños and other "southern Apaches." In July, 1852, Greiner and Colonel E. V. Sumner met the Gileño chiefs at Ácoma and negotiated a satisfactory treaty. In April of the following year Governor W. C. Lane of New Mexico reached new agreements with several Apache bands whereby, in return for an end to their raiding and looting, the government agreed to furnish them with corn, salt, beef and other subsistence over a three-year period. Meanwhile, near Santa Rita del Cobre, once the scene of bloody conflicts between the Tinde and Europeans, the Mimbreños established residence on a reservation under the sympathetic direction of Agent Michael Steck. Steck also reached agreements with the Coyoteros and Pinaleños and happily reported that they were now ready to accept government aid and to support themselves by farming and stockraising.

Eventually the reservation program might have been effective had it been carefully and consistently carried out, for it was not radically different from Gálvez' successful "pacification by dependency" which had brought peace in the last days of Spanish rule. But such was not to be. By the time the Anglos reached the Apachería, the United States government had radically revised its attitude with regard to Indian land rights. Although the government still set aside territory for the Apaches (and other western peoples), no definite boundaries were established and title to the land was not vested in the Indians. Thus, as Edward Spicer relates, a curious paradox existed whereby the Anglos "recognized the Indians as a political unit capable of making binding treaties" but without legal rights to the land they inhabited. White settlers remained free to infringe upon the reservations, and the government could, and did, move the Indians any time it wished to do so.

Congress, having "settled" the Apache problem, was slow to

appropriate the necessary funds for their maintenance; unscrupulous contractors were not reluctant to buy inferior supplies for the Indians and pocket the profits. On one reservation the agent reported that his people were being fed meat from diseased cattle, while at Santa Rita over half the Mimbreños died during the first few years of reservation life from a combination of hunger and disease. Many of the reservations were located on poor land where the Apaches could not support themselves even if they wished, and when they did manage to plant crops and accumulate some livestock, their white neighbors soon demanded removal of the Indians to other areas, so that the "superior" Anglos might utilize the fertile lands and water courses themselves.

As the white population increased, the Tinde grew wary and refused to negotiate further with U.S. agents. Small parties of warriors attacked immigrant trains, waylaid the Overland Mail, ran off livestock and generally made life miserable for the new inhabitants of the Apachería. Yet despite misunderstandings and bloodshed, there were men of good will on both sides who hoped to work out the problems between the two races. Many of the Tinde were tired of war and fighting and willing to locate in areas set aside for their use. Some civilian agents and military commanders held the Tinde in high regard and intended to see that they were treated fairly if they would give up their nomadic ways and live on the reservations.

Peace might have come to the Apachería had it not been for several unfortunate incidents. In 1851, for reasons that have never been clearly explained, a group of miners at Santa Rita seized the Mimbreño chief Mangas Coloradas, lashed him to a tree and whipped him. It was an unforgiveable insult which the Apache leader never forgot. Thereafter he devoted his life and energies to avenging himself and the honor of his race. A few years later, Lieutenant George N. Bascom, fresh out of West Point and not at all knowledgeable about Indians, attacked a peaceful band of Chiricahuas near Apache Pass in southern Arizona. Bascom later declared that he was sure that the band was holding some livestock and a young captive taken during an earlier raid on the nearby Ward ranch. But the Chiricahua leader, Cochise, knew only that he and his people had been attacked while they parleyed under a flag of truce. Cochise joined his father-in-law, Mangas Coloradas, in vowing revenge and war against the Pinda Lick-o-yi.

Meanwhile the Civil War began and many troops left the Southwest for battlefields in the east. While Confederate and Union forces occupied themselves with killing each other, the Tinde began a desperate effort to drive the Anglo invaders from the Apachería. Once again the dread cry, "Apaches!" echoed through the countryside. In the west and south the Mimbreños and Chiricahuas, joined by warriors from other once peaceful bands, systematically laid waste to Arizona and New Mexico. By the end of 1861, reported one newspaper, "nineteen-twentieths of the entire territory of Arizona is under the undisputed control of the Apaches." In Texas and eastern New Mexico, Gian-an-tah and Nicolás led Mescalero bands and a few Lipanes against Fort Davis and other frontier outposts and pushed the line of settlements back as much as a hundred miles. In scenes reminiscent of the earlier decades, deserted towns and abandoned ranches and farms dotted the countryside from the Colorado River in Arizona to the Nueces in Texas.

Imitating their Spanish and Mexican predecessors, Anglo frontier dwellers determined upon a war of extermination of their own. Local militia and volunteer companies, occasionally supplemented by regular troops, took to the field in pursuit of the elusive Apaches. In Texas both Confederate units and Ranger companies tried to stem the Apache tide, while in New Mexico and Arizona General J. H. Carleton and five companies of New Mexico volunteers, assisted by Colonel Kit Carson, began a relentless campaign to wipe out every Apache male in the Territory. Carleton's orders to his men were explicit: "The men are to be slain whenever and wherever they can be found. The women and children may be taken prisoners, but, of course, they are not to be killed."

No one was particular about obeying the final phrase of Carleton's order, but the rest of it was carried out with determination, deceit and treachery. In 1863 Captain Joseph Walker persuaded Mangas Coloradas to come to a parley and discuss terms for a new treaty. When the Mimbreño chief entered Walker's camp, he was taken prisoner and later murdered on specific orders from Colonel J. R. West, the commander at Fort McLean. In 1864 Colonel King S. Woolsey, aide to the governor of Arizona, lured a band of Coyotero Apaches to his camp, again on the promise of negotiating peace, and then killed Chief Para-mucka and eighteen of his people.

The Tinde struck back with acts of cruelty of their own. The horribly mutilated bodies of white men, women and children — brains roasted out, arms and legs hacked from the trunk, scalps gone — lay along the trails and beside smouldering cabins, mute testimony to Apache justice. But time was running out for the Tinde. The end of the War brought a new influx of prospectors, miners and settlers into the Apachería. The soldiers returned, re-established abandoned forts and built new ones. Hungry, tired, running out of room, the Apaches gradually gave way before overwhelming white population and military pressure.

By the end of 1870 many of the bands had surrendered and once again submitted to reservation life. But this did not save them from the schemes of rapacious Anglos. The U.S. government had no consistent policy but rather alternated between treating the Apaches as prisoners of war or friendly children to be cared for and protected. Always the Tinde were at the mercy of several contending forces. Between 1865 and 1871 military authorities, settlers and the Indian Bureau fought over control of the reservations and argued, often violently, about how the Indians were to be "managed." Greedy contractors, local inhabitants, some agents and even a few Congressmen, who supported themselves by supplying inferior goods and illegal items (including whiskey) to the reservations at exorbitant profits, worked hard to see that the Apaches did not become self-sufficient but remained dependent upon government handouts and supplies.

There were few real treaties between Anglos and Apaches, at least at the Congressional level, and these had long since become worthless pieces of paper. There were only easily broken local "arrangements" between individual field commanders, Indian agents and Apache band leaders. Even when the military and the Indian Bureau attempted to carry out the terms of such agreements, they were opposed by frontiersmen and civilian groups. Whites continued their old pre-War patterns of encroachment upon Indian lands and pressed for extermination or removal of the Tinde to other areas far from Anglo establishments. In 1871 a mob styling itself as the Tucson Committee of

Public Safety attacked a peaceful band of Arivaipa Apaches living and working under a military agent, Lieutenant Royal E. Whitman, at Camp Grant. The Tucson terrorists burned the village, raped several women and left the ground littered with the mangled bodies of eighty-five Apaches, mostly women and children.

Finally, even the government had had enough. A congressional investigating committee toured the western areas and reported the deplorable conditions on many of the reservations; humanitarians and reformers pleaded for a reassessment of the entire Indian program. In 1869 Congress authorized establishment of a new Board of Indian Commissioners; and during the next two years the Commissioners visited various tribes, met with Indians and agents and began working out recommendations for a new Indian policy. Vincent Colyer, secretary of the Board, toured the Apachería and became convinced that with adequate appropriations and honest and fair treatment even the most warlike Apaches could be persuaded to make peace. Meanwhile the Quaker leaders of the Orthodox Friends in the United States encouraged President Grant to appoint religious men as Indian agents and employees as a means to bring an end to graft and corruption on the reservations.

In 1871 the proposed reforms, known as Grant's Peace Policy, went into effect. In the same year Congress brought an end to further treaty-making (and thus breaking) with a law which stated "no Indian nation or tribe within the United States shall be acknowledged or recognized as an independent nation, tribe or power." The Board of Indian Commissioners removed a number of agents and contractors and turned control of the reservations over to various church groups, who were given the right to name new agents and direct future reservation activities. Congress also appropriated some funds for the creation of new reservations and increased aid to the Indians. In the Apachería, in addition to the existing reserves, four new areas — Camp Apache, the Tularosa Valley, Camp Grant and Camp Verde — were designated for the Tinde.

But a "Peace Policy" could not insure peace, and in the Apachería nothing really changed. The reservations were little more than concentration camps. Inexperienced agents from the church mission boards tried to enforce foolish and inane rules

which the Tinde did not understand. Once again the government neglected to live up to its pledges. Promised rations, tools and seed failed to arrive; no real reforms were made in the supply system which continued to be controlled by the infamous politico-economic group known as The Tucson Ring. The War Department, skeptical from the beginning of the peace policy, sent additional troops to the Apachería, and many military commanders, while giving lip-service to humanitarianism, worked for extermination. Even more detrimental to the success of the reformers' plans was the fact that the Apaches were often placed on lands far from their original homes, although many of the bands had agreed to make peace on the condition that they be allowed to take up residence near their traditional ranges.
Thus, even before the new program went into effect, Cochise and his band surrendered with the understanding that they would live at Canada Alamosa in southern New Mexico. But within a few months Cochise was ordered to take his people to Tularosa. The Chiricahua chief and many of his followers refused to move and returned to the warpath. Even those Chiricahuas who went to Tularosa were transferred within the year to Ojo Caliente. In fact, it seemed that whenever a promising start was made there was a new push for removal. Throughout the Apachería small bands of embittered warriors jumped the reservations and again took up their old ways, determined to be free of the white man's false promises. Perhaps the hostiles' sentiments were best expressed by Eskimo-tzin, the Arivaipa leader whose people had been massacred at Camp Grant. When asked why he had killed a white trapper known to be a good friend to the Apaches, Eskimo-tzin replied, "I did it to teach my people there must be no friendship between them and the white man."

At the time the peace policy was instituted, General George Crook arrived in the Apachería and began the enormous task of rounding-up all the Tinde bands and forcing them onto the reservations. Nan-tan Lupan (Chief Gray Wolf), as he was known to the Indians, attempted to carry out his assignment with firmness but fairness. Although an implacable foe in the field, Crook believed that the Tinde had been misjudged and mistreated. Shortly after his arrival in Arizona in July, 1871, Crook noted in a report to the Secretary of War:

Brig. Gen. George Crook on his mule "Apache"

> I think the Apache is painted in darker colors than he deserves. . . . Living in a country the natural products of which will not support him, he has either to cultivate the soil or steal, and as our vascillating policy satisfies him that we are afraid of him, he chooses the latter . . . being more congenial to his natural instincts.

Crook intended that the Tinde should give up "stealing" and learn to cultivate the soil, but he also believed that consistent and honest treatment would bring an end to sporadic raiding. Furthermore, convinced that Apaches were men and human beings, he insisted on treating them as such, demanded that the Tinde punish their own offenders and reservation jumpers and organized groups of Apache scouts to help in tracking down hostile bands. Between 1871 and 1875, assisted by the diplomatic and humane General O. O. Howard and agents Tom Jeffords and John Clum, who both understood and respected the Tinde, Crook completed his difficult task, winning the regard of white and red men alike.

But the efforts of Crook and his aides were consistently undermined by political scheming from the infamous Tucson Ring and stupid blundering in the Indian Office in Washington. Political leaders in the east favored a plan to concentrate all of the western Apaches on a single large reservation. Beginning in 1873, and despite the agreements made by Crook and Howard that they would be allowed to live at certain specified places, the various Tinde peoples were gathered up and moved to a new reservation at San Carlos. In 1875 fourteen hundred Tontos and Yavapais from Camp Verde were forced to leave their ripening crops and newly completed irrigation ditch and relocate on the new reserve. In 1877 Victorio's people and the Hot Spring Chiricahuas were taken to the reservation on the Gila River. Coyoteros, Pinaleños, Arivaipas, Tontos, Chiricahuas, Mimbreños — by 1878 more than five thousand Apaches had been concentrated at San Carlos.

Protests against the concentration policy and dissatisfaction with the miserable conditions at San Carlos — known in the army and Indian service as the "hell hole" of the West — led to new outbreaks under the legendary Apache leaders Gerónimo, Nana, Juh, Nachite and Victorio.

Crook, who had left Arizona in 1875 to take over the Department of the North Platte, returned to the Apachería and went in

Courtesy Amon Carter Museum, Fort Worth

Troop G, Tenth Cavalry, crossing Gila River at San Carlos with Apache prisoners.

pursuit of the hostiles. Once again, Nan-tan Lupan, by a wise balance of harshness and humane treatment, returned the hostiles to the reservation. By the time Crook left Arizona a second time in 1886 peace had come at last. The Tinde had run out of places to roam; everywhere in the once free and open Apachería were the villages, homes and roads of the Pinda Lick-o-yi. Only Mexico still beckoned, and in 1886 General Nelson Miles, assisted by Crook's Apache scouts, crossed the border and brought in Gerónimo's band. Thus ended three hundred years of Apache resistance.

Yet, even in their victory, the whites deceived the Tinde one last time. Miles had promised Gerónimo that he and his men would be sent to their families in Florida. But what was the word of an army general to a government that had already broken so many promises? The Apaches were sent to Florida, but they were not united with their families. Instead they were confined to prison and kept at hard labor. The crowning infamy was that peaceful Chiricahuas, who had refused to join Gerónimo, and the loyal Apache scouts who had risked their lives to help track him down, were rounded up as well and taken to Florida as prisoners of war! Crook, Howard and the newly organized Indian Rights Association protested vigorously, but not until 1913

Courtesy Amon Carter Museum, Fort Worth

Geronimo, mounted on left, and other Apaches

were the Chiricahuas allowed to return to New Mexico and settle on the Mescalero reservation. By then less than half of the seven hundred were still alive.

In the end the Tinde had little to show for their long, costly defiance — only prison, reservations and a trail of blood littered with the shreds of torn paper from a hundred broken pledges. Yet if the white man had broken his word, so had the Tinde. If the white man had refused to treat them as men, then how much more the Apaches scorned these pale-skinned white-eyes. They had led the Pinda Lick-o-yi a long and merry chase, had given as they had received. Out of the years of fighting and final defeat, the Tinde could take pride in one incontrovertible fact. They had defied and in defying sustained their right to call themselves The People.

The story should end here, but it does not. Although the long clash between Europeans and Tindes was over, the killing and

Courtesy Amon Carter Museum, Fort Worth

Geronimo, one of the last of the Chiricahua Apache hold-outs

Courtesy Amon Carter Museum, Fort Worth

Army and Apache scouts, 1886

bloodshed stopped, this marked only the end of one form of conquest and destruction and the beginning of another. For on the reservations began the last great humiliation of The People — a dehumanizing and deculturizing process that exceeded anything that had gone on before.

The new chiefs of the Indian Bureau began a systematic and efficient effort to destroy the Apaches' past, separate them from their language, culture and religion and make them into the Bureau's model W.A.S.P.'s. Assimilation became the new goal of U.S. Indian policy. Children were taken from their parents and shipped off to boarding schools many miles from home where they were beaten for using their native language, forbidden to wear their own costumes, and taught Anglo crafts, trades or skills which would force them into second-class jobs and second-class citizenship in the white man's world.

On the reservations poverty, disease, squalor and deculturization prevailed. One agent at the Mescalero reserve joyfully reported:

> [They] brought to me every educated Indian on the Reservation. . . . The Indian Office, at my request, issued a peremptory order for all to cut their hair and adopt civilized attire; and in six weeks from the start every male Indian had been changed into the semblance of a decent man, with the warning that confinement at hard labor awaited any backsliders.

Courtesy National Archives

Coyotero Apache scout, 1874

U. S. Scouts with Indian Scouts, in 1886.

Courtesy National Archives

Apache scouts, Fort Wingate, Arizona, probably 1870s

All reservation affairs were handled by the Indian Office and its employees, and decisions rarely, if ever, took into account what the Apaches wanted. The government was determined that the Tinde must become small-plot subsistence farmers and ranchers and did everything possible to force them to accept such a future.

Not until the 1920's was there any attempt at reform, first through a 1924 law which made all Indians citizens, whether they wanted to be or not, and later through the 1934 Indian Reorganization Act, intended as a kind of Red Man's Magna Carta, which did allow each tribe to have some voice in the management of its economic and political affairs. But even these modest reforms met opposition, especially at San Carlos, where the superintendent tried to circumvent the requirements of the Reorganization Act.

Unable to resist, divided, confined, relying on government supplies and government jobs to give them even the barest essentials of life, the Tinde went slowly along the white man's road. But they had learned much from their struggle for survival in an Anglo world, and they began subtly, weakly, but continu-

Courtesy Amon Carter Museum, Fort Worth

The notorious "Apache Kid" (center) as a scout with the army

ally, to reassert themselves. During the early years of the twentieth century, they consistently refused to carry out many of the government's plans and programs. Following the passage of the Reorganization bill, the Tinde set up a tribal council, which began a number of economic activities designed to meet the needs of the people rather than the wishes of the agents and superintendents. A few reservation-run schools began to appear, and a few of the Tinde once again practiced the old religion, taught the children the old crafts, the old language, the old ways.

During the later 1950's and throughout the 1960's the B.I.A. (Bureau of Indian Affairs), partly out of concern with overcrowding and poverty on the remaining reserves and partly out of pique at its gradually waning power to dictate reservation policy, suggested two new programs aimed at assimilation. These two programs — termination of the federal-tribal relationships and incorporation of the Indian lands into the states, and relocation of rural and reservation Indians to urban regions — met with strong resistance not only from the Tinde but other Native Americans as well. Indians began to fight back, to force the government, for the first time, to live up to its previous commitments. New organizations such as the National Congress of American Indians, various Intertribal Councils, the American Indian Chicago Conference and, later, the more militant National Indian Youth Council called for resistance to assimilation and acculturation and demanded that Indians be allowed to determine their own future. Young red militants sounded the call for unity and "Red Power."

The Spaniards tried to rule the Apachería for over three hundred years, the Mexicans for nearly one hundred, the Anglos for one hundred and twenty-five. All attempted, at one time or another to exterminate, assimilate, acculturate, destroy the Native Americans. But today, united with their red brothers, the Tinde speak again and demand that the white man listen. *Perhaps* this time they will succeed. The Tinde have endured and in enduring retained their right to be. They are still The People.

SUGGESTED READINGS:

Although relatively little has been written on modern Apache history, there is an extensive literature on Apache culture and on the pre-1900 period. Although old, Frank C. Lockwood, *The Apaches* (New York: 1938), is a good general summary, while A. H. Schroeder, *A Study of the Apache Indians* (New York: 1973) reflects more recent scholarship.

Among the many works on Apache culture are: Morris Opler, *Apache Odyssey* (New York: 1969) and *An Apache Life Way* (Chicago: 1941). Much more technical but of interest to the reader who wishes to delve more deeply are the essays in K. H. Basso and Morris Opler, (eds.), *Apachean Culture History and Ethnology* (Tucson: 1973). The chapters on the Apache in Ruth Underhill, *Red Man's America* (Chicago: 1953) and Harold E. Driver, *The Indians of North America* (Chicago: 1961) are also helpful.

The period of Spanish-Apache contact is well treated in Jack D. Forbes, *Apache, Navajo and Spaniard* (Norman: 1960). Anglo-Apache relations are traced in Ralph H. Ogle, *Federal Control of the Western Apaches, 1848-1886* (Albuquerque: 1970); C.L. Sonnichen, *The Mescalero Apaches* (Norman: 1966) and A. B. Bender, *A Study of Western Apache Indians, 1846-1886* (New York: 1973). Woodward Clum, *Apache Agent, The Story of John Clum* (Boston: 1936) details the efforts of a sympathetic white agent. A dramatic but balanced account of the Apache wars may be found in Paul Wellman, *Death in the Desert* (New York: 1935). A more recent account is Odie Faulk, *The Geronimo Cam-*

paign (New York: 1969). Particularly helpful in understanding the problems of the Apaches and other southwestern peoples throughout the period of contact with the white man is Edward Spicer, *Cycles of Conquest* (Tucson: 1962).

On contemporary Indian policy and land claims, W. E. Washburn, *Red Man's Land, White Man's Law* (New York: 1971) and Kirke Kickingbird and Karen Ducheneaux, *One Hundred Million Acres* (New York: 1973) deal with all of the tribes, but include sections on the Apache. Kenneth F. Neighbors, *Apache Ethnohistory: Government, Land and Indian Policies Relative to Lipan, Mescalero, Tigua Indians* (New York: 1973) is the most recent study directly related to the Apaches.

The government made treaties, gave presents, made promises, none of which were honestly fulfilled. . . . We took away their country and their means of support, broke up their mode of living, their habits of life, introduced disease and decay among them, and it was for this and against this they made war.

General Sherman, 1878

CHAPTER 12

The Eastern Pueblos

Eugene B. McCluney

THE FIRST EUROPEAN contact with the Eastern Pueblos occurred in the year 1540 when Coronado and his group of explorers pushed their way north into New Mexico. The background of the Eastern Pueblo and a point of origin for these people took place around 1300 A.D., when a series of very severe droughts caused the resettlement of the Eastern Pueblos from the northwest into the Rio Grande Valley.

These people carried with them two distinguishing traits. First, a socio-political organization that was highly autonomous, and second, a method of subsistence economy based upon intensive, irrigated agriculture. For two hundred forty years before the Spanish conquest and the arrival of Coronado, the Eastern Pueblos, composed of approximately seventy villages, were scattered from El Paso to Taos on both sides of the Rio Grande. Three language families made up the means of communication of these people, along with some half-dozen languages which had no immediate relation to the first three. In regard to population, Edward H. Spicer states, "What the Spaniards found in this two hundred fifty mile stretch of river valley was a large number of villages of very similar character. No village was large; the largest probably being less than two thousand inhabitants. Most of them were not over four hundred people." He goes on to say, "It is doubtful if the whole Rio Grande Valley had a population of forty thousand at the time the Spaniards entered it."

EUGENE B. McCLUNEY has studied the Indians of the Greater Southwest for many years and has participated in numerous archaeological excavations in New Mexico and Northern Mexico.

He received his B.S. and M.A. degrees in History from Texas Christian University, a second M.A. in Anthropology from the University of Colorado, and his Ph.D. in History from Texas Christian University.

During 15 years of teaching and research Dr. McCluney's interests have centered around the comparative ethnohistory of the Pueblo and non-Pueblo areas of New Mexico and West Texas.

He is currently Adjunct Professor of History at Texas Christian University, Director of the TCLL — Carswell Air Force Base Education Program, and a member of the Western Writers of America.

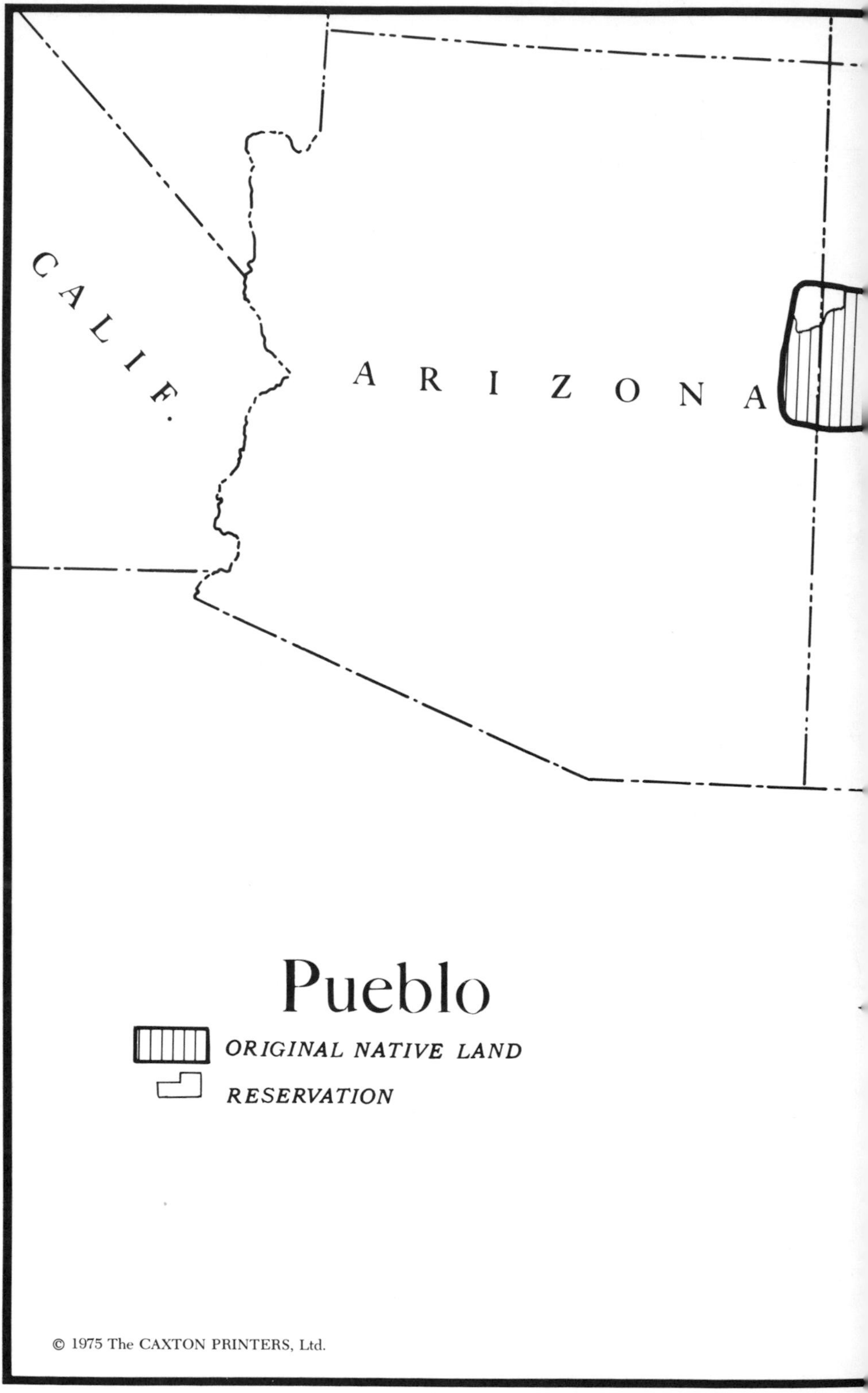
CALIF.
ARIZONA
Pueblo
ORIGINAL NATIVE LAND
RESERVATION

MEXICO
TEXAS
XICO
NWCI

Courtesy Amon Carter Museum, Fort Worth

Navajo woman and child

Prior to the arrival of Coronado in New Mexico in 1540, the Eastern Pueblo villages had undergone a series of attacks from the east by nomadic peoples who swept into the middle Rio Grande Valley periodically to raid the food stores of the Pueblo peoples. As a consequence, most of the Pueblo villages lying on the east side of the Rio Grande from El Paso to Socorro had been virtually wiped out prior to 1540, and the survivors had moved to the western shore and northward toward present Albuquerque, New Mexico.

The theory of conquest practiced by the Spaniards in New Mexico varied greatly from the administration of Cortez and his relations with the Indians of Mexico farther to the south. Coronado and his men dealt with the Eastern Pueblos very directly and harshly. He, and those Spanish Conquistadors who suceeded him, attempted to deal with the many autonomous Eastern Pueblo villages as a single political unit. The Spaniards felt that they could command and govern the Indians of the Rio

Courtesy Amon Carter Museum, Fort Worth

Navajo Indians

Grande Valley much as they had done with the Indian villages of Mexico, such as those of the Yaqui and Mayo tribes. The language differences, as well as the minor but highly important variations in the religion of the Eastern Pueblos, caused the Spanish a great deal of trouble with the Eastern Pueblos. Shortly after Coronado's party arrived in the middle Rio Grande valley, the Indians became aroused because of the Spanish pillaging for food and the treatment of the Indians of the Pueblos. Coronado and his party took some two hundred captives from among the rebelling villages of the Eastern Pueblos and burned them at the stake as a warning to the other Indians that the Spaniards would not tolerate any further acts of rebellion. By the spring of 1541 some twelve villages had been completely disrupted by Coronado and his men. Most of these villages were totally abandoned, and the people had allied themselves with other villages on both sides of the Rio Grande River north of Albuquerque. By the time Coronado decided to leave New Mexico, hundreds of Indians had been killed and dozens of villages had been totally destroyed or rendered uninhabitable.

In 1541 Coronado returned to Mexico to report to the viceroy on the expedition to New Mexico, and also to describe what he had found among the Eastern Pueblos. He had left behind a very thinly organized combination of military and religious administration, which proceeded to deal with the Indians as he had done in his first entry into New Mexico. The program was based primarily upon religious conversion, but whenever the Spaniards met with any resistance they applied military force to subjugate the Indians and force them into conversion by the Franciscan missionaries who had accompanied Coronado into the area. It was the decision of the viceregal government in Mexico City that the Pueblo Indians of New Mexico should undergo a continued direct conversion either peacefully or by military force. Several Spanish expeditions followed the Coronado entry. Among these were the expedition of Oñate, the Chamuscado-Rodríguez expedition, Espejo, and finally the expedition of Castaño de Sosa in 1590-91.

During this period of concentrated Spanish subjugation, the Indians began to build a formidable barrier between themselves and their Spanish masters. The Spanish suffered their first missionary losses with the murder of Padre Rodríguez and several

Courtesy Amon Carter Museum, Fort Worth

Navajo warrior with shield and lance

lay brothers by the Tiwa villages as a result of forceful conversion practices.

By 1600 the Eastern Pueblos had become partially acculturated. By using less force and making peaceful overtures the Spaniards gradually reduced the power of the Pueblos. Although Espejo adopted a more peaceful administrative attitude in his relations with the Indians, the program of missionary work continued to be difficult, and the Indians of the Eastern Pueblos continued to resent and defy the teachings of the missionaries.

Oñate was the first of the Spanish conquistadors of the 16th century to approach the Indians of the Eastern Pueblos diplomatically. Wherever he went he attempted to secure agreements or formal promises of obedience. He also told the various chiefs among the villages that the Spaniards were there to protect them against their enemies, and that by submitting to baptism by the Roman Catholic Church, the Indians would be assured of peace and prosperity. Paving the way by agreements, Oñate's colonization policy proved highly successful. He built a mission church on the banks of the Rio Grande above Santa Fe and named it San Gabriel. It was at San Gabriel that the first formal administrative framework for New Mexico was established. The area was divided into seven districts, each headed by an alcalde who in turn reported back to Oñate at San Gabriel. The Spanish sphere of influence by 1640 extended from El Paso to Taos in the north, and from Pecos east of the Rio Grande to some two hundred fifty miles west of the river. Spicer describes it as "a domain of eighty-seven thousand square miles, only spottily explored, but regarded by Oñate as properly subject to the King of Spain." Oñate's carefully laid colonization scheme, however, was to be short-lived.

Because of the geographical separation of Oñate's colonists from Mexico and the unfriendliness of the Indians who surrounded them in great numbers, the entire expedition began to falter and lose its grip upon the inhabited area. There followed a series of arguments between Oñate and the alcaldes of the various districts, a slowing of the missionary activity in the various hostile villages, and a general apathy caused by lack of food, and especially the failure of the Spaniards to find gold, silver, and other minerals in the area.

It appears that the military units of Oñate's expedition were

Courtesy National Archives

Navajo family, Canyon de Chelley, New Mexico, 1873

the first to lose heart, followed shortly by the missionaries. Gradually, the Indians north of Santa Fe began to drift away from the Spanish settlements to settle east of the Rio Grande, leaving San Gabriel isolated and open to attacks by other Indian tribes. West of the river the people of Ácoma lured a party of Spanish soldiers into their village by pretending to be friendly, and then annihilated them. The Spaniards formed a punitive expedition against the villagers of Ácoma and killed over five hundred of the men, resorting to the tactics of mutilation as practiced earlier by Cortez in his subjugation of the Aztecs. The village of one thousand five hundred souls was rendered virtually helpless, and with the defenses of Ácoma broken, the surviving villagers moved onto the mesas below. Regardless of the problems met by Oñate's colonists in the early 1600s, they did re-establish themselves in the year 1610, when Oñate ordered that the capital be moved from San Gabriel to present Santa Fe. Remembering what had happened at the village of Ácoma, the other Pueblos of the area gradually submitted to Spanish authority, and a period of colonization and conversion followed.

During the next twenty years the building of churches was successfully completed in most of the Pueblo villages along the Rio Grande. Conversion proceeded at a satisfactory rate to the point that several Indians were assigned secular service within the churches and given administrative responsibility, such as governors, *fiscales*, and other offices. The influx of Franciscan missionaries from Mexico continued and by 1630-35 there were an estimated fifty Franciscan missionaries at work among the Pueblos. They not only converted and baptised, but also trained the Indians in the ritual of the church and the responsibilities of administrative offices within the villages. Again, however, Oñate's progress was to be relatively short-lived. In 1641 the Indians again showed signs of unrest and feelings of hatred and retaliation against the Spaniards. By this time the missionaries found that they could not effectively maintain missionary service to the many scattered villages along the river. Coupled with this was the arrival of inquisition officials to investigate the practices of the church in New Mexico,. Their findings and the charges brought against the missionaries for malpractice, hurt church-Indian relations, and as a result of the inquisitional findings many mission stations were abandoned. The Indians were left without the teachings of the church, and more especially, the protection afforded them from their enemies by the Spanish military. It was during this time that the people of Taos killed their missionary and broke the power of the church in the northern area of the Rio Grande.

Before the year 1680 internal trouble spread throughout all of Spanish New Mexico. The trouble lay in the conflict of interest between the church and the civil authority. The governors of New Mexico pursued their self-interest rather than trying to create a successful colony, and this policy was bitterly opposed by the church authorities. The governors recruited large forces of Indian laborers, and put them to work for their own private gain. The missionaries took immediate offense at this practice, claiming that the Indians were being taken away from the influence of the church, and furthermore, were being barred from their own agricultural activities on which they and the missionaries depended. The governors considered the missions as well as the missionaries as a threat to their own administration and viewed the missionaries as creating empires of their own which limited the power of both civil and military authority throughout New Mexico. Although Oñate had been zealous in his attempt to create a peaceful coexistence between Spaniards and Indians, he had granted *encomiendas* of Indians to Spanish gentlemen, which gave them the right to use these Indians as servants and as laborers. The Spaniards had also encroached upon Indian agricultural lands, and as a result, the lands surrounding the Pueblos were being usurped by missionaries or civilians. The split between religious and civil authority among the Spanish colonists continued, and the Spanish governors charged the missionaries with malpractice and took the side of the Indians on such issues as punishment for non-attendance at mass, public whippings of Indians who either defied the missionaries or committed sins against church or community. In the end, the Spanish civil authorities accused the missionaries of contributing directly to the unrest of the Indians in New Mexico and blamed them for disruption of peaceful co-existence.

The Indians were confused by these disputes and regarded the promises made by the Spaniards for their protection and their Christianization as hollow and false. At the same time they began to realize that the warring factions within the Spanish government of New Mexico were weakening Spanish control, and that by marshalling the populations of the various villages they might be able to defeat the Spaniards and end Spanish rule.

From 1660 to 1680 the Indians gradually broke away from the church and reinstated their old religious practices and traditional mores within the villages. The masked religious dances grew in intensity and popularity, along with the use of the kiva, the ceremonial regalia, and the secret societies and priesthoods in the various villages in and around Santa Fe.

During the 1670s pressure from the Indians of the plains east of the Rio Grande Pueblos also intensified, and sporadic raiding began to take its toll among the Pueblos. The Indians appealed to the Spanish military for protection against their enemies, but the Spaniards were unable to defend them against attacks by the Comanches, Apaches, and other nomadic bands, who swept into the villages during the winter and carried off food, women, and children.

In 1680 the Pueblo Indians of New Mexico rebelled against their Spanish masters. Two leaders emerged at the head of the Indian population. One was Popé from San Juan, and the other was Catiti of Santo Domingo. The large Pueblo village of Taos had for several years been under close scrutiny by the Spanish of Santa Fe. There were many plots against the Spaniards hatched in this Pueblo, and it was considered a center of insurrection. The Indians of Taos broke out of the Pueblo and proceeded down river toward Santa Fe, gaining allies from northern villages as they travelled southward. The Spanish resistance in and around the northern area was quickly overwhelmed, and in order to save their lives, the Spaniards were forced, under the direction of Governor Otermín, to retreat southward to safety in the El Paso area. Many of the Spaniards, including citizens, military, and the missionaries, were unable to retreat quickly enough from their posts in northern New Mexico, and as a result, three hundred seventy-five of the almost three thousand Spanish colonists were either murdered or captured by the advancing Indians. The goal of Popé and Catiti was not total annihilation of the Spaniards, but the overthrow of the mission system and the expulsion of all Spaniards from New Mexico. As a result of the Pueblo revolt of 1680 the Spaniards lost control of New Mexico for the next twelve years, and although Governor Otermín made

Courtesy Amon Carter Museum, Fort Worth

Zuñi Pueblo

several attempts to reconquer the rebels, his efforts were not successful.

The revolt of 1680 was successful mainly because the Spaniards did not anticipate that the Pueblos could band together collectively to form a warrior force large enough to dislodge the garrison at Santa Fe. Although the Pueblo revolt did accomplish the two objectives for which it was organized, it failed in the end because the Pueblos, hampered by their own autonomous tradition, could not organize their forces into an effective administrative unit at Santa Fe after the Spanish had been forced out of New Mexico. The warrior forces of the Pueblos were not organized under central leadership, and the civil authorities of the Pueblos remained widely separated in their views of reorganization during the absence of the Spaniards. Lacking the knowledge of centralized organization, the various Pueblos returned to their traditional ways and went back into the villages to continue the aboriginal activities and pursuits they had known before the Spanish conquest.

The Pueblos soon found that the Apache raids were growing in force, and the winter raids became year-round activity. The Pueblo Indians around Santa Fe were forced to abandon the area south of Santa Fe and to take up defensive positions on mesa tops in the northern Rio Grande valley. Not only were the nomadic raids increased, but tension within villages and between villages became serious.

When Vargas re-entered New Mexico in 1692, many of the villages were abandoned and the people scattered throughout the northern area. His re-entry at the head of a strong punitive expedition met little resistance among the Pueblos who had formed the bulwark of the original rebellion in 1680. One of the few areas that defied Vargas was Black Mesa, near the Pueblo of San Ildefonso. Eventually the Indians of the Black Mesa area surrendered, and by 1694 the unity of the Pueblos against the Spanish reconquest was completely broken, never to reappear.

After the Pueblo revolt of 1680 the Spanish administration among the Eastern Pueblos continued as it had begun — economic exploitation on the part of the secular government and the continual growth of Christian conversion by the missionaries. The Indians, although neutralized by the Spaniards, still continued a program of non-cooperation, which had been

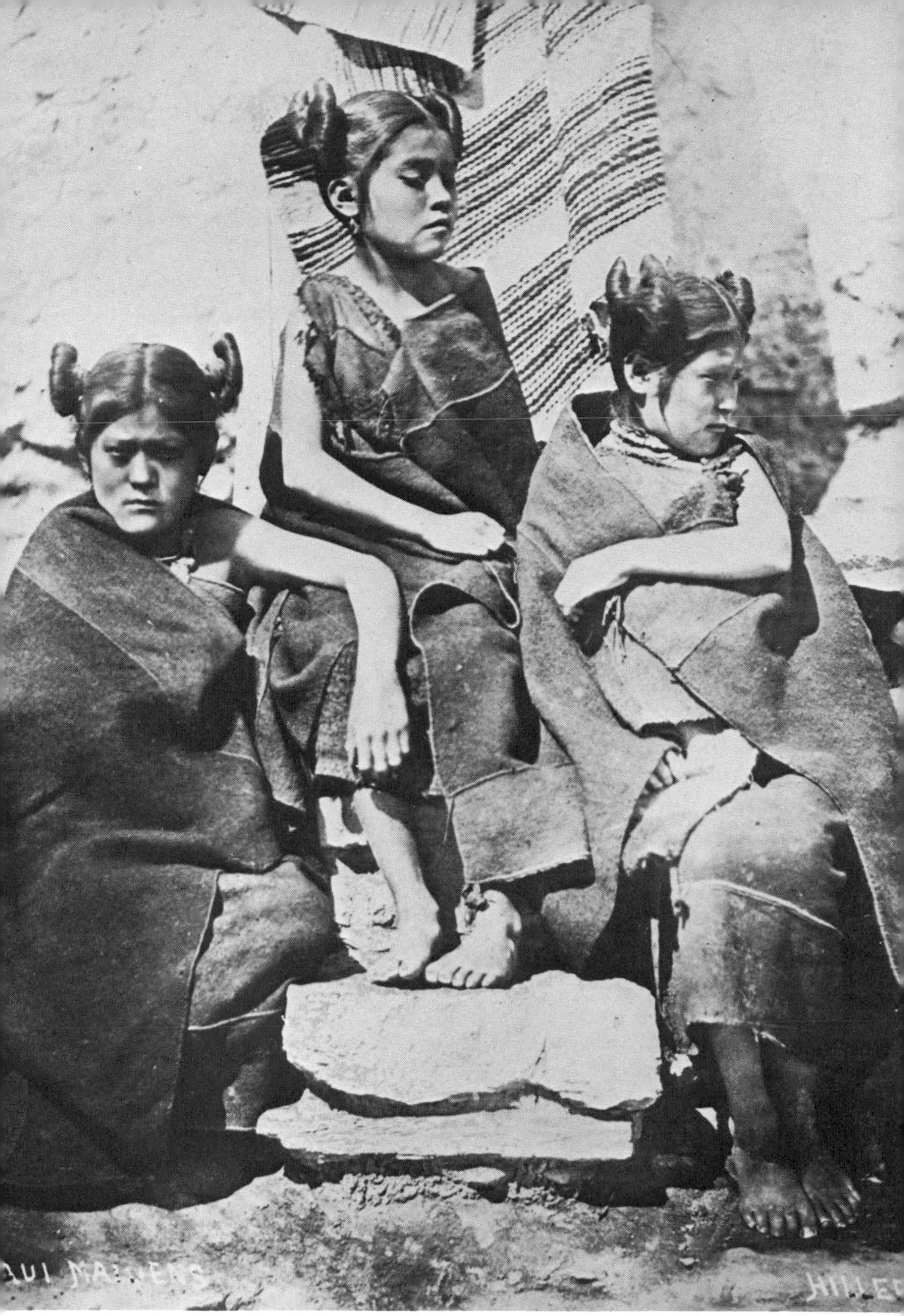

Courtesy Amon Carter Museum, Fort Worth

Hopi (Moqui) girls

Courtesy Amon Carter Museum, Fort Worth

House of Taos man married to Zuñi woman

reborn during the sixteen years of freedom from the Spaniards following the Pueblo revolt.

Between 1700 and 1750, a series of epidemics broke out among the Eastern Pueblo villages, reducing the population appreciably and forcing the Pueblo peoples to abandon small villages and move into larger inhabited areas. With the take-over by the Mexican government, after the Mexican revolution, the attitudes and governmental administration toward the Eastern Pueblos continued as before. The Mexican government was not faced so much with the problem of external and internal control of the Eastern Pueblo villages as it was with the continued raiding from the east by Apaches and from the west by large, heavily armed Navajo forces.

In 1846, when General Kearny and his troops marched into Santa Fe to take over New Mexico and to establish an Anglo-American government, he found that the raiding from both east and west by various nomadic groups had grown until the Pueblos were continually on the defensive. General Kearny made repeated attempts to check the raids but the necessity of maintaining an effective government in Santa Fe and Albuquerque distracted him.

Courtesy National Archives

Taos Pueblo, New Mexico, 1941

Colonel Doniphan was dispatched to lead punitive expeditions into the Navajo country for the purposes of ending the raiding in the west, and he was able to bring peace to the upper and middle Rio Grande valley. During this period, however, the Taos Indians rebelled, killed Governor Bent, and attacked Santa Fe. They were soon forced to retreat to their own Pueblo, where they remained a threat to Anglo-American occupation of New Mexico for some years afterward.

In 1847 the territorial legislature of New Mexico passed a law which recognized each Pueblo village as a separate entity and extended to each certain rights in perpetuity concerning land holdings. These grants had originally been formulated by the Spanish crown and extended through Mexican rule. They remained virtually unchanged and were considered binding.

A new Pueblo agency for the Rio Grande valley was established in the year 1849, which further extended peaceful dealings with the Eastern Pueblos. The Indians were armed in order to defend themselves against the raiding Apaches from the north and south. They were encouraged to remain at peace with the United States, and various chiefs of the Pueblo villages were invited to Washington to confer with the President and Congress and to lay before the government their grievances and desires to insure peaceful coexistence between themselves and the Anglo-Americans.

The nomadic raiding was finally brought to a close in the years 1864 and 1865, when the remaining Navajos and Apaches were subjugated and confined on widely scattered reservations. After the Civil War a new prosperity in New Mexico stimulated agricultural development as well as extended ranching and caused an upsurge in land development and land speculation. Encroachment on Pueblo land began as the influx of Anglo-Americans from east of the Mississippi River continued.

By 1890 cattle and sheep herds had developed to such a great degree that gradual encroachment was giving way to direct takeover of Pueblo Indian lands, which the Indians used for many years without title. Because of overgrazing, especially in the central Rio Grande valley, together with extensive timber and mining operations in the same area, flooding and land erosion began. Serious troubles also developed over water rights and water control in the Rio Grande valley area. By the early 1900s the Eastern Pueblo villages had lost virtually half their land because of flooding, overgrazing, and encroachments by the Anglo-American ranchers and farmers.

In 1876 the United States Supreme Court had ruled that the Pueblos of New Mexico were not Indians in the sense that the other aborigines of the United States were, and were not, therefore, entitled by law to receive the services of the United States government. They were not, furthermore, allowed protective rights for their property and their land holdings. The United States government held the opinion that the treaty of Guadalupe Hidalgo did not allow the government to interfere with Pueblo Indian policy as to restrain private individuals from recognizing the Eastern Pueblos of New Mexico as non-Indian groups.

During the early 1900s Pueblo Indians brought land suits against the government of the United States, ranging from squatting and other illegal trespass on the Indian lands by Anglos to extensive suits against wealthy cattle, sheep, and land companies which had infringed upon Pueblo rights. Meanwhile, the territorial legislature of New Mexico did not recognize the Eastern Pueblo Indians as citizens and, furthermore, federal legislation established recognition of the rights of squatters established

Courtesy Amon Carter Museum, Fort Worth

Hopi (Moqui) girl of Walpi Pueblo

Courtesy Amon Carter Museum, Fort Worth

Navajos at the last issue of rations, 1879

on Pueblo land. They placed any suits brought about by the Eastern Pueblos against the United States as the domain of the United States District Court rather than the Federal Court.

In 1924 the Congress of the United States, because of pressure brought about by the Santo Domingo Council of 1922, passed new legislation which was to be known as the Pueblo Lands Act. This was an attempt by the United States government to restore all of the lands granted to them by original Spanish land charters and to pay for land which could not legally be restored because of the lack of Indian title so mentioned in the original Spanish grants.

In the 1900s the United States government formulated a plan which proved to be a devastating, disruptive force among the Eastern Pueblos of New Mexico. The establishment of Indian schools, with forced recruitment of students for these schools, began as early as 1890 and continued to gain impetus until 1920.

Courtesy Amon Carter Museum, Fort Worth

Zuñi woman

The children of the Pueblos were compelled to attend these schools for a minimum of four years of training. Although no tuition was charged, the forced attendance program caused an internal breakdown and disruption of the family unit which further neutralized the Indian communities.

Competition developed between the various Protestant churches and the Roman Catholic churches of New Mexico over the administration of the schools and the various curricula which were to form the training basis for Indian children. In 1920 the Bureau of Indian Affairs attempted to end practice of Pueblo Indian religion. The government felt that this continuation of native religion was an encroachment upon the missionary activities of the Protestant and Roman Catholic churches. Teams of observers and reporters were sent into each Pueblo village to-make reports on Pueblo Indian religion, and these reports, which were greatly distorted and misinterpreted, denounced certain Indian religious practices as obscene, immoral, and damaging to standard Christian ethics. This was especially true of the aboriginal religious practices in the Pueblos of Taos and Santo Domingo. On the basis of these reports, the Commissioner of Indian Affairs decided that all children were to be retained in boarding schools and kept out of the Pueblos so that they could not be re-influenced by Pueblo religion once they had returned to their respective villages. A set of regulations was handed down by the Bureau of Indian Affairs called the *Religious Crimes Code*, which forbade the practice of aboriginal religious observances and further regulated the groupings of large numbers of Indians in the kivas and other religious ceremonial places within the Pueblos and in the surrounding areas.

As a result of the *Religious Crimes Code*, dissention and non-cooperation began to spread between the Pueblos and the United States government. Soon the *Religious Crimes Code* was rendered void because of American public opinion and also as a result of the growth and appreciation of the Indian way of life among anthropologists and artists, who were beginning to realize the value of preserving the artistic and religious traditions of the Pueblo communities of New Mexico.

Despite the impact of Spanish, Mexican, and Anglo influences, the Pueblo Indians today are attempting to preserve their identity, although acculturation has permeated most of the facets

Courtesy Amon Carter Museum, Fort Worth

Corn Dance, Pueblo Santo Domingo, New Mexico

of their everyday life. The lands on which the Eastern Pueblos maintained themselves prior to the coming of the Spaniards have now been isolated and over-used because of Mexican and Anglo agriculture and livestock activity. Today the various Pueblos of the eastern area, consisting of Ácoma, Cochití, Isleta, Jémez, Laguna, Nambe, Picuris, Pojoaque, Sandia, San Felipe, San Ildefonso, San Juan, Santa Ana, Santa Clara, Santo Domingo, Zia, Taos, and Tesuque, have become acculturated and are dependent upon the surrounding cities and towns for their livelihood. They participate in construction jobs, forestry, mining, the cattle industry, and other types of employment in the Hispano-Anglo communities.

Although each Pueblo still maintains its administrative organization consisting of its cacique or head, and its various priesthoods within the religious framework, the pure aboriginal subsistence pattern no longer exists. One of the few remaining attributes of the aboriginal tradition is manifest in the Pueblo religion. Because of the impact of the *Religious Crimes Code* and infringement by the United States government, as well as anthropological activity in the 1940s and 1950s, the Eastern Pueblos have isolated their religion and have attempted to maintain it in secret. Their religion is a binding force in the social and family organization of each Pueblo.

At present there is an attempt on the part of the Eastern Pueblos to rejuvenate and reinstate their traditional arts and crafts which has met with some success, although the original techniques and applications in certain cases have long been forgotten. Eastern Pueblo lands are now being purchased for water diversion and water control projects on the Rio Grande, and as a result, the agricultural practices of the Eastern Pueblos will soon be completely changed, and other means of subsistence will have to be found. The Eastern Pueblo tradition, which was once a powerful entity, is now threatened with extinction unless there is meaningful cooperation and deeper understanding on the part of the United States.

SUGGESTED READING

Beaglehole, Ernest "Notes on Hopi Economic Life". *Yale University Publications in Anthropology.* Number 15. 1937.

Bennett, John W. "The Interpretation of Pueblo Culture: A Question of Values." *Southwestern Journal of Anthropology,* II. 1946.

Brophy, William A. and Sophie D. Aberle *The Indian: America's Unfinished Business.* Norman. 1966.

Dozier, Edward P. "Rio Grande Pueblos," in Edward H. Spicer (ed.), *Perspectives in American Indian Culture Change,* Chicago. 1961.

Driver, Harold E. and Wilhelmine Driver *Indian Farmers of North America.* Chicago. 1967.

Driver, Harold E. and William C. Massey "Comparative Studies of North American Indians". *Transactions of the American Philosophical Society,* XLVII. 1957.

Eggan, Fred *Social Organization of the Western Pueblo.* Chicago. 1950.

Fisher, R. G. "An Outline of Pueblo Government," in D. D. Brand and F. E. Harvey (eds.), *So Live the Works of Men.* Albuquerque, 1939.

Foster, George M. "Culture and Conquest: America's Spanish Heritage." *Viking Fund Publications in Anthropology, No. 27.* 1960.

Parsons, E. C. *Pueblo Indian Religion.* 2 Vols. Chicago, 1939.

Spicer, Edward H. *Cycles of Conquest.* Tucson, 1962.

Courtesy Amon Carter Museum, Fort Worth

Governor of San Felipe Pueblo

A people once numerous, powerful, and truly independent, found by our ancestors in the quiet and uncontrolled possession of an ample domain, gradually sinking beneath our superior policy, our arts and our arms, have yielded their lands by successive treaties, each of which contains a solemn guarantee of the residue, until they retain no more of their formerly extensive territory than is deemed necessary to their comfortable subsistence.

John Marshall

CHAPTER 13

The Past Continues: Indian Relocation in the 1950s

Arthur H. DeRosier, Jr.

AMERICANS ARE INTERESTING, complex, and basically humanistic people. Sometimes we appear so complex that outsiders, such as Alexis DeTocqueville, Lord Charnwood, Gunnar Myrdal, and even Alistair Cooke, try their hand at explaining us to ourselves. Part of our mystery or charm is the fact that we enjoy mythologizing a great deal. In Indian affairs it seems to me that the myth most responsible for a good deal of mischief and even tragedy is the "melting-pot" myth. As much as anyone else, Hector St. John Crevecoeur stated the myth centuries ago. An American is a new man on the world scene, Crevecoeur wrote. "He is neither an European, or the descendant of an European. . . .[In America] individuals of all nations are melted into a new race of men. . . ." Since colonial days, we have labored under the assumption that all oppressed peoples of the world could journey to America, shed their past heritages, and become an entirely new creation — an American. Of course, it is true that most immigrants joined in the noble task of carving out a new, exciting, and impressive nation, but it is pure fancy to believe that they disowned their heritage in the bargain. Thousands of volumes have been written on the contributions of German-Americans, Jewish-Americans, Scottish-Americans, and others. It seems to be a favorite pastime of what we might call "heritage historians" to remind us continually of what some particular nationality has done to grace the rest of us. If one tried to catalog all of the Italian-American and other ethnic American clubs from coast to coast, I suspect his job would be monumental. In short, hardly anyone has forgotten that his ancestors played a significant role in insuring America's greatness: that is as it should be. If one does not possess pride in self, he likely will have pride in nothing else.

But the melting-pot myth that has persisted for centuries has been more deadly to Indians than bullets have. As Indians were here first and were obviously different from Europeans, it has been white America's goal since earliest times to make Native Americans over in their image. Perceptive Thomas Jefferson wrote for all of us when he suggested that the best way to conquer and transform Indians was to assimilate them. "Let our settlements and theirs meet and blend together, to intermix, and become one people," he wrote in 1803. "Incorporating themselves with us as citizens of the United States, this is what the natural progress of things will, of course, bring on, and it will be better to promote than retard it." Fortunately for Indians, we forgot Jefferson's advice in the nineteenth century and decided to try our hand at removing or killing them, and locking up the remnants on reservations. Strange as it may seem, I would like to suggest that our decision to isolate Indians on reservations was the best thing that happened to them since white Europeans arrived in 1492: it saved them from annihilation and total assimilation. Despite the inhumanity and corruption that accompanied the evolution of the reservation system, these prisons allowed Indians to remain united, in spirit and location, relatively free of an outside people plundering and profiting from Indian land. During those decades of subhuman existence on land too miserable to interest the interlopers around them, Indians survived and culturally prospered. They had nothing to hang on to save their heritage, and they did that with a tenacity that defies human explanation. And, more important, they entered this century as Indian as ever before. In fact, while blacks entered the twentieth century clamoring for admission to the American dream, Indians long since had decided they would forego the pleasure and would fight to the death any future effort to integrate them into the melting pot. While blacks cheered every victory on the road toward integration, Indians resisted white America's demand that they do likewise. Seen in this light, the gaining of citizenship in 1924 was no Indian victory. It was simply another step toward an undesired goal — integration.

The second major reason for the decade of termination and relocation is America's forgiving and humanistic nature. We fight to destroy Germans and North Vietnamese, then spend billions rebuilding them immediately. By this century, most Americans were ashamed of the Indian reservation system and wanted to remove the blot from their consciences. We could not and still cannot believe that Indians would rather remain together on seemingly useless land than live with us in Chicago and Los Angeles. The rest of us have left unsatisfactory rural conditions and journeyed to the big city, we reason. Why can't Indians? Probably our misconception stems from the fact that we have never realized the importance of land to Indians. Nothing is more sacred to "Indianness" than land. Until that fact is realized we will still ask questions rather than search for answers.

There are at least two schools of thought concerning the Indians' future in this country. Many believe we are headed toward a just reconciliation, as seen in the Indian Reorganization Act of 1934, and suggest the era of termination and relocation was simply an unfortunate interruption since rectified. The other school suggests that the I.R.A. was a momentary interlude, representative of the general confusion of the New Deal era. Reservation termination, they suggest, is the goal of America, and we must repeal the I.R.A. and return to the more traditional American path of assimilation. Therefore, I suspect the real question is: does the Indian Reorganization Act or termination and relocation represent the real desire of America? Unfortunately, history teaches that the latter is probably correct. The melting-pot myth, Jefferson's suggestion that assimilation is the way, and America's humanistic desire to end the reservation era are more comfortable suggestions to a majority of us. The idea of a nation of separate people within our nation is difficult to contemplate.

Seemingly, the tragic centuries of Indian cultural and physical abuse ended during the Coolidge years; at long last, we were dedicated to rectifying past mistakes. From 1924 to 1950, statutes favorable to Native Americans were passed and supplemented court and executive decisions which led many to prognosticate final accommodation. However, we had a problem; we could not agree on what the mistakes really were. Because of our national preoccupation with the integration syndrome and our belief that all will prosper together if given a chance to do so, the majority of Americans felt and still feel that our major past mistake was forcing tribesmen to live on unproductive reservations where they were isolated wards of a nation passing them by. If Indians were given citizenship, released from reservations, and granted all of the privileges and responsibilities that whites had and blacks wanted, the dilemma would be solved, they reasoned. But a minority, led by Franklin Roosevelt's Commissioner of Indian Affairs, John Collier, disagreed fervently with the integrationists. Collier argued that the major past mistake was robbing Indians of their identity and heritage. What we must do, he and his friends argued, is to allow Indians to remain Indians. Above all else, we must grant the various tribes the right to retain their reservations; it is upon this land that Native Americans will strengthen their bonds with the past, instill their children with tribal pride, and hopefully, prosper in their own way. It is important to reiterate that the argument was not between those who wished tribesmen good and evil; it was between two groups aiming at the same goal — Indian prosperity. One group equated happiness with integration; the Collierites were equally convinced that integration would destroy "Indianness." While John Collier was Commissioner of Indian Affairs from 1933 to 1945, the latter group held the field and pushed through Congress the Indian Reorganization Act and subsequent legislation supporting it. Hardly a session of Congress passed from the early New Deal through the Fair Deal without producing one or more bills protecting Indian rights in a variety of areas. And during those years Indians prospered as never before. They were consulted and their wishes respected. The integrationists grumbled, but in the main, they stood aside while seventy-four tribes transformed themselves into corporations and ninety-five tribes adopted constitutions accepted by the government.

Unfortunately, though the I.R.A. gave America's Indians their first glimmer of hope in four centuries, many believed that separation came too late in history to succeed. Even if a people wanted to remain separate or segregated, they argued, the concept could not be tolerated in Modern America. While President Truman was strengthening Indian separateness in his early presidential years, he was simultaneously displaying courage by leading the nation in an assault against the separatism that had long shackled black Americans. Though separation for Indians and integration for blacks were really complementary movements supported by the majority of both peoples, most white

Americans could not accept what seemed to be a dichotomy. If integration was right for blacks, it was also right for Indians.

In 1950 President Truman appointed Dillon S. Myer Commissioner of Indian Affairs. Myer had served as Director of the War Relocation Authority during World War II, supervising the dirty business of detaining one hundred thousand Japanese-Americans behind barbed wire because of the nation's illogical and racist fear of their possible disloyalty. Myer never got over that job; it was the crystallizing experience of his life. As Indian Commissioner he came to believe that Indian communities and land-reservations were prison camps from which the inmates had to be freed, as his previous Japanese-American wards had to be freed. He came to believe that the health services, educational opportunities, land restoration and conservation projects, freedom from taxes, and other privileges guaranteed to Indians by the government were discriminative over-privileges that deprived Indians of an opportunity to take their rightful place in society. Of course, these over-privileges were not over-privileges at all; they were legal treaty guarantees earned from previous land cessions. But Myer saw them as hindrances to respectability and he preached against Indian separatism; only total integration of tribesmen into society would set them free.

Fortunately for Native Americans, Myer was in office for only two years, and he was unable to transform his ideas into policies. However, when the Eisenhower appointees took charge of the Indian office in early 1953, they accepted Myer's logic and, as Collier put it, began "to translate the Myer fantasy into lethal reality." In truth, it made little difference insofar as Indian affairs were concerned whether Democrats or Republicans won the election of 1952; by that date both had decided on integration as the way of the future. In their platform, the Democrats promised to "remove restrictions on the rights of Indians individually and through their tribal councils to handle their own affairs," and the Republican platform stated that "all Indians are citizens of the United States and no longer should be denied full enjoyment of their rights of citizenship." Therefore, the new Commissioner of Indian Affairs, Glen L. Emmons (a banker from Gallup, New Mexico), set about charting a new course called "termination." The change began on August 1, 1953, with the adoption of House Concurrent Resolution 108. It stated, in part, that it was "the policy of Congress . . . to make the Indians . . . subject to the same laws and entitled to the same privileges and responsibilities as . . . other citizens . . . and to end their status as wards of the United States, and to grant them all of the rights and privileges pertaining to American citizenship."

A few days later Congress passed Public Law 280 empowering states to impose on tribes their own civil and criminal codes and enforcement machinery. The law encouraged states to set aside tribal codes and place all tribesmen under the laws that govern everyone else in that state. There followed in the Eighty-Third Congress a veritable flood of bills to "free" Indians from their so-called over-privileges. The identical pattern of all the bills was the same — to lift the federal trust from Indians and their property and subject them to the mercy of individual states. John Collier commented that Congress was trying to repeal the I.R.A. and "to resume forced individualization of Indian properties; and to make the Government-Indian treaties forgotten scraps of paper."

Collier's condemnation of P.L. 280 was appropriate. It was a bill that encouraged the termination of Indian communities in favor of integrating tribesmen into the various states. If the states had been willing to extend their laws over Indians residing within their boundaries, no other legislation or policy would have been necessary. But fortunately for most Indians, states were not anxious to comply. Indians were poor, illiterate, untrained, and without jobs; P.L. 280 would have transferred them from federal to state welfare rolls. States, of course, were repelled by that possibility. They would much rather allow the federal government to feed, clothe, and heal Indians. Or, to put it another way, states were more willing to allow tribal corporations and communities to exist within their bounds than to pay the high welfare costs that P.L. 280 made possible. But the Eighty-Third Congress persisted and passed over one hundred bills endeavoring to terminate various tribal units around the country. And they succeeded in a few cases.

The recalcitrance of the states left two courses of action open to federal lawmakers: they could remove the Indians from reservations to cities where they might find jobs, or they could enlarge the tribal domains and develop economic opportunities on or near the reservations. Today most realize that the latter course is the better one to follow; unfortunately, in 1953 the former idea seemed cheaper and less troublesome. Therefore, though termination remained the basic policy, it was transformed into what has since been called "relocation."

The few historians who have written about Indian policy in the 1950s have tended to place too much emphasis on termination and not enough on relocation. Simply to legislate tribal communities out of existence seems cruel. To achieve essentially the same goal by removing people from useless land to a glamorous urban setting seems kind and more American. So the idea of relocation was an easy one for Americans to accept. Also, Indian reservations were bad and were established decades earlier when it was necessary to confine recalcitrant tribesmen who had the nasty habit of killing people who were expanding onto their tribal lands. By and large these reservations were small. Not much land was really necessary to accommodate the dwindling number of natives ravaged by war and disease. However, once free of battlefield deaths and once government health services became available after 1926, the size of tribes grew by leaps and bounds, while the land available for use on reservations remained stationary. The growing size of Indian families became especially noticeable during the pleasant days after the I.R.A. became law. The increasing size of families caused overcrowding on the reservations which, for some tribes, became a real problem by the early '50s. It is not the least bit unusual, therefore, that the integration or termination-oriented leaders of 1953 seriously suggested that the best way to achieve termination was to use overcrowded reservations as an excuse to move Indians to cities. There was nothing to do on the reservation save propagate more tribesmen, they stated. If all Indians were influenced to seek success in a city, reservations might be terminated through abandonment. I want to reiterate, however, that another and more acceptable alternative was available in 1953 as it is today — increasing the size of reservations and establishing industries on or near them. But that would not have achieved the goal of terminating all reservations and integrating Indians into the general populace.

From its beginning in 1953, the Voluntary Relocation Program was a highly organized effort to terminate the reservation system. There was established in the Bureau of Indian Affairs the Relocation Division, an agency well stocked with bureaucrats who published two interesting manuals, an *Indian Affairs Manual* and the *Relocation Handbook*. Both were filled with statements about the need for relocation, the purposes of the program, and tips on how to influence Indians to leave the reservations. Directly under the Relocation Division in Washington were Relocation Offices on each reservation and among all of the non-reservation tribes of Oklahoma, and relocation began on individual reservations through the efforts of a Relocation Officer and his assistants. It was their job "to show to the Indian people that there is a better life awaiting them if they have the courage to request relocation."

They always had an abundance of pictures, posters, and pamphlets about the city to which that tribe would be sent. Though the BIA did try to discourage hard sell tactics after 1956, it is fair to say that urban America was depicted by energetic relocation officers as a haven for the oppressed where failure and poverty were unknown. Even loyal Chicagoans could not recognize Chicago in this literature designed to delight the fancies of poverty-stricken, uneducated people. In defense of the reservation officers, it must be added that each of them had an unpublished yearly quota to meet. Their jobs depended on how many Indians were sent to the cities forcing relocation officials to devise creative efforts to sell removal to all willing to listen. The Relocation Officer disseminated visual aids throughout the reservation, generated enthusiasm for seeking a meaningful life elsewhere, and passed out application forms. Supposedly, he was to screen all applicants carefully and subject each to a physical examination, but his need to meet a quota made it easy to disregard such formalities. It was also his job to hold numerous counseling sessions with migrants in order to acquaint them with the reality of city life and to advise them on what to take along, how to close out their tribal accounts, and to set a date for their departure. From the time an Indian filled out an application form until he departed for the city, approximately one month passed. Shortly before the time to leave, each migrant signed a permanent departure form requesting financial assistance which made him and his family eligible for one-way tickets to some predetermined city, fifty dollars moving expenses, and a small sum for subsistence enroute. Studies show clearly that, especially during the early '50s, Indians were not prepared in one short month for the shock that accompanied migration to a major urban center. Not until 1956, when national criticism became unbearable, did the government try to reform the preparation process followed on most reservations.

Upon arrival, the migrants were either met at the railroad or bus station, or they reported directly to the city Relocation Office. There they received a number of services designed to help make the transition from reservation to urban life successful. Temporary housing was arranged until the relocatee had regular employment. After he was established in a job, he was assisted in securing permanent quarters commensurate with his income and place of employment. In between job interviews, the relocatee attended counseling and guidance sessions designed to explain economic opportunities, the mores of the community, and educational opportunities for the family. Supposedly, counseling services were available for a full year after arrival, but because of insufficient staff members the city Relocation Office usually ended these services after a job and permanent housing had been secured by the relocatee. Lastly, all relocatees were eligible for one month's financial assistance after arrival. A single person, or a man and his wife, was eligible for forty dollars per week. The amount of help increased from that minimum payment to one hundred dollars per week for a family unit of ten or more. In addition to financial assistance for one month, all relocatees were eligible for an undetermined amount of emergency subsistence for three weeks, if they lost their jobs through no fault of their own. Since Indians were seldom able to prove that they were not responsible for the loss of employment, and since the amount of aid was never spelled out and Relocation Officers operated on tight budgets until 1956, this assistance was seldom available.

On paper, especially in the Annual Reports of the Secretary of the Interior, the relocation experiment of the '50s was acclaimed a resounding success. Reservation Relocation Officers advertised with the fervor of Madison Avenue hucksters and enticed thousands of poor, illiterate tribesmen to apply for relocation in an increasing number of cities. The three earliest relocation cities were Los Angeles, Chicago, and Denver; by 1958 the government added Cincinnati, Oakland, San Jose, San Francisco, Cleveland, St. Louis, and Dallas for a total of ten. Chicago and Los Angeles were always the major relocation cities. Though BIA statistics were always padded to exaggerate the number of persons migrating to urban areas during the '50s, the number was significant. We can account for at least thirty-five thousand migrants from 1953 through 1960. During the first year (1953), two thousand six hundred relocated; in the peak year (1957), six thousand nine hundred sixty-four joined the trek to the city — an increase of more than one hundred fifty percent in four years. Also, in 1953, one thousand three hundred received financial assistance, while six thousand five hundred forty-three received help in 1957 — an increase of four hundred percent.

In 1956, reacting favorably to the apparent success of the program, Congress increased significantly appropriations for relocation. Until that year, relocation was carried out on a shoestring. For example, the relocation budget for fiscal year 1955-56 was only $1,016,400. But the following budget was increased more than threefold to $3,472,000. Indeed, as far as Congress and the BIA were concerned, relocation was proving to be the long-sought-after magical way to terminating Indian reservations.

But the success of relocation was more apparent than real; in fact, it was limited to BIA reports. At the very time that Congress was tripling the budget for relocation, serious flaws in the undertaking were coming to light. Most important was the fact that urban life was not proving very beneficial to Indians; they were failing in the cities. From the time they learned about relocation in their tribal communities until they were turned loose in Chicago on their own, an average time of only two months elapsed. In the meantime, Native Americans forsook all of the health, educational, and welfare advantages due them in their home communities in favor of life in a technologically oriented urban center. They were unskilled and untrained, land and family oriented, and totally unfamiliar with the tempo of city life. They brought large families and no special skills to the cities and quickly drifted into the lowest paying jobs and homes in filthy, degrading urban ghettos. Upon arrival in the city, Indians were assisted in acquiring a job and housing, but that was all. Before 1957 counselors were few and assistance beyond initial orientation unavailable, not because city relocation personnel were unsympathetic but because funds were not available for staffs adequate to meet the needs of an ever-growing number of Indians sent by quota-hungry bureaucrats. Inadequately prepared for their new environment and totally frustrated and lost, Indians tended to drift from job to job and bottle to bottle. The lucky ones got some money and returned home. Even the BIA admitted that one out of three Indians eventually returned to the reservation, but then added that such evidence was encouraging because it showed that "the great majority of . . . relocated Indians are making satisfactory adjustments . . . " in the cities.

By 1959 even the government had to admit the utter failure of its experiment to terminate reservations. The 1959 Annual Interior Report contained the first admission that all was not well with relocation. Secretary Emmons wrote, "because the market for unskilled and semi-skilled workers was quite limited in most relocation cities . . . , the Relocation Services . . . [will be] carried forward at a somewhat reduced tempo during the fiscal year." And indeed it was. In 1959, the Cincinnati relocation office was closed; the next year the St. Louis office met the same fate. Also, the number of Indians relocated took a drastic downward swing after a high of six thousand nine hundred sixty-four in 1957. The following year five thousand seven hundred twenty-eight migrated, and the 1959 and 1960 figures did not reach four thousand a year.

However, the decreasing numbers and increasing appropriations after 1957 did allow reservations and city Relocation Officers to do a better job of training Indians for city life. Hard–sell advertisement was replaced on the reservation with short courses on problems of city living. The requirement to give each Indian a careful physical examination before migration was enforced, in addition to inaugurating the use of a battery of tests to determine job skills. Family counseling sessions were introduced to prepare all members of the family unit for the adjustment necessary to succeed in the city. Also, extended services were provided in the cities. Relocation personnel were assigned individual families for a full year and during that period they spent considerable time and effort in job placement, improving housing accommodations, training Indians in money management and banking procedures, encouraging adult training programs, and stimulating interest and participation in community activities. Increased personnel and services cost money.

Whereas the estimated cost of relocating a family before 1957 was $196.00; it cost $347.20 thereafter. Also, before 1957, government services to relocated Indians cost a total of $408,800 per year; after that date more than three times as much—$1,367,700.

Despite improvements after 1957, history has remembered, and I believe will continue to remember, the era of termination by relocation as a failure of tragic proportions. It is important to note in passing that measurable increases in alcoholism among Indians has always accompanied concerted American efforts to destroy them as viable entities in our society. By using what we might call the alcohol index, it seems obvious that the Indian Removal Act of 1830, the Dawes Act of 1887, and relocation of the 1950s are the most destructive actions taken against Native Americans in the last two centuries — all were supported by "Indian friends" and accompanied by an unprecedented rise in alcoholism. A study of the files of Relocation Offices around the country reveals that one problem stands clearly above others among Indians in all the cities — alcoholism. We are told by scholars who study the reasons for and results of alcoholism that the disease is usually the result of other stresses. For Native Americans alcoholism is symptomatic of the number of basic problems they face when forced to adjust to a profound change in their relationships with the world beyond the tribe. To move from a rural to a highly urban environment creates tension enough — to move from a tribal society into the center of a great city must be, for many, a traumatic experience. The trauma was deepened by the fact that the government seemed concerned only with acquiring initial housing and employment for the relocatee. As Jack Forbes wrote, the Indians' "social-psychological adjustment is of little moment, and if a meaningful life is to be discovered in the city, the Indians must discover it. Perhaps to be truly 'assimilated' every minority group must become urban slum-dwellers, sinking into the whirlpool of a great city and becoming absorbed in the mass of humanity around them. How many private tragedies occur in the whirlpool, and how many useful lives are lost along the way?"

In 1956 the Association of American Indian Affairs, Inc. studied relocation efforts and cataloged forty-eight significant criticisms of the program. Three of the criticisms most often levied by Indians, white critics, and even some government officials were that training for urban living was neglected before, during, and after removal; urban stresses drove Indian men and women to alcoholism; and the U.S. government was using relocation as a device for emptying Indian reservations and ending its obligations to the tribes. My research has led me to agree with these and most of the other forty-five criticisms. Therefore, it was a glorious day for Indians when both political parties in the presidential election of 1960 forsook termination by relocation. Candidate John F. Kennedy promised that if he became President no change in any treaty or contractural relationship would take place without the consent of the tribes concerned. He also promised to protect the Indians' land base and to do all in his power to protect the cultural heritage of Native Americans. He won and the era of termination by relocation came to an abrupt end. But no Indian has since forgotten the 1950s, nor is he likely to in this century. It is true that termination as a government-sponsored policy ended in 1960. But Indians know full well that white Americans have an uncanny ability to state one thing while doing the opposite. If the government of the U.S. and its people had not broken previous treaties with such regularity, Indians could have relaxed in 1960 and taken comfort from the knowledge that another insidious and thinly-disguised effort to terminate Indianness had ended in failure. But history has taught Native Americans vigilance; they know that words on paper, public and private utterances, and good intentions have not tempered the thrust of white aggression in the past and are not likely to do so in the future. Maybe the future will be different; only time will tell.

Actually, the movement of tribesmen from a rural to an urban environment in the 1950s insured that the future would have to be different. The events of that decade willed us urban Indians and rural Indians now about equal in number and more Indian problems to solve than ever before in history. Whereas prior to 1953, rural Indians were willing to accept orderly progress secure in the fact that the I.R.A. of 1934 protected them, urban Indians live with no such fanciful illusions today. They want justice now, and they will burn the BIA or occupy Wounded Knee to get it. And like the cities that have molded them for the past two decades, they are impatient, vocal, and easy to anger. If they do indeed become violent in the days ahead, maybe we snould reflect momentarily and remember that Dillon Myer, H.C.R. 108, P.L. 280, and the melting-pot myth many cherish have helped, in our lifetime, to turn orderly and dignified progress into a tragic nightmare for thousands of people.

SUGGESTED READING

Cohen, Felix S. "The Erosion of Indian Rights, 1950-1953: A Case Study in Bureaucracy," *The Yale Law Journal,* Vol. 62, No. 3 (February, 1953).

Collier, John. *Indians of the Americas.* New York: New American Library, 1947.

Collier, John. "Return to Dishonor," *Frontier* (June, 1954).

Debo, Angie. *A History of the Indians of the United States.* Norman: University of Oklahoma Press, 1970.

Deloria, Vine, Jr. *Custer Died for Your Sins: An Indian Manifesto.* New York: Avon Books, 1970.

Fey, Harold E. "Our National Indian Policy," *The Christian Century,* Vol. 72, No. 13 (March 30, 1955).

Harmer, Ruth Mulvey. "Uprooting the Indians," *Atlantic,* Vol. 197, No. 3 (March, 1956).

"Indian Reservations May Some Day Run Out of Indians," *The Saturday Evening Post* (November 23, 1957).

LaFarge, Oliver. "Termination of Federal Supervision: Disintegration of the American Indians," *The Annals of the American Academy of Political and Social Sciences,* Vol. 311 (May, 1957).

LaFarge, Oliver (ed.). *The Changing Indian.* Norman: University of Oklahoma Press, 1942.

Nader, Ralph. "American Indians: People without a Future," *Harvard Law Record,* Vol. 22, No. 10 (May 10, 1956).

The Kinzua Dam Controversy. Philadelphia: Philadelphia Yearly Meeting of Friends, 1961.

U.S. Congress, Senate. "Indian Policy: The Goal Is Freedom as an American Citizen," *Congressional Record,* Vol. 103, Pt. 8, 85th Cong., 1st sess. Washington: U.S. Government Printing Office, 1957.

Index